THE HISTORY OF GOTHIC FICTION

THE HISTORY OF GOTHIC FICTION

MARKMAN ELLIS

EDINBURGH UNIVERSITY PRESS

© Markman Ellis, 2000

Edinburgh University Press Ltd
22 George Square, Edinburgh

Typeset in Goudy Old Style by
Florence Production Ltd, Stoodleigh Devon, and
printed and bound in Great Britain by
MPG Books Ltd, Bodmin

A CIP Record for this book is available from the British Library

ISBN 0 7486 1195 9 (paperback)

Contents

Acknowledgements

I would like to thank everyone who has helped in the production of this book. For the book's shape and conception, I am indebted to Vanessa Smith, Darran Whatmore, Chris Reid, Richard Hamblyn, and the students of my classes on gothic fiction from 1993 to 1999. Numerous others have willingly given up their time and assistance: Ava Arndt, Annette Ashley, Rebecca Beasley, Marilyn Butler, Brycchan Carey, Dierdre Coleman, Elizabeth Eger, Eliane Glaser, Charlotte Grant, Margaret Harris, Megan Hiatt, Margaret Homberger, Peter Hulme, Gavin Jones, Leya Landau, John Mullan, Vic Sage, Nicholas Smith, Vivian Smith, Nicola Walker and James Watt. Noting the kind generosity of these people does not alter the fact that the mistakes and confusions are all my own. At Edinburgh University Press, I would like to thank Nicola Carr and Jackie Jones, Sarah Burnett, and the two anonymous readers. I would like to thank all my colleagues at Queen Mary and Westfield College, University of London, for their support over the years, especially Cornelia Cook, Paul Hamilton, Anne Janowitz, Lisa Jardine, Jacqueline Rose and Morag Shiach; and Andrew Penman, Sue Cook and Pat Hamilton. Thanks are also due to the staff and librarians at the British Library, the University of London Library, the Queen Mary and Westfield College Library, the Cambridge University Library, the Fisher Library of the University of Sydney, and the Mitchell Library, Sydney. Finally, thanks of a more personal kind are due to Sharon Ellis, Stead Ellis, Briony Ellis, Sybille Smith, Gabrielle Smith, Jo Lynch, John Mitchinson, Simone Horrocks, Patrick Reynolds, Maria Majsca, and above all, Vanessa Smith.

Sections of Chapter 4 have previously appeared as 'Fictions of Science in Mary Shelley's *Frankenstein*', *Sydney Studies in English*, 25 (1999), pp. 27–46.

Illustrations

Figure 1. Frontispiece: Henry Fuseli, The Nightmare, engraved W. Raddon (London: W. Raddon, 1827); British Museum, Department of Prints and Drawings, London.

The history of gothic fiction

In 1799, a French natural philosopher, Barthélemy Faujas de Saint-Fond, in his account of his travels in Britain, reported a strange encounter in the Cabinet (scientific collection) of John Sheldon, a surgeon in London.

> I was introduced to a very handsome bed-room; a mahogany table of oblong form, stood in the midst of it, facing the bed.
>
> The top of the table opened by a groove, and under a glass-frame I saw the body of a young woman, of nineteen or twenty, entirely naked. She had fine brown hair, and lay extended as on a bed.
>
> The glass was lifted up, and Sheldon made me admire the flexibility of the arms, a kind of elasticity in the bosom and even in the cheeks, and the perfect preservation of the other parts of the body. Even the skin partly retained its colour, though exposed to the air.

Sheldon was very impressed by this dead woman, although he managed a few critical remarks about a certain 'tenseness of the muscles' which, he said, 'gave to the figure, though it still possessed the remains of beauty, a meagre or feeble air, which considerably diminished the delicacy of its traits'. Faujas de Saint-Fond undertook his journey, he announced, 'for the purpose of examining the state of the Arts, the Sciences, Natural History and Manners, in Great Britain'. As a gentleman of curiosity, Faujas de Saint-Fond took an interest in the science of Sheldon's woman, summarised in two pages describing the techniques of embalming. But his curiosity also led him to examine the effects the experience had on his thoughts and feelings.

> A sentiment of curiosity made me ask Sheldon, at this moment when he was closing up the table, who this young woman was, whose remains he had preserved with so much care. He replied frankly, and without any hesitation, 'It is a mistress whom I tenderly loved. I paid every attention to her during a long sickness, and a short time before her death, she requested that I should

make a mummy of her body, and keep her beside me – I have kept my word
to her.'
I was glad that Sheldon had not informed me of this circumstance sooner,
for I confess I could not have avoided a disagreeable feeling at seeing a
lover so coolly describe the anatomical operations which he had made on
the object of his most tender affection; on a charming young woman whom
he had lost, and whose disfigured image could only excite in him the most
painful recollections.

In response to the 'mummy' – as Sheldon calls her – Faujas de Saint-
Fond records a 'disagreeable feeling' engendered by the disparity between
the 'cool' gaze of the scientist, engaged in the bloody anatomists' work
of the embalmer, and the tender emotions of love inspired by the woman
of his affections. He asks 'but who would, with his own hand, perform
the disgusting operations which must be necessary to preserve the body
of his friend'. Indeed, as Faujas de Saint-Fond describes it, the experience of seeing the woman is most interesting for this feeling between
love and pain.[1]

It might be useful here to draw a contrast between Faujas de Saint-
Fond's scientific *sang froid* and the suggestible mind of Emily St Aubert,
the heroine of Ann Radcliffe's novel *The Mysteries of Udolpho* (1794).
Agitated by plots against her virtue and life, a fearful Emily is shown
into a chamber of the castle of Udolpho furnished with an iron chair
'immediately over which, depending on a chain from the ceiling, hung
an iron ring'. In her state of 'wonder and horror', Emily concludes that
these were 'instruments of torture', a thought which causes her such 'acute
pain' that she involuntarily seats herself in the very chair. Starting up,
she 'perceives only a dark curtain, which descending from the ceiling to
the floor, was drawn along one whole side of the chamber'. Radcliffe's
careful delineation of space, through an almost diagrammatic attention
to the relation between objects, places the reader in an analogous position to Emily. In this way Radcliffe invites sympathetic identification,
and maintains distance through the third-person narrator. The curtain
exerts a fascination:

Ill as she was, the appearance of this curtain struck her, and she paused to
gaze upon it, in wonder and apprehension.
It seemed to conceal a recess of the chamber; she wished, yet dreaded, to
lift it, and to discover what it veiled: twice she was withheld by a recollection of the terrible spectacle her daring hand had formerly unveiled in
an apartment of the castle, till, suddenly conjecturing, that it concealed the
body of her murdered aunt, she seized it, in a fit of desperation, and drew
it aside.

In this drama of sensibility, Emily sorts and resorts the contradictory feelings in her mind: curiosity (wonder and apprehension), fear (dread and horror), recollection (memory). The war of emotions ends when curiosity wins out: her desire for information overwhelms her fear of what she might discover. When she draws aside the curtain,

> Beyond, appeared a corpse, stretched on a kind of low couch, which was crimsoned with human blood, as was the floor beneath. The features, deformed by death, were ghastly and horrible, and more than one livid wound appeared in the face.

Emily 'gazed' briefly at this sight, before 'she fell senseless at the foot of the couch' (see Figure 2). Emily's fainting response, demonstrating her refined sentimental capacity, has an interesting consequence for the narrative: when her 'senses' return, she is being removed from the chamber in a state of such 'extreme languor' that she could not feel any distinct fear.[2] The fainting fit occludes conclusions and analysis (a convention of sensibility) and concentrates the reader onto the theatrics of emotional excess. Emily proves her sensibility in her demonstration of terror: the reader is invited to experience her terrified state. However, for the reader, terror operates on a secondary level, exposing the reader's curiosity about, and pleasure in, such feelings of terror. In the end, this scene does not meet its final conclusion for several hundred pages – nearly two volumes later in the first edition – when, eventually, the reader discovers that the dead body is a wax effigy. The narrator recaps:

> It may be remembered, that, in a chamber of Udolpho, hung a black veil, whose singular situation had excited Emily's curiosity, and which afterwards disclosed an object, that had overwhelmed her with horror; for, on lifting it, there appeared, instead of the picture she had expected, within a recess of the wall, a human figure of ghastly paleness, stretched at its length, and dressed in the habiliments of the grave. What added to the horror of the spectacle, was, that the face appeared partly decayed and disfigured by worms, which were visible on the features and hands. On such an object, it will be readily believed, that no person could endure to look twice. Emily, it may be recollected, had, after the first glance, let the veil drop, and her terror had prevented her from ever provoking a renewal of such suffering, as she had then experienced. Had she dared to look again, her delusion and her fears would have vanished together, and she would have perceived, that the figure before her was not human, but formed of wax.

The narrator's admonition to Emily to 'look again' serves as a warning against excess sensibility. As well as indicating that the corpse is a

Figure 2. 'Mysteries of Udolpho, Vol. 3, Ch. 4, p. 21', in Ann Radcliffe, The Mysteries of Udolpho, A Romance; interspersed with some pieces of poetry. Illustrated with copper-plates, *4 vols, 4th edn (London: G. G. and J. Robinson, 1799), III, opp. p. 21; British Library, London.*

wax-work fake, the reader's second look behind the curtain supplies additional information about its appearance, clothes and the disfiguring worms.[3] By prolonging the moment of clarification, Radcliffe reinforces the extent to which the narrator positions the reader as Emily (unable to take a second look). When the reader finally understands, the mystery behind the curtain becomes an experience not of terror, but of comedy and disappointment, of bathos.

The creative potential located by the gothic in problems of realism is further examined in John Henry Fuseli's painting *The Nightmare* (1782). A Swiss painter resident in London, Fuseli (1741–1825) exhibited *The Nightmare* at the Royal Academy in 1782, where it 'excited . . . an uncommon degree of interest'.[4] The image's popular success was established by a monochrome print, engraved in several versions (by T. Burke (1781), T. Holloway (1791), and twice by W. Raddon (1802 and 1827) (see Figure 1). As the title suggests, the painting represents a nightmare, but it does so in a curious way, depicting it as both a dream image and the image of a dream. It represents a moment of terror: at one level it depicts the effect of a nightmare on a sleeping woman (an empirical observation); but at another level, it seeks to represent to us the disturbed sleeper's mind (a symbolic portrayal of the nightmare). Fuseli's hybrid style, mixing innovation and tradition, was described by Peter Tomory as a Germanic '*Schwarzkunststudie*' or 'moment of terror' painting.[5]

The painting's scene of action is a well-ordered, even fashionable, room, draped with thick red curtains encircling a low, gilt sofa, hung with luxurious red and gold rugs. On a bedside table is a book, a phial of liquid – perhaps laudanum or a sleeping potion – and a mirror. In Raddon's 1827 engraving, the table sports hair ornaments and a pair of fanciful fairy figures, admiring their reflection in the mirror (reinforcing the theme of female vanity). The atmosphere is dark and heavy, but this oppressive and claustrophobic quality belies the scene's contemporary and modern situation. The painting's gothic effects rely on oddly classicising aspects of composition and allusion.[6] Fuseli's naturalistic painting technique, felicitously recording the detail of objects and figures, can be initially equated with a novelised variety of realism. The sleeping figure of the woman is figured in a pose of passive abandon, stretched out on the couch, her arms flung above her head. Her fashionable dress is also modern, revealing an expanse of white skin on her bizarrely elongated neck and revealing *décolletage*. The woman's wanton pose could be explained as deep sleep, but it seems suggestive of a deeper insensibility: a trance, a narcotic sleep, an erotic fit, or even death. On her torso sits a grotesque gargoyle-like figure, the incubus, figured as a small devilish monster staring out at the viewer with a challenging gaze, as if disturbed in some preternatural ritual. Even more disturbing is the goggle-eyed horse watching from behind the red curtain. These two figures set up a disturbing resonance in the painting.

The painting's ambiguity centres on the incubus sitting on the woman's chest, who either represents or is the nightmare of the painting's title. In his *Dictionary* of 1755, Dr Johnson established that the etymology of 'nightmare' was a conjunction between *night* and *mara*, 'a spirit that, in the northern mythology, was related to torment or suffocate sleepers'. Johnson defined 'nightmare' as 'A morbid oppression in the night, resembling the pressure of weight upon the breast'.[7] Johnson's definition establishes how the phenomenon of the nightmare, on the cusp between physiology and folklore, probed a curious epistemological problem for eighteenth-century medical science, centring on how to make use of popular tales (folklore or myth) in their empirical research. But in medieval theology, the incubus referred to a demon who lay upon men and women in their sleep.[8] Recognised by the courts in ecclesiastical and civil cases of witchcraft, the incubus was believed especially to seek carnal intercourse with women. John Bullokar, in his dictionary of 1616, states that 'The vulgar thinke it [the incubus] some spirit, but the Phisitions [physicians] affirme it to bee a naturall disease, caused by humours undigested in the stomacke, which fuming up to the braine, doe there trouble the animall spirits'.[9] Such demon figures could be connected to the nightmare by etymology too. Italian travellers in Dalmatia (now in Croatia) reported a belief amongst the uneducated peasants that connected the incubus with a word among the Morlacchi, 'morra', for a vampire-like witch (*stregha*) that sucked blood from people at night.[10] Nonetheless, from the sixteenth century on, the incubus came to refer to a nocturnal phenomenon occurring in sleep, like that of having a heavy weight on the chest, inducing a trance-like immobility.

John Bond, a Scottish doctor, in his medical treatise called *An Essay on the Incubus, or Night-mare* (1753), declared that the name 'Night-mare' was a 'strange term' which 'arose from superstitious notions' even amongst the British. Himself 'much afflicted' by nightmares, Bond is aware of the superstitions concerning the experience, and signals the different 'quaint names' given to the disorder. Nonetheless, his purpose is to establish its cause, and thereafter, to suggest the cure.

> The Night-mare generally seizes upon people sleeping on their backs, and often begins with frightful dreams, which are soon succeeded by a difficult

respiration, a violent oppression of the breast, and a total privation of voluntary motion. In this agony they sigh, groan, utter indistinct sounds, and remain
in the jaws of death, till, by the utmost efforts of nature, or some external
assistance, they escape out of that dreadful torpid state.

As soon as they shake off that vast oppression, and are able to move the body,
they are affected with a strong Palpitation, great Anxiety, Languor, and
Uneasiness; which symptoms gradually abate, and are gradually succeeded by
the pleasing reflection of having escaped some imminent danger.[11]

The seventeenth-century physician John Floyer – a man with occult interests, and an apologist for angels – nonetheless explained the incubus as
a physiological effect: 'The *incubus* is an inflation of the membranes of
the stomach, which hinders the motion of the diaphragma, lungs, pulse,
and motion, with a sense of a weight oppressing the breast.'[12] Bond himself
argued that the oppression occasioned by the nightmare was caused by
the pressure of blood on the heart:

> When the body lies supine [on the back] the Heart necessarily falls on the
> Vertebræ of the Spine; and therefore, by its own gravity, must compress
> the left Auricle and Pulmonary Veins, which, at that time, lie directly under
> its basis; and, by that means, the course of the Blood through the Lungs will
> be stopped.[13]

By 1780, the *Encyclopaedia Britannica* had further re-Latinised 'nightmare'
into 'Oneirodynia' or 'Uneasiness in Sleep', and determined the demon
incubus to be imaginary: those 'seized with it . . . sometimes . . . imagine
they see spectres of various kinds which oppress or threaten them with
suffocation'.[14]

To represent the nightmare, Fuseli has literalised the incubus of both
accounts: as a bug-eyed hairy demon with pointy ears whose muscular
weight oppresses his victim's exposed breast. In this way, Fuseli also
exploits the notion of the incubus as demon lover recorded in the popular
tales. But as he does so, he also articulates recent medical theory that
identified the nightmare as a mental fit, occasioned by 'frightful Dreams',
and caused by a Plethora, or a too great quantity of Blood'. Those who
are most subject to the nightmare are 'young persons of gross habits, the
robust, the luxurious, the drunken, and they who sup late . . . Also Women
who are obstructed; Girls of full, lax habits, before the eruption of the
Menses [menstruation]'. Young unmarried women about to enter into the
sexual world experience nightmares as an expression of their awakening
sexuality. Robert Burton, in *The Anatomy of Melancholy* (1621), stated
that 'maids, nuns and widows' were particularly subject to 'terrible dreams

at night'. Burton proposed marriage – that is to say, an active sexuality – as a cure. Bond provides several examples:

> A robust servant Girl, about eighteen years old, was severely oppress'd with the Night-mare, two or three nights before every eruption of the Menses, and us'd to groan so loudly as to awake her Fellow-servant, who always shook or turn'd her on her Side; by which means she recover'd. She was thus afflicted periodically with it, 'till she took a bedfellow of a different sex, and bore Children.[15]

The pose of sexual abandon of Fuseli's young woman's suggests this conjunction of nightmare and sexual longing.

The horse makes all this rather more disturbing. The horse is a liter-alisation of the night-mare – a horse that comes by night – but also feeds into the incubus myth. The incubus rides the sleeper, in a way that is suggestive of equestrian as well as sexual mounting. But the connection between the horse and the nightmare is a false etymology: the night-mare is not a horse but a spirit, a 'mara', as Johnson declared. The figure of the horse then is a pun or joke on the title of the painting as a whole: a literalisation that disturbs the topic more than it centres it. *The Nightmare* offers a telling example of how the gothic articulates unstated or inexpressible themes in excessively ornate rhetorical gestures, such as puns or jokes. Horace Walpole, when he saw *The Nightmare* at the Royal Academy in 1782, thought the painting 'shocking'.[16] Perhaps part of the reason he was shocked is that the image makes little attempt to distance this gothic tone by adopting an exotic setting or a location in the medieval past, like his own novel *The Castle of Otranto* (1764). Fuseli's *Nightmare* is a powerful image that achieves its power in an interesting way: it describes a disturbing scene (a moment of terror, articulated through the woman's abandoned sexuality and the monstrous figure of the incubus). But the scene is made more unsettling by the epistemologically prob-lematic figure of the horse, a weak pun that literalises the ambiguities of the *mise en scène*. It is this instability that makes the image so tellingly 'gothic' in tone.

ON THE PLEASURE DERIVED FROM OBJECTS OF TERROR

These three anecdotes about the dead and near-dead exemplify how the gothic is not simply a narrative of terror or a set of properties, but is also a tone or mood that is, in its own way, quite experimental. These exam-ples indicate that the gothic is particularly interested in exploiting the emotions, both by detailing the protagonist's thoughts and feelings, and by asking that the reader identify with them. The principle of pathos, arousing feelings in the reader, is established as the primary pattern for consumption of these works, both fictional and visual. The gothic novel's varied responses to this 'affective fallacy' reminds the critic of its inheritance of the strategies and interests of the late-eighteenth-century culture of sentimentalism.

Such a theory was offered by Anna Letitia Aikin, in an essay entitled 'On the Pleasure Derived form Objects of Terror', published in a collection of essays written with her younger brother John Aikin, entitled *Miscellaneous Pieces in Prose* (1773). Later known by her married name, Barbauld, Aikin's essay explores a 'paradox of the heart' she has identified by 'daily observation', that reading about terrible things is a different order of experience from actually being terrified. While the former can arouse a feeling of pleasure, the latter cannot. She notes 'the apparent delight with which we dwell upon objects of pure terror, where our moral feelings are not in the least concerned' and observes that 'The greediness with which the tales of ghosts and goblins, of murders, earthquakes, fires, shipwrecks, and all the most terrible disasters attending human life, are devoured by every ear, must have been generally remarked.' In her analysis of the source of this appetite, Aikin suggests that mere entertainment or avoidance of boredom are insufficient cause. Rather, she concludes that:

> A strange and unexpected event awakens the mind, and keeps it on the stretch; and where the agency of invisible beings is introduced, of 'forms unseen, and mightier far than we', our imagination, darting forth, explores with rapture the new world which is laid open to its view, and rejoices in the expansion of its powers. Passion and fancy co-operating elevate the soul to its highest pitch; and the pain of terror is lost in amazement.

The supernatural, Aikin argues, offers an expansive field of the imagination in which anything may happen. In part, then, terror and the supernatural is an issue of epistemology: an opening out of imagination that leads to amazement and bewilderment. In this sense, such scenes must avoid an overly close approximation of ordinary experience (realism) in order to achieve this effect of pleasure in terror.

> Hence, the more wild, fanciful, and extraordinary are the circumstances of a scene of horror, the more pleasure we receive from it; and where they are too near common nature, though violently borne by curiosity through the adventure, we cannot repeat it or reflect on it, without an over-balance of pain.[17]

If it is too realistic, 'too near common nature', the gothic becomes terror and cannot be suffered.

Aikin's theory of the gothic is clearly indebted to some aspects of Edmund Burke's theory of the sublime offered in his *Philosophical Enquiry into the Origin of our Ideas of the Sublime and Beautiful* (1757). However, by working in the domestic scale of the Johnsonian essay, Aikin avoids the posturing philosophising, manic classifying and masculine style of Burke's dissertation. Burke had argued that,

> Whatever is fitted in any sort to excite the ideas of pain, and danger, that is to say, whatever is in any sort terrible, or is conversant about terrible objects, or operates in a manner analogous to terror, is a source of the *sublime*; that is, it is productive of the emotion which the mind is capable of feeling.

The innovation of Burke's account of the sublime – a concept of classical rhetoric resuscitated in the seventeenth century – was the dynamic he established between pain and pleasure.

> When danger or pain press too nearly, they are incapable of giving any delight, and are simply terrible; but at certain distances, and with certain modifications, they may be, and they are delightful, as we everyday experience.[18]

Burke's analysis of the representational logic of the sublime – a contradictory feeling, that derives a certain pleasure from the depiction of events or effects that are in themselves terrible[19] – had considerable influence on gothic novelists.[20] Aikin's domesticated version, and her subsequent elucidation of a practical rhetoric of pleasurable terror in her parodicly-titled essay 'An Enquiry into those Kinds of Distress which Excite Agreeable Sensations', was arguably better suited to the particular effects of the gothic novel.

'Objects of terror', Nathan Drake argued in *Literary Hours* (1800), are divided into two kinds: 'those which owe their origin to the agency of super-human beings' and 'those which depend upon natural causes and events for their production'. Terror produced by 'simple material causation', he cautions, requires the 'skills and arrangement' of art to 'prevent its operating more pain than pleasure'. Drake certainly believed that 'a poem, a novel, or a picture' could 'unfold a scene so horrid, or so cruel, that the art of the painter or the poet is unable to render it communicative of the smallest pleasurable emotion'. Drake's essay, however, explores those works in which the viewer perceives a feeling of terror as pleasurable.

No efforts of genius . . . are so truly great as those which approaching the brink
of horror, have yet, by the art of the poet or painter, by adjunctive and
pictoresque embellishment, by pathetic, or sublime emotion, been rendered
powerful in creating the most delightful and fascinating sensations.

Of all the writers who attempted this, Drake argues that Ann Radcliffe
is the most effective.

In the productions of Mrs Radcliffe, the Shakespeare of Romance Writers,
. . . may be found many scenes truly terrific in their conception, yet so soft-
ened down, and the mind so much relieved, by the intermixture of beautiful
description, or pathetic incident, that the impression of the whole never
becomes too strong, never degenerates into horror, but pleasurable emotion is
ever the predominating result.[21]

By championing Radcliffe's example, Drake argues that even without the
supernatural element, the gothic can achieve its curious effect by the
studious deployment of picturesque language. Burke, Aikin and Drake
agree that gothic fiction (not their term) does not excite terror itself but
rather this curious hybrid, the pleasure of terror. The delicate and vague
line that the gothic has to maintain between distant and enchanted other-
worldliness and realistic portrayals of terror remains fraught and essentially
subjective. Nonetheless, as the history of gothic fiction demonstrates, this
difficult line is deeply historicised and dependent on the expectations of
readers.

— GOTHIC AND HISTORY —

The chapters that follow do not attempt a comprehensive history of the
gothic novel, but rather, offer a series of readings of the use of history
in the gothic novel. Describing how history is adopted and recycled in
the gothic novel, the book considers how 'the gothic' is itself a theory
of history: a mode for the apprehension and consumption of history.
In this book, I use the term 'history' in the sense now commonplace in
English studies, as something more than context or backdrop, or a simple
record of events. History here is a methodology for literary criticism in
which the reader is asked to consider the mutability of ideas and language.
The book does not stop at describing the gothic novel's signature effects,
but goes on to consider when these effects have worked. It asks the reader
of gothic novels to consider not only what the novel means, but when
this meaning evolved, and how it has changed. It relates particular historical events, takes an interest in the publication of books and editions,

and traces contemporary responses to gothic novels. Furthermore, it examines how some critical assumptions about the gothic, established as timeless or natural, have their origin in particular events and debates. Recovering the horizon of expectations of these controversies can not only throw into perspective the modern understanding of gothic texts, but also show how this particular history is frequently suppressed or elided.[22] It is in this sense that the book relates historical events, takes an interest in the publication of books and editions, and traces contemporary responses to gothic novels. In this sense, too, it makes some sense to speak not only of history in gothic fiction, but also of gothic fiction as history.

Certainly, the history of gothic fiction is of comparatively recent invention. Literary criticism first located the gothic novel as a separate and discrete entity in the 1920s in a series of critical studies by Edith Birkhead, Eino Railo and, later, Montague Summers.[23] These first critics practised a variety of literary history whose concern was as much bibliographical and classificatory as it was hermeneutic. Such work established and also produced the canon of gothic texts, reinforced by later decisions – from the 1960s on – to publish paperback editions of these now 'neglected' classics. Decisions taken in this period have largely built the orthodox view of the 'rise' of the gothic as a series of novels beginning with Walpole and Radcliffe. This notion of the gothic novel (and its history), as James Watt has convincingly argued, was almost unknown to writers in the late eighteenth century. As Watt observes, the term 'gothic' is now made to accommodate a wide variety of works, even though, in the 1790s, those novels now known as gothic would have been categorised – if at all – under various names, such as 'the romance' or even 'German' novels (signalling their debt to the *Shauer-roman*).[24] It is in this sense that Matthew Lewis, for example, explained to Goethe in 1799 that 'German Literature is at present the prevailing taste in England'.[25] That British and American critics in the 1920s shied away from terms such as 'Germanic' and 'romance', and hit upon another, 'gothic', to describe these novels, is not accidental. Despite its anachronism, the ubiquity of the term 'gothic' gives critics little choice but to use it: an analogous example is afforded by the term 'novel', unavoidably used to describe the bulk of eighteenth-century prose fiction.

For most of its history the institutions of literary criticism have largely ignored the gothic novel, even though the nineteenth century witnessed a steady gain in prestige and critical notice for the historical novel, implicated, as it was, in the ideology of the nation state. Although the genre was dismissed to the marginal reaches of popular entertainment by critics, booksellers and readers, writers continued to find the gothic mode a rich field of creative potential. The extensive stream of gothic novels that have issued from the presses since the 1790s constitutes its own form of criticism, and theory, of the gothic. Manifestations of 'the discourse of the gothic', to use Robert Miles's phrase, supplemented the novel with poetry, painting and, later, film.[26] The chapters which follow provide some outline of this flow of creativity, and, moreover, trace how this series of novels and fictions criticise their forebears by debts of allusion and influence. Revising plots, revisiting themes, reanimating characters, these gothic fictions recall their predecessors as much as they innovate and modernise. Connected by explanatory prefaces, footnote references, textual allusions, the gothic novel effectively historicises itself.

As will become apparent, the gambit of this book is to offer an account of gothic fiction without recourse to the language or theory of psycho-analysis. In part, this stems from the simple observation that writers of gothic fiction of the eighteenth and nineteenth centuries did not have access to this language. As the term 'psychoanalysis' was first coined by Freud in 1896 – first in French, then German, and only later in English[27] – it could be concluded that the gothic inhabits a world of representa-tion categorically pre-Freudian. Nonetheless, critical accounts of gothic fiction have been dominated by psychoanalytic theory. There are solid reasons for this, as well as reasons to be wary. The effect of psychoanalysis was to universalise the lessons of the gothic novel, oddly increasing its cultural significance and prestige by explicating its relevance and impor-tance. Maggie Kilgour suggests that,

> With its theory of an underlying reality, psychoanalysis helped give the gothic a new 'profundity', by seeing it as the revelation of the private life of either the individual or his culture that had been buried as habit, the conscious will, and forces of individual and social repression.

Some of the structural assumptions and key terms of value of psycho-analysis (the uncanny, the unconscious, repression) are predicated on, determined by, or theorised in the discourse of gothic fiction, with its secret family histories, curtained recesses, subterranean passages, and dingy vaulted dungeons. Recent criticism, on both sides of this critical debate, has observed how the gothic repertoire informs the psychoanalytic: the historicist Kilgour ironically notes that 'Psychoanalysis is itself a gothic, necromantic form, that resurrects our psychic pasts';[28] while Robert Miles observes more enthusiastically that 'as narratives, psychoanalysis and the Gothic are coeval. They both begin to take shape around the end of the eighteenth century.'[29] Terry Castle's historicist and sympathetic exploration of Freud's account of the uncanny as a moment of subversion between the 'real and the phantasmic', constructs the uncanny as an invention of the eighteenth century, and a commentary on enlightenment categories of knowledge.[30] Nonetheless, there remains a gap between the kinds of insight derived from the psychoanalytic criticism and the kinds of knowledge articulated in the gothic text. Even when both the theory and the text are adequately historicised, it is not always clear that the same can be said of this gap. The conclusions of psychoanalytic theory articulate kinds of knowledge about which the text is itself ignorant, conclusions which can remain inviolable by dint of their disinterest in the forms of knowledge of the text's own conclusions.

Gothic fiction, in its formal structures, mode of discourse and its narrative patterns, hosts a contest between different versions of history. On the one hand, the aura of dark irrationality and pleasurable terror enveloping gothic fiction offers a critique of the enlightenment construction of history as a linear account of that which William Godwin characterised as the 'progress and varieties of civilisation'.[31] The scenes of terror and pleasurable fear entertained by gothic fiction indulge a kind of creative anachronism, proposing untoward, perverse connections between the deep past and contemporary life and politics. On the other hand, the novelising strategies of gothic fiction, even when presented within the formal structure of the romance, propose a scepticism not only towards supernatural experience and superstitious belief but towards all naive forms of credulity. Entertaining enchantment is served up in a self-conscious mode of questioning criticism that professes its own allegiance to enlightenment strategies. The unresolved nature of this contest, played out over forms of knowledge and kinds of history, is given extended space in the fictional landscape of the gothic. In this sense, gothic fiction is itself is a mode of historicist criticism. The distinctive tone of the examples surveyed above, from Faujas de Saint-Fond, Ann Radcliffe and Henry Fuseli to Anna Letitia Aikin and Nathan Drake, is redolent of the simultaneous ambivalence and particularity of this gothic historicism.

— NOTES —

1. Barthélemy Faujas de Saint-Fond, *Travels in England, Scotland, and the Hebrides*, 2 vols (London: James Ridgway, 1799), I, pp. 43–4, 46–7.
2. Ann Radcliffe, *The Mysteries of Udolpho*, ed. Bonamy Dobrée and Terry Castle (1794; Oxford: Oxford University Press, 1998), p. 348.
3. Radcliffe, *The Mysteries of Udolpho*, p. 662.

4. John Knowles, *The Life and Writings of Henry Fuseli, Esq*, 3 vols (London: Henry Colburn and Richard Bentley, 1831), I, p. 64. Over the next forty-five years, Fuseli completed four versions in oil of *The Nightmare*, and three engravings were published. Gert Schiff, *Johann Heinrich Füssli, 1741–1825: Abbildungen* (Zurich: Verlag Berichthaus, 1973), Nos 757, 757a, 928, 975, 1789, 1502, 1503.

5. Peter Tomory, *The Life and Art of Henry Fuseli* (London: Thames and Hudson, 1972), pp. 92–3.

6. Nicolas Powell, *Fuseli: 'The Nightmare'* (London: Lane, 1973); and Miles L. Chappell, 'Fuseli and the "judicious adoption" of the antique in the "Nightmare"', *Burlington Magazine*, 126 (1986), pp. 421–2.

7. Samuel Johnson, *Dictionary of the English Language* (London: W. Strahan, 1755).

8. Nicolas Kiessling, *The Incubus in English Literature: Provenance and Progeny* (Washington State University Press, 1977).

9. I.B [John Bullokar], *An English Expositor: teaching the interpretation of the hardest words in our language* (London: John Legatt, 1616).

10. Giovanni Lovrich, *Osservazioni di Giovani Lovrich sopra diversi pezzi del viaggio in Dalmazia del Signor Abate Alberto Fortis* (Venice: Francesco Sansoni, 1776), p. 201.

11. John Bond, *An Essay on the Incubus, or Nightmare* (London: D. Wilson and T. Durham, 1753), pp. 2–3.

12. 'John Floyer on the Humours', quoted in Johnson, *Dictionary*.

13. Bond, *Incubus*, p. 19.

14. 'Oneirodynia', *Encyclopaedia Britannica*, 2nd edn (Edinburgh: J. Balfour et al., 1780), VI, p. 4809.

15. Bond, *Incubus*, pp. 21, 46–7, 49.

16. Algernon Graves, *The Royal Academy: A Complete Dictionary* (1905–6; Bath: Kingsmead Reprints, 1970), II, p. 184.

17. Anna Letitia Aikin, 'On the Pleasure Derived from Objects of Terror', in John and Anna Letitia Aikin, *Miscellaneous Pieces in Prose* (London: J. Johnson, 1773), pp. 120–1, 125–6.

18. Edmund Burke, *Philosophical Enquiry into the Origin of our Ideas of the Sublime and Beautiful*, ed. J. T. Boulton (London: Routledge and Kegan Paul, 1958), pp. 39–40.

19. For further discussion of the sublime in the eighteenth century, see: Samuel Holt Monk, *The Sublime: A Study of Critical Theories in Eighteenth-Century England* (1935; Ann Arbor: University of Michigan Press, 1962); and Peter de Bolla and Andrew Ashfield, *The Sublime: a Reader in British Eighteenth-century Aesthetic Theory* (Cambridge: Cambridge University Press, 1996).

20. Vijay Mishra, *The Gothic Sublime* (Albany: State University of New York Press, 1994); David Morris, 'Gothic Sublimity', *New Literary History*, 16 (1985), pp. 299–319.

21. Nathan Drake, 'On Objects of Terror', *Literary Hours: or Sketches Critical and Narrative*, 2 vols, 2nd edn (Sudbury: T. Cadell & W. Davies, 1800), I, pp. 353–6, 359.
22. The term horizon of expectation is defined (more rigorously than here) by Hans Robert Jauss in *Toward an Aesthetic of Reception*, trans. Timothy Bahti (Brighton: The Harvester Press, 1982), pp. 9–45. See also Jerome McGann, *The Beauty of Inflections: Literary Investigations in Historical Method and Theory* (Oxford: Clarendon Press, 1985), pp. 17–65; and Paul Hamilton, *Historicism*, (London: Routledge, 1996).
23. Edith Birkhead, *The Tale of Terror: a Study of Gothic Romance* (New York: Russell & Russell, 1921); Eino Railo, *The Haunted Castle: a Study of the Elements of English Romanticism* (London: George Routledge & Sons, 1927); and Montague Summers, *The Gothic Quest* (London: Fortune Press, 1938).
24. James Watt, *Contesting the Gothic: Fiction, Genre and Cultural Conflict, 1764–1832* (Cambridge: Cambridge University Press, 1999), pp. 68–76.
25. M. G. Lewis to Goethe, 21 April 1799, *Some English Correspondents of Goethe*, ed. D. F. S. Scott (London: Methuen & Co., 1949), p. 1.
26. Robert Miles, 'The Gothic Aesthetic: The Gothic as Discourse', *The Eighteenth Century*, 32, 1 (1991), pp. 39–57.
27. Peter Gay, *Freud: a Life for our Time* (London: J.M. Dent & Sons, 1988), p. 103.
28. Maggie Kilgour, *The Rise of the Gothic Novel* (London: Routledge, 1995), p. 220.
29. Robert Miles, *Ann Radcliffe: The Great Enchantress* (Manchester: Manchester University Press, 1995), p. 108.
30. Terry Castle, *The Female Thermometer: Eighteenth-Century Culture and the Invention of the Uncanny* (New York and Oxford: Oxford University Press, 1995), p. 5.
31. William Godwin, 'Of History and Romance' (1797), in *Things As They Are; or, The Adventures of Caleb Williams*, ed. Maurice Hindle (London: Penguin, 1988), p. 360.

CHAPTER ONE

History and the gothic novel
Horace Walpole, The Castle of Otranto (1764)

I. WHAT'S GOTHIC ABOUT — THE GOTHIC NOVEL?

In answering a simple question like 'what is a gothic novel?', critics and readers have long been struck by the tension between these two key terms 'gothic' and 'novel'. While 'gothic' invokes an historical enquiry, 'novel' implicitly refers to a literary form; while 'gothic' implies the very old, the novel claims allegiance with 'the new'. As Ian Watt jokes, 'It is hardly too much to say that etymologically the term "Gothic Novel" is an oxymoron for "Old New"'.[1] In this chapter, the tension between these terms will be explored by examining each within a defining opposition: the first between the gothic and the enlightenment; and the second between the novel and the romance. Both oppositions reveal a complex and enlightening history of their usages (etymology) and also demonstrate how the gothic novel encodes debates about history. It is clear that to eighteenth-century readers, the term 'gothic' identified a complicated and slippery topic connoting a number of related but distinct judgements about medieval culture, national history, civic virtue and the enlightenment. Judgements about the propriety and value of the gothic lay behind Horace Walpole's decision to rename the second edition of his novel, *The Castle of Otranto*: when it had first appeared on 24 December 1764, the anonymous novel was subtitled 'A Story'; the second edition, published in April 1795, prompted by the rapid sale of the first 500 copies, was subtitled 'A Gothic Story'. In later decades, other writers followed Walpole by identifying their work as 'gothic', such as Clara Reeve's *The Old English Baron: A Gothic Story* (1778), but as James Watt observes, these only ever amounted to a handful.[2] Walpole's use of the term was not without precedent, although there was no contemporary agreement about what it might mean when applied to a prose fiction.

— QUESTIONS OF FORM: THE NOVEL AND THE ROMANCE —

It was only in the 1790s that some agreement between readers, critics, booksellers and writers emerged about the constitution of the novel as a form. Throughout the eighteenth century, most prose fictions referred to themselves as histories, memoirs, or romances; while 'the novel' was a short tale of romantic love. Nonetheless, it is of the period from the late seventeenth to the mid-eighteenth century that literary history has come to speak of the rise of the novel. As a new genre, the novel was not burdened by precedent: the form had no strict set of rules, no long heritage of writers. Writers and readers were, in comparison with more prestigious genres of verse and drama, unconstrained by expectations of what was possible or permitted. It seemed to many that the novel consciously rejected the rules and conventions of prior literary forms, neglecting older plots in favour of innovative stories drawn from news, gossip and scandal. In consequence, the writing of novels was not perceived to be difficult, implying that there were few educational or status barriers to willing writers. By appealing to a wide public readership, the novel became associated with the nascent consciousness of the culture of the people.

Ian Watt's *The Rise of the Novel* (1957), the seminal account of this history, connected the novel's accessibility to writers, and its address to a new wide, popular audience, with the 'rise of the middle class' in eighteenth-century Britain.[3] The property that clearly identified the novel as new, Ian Watt argues, was the formal property of realism, derived especially from a reading of the novels of Daniel Defoe, Henry Fielding and Samuel Richardson. The techniques of formal realism shared the empirical method of science, based on the observation of events in everyday ordinary life. As the critic and novelist Clara Reeve observed in 1785, events in novels should transpire in ways that are recognisably like events in the real world. She observed:

> The Novel is a picture of real life and manners, and of the times in which it is written. [. . .] The novel gives a familiar relation of such things, as pass every day before our eyes, such as may happen to our friend, or to ourselves; and the perfection of it, is to represent every scene, in so easy and natural a manner, as to make them so probable, as to deceive us into a persuasion (at least while we are reading) that all is real, until we are affected by the joys or distresses, of the persons in the story, as if they were our own.[4]

By valuing the experience of the individual and privileging information accessed through the senses, the novel helped to theorise a new conception of the self. The novel's experiential bias gave unprecedented access to the interior thoughts and emotional status of character, providing extended space to the deliberations of private feeling, often played out in difficult, complex moral dilemmas. As an experiment in conduct, the novel played an important part in forming and refining the concerns and morality of the emergent middle class.

The title of Clara Reeve's study, *The Progress of Romance* (1785), suggests the early history of the novel offers an illuminating contrast with the genre of the romance. Although the genre of the romance had an established history extending back to the fourteenth and fifteenth centuries, by the seventeenth century, the romance was declining in relevance and popularity. In the eighteenth century, the general hypothesis was that the romance had been eclipsed in importance by other varieties of prose fiction, in particular the novel. The medieval romance was conventionally located at a distance from the contemporary scene of everyday life: in a socially remote society (amongst the nobility and aristocracy); in the distant past and exotic locations; and revising well-known stories. Romance characterisation, tending towards idealisation of particular traits, expressed the essence of its heroes and villains in generalised portraits depicted in the most profuse and sensuous detail. In romance's mode of excess and extreme, the supernatural, miraculous and wonderful are given ample attention.[5] Despite becoming a by-word for corrupting entertainment, the genre of the romance did not completely disappear in the mid-eighteenth century. Readers retained the taste for medieval romance, and publishers kept many in print to satisfy this demand (Smollett's translation of *Gil Blas* was published in 1755, for example). Ann Radcliffe proposed an allegiance to the romance, at once legitimating and critical, in the titles of her novels.

The persistence of romance poses a significant question to the historiography of the 'rise of the novel'. The progressive teleology of this account suggests that the rise of the novel leads to the extirpation of romance. The revival of romance characteristics in the late-eighteenth century, of which the gothic novel is but one signal, suggests the argument needs refinement. Some recent critics, such as William Beatty Warner and Homer Obed Brown, have argued that the 'rise of the novel' was not the result of an orderly progress of superior technique but was secured by the active critical intervention of key writers. Richardson wrote that *Pamela* (1740–1) was a 'New Species of Writing',[6] and Fielding similarly noted that his novel *Joseph Andrews* (1742) was a 'kind of writing, which I do not remember to have seen hitherto attempted in our language'.[7] In their fiction and criticism, these writers sought to revise and refine the novel to a more moral project, in the course of which they worked to distance their work from the fiction-making of the previous generation of writers. Richardson remarked that his reformed novel 'might possibly turn young people into a course of reading different from the pomp and parade of romance-writing, and dismissing the improbable and marvellous, with which novels generally abound.'[8] Warner argues that the emergence of the domestic novel was rather the effect of a violent, aggressive and deliberate suppression of earlier popular traditions of fiction (such as the secret history and scandalous memoir of Aphra Behn and Eliza Haywood) in the name of a new moral fictional discourse, self-consciously sentimental and ethically proper. Richardson and Fielding, Warner concludes, 'successfully hegemonize the novel through a series of articulatory moves that reshape what their culture takes the novel to be'.[9] The popular fictions of Aphra Behn, Daniel Defoe, Delarivier Manley and Eliza Heywood, for example, were denigrated as both aesthetically weak and morally corrupt. In particular this type of fiction writing was constructed as distinctively feminine (contrasting its entertaining indulgence with their own civic and masculine literary project) and hence associated with the discredited genre of the romance.

As some eighteenth-century critical writing stated, the novel in its gothic mode effected the reconciliation of certain romance conventions with those of the novel. Horace Walpole, in the preface to the second edition of *The Castle of Otranto* (1764), explained that his 'Gothic Story', as he called it, 'was an attempt to blend the two kinds of romance, the antient and the modern'. This enigmatic distinction between them offers an imprecise analogy between twentieth-century categories of the romance and the novel. Walpole continues:

> In the former, all was imagination and improbability: in the latter, nature is always intended to be, and sometimes has been, copied with success. Invention has not been wanting; but the great resources of fancy have been dammed up, by a strict adherence to common life. But if in the latter species Nature has cramped imagination, she did but take her revenge, having been totally excluded from old romances. The actions, sentiments, conversations, of the heroes and heroines of antient days were as unnatural as the machines employed to put them into motion.[10]

It was not clear, in contemporary terms, that Walpole's distinction was anything more than instrumental. For one early reviewer, the difference lay in history: *The Monthly Review* stated that the book was 'an old Italian romance' when 'published as a translation'; but included it in the category of 'Novels' when they discovered that Walpole was the author.[11] Walpole's preface describes a theoretical *rapprochement* between the modes of fiction writing that the Richardson and Fielding debate proposes as antithetical. His innovatory, almost paradoxical subtitle, 'A Gothic Story', re-invigorates some significant romance attributes by incorporating them into the genre of the novel. As romance elements dilate the definition of the novel, they also enliven and energise it.

In her essay 'On Romances' (1773), Anna Letitia Aikin considered romance as a mode of discourse rather than a genre, as a tendency towards whimsical fictionality. 'To the writer of fiction alone, every ear is open, and every tongue lavish of applause; curiosity sparkles in every eye, and every bosom is throbbing with concern.' The supernatural power of fictional fancy, then, allows experiences beyond the rational.

> To follow the chain of perplexed ratiocination, to view with critical skill the airy architecture of systems, to unravel the web of sophistry, or weigh the merits of opposite hypotheses, requires perspicacity, and presupposes learning. Works of this kind, therefore, are not so well adapted to the generality of readers as familiar and colloquial composition; for few can reason, but all can feel; and many who cannot enter into an argument, may yet listen to a tale.

The free play of romance gives prose its quality of 'enchantment', transporting the readers imagination to:

> the fairy land of fiction, where every bank is sprinkled with flowers, and every gale loaded with perfume ... Invited by these flattering scenes, the student quits the investigation of truth, in which he perhaps meets with no less fallacy, to exhilarate his mind with new ideas, more agreeable, and more easily attained.[12]

Clara Reeve argued that romance inspired a 'delight' in 'Fictitious Stories' that extended across 'all times and all countries, by oral tradition in barbarous, by writing in more civilised ones'.[13]

The return of romance elements does, however, present a formal problem to these fictions. Ian Watt's identification of 'formal realism' as the hallmark of the novel cannot completely describe the range of formal effects attempted by gothic fiction, for they frequently, and as a matter of course, represent events outside of nature. As a novel, the gothic ought to rely on a contemporary setting and an empirical understanding of how the world operates. However, the gothic is often located in the distant past or a distant foreign location. It often incorporates older or traditional plots, and it has recourse to fantastical or supernatural events, that cannot be justified or analysed by empirical method. As Anna Letitia Aikin suggests, the marvellous and the supernatural exposes a significant problem for the novel's regime of formal realism. Techniques of realism cannot describe the marvels and wonders of the supernatural, which are by their nature unknown to empiricism. Nonetheless, the gothic consistently approaches the supernatural as if it can be described or observed in the mode of formal realism. By novelising the supernatural, the monstrous and the unspeakable, the gothic attempts to inscribe the passions of fear and terror. In the coming chapters, different responses to this problem are canvassed. Ann Radcliffe and Charles Brockden Brown consistently provide rational, empirically observable, material solutions to the supposedly supernatural events described by her novels. Matthew Lewis and Charlotte Dacre, on the other hand, offer narratives in which things happen that can only be ascribed to the supernatural. The contest these novels stage between credulity and reason, superstition and rationalism signals the novels' engagement in a discourse of enlightenment historicism.[14]

QUESTIONS OF HISTORY: GOTHS AND THE AGE OF ENLIGHTENMENT

History relates that the Goths were the barbarians who destroyed classical Roman civilisation and plunged the civilised world into centuries of ignorance and darkness. The Goths were a German tribe who lived on the northern and eastern borders of the Roman Empire, who, after long-running border disputes, launched a widespread invasion of the empire in 376 AD. The Goths and Lombards, Vandals and Huns crossed the Danube, and repeatedly defeated the Roman forces, before sacking Rome in 410 AD. Although the Goths established their own kingdoms in France and Italy, the history of these events is typically (but unfairly) depicted as a sordid tale of pillage and plunder, of destruction and tyranny: it is a narrative of the fall of empire, not the rise of something new in its place.

By the eighteenth century, 'Goth' was a blanket term for any of the German tribes, as if distinctions between individual tribes were not significant. Following the sixth-century historian Jordanes, the name Goths referred to the Germanic tribes in general, including the Angles, Saxons and Jutes who had settled England after 449 AD. The term 'gothic' came to stand for medieval culture, and thus for the culture dominant in England in the 'Dark Ages' (in the period from the seventh to the thirteenth centuries). As the eighteenth-century literary critic Nathan Drake argued, 'the Dark Ages of Christian Europe' – which he dated from the eighth to the tenth centuries – were characterised by the 'barbaric ignorance' of its 'rude and untutored conquerors.'[15] As a consequence of their significant role in the collapse of the Roman Empire, regarded as the greatest civilisation the world had known, the word gothic came to mean 'barbarous' – a connotation that can be found in Chaucer and Shakespeare, and which survives into the eighteenth century. Dr Johnson, in his *Dictionary* of 1775, defined a Goth as 'one not civilised, one deficient in general knowledge, a barbarian'. As Edward Gibbon notes, 'the name of Goths is frequently but improperly used as a general appellation of rude and warlike barbarism.'[16] As this implies, the surviving examples of medieval culture, such as architecture or literature, were regarded as barbarous.[17] By a reversal at once metaphorical and significant, that which was barbarous became known as gothic, including the surviving fragments of medieval culture, such as architecture and poetry. Samuel Taylor Coleridge, in his 'Lectures on Literature' in 1818, devoted the first lecture to 'a portrait of the (so called) Dark Ages of Europe', which he entitled the 'General Character of the Gothic Mind in the Middle Ages'.[18]

In the eighteenth century, the term gothic was revised and transformed from a term connoting the unfavourable, unhappy and ruined, to a more positive and confident understanding. The emergence of gothic fiction represents one of the defining moments when an older chivalric past was idealised at the expense of a classical present. The gothic is then a conscious anachronism, presented not as an error of taste or a corrupting influence, but as a positive attribute. The past is re-valued and found to be superior to the present, a process that wears a nostalgic aspect. The revision of the meaning of gothic culture in the eighteenth century placed increasing value on the significance of gothic history and culture. There were a number of fields where this medieval gothic culture was still alive to eighteenth-century people, for instance architecture, political theory, religion, literature, and popular customs. The eighteenth-century rediscovery of medieval culture, an endeavour collectively known as antiquarianism, completes this revaluation of gothic culture. Richard Hurd, for example, in his *Letters on Chivalry and Romance* (1762), launched a complex defence of medieval literary culture from the attacks of neoclassical criticism, opposing gothic manners and culture with Roman and Grecian: 'The ages, we call barbarous, present us with many a subject of curious speculation. What for instance, is more remarkable than the Gothic Chivalry? or than the spirit of Romance, which took its rise from that singular institution'. Just as the ritualised ceremonies of chivalry had civilised war without destroying the manly vigour of the warrior, so the 'old Romances' preserved in their 'barbarous volumes' something of the heroic energy of the exploits they record.[19]

Hurd associates the gothic with highly-valued medieval characteristics like gallantry, loyalty, heroism and chivalry. He also associates these valuable characteristics with medieval literary production, even when they relate low tales of 'popular superstitions' and '*grisly specters*'. Familiarity with this material can revivify and enchant the creative productions of the modern age.

> The fancies of our modern bards are not only more gallant, but, on a change of the scene, more sublime, more terrible, more alarming, than those of the classic fables. In a word, you will find that the *manners* they paint, and the *superstitions* they adopt, are the more poetical for being Gothic.

As Hurd demonstrates, there were telling analogies between gothic literature and gothic history. Coleridge's lectures on medieval literature in 1818 also reinforced these connections. Coleridge argued that the rude and uncivilised manners of 'our remote ancestors from the forests of Germany, or the deep dells and rocky mountains of Norway' made an important contribution to the predilections and general tone or habit of thought or feeling of English literature and culture. Their gothic contribution, he claimed, was

> the love of the marvellous, the deeper sensibility, the higher reverence for womanhood, the characteristic spirit of sentiment and courtesy; – these were the heir-looms of nature, which still regained the ascendant, whenever the use of the living mother-tongue enabled the inspired poet to appear instead of the toilsome scholar.[20]

The gothic is not the destroyer of the civilised values of classical Rome, but rather is perceived as the source and repository of some of the unique, valuable and essential elements in English culture and politics. Roman civilisation, and the neoclassical metaphor of the Augustan age in England, was recast as the source of luxury, corruption and despotism, while 'the hardy habits, the steady perseverance, the better faith' constructed the gothic as the repository of virtue and liberty. The 'gothic enlightenment', as Samuel Kliger designates it, politicised a revaluation of deep British history to reinforce British cultural solidarity in the present.[21]

— READING HISTORY AND THE GOTHIC CONSTITUTION —

During the English civil war in the 1640s, political theorists wanting to distance themselves from the old monarchist constitution clothed themselves in the rival political discourse of republicanism. These theorists invoked the glories of the republican tradition, which, in their view, encompassed not only ancient Rome and Greece, but also contemporary republican states such as Florence and Venice. Writers such as James

Harrington, in *Oceana* (1656), identified and repudiated the monarchist past as 'gothick', by which he implied it was both barbarian and ruined. Harrington argued that ancient wisdom and civilisation had been destroyed in Europe by Gothic barbarians, and that England's civil wars had liberated her from Gothic forms of government. Harrington, like other English republican writers, positively identified the republican future as neoclassical (Roman, civic and austere), and deprecated the monarchist past as gothic (barbarian, corrupt, and despotic).

With the restoration of the monarchy in 1660 (and again, during the Revolution of 1688), political theorists worked to develop a counter argument to this republican neoclassicism. Many writers sought to distance neoclassical culture (especially architecture) from its construal as a republican mode. But they also worked to revalue the gothic tradition. Specifically, they sought to identify the valuable aspects of the British constitution, such as its common law tradition, its preservation of liberty, and especially its restriction of the rights of the crown. These were figured as aspects of the constitution that had endured over a long period of history: they were, in other words, gothic elements. As Pocock explains,

> Belief in the antiquity of the common law encouraged belief in the existence of an ancient constitution, reference to which was constantly made, precedents, maxims and principles from which were constantly alleged, and which was constantly asserted to be in some way immune from the king's prerogative action; and discussion in these terms formed one of the century's chief modes of political argument.[22]

Pocock established that discussion of the ancient English constitution was used instrumentally, or strategically, in a variety of political debates to different ends. There is an important lesson for students of the gothic novel in Pocock's approach: in discourse such as this, key terms of value or resonant images – such as the ancient constitution or the gothic castle – may be both crucially significant and deeply flexible (or even ambiguous) in their meaning, even within one work.

The nature of the gothic legacy in the English constitution was the subject of fierce and complex debate amongst political theorists of the eighteenth century. Significant political philosophers like David Hume, Adam Smith and Edmund Burke debated the issue, arguing that the English constitution was the product of progressive evolution. It preserved elements of the simple and barbarous gothic system of government, while at the same time revising and refining the laws for a modern and politer era, resulting in a 'mixed' or 'balanced' constitution that was presented as the envy of the world. The gothic elements were nonetheless important and valuable because they indicated the historically remote origins of the constitution. It had existed since time out of mind, a deep past that validated the power of the constitution through a continuity established by the law and the church. To Burke, this enduring continuity in the constitution presented powerful arguments for its further continuance.[23] In Burke, then, the gothic constitution is a conservative mode, but, as we shall see, at the hand of other writers, gothic novelists amongst them, it need not be.

The debate over the gothic constitution was played out in a richly figurative manner. In the same way that the republican senate was figured as residing in Roman and classical architecture, the gothic constitution was identified with gothic architecture. The medieval castle, in particular, offered a potent symbolism, diverse and fully exploitable, to political theorists as much as gothic novelists. The castle could represent the site of the monarchy's power, but it could also figure within a more popular tradition as the place of refuge, where the entire community found protection and succour. The political symbolism of the castle was, of course, reinforced by the surviving splendours of real medieval castles (the Tower of London or Windsor Castle, for example), buildings made the subject of focused study in the late eighteenth century by architectural antiquarians. In 1765, William Blackstone deployed this image of an ancient gothic castle in his discussion of the 'the intricacy of legal process' in England. 'Dread of innovation', he remarks, has led to labyrinthine 'fictions and circuities' in the English constitution, as historically enduring structures are revised but preserved in the polite and sociable era.

> We inherit an old Gothic castle, erected in the days of chivalry, but fitted up for a modern inhabitant. The moated ramparts, the embattled towers, and the trophied halls, are magnificent and venerable, but useless. The inferior apartments, now converted into rooms of convenience, are chearful and commodious, though their approaches are winding and difficult.[24]

Blackstone's portrait of the ancient constitution as a gothic castle is an affectionate portrait, in which the castle's age, read through the picturesque aesthetic, serves a legitimating function. The apparent conservativism of Blackstone's image could also bear a common-law interpretation. Ancient constitutionalism was deployed against regal tyranny and the royal threat of absolutist government by demonstrating that the law, incorporated in the commonalty of its usages, had precedence over the monarchy. In this reading, arbitrary government by command of the sovereign was figured as a modern innovation only recently 'sprung up amidst the decaying Forms of *Gothick Policy*'.[25] The figure of the ancient gothic building of Parliament could be deployed in this defence of common-law constitutionalism. The symbolic association of the castle with political power and established authority was re-appropriated in many contexts, including the gothic novel, where it could also serve as an image of the oppressive restraint of the old order on modern innovations and change. The tensions between the polyvalent symbolism of the ancient constitution debate can be witnessed in the early gothic fictions by Walpole, Reeve and Radcliffe.

II. READING GOTHIC HISTORIES: WALPOLE'S *THE CASTLE OF OTRANTO*

Horace Walpole's *The Castle of Otranto* is widely regarded as the first gothic novel, and therefore as the source of one of the major strands of modern literary history. It was published in December 1764 by the London publisher Thomas Lownds. It was reasonably popular at the time, particularly in Walpole's own circle of sophisticates and wits, but its publication history suggests that it was most popular with a general audience twenty to thirty years later in the 1790s, when at least nine editions were published, against only two in the previous two decades. Against the context of Radcliffe's gothic, Walpole's weird mixture of genres was stabilised and contained. To Radcliffe's contemporaries, Walpole's novel stopped being odd, and became an origin. The Tory critic Thomas Matthias complained in *The Pursuits of Literature* (1796) that, 'The spirit of enquiry which he [Horace Walpole] introduced was rather frivolous, though pleasing, and his Otranto Ghosts have rather propagated their species with unequalled fecundity. The spawn is in every novel shop.'[26]

The novel presents its own elaborate fictional account of its origins, which pretends that it is an authentic product of the period in which it is set. In a complicated framing structure, the novel claims to be itself a gothic document, reproduced by a process of transmission into the form presented by Walpole. The title-page of the first edition initially made these claims: *The Castle of Otranto, a story. Translated by William Marshal, Gent. From the Original Italian of Onuphrio Muralto, Canon of the Church of St Nicholas at Otranto*. The 'Preface' to the first edition, supposedly written by the translator of the Italian gothic document, William Marshal, elaborated this fiction of origin.

> The following work was found in the library of an ancient catholic family in the north of England. It was printed at Naples, in the black letter, in the year 1529. How much sooner it was written does not appear. The principal

incidents are such as were believed in the darkest ages of christianity; but the language and conduct have nothing that favours of barbarism. The style is purest Italian.[27]

Marshal judges that the text was written by an Italian clergyman in the period of the crusades, at some time in the eleventh to thirteenth centuries. The version seen by Marshal was supposedly a sixteenth-century Italian transcription of the original text. Marshal translates and disseminates the text to its modern eighteenth-century English audience; the comfortable and relaxed readership is thus triply removed from the scene of action. Marshal's chronology, with its inconsistent dates and misleading scholarship, satirises the speculative imprecision of the learned scholarship. The early reviews of the still-anonymous novel credulously entertained the premise that it was a genuine medieval document. The Monthly Review praised Marshal's judicious remarks about the original manuscript, 'on the supposition that the work really is a translation'; although it commented that only entertainment was to be found amongst 'the absurdities of Gothic fiction'.[28] After the second edition declared it to be 'a modern performance', the same journal stated that the novel instanced 'a false taste in a cultivated period of learning', and accused Walpole of being an 'advocate' for 'the barbarous superstitions of Gothic devilism!'[29] The Critical Review, praising Marshal as 'the ingenious translator of the very curious performance', expressed concern that the supernatural wonders suggested a 'modern fabrick', but concluded with an air of jaded insouciance that 'whether he speaks seriously or ironically, we neither know or care'.[30]

The editorial fiction of Marshal's framing device, technically known as a discovered manuscript, was a common authenticating procedure in eighteenth-century fiction. The 'Preface' suggests that the circumstantial realism of the narrative argues that it is founded on fact.

> Though the machinery is invention, and the names of the actors imaginary, I cannot but believe that the groundwork of the story is founded on truth. The scene is undoubtedly laid in some real castle. The author seems frequently, without design, to describe particular parts.[31]

The realism of the narrative testifies to its truthfulness as historical text, yet paradoxically, it also undoes the claim to truthfulness, because such circumstantial realism is what makes it a novel, a quintessentially modern genre. In any case, the 'Preface' argues that this circumstantial authenticity of time and space (a variety of formal realism) is balanced against the magical or supernatural aspects of the text, that which the novel calls 'the air of the miraculous'. The novel is actively credulous in the super-natural. The supernatural is categorically an unnovelistic aspect of the gothic – it cannot be reconciled with the empirical observation of the novel. As the theoretical conjectures of the two prefaces explore, Walpole demonstrates that he has a sophisticated understanding of the divergent conventions of writing in the mode of the novel and the romance. However, the ambivalence as to which course to follow renders the text structurally unstable, with the pastiche of medieval narrative undercutting the mode of formal realism. As Walpole's 'Preface to the Second Edition' notes, the success of the subterfuge muddled his polit-ical virtue with his fictional prowess, and as himself ('H. W.') he asked for pardon for publishing under the 'disguise' of 'the borrowed personage of a translator'.[32]

Walpole later offered an anecdotal account of how he came to write 'the little story book'; a biographical account that supplements the bibli-ographical account offered by the text itself. During the 1750s, Walpole had been engaged in an antiquarian project that he referred to ironically as 'Gothicising'. Visiting old country churches and the seats of ancient families, renovating his villa at Strawberry Hill with galleries and cloisters, and collecting paintings, Walpole nonetheless expressed a gentlemanly distaste for the pedantic erudition of the 'learned man'. The anecdote was related by Walpole in a letter he wrote to his friend, the antiquarian clergyman Rev. William Cole, on 9 March 1765, after the novel was published, in which Walpole offered to confess 'the origin of this romance'.

> I waked one morning in the beginning of last June, from a dream, of which, all I could recover was, that I had thought myself in an antient castle (a very natural dream for a head filled like mine with Gothic story), and that on the uppermost banister of a great staircase I saw a gigantic hand in armour. In the evening I sat down, and began to write, without knowing in the least what I intended to say or relate. The work grew on my hands, and I grew fond of it – add that I was very glad to think of anything, rather than politics.

Such an account locates the novel in the realm of fiction, as a fable of romance, to use a contemporary construction. Characterising it with the diminutive tag of a 'little story-book' and a 'trifle', and confessing his preference for 'romantic scenes of antiquity', Walpole locates the text as an entertainment, a vulgar and inconsequential indulgence: 'if I have amused you, by retracing with any fidelity the manners of ancient days, I am content, and give you leave to think me as idle as you please'.[33]

Walpole's *post facto* account of the dream origins of the story has formed the back-bone of many psychoanalytic readings of the novel.[34] More instrumentally, his explanation to Cole belittles the political resonances of his text, perhaps because he is embarrassed by them, and perhaps because he realised the novel's popular success as entertaining romance was overtaking an alternative reading as satire. The prominent role Walpole played in contemporary politics, especially his part in a localised political scandal of the years 1763–4, had meant that a period out of public notice was prudent. Attacked in the disputes of Westminster party politics, Walpole turned his back on the intrigues of political faction, and retired to his house at Twickenham, where he took refuge in writing and the past. He later explained,

> Visions, you know, have always been my pasture; and so far from growing old enough to quarrel with their emptiness, I almost think there is no wisdom comparable to that of exchanging what is called the realities of life for dreams. Old castles, old pictures, old histories, and the babble of old people make one live back into centuries, that cannot disappoint one.[35]

Walpole argues that the study of history can provide an escape from the cares of the present day, a present that by comparison seems degraded and corrupted, a tawdry copy of past glories. Many readers have been happy to take Walpole at his word here, and have concluded that, indeed, the novel is a dream in which anything can happen, where the supernatural is expected, where fears can be expressed with safety, and all is entertainment – a light-hearted romp through the dungeons of an old castle, full of skeletal spectres and sleeping giants. If the novel is 'just a dream' as Walpole argues, then it is not 'political'. This is something of an under-reading.

The novel is tightly drawn, fitting into a strict structure that is not allowed to dissipate or become uncontrolled. As one contemporary reviewer remarked, 'the narrative [is] kept up with surprising spirit and propriety'.[36] The novel's brevity, pace and control invite comparison with the work of Defoe or Richardson, where detail and digression continually prolong the action, swelling the novel to sometimes inordinate length. *Otranto* is short, fast, and controlled. The supposed translator, Marshal, comments on this in the first 'Preface':

> Every thing tends directly to the catastrophe. Never is the reader's attention relaxed. The rules of the drama are almost observed throughout the conduct of the piece. The characters are well drawn, and still better maintained. Terror, the author's principal engine, prevents the story from ever languishing; and it is so often contrasted by pity, that the mind is kept up in a constant vicissitude of interesting passions.

As Marshal signals, the novel almost observes the 'rules of the drama', the 'three unities' of action, place and time established in neoclassical drama criticism by Aristotle in his *Poetics*. The tightly restricted field of action (the castle, the convent, the forest) certainly gives the novel a theatrical feel, and, like a tragedy, the action is sequential (without flash-backs or interpolated digressions). The tone, he suggests, has elements of Shakespearean tragedy too, specifically in its attempt to graft the height-ened passions, elemental situations and stylised poetic techniques of Elizabethan tragedy onto the contemporary and everyday structures of the novel. The five-chapter structure is borrowed, in a broad sense, from a Shakespearean tragedy, typically cast in five acts. This further reproduces the narrative conventions of dramatic tragedy: chapters one and three develop the main plot, chapters two and four develop the sub-plot. In the fifth chapter, like the fifth act, the two plots are resolved, the one providing the key to the other. William Warburton defended *The Castle of Otranto* for effecting 'the full purpose of the *ancient Tragedy, that is, to purge the passions by pity and terror*'. Despite this deployment of Aristotle's theory of catharsis, Warburton argued that Walpole's 'Master-piece' was 'of a new species'.[37] In the 'Preface to the second edition', given in the voice of the historical Walpole, this is made the basis for a profound innovation, where he claims, recalling Richardson, to have 'created a new species of romance'. As such, he says, 'I was at liberty to lay down what rules I thought fit for the conduct of it', even though he recognises the master pattern of Shakespearean romance. The self-conscious radicalism of his stance, demonstrating his 'genius' and 'originality', reinforces the violence of his hybridisation of romance and novel.[38]

The novel is located in the environs of the castle of Otranto, and concerns a complicated history of succession and legitimacy in the ruling elite of the principality. The main plot of *The Castle of Otranto* narrates the history of Manfred, Prince of Otranto, while the sub-plot follows a story of romantic love centred on his daughter Matilda. The main plot's primary motivating factor is established in the first page. Manfred's reign is autocratic and severe, a policy that his 'tenants and subjects' attribute to his 'dread' that his family's grasp on the throne is tenuous. His fear is exacerbated by an ancient prophecy that casts doubt on the legitimacy and extent of his entitlement to the throne. The prophecy is, however, enigmatic: '*That the castle and lordship of Otranto should pass from the present family, whenever the real owner should be grown too large to inhabit it.*' It is not clear to Manfred how he should protect himself from this fate, except that he recognises that he should ensure his family's grasp on the throne by ensuring he has an heir to succeed both him and his sickly son Conrad. In order to secure an heir, he attempts to marry his son to a beautiful young woman, Isabella, the daughter of a rival nobleman, Frederick, the marquis of Vicenza. At the opening of the novel, Manfred's intentions are thwarted when his son is suddenly killed in a most extraordinary manner: 'He beheld his child dashed to pieces, and almost buried under an enormous helmet, an hundred times more large than any casque ever made for human being.'[39] This event, despite its surpassing strangeness, resonates with the threats offered by the prophecy promising Manfred's downfall. Undeterred, Manfred renews his attempts to secure himself an heir by deciding he must himself marry Isabella, despite the fact he already has a wife, Hippolita. His wishes, perhaps better termed desires, also overlook the fact that Isabella is most unwilling.

The helmet is the first sign of the supernatural in the novel, although in truth, the handling of these elements is somewhat unusual. Walpole's supernatural is peculiarly enigmatic: it is not easy for the reader to imagine or literalise the events described. Conrad is crushed by a giant helmet, but it is not even clear that it has fallen out of the sky. A peasant, later named as Theodore, observes that the helmet resembles that on the statue of Alfonso the Good in the Church of St Nicholas. Manfred is enraged further by the news that the helmet has gone missing, and imprisons Theodore beneath the helmet. But the supernatural events proliferate: a portrait sighs and leaves its panel to walk about the castle. Later, a giant leg is reported in the galleries of the castle. The supernatural events in *The Castle of Otranto* rarely precipitate tension or fear in the reader: indeed the dominant effect they create is low comedy. A notable exception, which only seems to demonstrate that this effect is not tried elsewhere in the novel, is Frederic's encounter with the 'fleshless jaws and empty sockets' of the skeletal monk of Joppa, who reminds him of his duty.[40] Here, Walpole varies his strategy of terror by deliberately withholding information from the reader, delivering a carefully controlled tension which is finally dissipated in a shock effect that engenders the feeling of horror.

The mysterious and seemingly supernatural events pervading the castle establish an enigmatic tone of conjecture in the novel that equates readerly incomprehension with political subversion. Not knowing the meaning of the supernatural nourishes a growing sense of disquiet about Manfred's legitimacy. The arrival of a cavalcade of silent knights bearing an enormous sword from the Holy Land reinforces this subversive conjecture. On the sword's blade is written a further enigmatic prophecy:

Wher'er a casque that suits this sword is found,
With perils is thy daughter compass'd round:
Alfonso's blood alone can save the maid,
And quiet a long-restless prince's shade.[41]

This prophecy now appears decipherable, especially to Theodore. The sword appears to all to be the counterpart of the giant helmet (or casque) that killed Conrad. The deciphered prophecy unravels the political quarrel: proposing that the imperilled daughter must be Isabella, it suggests in turn that the daughter of the leader of the knights (Frederick), who is saved by Theodore, is thus the repository of Alfonso's noble blood. The solution to this enigma confirms the prediction that Manfred will fall at the hand of an over-sized force ('*whenever the real owner should be grown too large*'). The enigma is unravelled when it is related that Manfred has inherited the title only through the treachery of his grandfather, Richard, who was Alfonso's chamberlain (a minister in the government, but also a servant). Richard poisoned his master and made himself owner of Otranto by forging a will. Unbeknownst to Manfred, Alfonso's secret but true heir still lives in Theodore, who is restored eventually to the princely throne as the 'real owner' mentioned in the prophecy. The particular manipulations of the plot are controlled by the force of the supernatural, which exercises authority over the normal events of the everyday world.

The narrative of Otranto thus depends on two secret and enigmatic family histories: those of the families of Manfred and Theodore. The characters are totally helpless in the face of these hidden histories, which are revealed by forces not only outside their control but outside the natural (the supernatural in fact). These supernatural events seem to happen in order to allow historical revelations and hence, to rectify past crimes. Ian Watt concludes, 'The anterior past has all the power. Whenever the present generation attempts to avoid its fate . . . its effort is wholly ineffectual.'[42] The dominance of the past over the present seems unusually resonant in a novel that is itself presented as a version of the past. The past is the repository of the truth, a truth that the present has disregarded, but whose force will nonetheless be manifested in the present.

This sort of nostalgia is, it might be argued, a conservative gesture. One critic, Ronald Paulson, writing about the gothic representation of the French revolution, described *The Castle of Otranto* as 'a fable of the *ancien régime*', the story of one man trying to hold together 'his crumbling estate and cheat others of their rightful inheritance' (anachronistically figuring Manfred as Louis XVI).[43] This conservative or reactionary reading of the novel is not uncontested. *The Castle of Otranto* could be read as a study of revolutionary politics: it celebrates the overthrow of a tyrant, after all. Manfred is consistently described as a 'tyrant' and a 'despot', who attempts to exercise an absolute power over his servants and subjects. He also, of course, consistently abuses this power, most obviously in his attempt to force Isabella to marry him. The overthrow of Manfred by Theodore represents a radical, even revolutionary aspect. Theodore's initial appearance as a 'young peasant' allied him, in the eyes of Manfred and the reader, as one of the 'vulgar spectators' of Conrad's death.[44] Theodore's self-presentation as peasant barely masks his natural nobility revealed in the winding-up of the story: Theodore turns out to be the rightful prince usurped by Manfred. Despite Theodore's inconsistent status, Walpole's peasant prince suggests that the common people are the repository of liberty, truth and justice. Like the recumbent form of the giant Alfonso, Theodore's delayed revelation as rightful prince has echoes of the trope of the Sleeping Hero familiar in ancient constitution discourse, defined by Christopher Hill as 'the leader who has not really died, but will return one day to rescue his people'.[45]

The central role occupied by the royal family in *The Castle of Otranto* establishes that the novel is located in a high social setting. But curiously, at the same time that it details the social distance of the royal world (the rulers) from the world of servants and peasants (the ruled), it simultaneously represents the royal household as a domestic family. The novel offers a sentimental construction of the domestic family: a homely unit that ought to be, but is not, bound by ties of love and affection as much as parental authority. The novel focuses on the family and familial relations as the place where political issues and tensions may be articulated, understood and resolved. It almost seems that although this gothic novel is about dreams of ghosts and monstrous calamities, it is actually about families and children. *The Castle of Otranto*'s themes of usurpation and bastardy contest, but ultimately reinforce, the system of legitimate patriarchal inheritance – known as primogeniture – which ought to ensure the proper transmission of value between generations.[46] The novel also argues that there is nothing outside the sexual: as Isabella and Matilda show, innocence is not a proof against the evil intentions of sexual predators. Innocence is just ignorance in this novel, not an admirable moral quality, and the ignorant are at the mercy of the cunning. Isabella's narrative, especially her rejection of Manfred's unwelcome advances, suggests it is possible, and even valid, for young women to rebel against autocratic fathers. The novel argues that the parent-child relationship is a two-sided contract, not a relation of absolute power, where the father can expect complete submission.

Matilda's story dramatises this complex vindication of sentimental passion. She falls in love with Theodore, the 'noble peasant', before she is aware of his concealed aristocratic origins. Her love for someone so low in the scale of power demonstrates that she trusts her own belief in his value, rather than the value placed on him by her father. The revelation of his aristocratic origins suggests that she is vindicated in this self-trust. Learning that her father has imprisoned Theodore in a characteristic fit of paranoia (he thinks Theodore is a rival for Isabella), Matilda resolutely refuses to abandon her ostensibly humble peasant lover. She says, 'Though filial duty and womanly modesty condemn the step I am taking, yet holy charity, surmounting all other ties, justifies this act. Fly; the doors of thy prison are open.'[47] By setting her lover free, and directly countermanding the voice of the father, Matilda argues both for the redemptive power of love and (pace Clarissa) maintains the independent moral agency of women.

The novel works hard to merge the strands of the familial and the political; and, in fact, the romantic love narrative converges at the end with the history of political usurpation. Walpole uses sexuality as a significant motivating force in the novel: the passions are heightened to the extent that they become ruling passions. Characters express emotions wire-drawn to the most hyperbolic extremes. At times, sexuality is capable of resisting, or even dominating, historical forces. Typically, when characters fall in love, they do so in a totalised way: Manfred's love for Isabella, for example, is a total, blinding passion that is destructive not only to his own self-interest but also to the family he so much wants to defend. Manfred is 'enraged' by Frederic's rejection of his marital conspiracy, leaving him 'in a frame of mind capable of the most fatal excesses'. Informed by a domestic spy that Theodore is in 'private conference' with an unnamed lady at the tomb of Alfonso in St Nicholas's Church, he hurries with 'inflamed' 'spirits' to intercept them. At the church, he overhears the woman complain that Manfred would never permit her union with Theodore. Misinformed, and impetuous with passion, Manfred acts on his conjecture that Theodore's companion is Isabella by plunging his dagger into the woman's bosom. He discovers too late that he has slain his daughter Matilda (see Figure 3). As she dies with a passive resignation, 'bathed in innocent tears', Theodore imprecates Manfred's behaviour as the necessary consequence of his parental and political tyranny, crying 'Now, tyrant! behold the completion of woe fulfilled on thy impious and devoted head!'[48] Manfred's destruction of his daughter, a desperate act of self-injury, suggests providence is against him, and indeed Theodore connects the disaster with Alfonso's call for vengeance.

Figure 3. J. W. Meil, 'No. 4: [Manfred stabs Matilda]', [Horace Walpole], The Castle of Otranto. A Gothic Story (Berlin: Christ. Fred. Himbourg, 1796), opp. p. 142; British Library, London.

Manfred's political deviance, his abuse of power, his tyrannical behaviour and his usurpation of the throne, are mirrored or expressed in his perverse sexual behaviour: his adulterous, bigamous and incestuous designs on Isabella, his mad jealousy and supposed infidelity, and, most of all, his automatic recourse to violence (sexual violence) to resolve these problems. His threat to marry Isabella is a covert, and legal, attempt to rape her. Manfred's status as the violator of history, then, is expressed as a variety of sexual deviance (he wants to rape his son's wife). To some extent the novel suggests that the passions and sexuality have a force that could counter the historical motivations of the plot (usurpation). The characters operate at the behest of historical events, but they also are powerfully affected by their passions, their loves and erotic desires. Unlike the power exercised by the past, sexuality articulates a power in the present generated by the present. Manfred is a notable forerunner of a character typical of later gothic fiction (like Montoni in *The Mysteries of Udolpho* and General Tilney in *Northanger Abbey*): a tyrant who offers the reader models of both political and domestic tyranny.

— PATRIOTISM, WILKES AND THE GOTHIC —

In the second edition of the novel, Walpole elaborated his account of the novel's project, as we have seen, by examining his method of blending the genres of the romance and the novel. He defended the faults of the work – such as the comic behaviour of the servants – using an elaborate analogy with Shakespeare. According to Walpole, Shakespeare's intermixing of comic and tragic elements in works like *Hamlet* and *Julius Caesar* served as the 'model' he 'copied'.[49] The beauties of Shakespeare, he notes, are achieved because of this mixture of genres, not despite them. He explores this idea in an extensive analysis of the French critic Voltaire's criticism of Shakespeare, which he accuses of being dominated by regard for dry rules and restrictive regulations. To Walpole, literature cannot be 'reduced' by such 'fetters'. Walpole's discovery of an authoritative precedent legitimates his work: he finds 'shelter ... under the cannon of the brightest genius this country ... has produced'.[50] Such a precedent, he finds, legitimise his claims to the originality and genius of a 'new species of romance'.[51]

The claims to innovation made on behalf of *The Castle of Otranto* belie its reliance on the national tradition. Walpole's imitation of Shakespeare's 'masterly' 'pattern' associates him with a peculiarly English sense of literary creativity, at liberty from the fetters of French rule books. His defence of Shakespeare, and his spirited attack on Voltaire, was read by contemporaries as a species of patriotism that reflected creditably upon Walpole.

The Critical Review, induced into second review upon discovering the identity of the author, applauded 'the noble warmth which our author has expressed in defence of Shakespeare against Voltaire'. Against the backdrop of British victories in the recently concluded Seven Years War with France (1757–63), this critic enlisted Walpole's gothic 'in defence of the glory of this country'.[52] Even though the story is set in a feudal and Catholic Europe, the novel's championing of gothic virtue could be understood as a defence of Protestantism and British liberty.

Walpole consistently denied he had any serious ambitions – political or literary – in writing the novel: in a letter to a friend in 1780, he claimed that he could not 'affirm that I had any intention at all but to amuse myself'.[53] He, of course, explicitly rejected the idea that the novel might in some sense be about politics. But if *The Castle of Otranto* expresses anxiety about history through a forthright attack on political despotism, we might expect to be able to read it against the contemporary politics Walpole abjures. Emma Clery has argued that the novel can be located against a contemporary critique of aristocratic institutions and property rights, especially inheritance. Clery argues that the novel 'invites the reader to revel in the nightmarish collapse of a system of power that contains the seeds of its own destruction'.[54] The novel's focus on Otranto's succession crisis points the reader back to Britain's tumultuous politics of the previous century, during which two kings were deposed. The novel offers tacit support for the political settlement of the Glorious Revolution of 1688, in which the Dutch Protestant prince, William of Orange, deposed the catholic king, James Stuart – figuring Theodore as William and Manfred as the autocratic James. In terms of contemporary political discourse, Manfred's autocratic rule would have appeared as a curiously resonant political settlement, reminiscent of the Jacobite crypto-Stuart conspiracy against the Whig constitution, and the notorious abuses and corruption of the Whig ministry (1727–41) of Walpole's father, Sir Robert Walpole. Certainly, once the author's name was known, the moral offered by the supposed editor Muralto seems unusually full of resonance: 'that *the sins of the fathers are visited on their children to the third and fourth generation*' – despite the fact that Walpole's inheritance was from the first generation.[55]

Walpole opposes notions of liberty, associated with Britain's ancient 'gothic' constitution, with notions of despotism, associated with the corrupt tyranny of Britain's contemporary government. It is in this sense that Walpole's claims to have turned his back on party politics in the writing of the novel are open to conjecture. Walpole was a member of parliament, and identified with the Whigs, who formed the ministry under the leadership of Pitt (until October 1761). The subsequent ministry, led by the George II's favourite, the Earl of Bute, was widely attacked, not only for its incompetent conclusion of the Treaty of Paris, but also for its indebtedness to the King's interest. The parliamentary opposition, including Walpole, was loyal to the constitution and perceived the actions of the King and Bute as a threat to liberty: Walpole, for example, characterised Bute's brief ministry as 'a plan of absolute power'.[56] Although, like many Whigs, Walpole was given to hyperbolic statements in defence of liberty, he had long articulated anti-Court sentiment and parliamentary loyalism. Describing himself as a 'quiet republican' in 1756, he defended 'the least bad of all murders, that of a King' by hanging up a copy of the execution warrant for Charles I above his bed at Strawberry Hill.[57]

The themes and interests of *The Castle of Otranto* have warm echoes of political events in the period 1763–4 surrounding the arrest of the radical MP John Wilkes for seditious libel. This scandal, as John Samson has shown, eventually enveloped Walpole too, through his cousin Henry Conway.[58] 'The Wilkes affair', by raising issues of political liberty, freedom of expression and the actions of the London mob, expressed concerns that the period found of the utmost significance.[59] The controversy brought together a number of important strands of dissent, uniting London politicians, the crowd and disgruntled parliamentarians in an innovative alliance. Through his weekly newspaper called *The North Briton*, Wilkes had expressed a popular variety of a widespread anti-government feeling. The scandal exploded on publication of the forty-fifth edition of *The North Briton* (23 April 1763), which attacked the preliminaries for the peace treaty between Britain and France, and denounced the King's Speech. The Secretary of State (George Montague Dunk, Earl of Halifax) declared the paper 'seditious and treasonable' and had 'the authors, printers and publishers' of the newspaper arrested, using a legal device that ordered officers to 'apprehend and seize' the men, 'together with their papers, and to bring in safe custody before me, to be examined concerning the premisses'.[60] This was called a 'General Warrant' as it named no individuals, and allowed for the seizure of papers, both printed and manuscript, associated with the publication.

Throughout 1762, Walpole's biographer states, Walpole became 'increasingly sympathetic' to the point of view represented by Wilkes[61] despite being mocked in Wilkes's newspaper as part of a vindictive attack on Henry Fox, the government Paymaster.[62] Walpole was one of the voices raised against the General Warrants, arguing that their non-specific nature made them a dangerous extension of the Secretary of State's power, although such warrants had been used many times before. Wilkes and others were arrested, and secured in the Tower of London. In court, Wilkes's defence attacked the legality of the warrant, and claimed, as an MP, the privilege of being free from arrest on a charge of libel. Legal opinion swung against the warrants. As Walpole argued, 'the warrants were universally allowed to be illegal: the most profligate lawyer in the H[ouse of Commons] could not say the contrary; they were contrary to *magna charta* and the bill of rights, [. . .] those great pillars of our liberty'.[63] Writing as a 'friend to liberty' against 'despotism and corruption', Walpole deploys the language of the gothic constitution in his argument, as did many others. Although the General Warrants were established by common law precedents, this only went as far back as the 1688 revolution. This, as Lord Chief Justice Camden declared, was insufficient: 'If the practice began then, it began too late to be law now.' The language of his ruling invoked the image of the antient constitution as a gothic castle:

> The Revolution restored this [ancient] constitution to its first principles. It did no more. It did not enlarge the liberty of the subject; but gave it a better security. It neither widened nor contracted the foundation, but repaired, but perhaps added a buttress or two to the fabric; and if any minister of state has since deviated from the principles at that time recognised, all that I can say is, that, so far from being sanctified, they are condemned by the Revolution.[64]

In parliament, Walpole contributed to the defence of Wilkes from the attacks of the court party. He enlisted the support of his cousin, Henry Conway, a general in the army and a fellow MP. Throughout the winter of 1764, says his biographer R. W. Ketton-Cremer, Walpole, 'consistently voted and spoke against the Government in general warrants, the persecution of Wilkes, and all related questions of privilege and liberty.'[65] Walpole himself commented, in his *Memoirs of the Reign of King George the Third*, that, 'The tone of the ruling Administration was despotic, nor had they forgotten how lately they had trembled with apprehension of losing their power.'[66] As a result of voting with the opposition in parliament, however, Conway lost a lucrative sinecure (his command of a regiment and his position as Groom of the Royal Bedchamber), which aroused Walpole's resentment. When Conway was attacked in a pamphlet by a government hack, William Guthrie, Walpole wrote a reply that inspired Guthrie to harsher criticism.[67] Walpole attacked the constitutionalism of Conway's dismission, suggesting it was 'the business of those who mean to govern by a system of slavery and corruption'.[68] Guthrie's reply rounded on Walpole in a ferocious personal attack. Without naming

Walpole directly, Guthrie noted the 'most lady-like form of speaking' of 'the Author of the Counter Address', further suggesting that the attack was made from 'a neutral quarter, from a being between both, neither totally male or female, whom, if naturalists were to decide on, they would most likely class him by himself, by nature maleish, by disposition female, so halting between the two that it would very much puzzle a common observor to assign him his true sex.'[69] Guthrie's personal attack on Walpole's sexuality – like a 'hermaphrodite horse' who had made an attempt 'on the general's virtue' – suggested that Walpole and Conway were lovers. This grave charge (sodomy was a hanging offence) compromised Walpole's continued engagement in the opposition attack on the government.[70] As a result, Walpole retired to Strawberry Hill, where, claiming to be sick of politics and faction, he wrote *The Castle of Otranto* between 12 June and 6 August 1764, before publication on 24 December 1764. Writing to Conway on 1 September, Walpole complained that 'they have nothing better to say than that I am in love with you, have been so these twenty years, and am no giant.'[71] Walpole's reference to himself as no giant (of politics) has curious resonance in the use of the giant in the novel, as one of the preternatural signals of Manfred's illegitimate rule. Diego reports that he has seen a giant 'all clad in armour, for I saw his foot and part of his leg, and they are as large as the helmet below in the court;' although Hippolita assures Manfred that the 'vision of the gigantic leg and foot was all a fable'.[72] In the novel's conclusion, the giant is reified in 'the form of Alfonso, dilated to an immense magnitude', who appears amongst the ruins of the castle. Viewed only in fragmentary glimpses, the giant figures as the overarching omen of the ancient constitution.[73]

Wilkes, who was released from the Tower after a week, considerably broadened the issue, raising a popular cry addressed to 'all the middling and inferior set of people'. On his release, the mob escorted him to his house crying 'Wilkes and Liberty'. Wilkes had, however, anonymously printed a pornographic poem called 'The Essay on Women', which was bound and sold with No. 45 of *The North Briton*. The prime minister, George Grenville, accused him (probably correctly) of being the author, and summoned him to appear before the House of Commons on a charge of blasphemy. In an extraordinary move, the ministry ordered the common hangman to burn all available copies of No. 45, but when he attempted to do this outside the Royal Exchange, a mob of 500 gathered and pelted the sheriffs with stones. The tumult prevented the ritual happening, while the mob took the newspaper in triumph to Temple Bar where they lit a bonfire, burnt members of the government in effigy and shouted 'Wilkes and Liberty'. Wilkes evaded arrest by escaping to France, where he lived in exile until 1768. During Walpole's sojourn in Paris in 1765, Wilkes visited him twice: 'He was very civil,' Walpole remarked, but 'his conversation shows how little he has lived in good company, and the chief turn of it is the grossest bawdy.'[74]

There are numerous connections between the Wilkes affair and the story of Manfred's destruction in *The Castle of Otranto*. Samson argues that 'Manfred himself is almost directly a portrait of [the prime minister] Grenville',[75] identifying the book as a political satire. Bute too may have been a target. Manfred's imprisonment of Theodore under the giant helmet has confused echoes of the detainment of Wilkes in the Tower, especially the unruly behaviour of the crowd, possessed of the 'bewildered reasonings' of the 'mob' catching cries from their superiors.[76] Both Wilkes and Theodore suffer arbitrary imprisonment within the symbolic embodiment of ancient liberty: the Tower of London suggesting the royal perversion of the gothic constitution just as the giant helmet reifies the claim of Alfonso's true heirs to Otranto. Both the novel and history have recourse to a common-law argument, on a principle that something is true because older. The arguments of the Wilkes affair had frequent recourse to notions of the ancient constitution. In the novel, Walpole signals that, although the established order (Manfred's reign) appears stable and legitimate, it is not so unless founded in an original legitimacy (such as that enjoyed by Alfonso the Good). Manfred's legitimacy is insubstantial, as were the General Warrants, because it rests in recent history. Innovation – political or literary – is read as a variety of usurpation.

The novel, then, was available for a reading as a serious satire written against the government, attacking the administration's unwarranted and despotic attempts to silence its enemies. But it is noticeable that no contemporary readers read the novel in this way. The reviewers worried more about its curious tone and credibility as a discovered gothic manuscript: and in the 1790s, when the novel garnered even more popular success, the resonance of the Wilkes affair would have dissipated. Nonetheless, the general aspects of this satire remained cogent to later readers. Questioning the constitutional settlement by throwing into crisis notions of succession and legitimacy, Walpole invigorates the gothic as a political problem by introducing the ambiguous and disturbing factor of sexuality, most particularly the problem of women, a concern for later gothic novelists too.

The satiric opacity of Walpole's novel seems to confirm the hermeneutic *impasse* contemporary readers located in the novel's tone. In 1765, Walpole's friend George Williams wrote to George Selwyn,

How do you think Horry Walpole has employed that leisure which his political frenzy has allowed of? In writing a novel . . . and such a novel, that no boarding-school Miss of thirteen could get half through without yawning. It consists of ghosts and enchantments . . . He says it was a dream, and I fancy one when he had some feverish disposition in him.[77]

The nightmarish quality of Walpole's 'novel', as Williams calls it, reinforced by its reliance on the 'enchantments' associated with romance, was the antidote to 'political frenzy'. When in 1780 Robert Jephson adapted the novel for the stage, as a tragedy entitled *The Count of Narbonne*, Walpole replied that making a 'regular' neoclassical tragedy was 'an intention I am sure I do not pretend to have conceived'. Although Walpole was amused at Jephson having made 'so rational a play out of my wild tale', he regretted the omission of 'the marvellous', upon which so much depended.[78] However, in general, the novel's first readers and critics were perplexed by its unstable and eccentric tonal range. Clara Reeve, in her estimation of *The Castle of Otranto* in the preface to her own 'gothic story' *The Old English Baron* (1788), found that Walpole's supernatural tested certain limits of credibility and caused a disturbing comic effect: 'When your expectation is wound up to the highest pitch, these circumstances take it down with a witness, destroy the work of imagination, and, instead of attention, excite laughter.' As Reeve concludes, she was 'surprised and vexed to find the enchantment dissolved', a 'disappointment' that she reports she shared with several readers.[79] A clearly irritated Walpole replied that her own novel was not only 'devoid of imagination and interest', but 'admitted a ghost' despite having 'condemned the marvellous'.[80] Later in the century, although the novel was already celebrated as the origin of the gothic tale, some readers found it less than compelling. In 1797, Thomas Green noted in his diary that he had read *Otranto* 'which grievously disappointed my expectations. The tale is, in itself, insipid.' By contrast, 'Mrs Radcliffe . . . evokes scenes of far more thrilling horror, than are attained by the supernatural and extravagant machinery.'[81]

— Notes —

1. Ian Watt, 'Time and Family in the Gothic Novel: *The Castle of Otranto*', *Eighteenth-Century Life*, 10, 3 (1986), pp. 159–71, p. 158.
2. James Watt, *Contesting the Gothic: Fiction, Genre and Cultural Conflict, 1764–1832* (Cambridge: Cambridge University Press, 1999), p. 70.
3. Ian Watt, *The Rise of the Novel: Studies in Defoe, Richardson, and Fielding* (London: Chatto, 1957). See also Michael McKeon, *The Origins of the English*

Novel, 1600–1740 (Baltimore: The Johns Hopkins University Press, 1987); and J. Paul Hunter, *Before Novels, The Cultural Contexts of Eighteenth-Century English Fiction* (London: Norton, 1990).

4. Clara Reeve, *The Progress of Romance, Through Times, Countries, and Manners*, 2 vols (London: the Author, 1785), I, p. 111.

5. Gillian Beer, *The Romance* (London: Methuen, 1970), p. 3.

6. Samuel Richardson to Aaron Hill, 26 January 1746/7, *Selected Letters*, ed. John Carroll (Oxford: Clarendon Press, 1964), p. 78.

7. Henry Fielding, *The History of the Adventures of Joseph Andrews, and of his Friend Mr. Abraham Adams*, ed. R. F. Brissenden (1742; London: Penguin Books, 1985), p. 25.

8. Richardson to Hill [1741], *Letters*, p. 41.

9. William B. Warner, 'The Elevation of the Novel in England: Hegemony and Literary History', *ELH*, 59 (1992), pp. 577–96, p. 581. See also Ian Duncan, *Modern Romance and Transformations of the Novel: The Gothic, Scott, Dickens* (Cambridge: Cambridge University Press, 1992), pp. 6–15.

10. Horace Walpole, *The Castle of Otranto*, ed. Emma Clery (1764; Oxford: Oxford University Press, 1994), p. 9.

11. *The Monthly Review*, 32 (May 1765), p. 394.

12. Anna Letitia Aikin, 'On Romances', *Miscellaneous Pieces in Prose* (London: J. Johnson, 1773), pp. 41–3.

13. Clara Reeve, 'Preface', *The Old English Baron: a Gothic Story*, 2nd edn (London: Edward and Charles Dilly, 1788), p. iii.

14. John Bender, 'A New History of the Enlightenment', in Leo Damrosch (ed.), *The Profession of Eighteenth-Century Literature: Reflections on an Institution* (Madison: The University of Wisconsin Press, 1992), pp. 62–83; and David Richter, *The Progress of Romance; Literary Historiography and the Gothic Novel* (Columbus: Ohio State University Press, 1996).

15. Nathan Drake, *Literary Hours: or Sketches Critical and Narrative*, 2 vols, 2nd edn (Sudbury: T. Cadell & W. Davies, 1800), pp. 258–9.

16. Edward Gibbon, *The History of the Decline and Fall of the Roman Empire*, ed. David Womersley, 3 vols (1766–88; London: Allen Lane The Penguin Press, 1994), I, x, p. 255.

17. Alfred Longueil, 'The word "gothic" in eighteenth century criticism', *Modern Language Notes*, 38 (1923), pp. 453–60, p. 453

18. S. T. Coleridge, 'Lectures on Literature (1818)', *Coleridge's Miscellaneous Criticism*, ed. Thomas Middleton Raysor (London: Constable & Co., 1936), pp. 3, 6.

19. Richard Hurd, *Letters on Chivalry and Romance* (London: A. Millar, 1762), pp. 1, 24, 54–5.

20. Coleridge, 'Lectures on Literature', pp. 20–1.

21. Samuel Kliger, *The Goths in England: a Study of Seventeenth and Eighteenth Century Thought* (Cambridge, MA: Harvard University Press, 1952), pp. 33–4.

22. J. G. A. Pocock, *The Ancient Constitution and the Feudal Law* (Cambridge: Cambridge University Press, 1987), p. 46.
23. R. J. Smith, *The Gothic Bequest: Medieval Institutions in British Thought, 1688–1863* (Cambridge: Cambridge University Press, 1987), pp. 71–96. See also John Phillip Reid, 'The Jurisprudence of Liberty: the Ancient Constitution in the Legal Historiography of the Seventeenth and Eighteenth Centuries', *The Roots of Liberty: Magna Carta, Ancient Constitution, and the Anglo-American Tradition of Rule of Law*, ed. Ellis Sandoz (Columbia and London: University of Missouri Press, 1993), pp. 147–231.
24. William Blackstone, *Commentaries on the Laws of England*, 4 vols (Oxford: Clarendon Press, 1765–69), III, 17, pp. 267–8.
25. *The Spirit and Principles of Whigs and Jacobites Compared* (London: R. Dodsley, 1746), p. 29.
26. Thomas J. Mathias, *The Pursuits of Literature: a satirical poem in dialogue*, 3rd edn (London: T. Becket, 1797), IV, p. 87n.
27. Walpole, *Otranto*, p. 5.
28. *The Monthly Review*, 32 (January 1765), pp. 97–9.
29. *The Monthly Review*, 32 (May 1765), p. 394.
30. *The Critical Review*, XIX (January 1765), pp. 50–1.
31. Walpole, *Otranto*, pp. 7–8.
32. Walpole, *Otranto*, p. 9.
33. *The Letters of Horace Walpole*, ed. Helen Paget Toynbee, 19 vols (Oxford: Clarendon Press, 1903–25), VI, pp. 194–5, 198.
34. Watt, 'Time and Family', pp. 164–8.
35. Walpole to George Montagu, 5 January 1766, *Letters*, VI, pp. 387–8.
36. *The Critical Review*, XIX (January 1765), p. 51.
37. William Warburton, *The Works of Alexander Pope Esq.* (London: C. Bathurst, W. Strahan, J. and F. Rivington et al., 1770), IV, pp. 166–7.
38. Walpole, *Otranto*, pp. 6, 14.
39. Walpole, *Otranto*, pp. 17, 19. A casque is a piece of armour that covered the head, that is to say, a helmet.
40. Walpole, *Otranto*, pp. 106–7.
41. Walpole, *Otranto*, p. 82.
42. Watt, 'Time and Family', p. 161.
43. Ronald Paulson, *Representations of Revolution (1789–1820)* (New Haven and London: Yale University Press, 1983), p. 221.
44. Walpole, *Otranto*, pp. 20–1.
45. Christopher Hill, 'The Norman Yoke', in John Saville, *Democracy and the Labour Movement: Essays in honour of Dona Torr* (London: Lawrence & Wishart, 1954), pp. 11–66, p. 15.
46. See Emma Clery, *The Rise of Supernatural Fiction 1762–1800* (Cambridge: Cambridge University Press, 1995), pp. 68–79.
47. Walpole, *Otranto*, p. 72.
48. Walpole, *Otranto*, pp. 108–10.

49. Walpole, *Otranto*, pp. 10–11.
50. Walpole, *Otranto*, p. 14.
51. Walpole, *Otranto*, p. 14.
52. *The Critical Review*, XIX (June 1765), p. 469.
53. Walpole to Robert Jephson (27 January 1780), *Letters*, XI, p. 112.
54. Emma Clery, 'Introduction', Walpole, *Otranto*, p. xxxii–xxxiii.
55. Walpole, *Otranto*, p. 7.
56. Walpole to George Montagu (8 April 1763), *Letters*, V, p. 301.
57. Walpole to George Montagu (14 October 1756), *Letters*, IV, p. 1.
58. John Samson, 'Politics Gothicised: The Conway Incident and *The Castle of Otranto*', *Eighteenth-Century Life*, 10, 3 (1986), pp. 145–58.
59. This account of the Wilkes affair is based on George Rudé, *Wilkes and Liberty: A Social Study of 1763 to 1774* (Oxford: Clarendon, 1962). See also John Brewer, *Party Ideology and Popular Politics at the Accession of George III* (Cambridge: Cambridge University Press, 1976), pp. 163–200; and John Stevenson, *Popular Disturbances in England, 1700–1832* (1979; 2nd edn, London: Longman, 1992).
60. Dunk Halifax, 'General Warrant', 26 April 1763, in T. B. Howell (compiler), *A Complete Collection of State Trials and proceedings for high treason and other crimes and misdemeanours*, 26 vols (London: T. C. Hansard, 1809–26), XIX, p. 981.
61. R.W. Ketton-Cremer, *Horace Walpole: A Biography* (1940; 2nd rev. edn London: Faber and Faber, 1946), p. 215.
62. *The North Briton*, No. 36 (5 February 1763).
63. Horace Walpole, *The Question on Some Late Dismissions Truly Stated. By a Friend to the Army and the Constitution* (London: J. Wilkie, 1764), p. 15.
64. Howell, *State Trials*, XIX, pp. 1067–8.
65. Ketton-Cremer, *Walpole*, pp. 171–8.
66. Horace Walpole, *Memoirs of the Reign of King George the Third*, ed. G. F. Russell Barker, 4 vols (New York: George Putnam's Sons, 1894), I, p. 320.
67. William Guthrie, *An Address to the Public on the late Dismission of a General Officer* (London: W. Nicoll, 1764).
68. Horace Walpole, *The Question on Some Late Dismissions*, p. 35.
69. William Guthrie, *Reply to the Counter-Address; Being a Vindication of a Pamphlet entitled, An Address to the Public* (London: W. Nicoll, 1764), p. 7.
70. Timothy Mowl, *Horace Walpole: The Great Outsider* (London: John Murray, 1996), claims that Guthrie's attack amounts to Walpole's 'outing' as a homosexual, though, of course, both terms were unknown in the period.
71. Walpole, *Letters*, VI, p. 119.
72. Walpole, *Otranto*, pp. 35, 37.
73. Walpole, *Otranto*, pp. 112–13.
74. Walpole, *Letters*, VI, pp. 326–7.
75. Samson, 'Politics Gothicised', p. 146.
76. Walpole, *Otranto*, p. 21.

77. Gilly Williams to George Selwyn, 19 March 1765, *George Selwyn and his Contemporaries*, ed. John Heneage Jesse, 4 vols (London: Richard Bentley, 1882), I, p. 372.
78. Walpole, *Letters*, XI, pp. 110, 112–13.
79. Reeve, *Old English Baron*, pp. vi–vii.
80. Walpole, *Letters*, XI, p. 113.
81. Thomas Green, 'February 1, 1797', *Extracts from the Diary of a Lover of Literature* (Ipswich: John Raw, 1810), p. 23.

CHAPTER TWO

Female gothic and the secret terrors of sensibility

Ann Radcliffe, The Romance of the Forest (1791);
Ann Radcliffe, The Mysteries of Udolpho (1794);
Jane Austen, Northanger Abbey (1817);
Mary Wollstonecraft, The Wrongs of Woman (1798)

Soon after the death of Ann Radcliffe in 1826, an anonymous critic writing in *The New Monthly Magazine*, eulogised her hold over her readers:

> Mrs Radcliffe's best works have continued to excite the girl's first wonder, and to supply the last solace to her grandame's age, thumbed over, begged, borrowed, and thought of as often as ever! To the fancies of her numberless readers, she seems to hold august sway over the springs of terror.[1]

The essayist understood Radcliffe's readership to be largely, if not completely, composed of women. The vulgar entertainment of gothic romance was not only compatible with the reading and writing of women, but confirmed in the publishing market and the circulating library. This homology between women's reading and gothic fiction had a political as well as literary critical note, as the gothic novel became the site of a heartfelt and, at times, bitter debate about the nature and politics of femininity. This debate is carried out in her novels' eloquent plots, but also in their form and tone. Although the eighteenth century had witnessed the emergence of a decorous and virtuous corpus of writing by women, it remained the case that publication exposed a female author to vicious personal assaults. In the 1760s, the Bluestocking group around Elizabeth Montagu had constructed their scholarship, literary criticism and moral enquiry as virtuous, in contrast to those 'low' and popular genres, such as the novel, in which women were said to excel.[2] The novel's attraction to women writers remained, not only because its conventional topics and settings occupied a world that reflected women's interests, but also because the genre required little formal polish or learned knowledge to produce or consume. In 1773, *The Monthly Review* had remarked of novels that, 'this branch of the literary *trade*, appears now to be almost entirely engrossed by the Ladies.'[3] This 'expansion of women's professional writing', which Jane Spencer describes as the 'feminization of literature',[4] extended in the late eighteenth century to gothic novels, which were particularly associated with female writers and readers.

Ann Radcliffe (1764–1826) never aspired to fame as an author, nor did she seek entrance to the literary establishment in London, despite the undoubted commercial success of her fictions. Rather, it was the domestic tranquillity of marital life, writing by the fireside, that she claimed to enjoy most. Ann Ward was born into a dissenting family who operated a showroom in Bath for Thomas Wedgwood's Derbyshire pottery. Radcliffe's most recent biographer, Rictor Norton, argues however that she largely grew up in London at the house of her uncle, Thomas Bentley, a fellow dissenter, patron of the arts and enlightenment science, and a business partner of Wedgwood.[5] Her husband, William, whom she married in 1784, was an Oxford graduate with literary and antiquarian interests, employed as a parliamentary reporter for the *Gazetteer*, a newspaper with links to the radical Whig circles of Charles James Fox. Ann Radcliffe's publications, beginning with the Scottish tale *The Castles of Athlin and Dunbayne* in 1789 and *A Sicilian Romance* in 1790, soon overtook her husband's fame. The popular acclaim of *The Romance of the Forest* in 1791 was translated into financial and critical success. She was paid £500 for *The Mysteries of Udolpho* (1794) and £600 for her last novel *The Italian* (1797), enormous sums for the period. Such reward had its own problems.

Like many who aspired to the upper fringes of the middle station of life, she had a profound aversion to the unavoidable public notoriety of authorship. The Bluestocking model of the virtuous and genteel professional woman writer did not erase the profound unease about the propriety of women's writing, which risked equating the writer with another professional woman encountered in public, the prostitute. Radcliffe, who was in any case 'a female of diffidence, approaching to shyness', found the public status of the writer distinctly embarrassing, especially the attentions of male literary critics. This unease was intensified when other writers, such as Matthew Lewis and Charlotte Dacre, fleshed out her virtuous gothic vision with more salacious and libertine material in the following decade. Radcliffe found a public persona unavoidable, and as it began to impinge on her private self she responded by a retreat into domestic privacy.

> The very thought of appearing in person as the author of her romances shocked the delicacy of her mind. To the publication of her works she was constrained

by the force of her own genius; but nothing could tempt her to publish herself; or sink for a moment, the gentlewoman in the novelist.[6]

Publishing her novels, Talfourd suggests, amounted to publishing her self. The problem of the female writer, exposing herself to public view, expressed a significant *impasse* in the contemporary construction of femininity, one that is played out and tested in her novels' obsessive interest in the value of retirement and domesticity. Radcliffe's determination to keep her private life secret is reflected in the role of family secrets in her novels, secrets which the narrative works to uncover. Radcliffe's fiction structures itself around a discourse on women that sought to regulate both women's behaviour and their representations, by outlining and regulating a model of feminine virtue and propriety.

Readers associated Radcliffe with a type of writing about terror, a mode in which she was held to be unsurpassed. Hazlitt observed, in his estimation of novelists in 1818, that, 'In harrowing up the soul with imaginary horrors, and making the flesh creep and the nerves thrill with fond hopes and fears, she is unrivalled among her fair country-women.'[7] After her death, one critic remarked she had 'a fine knowledge of the pulses of curiosity and fear in the human heart; and a nice discrimination in apportioning the degree and the kind of excitement which would call forth their fondest throbbings.'[8] Nathan Drake, as noted in the introduction, described Radcliffe as 'the Shakespeare of Romance Writers', associating her with a distinctly nationalist school of writing.[9] To her contemporaries, Radcliffe's combination of fear and the familiar created a horror that could not be dismissed as mere 'melodramatic artifice and ingenious trickery'. Talfourd reckoned that she had a particular skill in addressing the thought and feeling of her young and feminised audience, at 'that delightful period of youth, when the soft twilight of the imagination harmonizes with the luxurious and uncertain light cast on their wonders'.[10] Her novels intimately explore fears and horrors endemic to the private lives of her female readership: so much so that an anonymous critic suggested that 'her readers are the virtual heroes and heroines of her story'.[11] Despite or because of her seductive charm for women readers, the serious weight Radcliffe's fiction gives to questions of female conduct and status can be overlooked. Rather than mere entertainments, her novels direct her readers to consider one of the central issues of the 1790s: the status of women. Radcliffe pursues this contemporary and particular question in her signature manner, by locating the story in a distant society. Excepting the first, her novels are set in exotic locations – in southern Europe, around the Mediterranean – and in the deep past.

This doubly-distanced setting is detailed with much feeling loco-description, although Radcliffe, circumscribed by the French Revolutionary Wars of the 1790s, never visited these locations.

I. RADCLIFFE AND THE POLITICS OF FEMALE SENSIBILITY

Radcliffe first found popular success with *The Romance of the Forest* in 1791, which saw four editions in the next three years.[12] Coleridge praised its hold over the reader, in which 'the attention is uninterruptedly fixed, till the veil is designedly withdrawn'.[13] Published anonymously at first, the second edition added her name, but in a form, 'Ann Radcliffe', that left the reader to speculate about her marital status, and later editions moderated it to Mrs Radcliffe. *The Mysteries of Udolpho* followed in 1794, and was announced in the sub-title as 'A Romance'. It too met with popular success, going through ten editions in its first decade, including those published in Dublin, Boston and Philadelphia, and receiving wide coverage in the periodical press.[14] Although *Udolpho* quickly became her most famous work, Coleridge, in *The Critical Review*, argued that the earlier novel was superior: 'while we acknowledge the extraordinary powers of Mrs Radcliffe, some readers will be inclined to doubt whether they have been exerted in the present work with equal effect as in *The Romance of the Forest*.'[15] The plots of both *The Romance of the Forest* and *The Mysteries of Udolpho* are constructed as marriage romances, but they also concern the legitimacy of proper inheritance, explored through the female victims of these usurpations, Adeline and Emily. As we will see, the novels' historicist mode, their narrative technique of suspended tension and their plots all combine in a thorough examination of contemporary constructions of gender.[16]

Adeline, the heroine of *The Romance of the Forest*, is nineteen years old, possessed of a 'good understanding and an amiable heart'. Her ethereal fragility recalls the protagonist of sentimental novels: a figure of 'exquisite proportion', 'attractive' melting eyes and a form which had the 'airy lightness of a nymph'.[17] Her own account relates that upon her mother's death, when she was seven, her father sent her to a convent. Later recalled from the convent's harsh regime, Adeline finds her father a melancholy and cruel man, who does not enjoy her company. The novel's sudden and violent beginning sees her threatened by ruffians and placed in the hands of a stranger, Pierre de la Motte, whose kindness somewhat pacifies her fears. The novel's motivating enigma is the violent cruelty of Adeline's past with its repeated examples of patriarchal severity, an enigma further explored in Adeline's search for her place in society. Without family, guardian or friend, Adeline fortifies her contested virtue by seeking an advantageous marriage. Patriarchy appears both the cause and the solution to her difficulties. The patriarchal model identified political congruencies between the authority of the father over the household and that of the king over society. In this mutually authorising relationship, the state was imagined as a family presided over by the king whose authority was like that of a father: paternal, benevolent and absolute. The model received some of its force from Old Testament Protestant theology, where narratives of female submission in worldly matters established a gendered pattern of dominant and subordinate positions. Within the family, husbands properly dominated wives, parents dominated children, and masters dominated servants.[18] In the novel, patriarchal structures are shown to be violent, corrupt and ruined, but also, oddly like the haunted abbey where La Motte seeks refuge with his family, the only secure place of refuge.

Adeline's search for an empowered femininity is pursued through a study of her origins, in particular the fate of her mother. Her enquiries examine how women act independently in a patriarchal society which does not accord them agency, freedom of movement and liberty of sexual choice. The focus of male desire in the abbey, Adeline attracts the attention of La Motte's son Louis, and an aristocratic schemer, the Marquis de Montalt. Men consistently conspire against her virtue: Louis by means of love; Montalt by conspiracy and bribery; and even La Motte, dithering between benevolence and mercenary self-interest. The test of Adeline's femininity is thereby simultaneously constructed as a test of the discourses of masculinity.

In constructing the character of Emily St Aubert, the heroine of *The Mysteries of Udolpho* (1794), Radcliffe again turns to the sentimentally validated qualities of chastity, humility, innocence and modesty. Repeating a paradox typical of the eighteenth-century sentimental novel and practical guides to women's behaviour (conduct books), *Udolpho* describes how Emily achieves her innate innocence and virtue by a course of education and advice, and furthermore, it offers itself as a way of disseminating this advice and education to its own readers. The prolonged test of her moral qualities in later volumes offers itself as a study of the nature and origin of that virtue. The novel's test of Emily's virtue establishes its authenticity, but also questions its practical force in the world. The modernity of these concerns occasionally conflict with the exotic location in deep history, reinforcing Radcliffe's characteristic tone of creative anachronism.

In the first volume, the novel articulates and justifies an idealised vision of a stable paternalistic society, in which the sentimental female virtues of innocence, virtue and feeling reinforce the loving care of her father St Aubert in the family chateau of La Vallée in Gascony. Within these protective enclosures, Emily cultivates a range of desirable sentimental virtues, such as responsiveness to nature, unreflecting generosity, unaffected trust, artless friendliness, sincerity and truth, humility and chastity. To articulate these virtues, she develops the emotional susceptibility advocated by the sentimental novel. In her encounters, she exhibits a simplicity of response and tenderness that speaks highly of the quality and refinement of her sentimental feelings. Moreover, she learns how to display this sensitivity in a rhetoric of bodily feeling. Using the full range of emotional signifiers such as tears, blushes, and swooning (familiar from earlier novels of sensibility), she is able to register the most sophisticated and subtle emotional responses to the world around her. Using her body as a signifying surface allows it to say things the mind cannot admit, a useful technical device for the novelist. St Aubert teaches her how to channel her reserves of feeling:

> With anxious fondness, he endeavoured, with unremitting effort, to counteract those traits in her disposition, which might hereafter lead her from happiness. She had discovered in her early years uncommon delicacy of mind, warm affections, and ready benevolence; but with these was observable a degree of susceptibility too exquisite to admit of lasting peace.

Emily's 'sensibility', as Radcliffe calls it, is the foundation of her beauty and appeal, but it also renders her temperament precariously unstable. St Aubert counters her sensibility with lessons designed 'to strengthen her mind' and 'to inure her to habits of self-command'. Against the allure of a benevolent and refined sensibility, the novel proposes an austere and rational self-command. But even when St Aubert cautions against the 'dangers of sensibility', he does so in a sentimental mode:

> 'Above all, my dear Emily,' said he, 'do not indulge in the pride of fine feeling, the romantic error of amiable minds. Those, who really possess sensibility, ought early to be taught, that it is a dangerous quality, which is continually extracting the excess of misery, or delight, from every surrounding circumstance. And, since, in our passage through this world, painful circumstances occur more frequently than pleasing ones, and since our sense of evil is, I fear, more acute than our sense of good, we become the victims of our feelings, unless we can in some degree command them.'[19]

St Aubert's corrective to Emily's sensibility is advice that she finds difficult to apply outside her father's benevolent patriarchal protection, although her eventual discovery of security and happiness, much later in the novel, depends on the agency inspired here.

Radcliffe's fiction is embedded in a long-term and significant contestation of the status of women. Radcliffe's association of innate domestic virtues with the youthful innocence of her heroine Emily articulates the new sentimental domestic construction of femininity that had emerged in the mid- to late eighteenth century.[20] The sentimental revolution identified by some historians in this period identifies a widespread transformation in lived experience, encompassing changing notions of gentility, politeness and manners in all spheres of life, commercial or social, public or private.[21] The changing status of women in the period was dependent upon and a part of wider patterns of changing economic and cultural structure. A new model of female behaviour, described here as the sentimental construction of femininity, gave evidence of a new climate of thought.[22] Schemes of education and moral reform not only revalued women's accomplishments but celebrated the notions of politeness and manners with which they were associated. To address these concerns, moralists composed books of advice and instruction to reproduce the desired female attributes. These conduct books were aimed primarily at young women (and their mothers) in the middle station of life, although some were written for young men too. Amongst the most popular were Lady Sarah Pennington's *An Unfortunate Mother's Advice to her Daughters* (1761), Dr John Gregory's *A Father's Legacy to his Daughters* (1774), and Hestor Chapone's *Letters on the Improvement of the Mind, Addressed to a Young Lady* (1773). The conduct books educated this audience in the behaviour 'proper' for a young lady; offering a model of feminine behaviour consciously different from the aristocratic codes they criticised as ornamental, luxurious and exhibitionist, and the plebeian codes they recognised as vulgar and coarse. By contrast, the conduct books located virtue as an interior moral quality articulated by the emotions. Sentimental moral theory – as in Shaftesbury and Hutcheson – projected the idea that society was, or ought to be, based on mutual love and benevolence. It promoted a heightened sensitivity to the social and moral problems of economic change, and engaged actively in the promotion of philanthropic institutions to relieve distress. While some women, such as Mary Wollstonecraft, attacked the moral worth of sensibility, others, including many novelists, defended sensibility for the enhanced emotional life that seemed to reconcile the domestic agenda to deeply felt and powerful feelings.

Radcliffe's novels explore these antithetical and inconsistent principles: they lay bare the contradictions of sensibility, showing how a sentimental heroine like Emily succeeded in being the virtuous centre of a paternal-istic and domestic family, yet at the same time, using the sentimental novel's recognition of the deep power of the emotions and the passions, opened that domestic economy to wilder currents of sexuality and feeling. Emily's sensibility then, restricts her ability to take action in her life, leaves her defenceless against aggressive masculine predators, and renders her listless and enervated. At the same time it provides her with a powerful new emotional life, an arena of feeling action, where heightened passions are recognised, rewarded and explored. Emily's coherent and successful social self in the sentimental model only has solidity when she demon-strates that this self has strength and power to resist the world's predations. Emily first has to achieve this sentimental femininity and then has to defend it, primarily from forces that emanate from within herself.[23] Emily's achievement of marriage initially argues that she is able to find a way to command the passions, sexual and selfish.

Moralists, however, were not convinced that the lessons of their conduct books were safely promoted by the novel. The novel attracted criticism both because it was consumed in private in a spirit of leisure, and because it was an entertainment that held a special fascination for society's most corruptible: the young, the female and the less educated. The gothic novelist Clara Reeve argued that the leisured consumption of novels suggested not only idle frivolity but also a threat to virtue. Through novels, Reeve argued,

> The seeds of vice and folly are sown in the heart, – the passions are awak-ened, – false expectations are raised. – Young woman is taught to expect adventures and intrigues, – she expects to be addressed in the style of these books, with the language of flattery and adulation.[24]

Sarah Pennington advised her daughters to forbear reading novels, because the powerful attractions of the narrative form made them 'apt to give a romantic Turn to the Mind, that is often productive of great Errors in Judgement, and fatal Mistakes in Conduct'.[25] The Rev. Edward Barry argued in 1791 that novels were an 'incentive to seduction' because the 'main drift of such writing is to interest, to agitate, and convulse the passions, and is but too prone, by a sympathy of sentiment, to lead the mind astray'.[26] Mary Wollstonecraft even suggested that 'novel reading' was 'a principal cause of female depravity'.[27]

The gothic novel in particular attracted condemnation. One anony-mous critic (recapitulating Reeve) argued that if the novel is to be 'useful', it 'ought to be a representation of human life and manners, with a view to direct the conduct in the important duties of life, and to correct its follies'. The gothic novel, though it 'is calculated to "elevate and surprise"' must be 'hurtful' because it 'carries the young reader's imagination into such a confusion of terrors'. In this way, it fails the great dictum of instruction through entertainment. The critic laments, 'What instruction is to be reaped from the distorted ideas of lunatics, I am at a loss to conceive.'

> Are the duties of life so changed, that all the instructions necessary for a young person is to learn to walk at night upon the battlements of an old castle . . .? Is the corporeal frame of the female sex so masculine and hardy, that it must be softened by the touch of dead bodies, clay-cold hands and damp sweats? Can a young lady be taught nothing more necessary in life than to sleep in a dungeon with venomous reptiles, walk through a ward with assassins, and carry bloody daggers in their pockets, instead of pin-cushions and needlebooks?[28]

This critic supposes that reading the gothic novel as a discourse of conduct is a foolhardy enterprise. Yet even this passage assumes that the problem of the gendered construction of manners (the 'duties of life') was central to Radcliffe's fictions, and that the best way to inculcate moral lessons was not always polemic pedagogy.

RADCLIFFE AND GOTHIC MASCULINITY: BANDITTI AND TYRANTS

Radcliffe's representation of the patriarchal tyrant – such as Montalt and Montoni, as well as Schedoni in *The Italian* – identifies both the power and the weakness of this mode of masculinity. Adeline, in *The Romance of the Forest*, is subject to the bewildering conspiracies of the Marquis of Montalt. From the murderous attack by hired assassins in the opening chapter, to his corrupting attempts to bribe La Motte to gain access to her, he is shown to be the secret architect of her misfortunes. This is finally confirmed when it emerges she is the daughter of Montalt's brother Henry, whom Montalt had murdered to secure his extensive fortune. Montalt's crimes and vices – libertinism, corruption, blackmail, fratricide – are 'rewarded' by the narrative when he commits suicide by poison rather than face the public exposure of his treachery. The test of Emily's virtues is primarily undertaken by the tyrant Montoni, whose worldly and cynical ideology of libertine sexuality defines him, in opposition to Emily, as a counter-sentimental avatar of patriarchal corruption. Radcliffe depicts Signor Montoni as a virile and intelligent man: 'an uncommonly handsome person, with features manly and expressive, but whose countenance exhibited, upon the whole, more of the haughtiness of command, and the quickness of discernment, than of any other character'. Montoni's terror derives not merely from his physical strength or his social position, but from his mental talents: 'Montoni had an air of conscious superiority, animated by spirit, and strengthened by talents, to which every person seemed involuntarily to yield. The quickness of his perceptions was strikingly expressed on his countenance.' That Montoni is able to assert power almost without effort occasions feelings within Emily that she is unable to account for and which the reader is invited to identify as enigmatically sexual: 'Emily felt admiration, but not the admiration that leads to esteem; for it was mixed with a degree of fear she knew not exactly wherefore.'[29]

The death of her father destroys Emily's sentimentally valorised life at La Vallée and she is forced to take up residence with her aunt, whose marriage to Montoni places Emily under his protection. Her romantic attachment to Valancourt, a man of sensibility encountered wandering in the mountains, is broken off. Obeying Montoni's will, Emily removes to Venice, where an attempt is made to marry her to Count Morano, an associate of Montoni. Thereafter she is taken to Montoni's decaying castle of Udolpho in the Apennines:

> Emily gazed with melancholy awe upon the castle . . ., for, though it was now lighted up by the setting sun, the gothic greatness of its features, and its moul-dering walls of dark grey stone, rendered it a gloomy and sublime object . . . Silent, lonely and sublime, it seemed to stand the sovereign of the scene, and to frown defiance on all who dared to invade its solitary reign.[30]

The castle is made here to figure a kind of outlaw masculinity: patriarchal but illegitimate, an aberration within the proper order. Montoni's absolute rule exercises unrestrained power over his masculine political domain.

The castle of Udolpho can usefully be compared with St Aubert's house at La Vallée. The chateau was notable for its 'neat simplicity', a cottage ornée forming a 'simple and elegant residence' whose principle room is its library 'of the best books in the ancient and modern languages'. The house is nestled in the protective shelter of its mountain valley, unlike Udolpho, perched amongst the mountains. Upon first sight, Emily impressed by Udolpho's sublime appearance: its 'massy ramparts' she finds 'vast, ancient and dreary', its ruined state suggests 'desolation' and told of the 'ravages of war'. While La Vallée existed outside history, Udolpho is a centre of political intrigue. When she enters the castle, 'Emily's heart sunk, and she seemed as if she was going to her prison; the gloomy court, into which she passed, served to confirm the idea, and her imagination, ever awake to circumstance, suggested even more terrors, than her reason could justify'.[31] Whereas her father's house offered Emily a domestic protective enclosure, Montoni's castle is only a prison or grave in which Emily is incarcerated or buried alive. La Vallée kept the troubles of the wider world at bay, while Udolpho keeps Emily locked up with her troubles (in particular, with the threat of sexuality and passion). Udolpho is a prison away from all social virtues of love and compassion, ruled by viciousness and hatred. Or so Emily would have the reader believe; it must be said that Emily's comprehension of Udolpho's terror is more imaginary than real. Udolpho's ruined state and general gloom provide an atmosphere of crepuscular terror to which Emily's sensibility is finely attuned, further provoked by her perception of threats to her innocence and chastity, portending murder, violent rape, or at least forced marriage. These threats are obscure, and in their obscurity, they take on strong hues.

Udolpho and its male inhabitants provide Radcliffe with a intoxicating mode of describing history as both libertine and sublime. Emily's rapturous appreciation of the castle and mountains sensually evokes a setting both Mediterranean and historical (albeit in the anachronistic mode of the picturesque). The inhabitants of the castle, Montoni's entourage, are described as cavaliers or soldiers of fortune, employed by Montoni for his personal protection and to prosecute his political intentions. However, to Emily's 'timid' fancy, their 'expression . . . of wild fierceness, of subtle design, or of licentious passion' makes them seem more like 'banditti', which is to say, a company of criminal outlaws. Their conversation, like Montoni's world in general, turns on 'war and politics', in particular the contest between Venice and Rome in which Montoni has secretive 'exploits' to pursue.[32] Montoni and his men, as cavaliers or banditti, are an outlaw community of political insurgents. The men are heavily armed, passionate in their opinions, and quick to take offence – a masculinity which is the proper gender expression of their political status. In Emily's eyes, they are an explicit threat to her sexual safety.

Banditti had emerged as one of the stock properties of gothic fiction in the 1790s. Derived from an Italian word *bandito* meaning 'proscribed or outlawed', banditti had come to mean, in the seventeenth century, an organised gang of marauding brigands who lived in mountainous districts of Southern Europe, especially Italy. Thomas Coryat, travelling in Italy in the first decade of the seventeenth century, observed of the 'bandits' who had made the castle of Mirandula their 'Sanctuary' and 'aboad', that they are 'the murdering robbers upon the Alpes, and many places of Italy'.[33] As Eric Hobsbawm has argued, bandits are outlawed by authority, and often retain popular support as heroes and 'free robber-liberators'.[34] By the 1790s, the banditti were another picturesque example of Italian customs. As one traveller remarked, 'These banditti are very numerous and enjoy the protection of the people of quality.' Despite their murdering ways, he adds, 'it would be a matter of mistake to consider these banditti as *monsters*,' because they understand their 'black' profession to be 'justified by education, laws and religious notions.'[35] Although Radcliffe herself had explored the picturesque world of Italian banditti in her second novel *A Sicilian Romance* (1790), the seminal portrayal was the band of banditti led by Charles de Moor in Schiller's drama *The Robbers* (1781, translated 1792), whose outlawry takes on a pronounced tincture of political rebellion and libertinism.[36]

Montoni's banditti also reflect Radcliffe's painterly interests. In the 1770s, the highly regarded English painter John Hamilton Mortimer (1740–79) had made many studies of groups of banditti in unnamed Italian settings. Mortimer exhibited a pair of drawings on the theme at the Society of Artists in 1772, and painted them in oil in 1775. 'Banditti Returning' (see Figure 4) depicts the banditti as men of haughty virility heavily armed with archaic medieval weapons, and clothed in flowing armoured tunics. Returning from a raid with their plunder, they escort their orientalised captives, including a beautiful young woman, whose dishevelled clothing, revealing her breast, casts a libertine note.[37] Mortimer's renown as 'the English Salvator', recognises that banditti drawings were a response to the works of the sixteenth-century Italian painter Salvator Rosa (whose landscapes were repeatedly mentioned by Radcliffe). Other artists, such as Phillipe de Loutherbourg and Joseph Wright of Derby, completed banditti landscapes. However, as Benedict Nicolson argues, the 'bandits who people his [Mortimer's] Rosa-like landscapes are not to be discovered in Rosa's own work, but belong to the mythology of the mid-eighteenth century'.[38] In Mortimer's work, the banditti are translated from staffage (figures in a landscape) to the central actors of history painting.[39] The groups of wild yet uniformed men, committing crimes or holding captives, exude a lawless sexual excitement that hybridises picturesque landscape into gothic.

The events in the castle conspire to heighten Emily's sense of her imperilled virtue when Montoni requests that she wear an immodest dress to dinner with his comrades. Declaring her own simple dress is 'prudish', Montoni forces her to wear one of Neapolitan cut that 'set off the shape and figure, to the utmost advantage'. As Emily is aware, the dress had been prepared for the forced marriage Montoni had plotted in Venice. The memory of this 'offensive purpose' taints the dress, but his 'absolute command' prevails. The dinner, at which blushing Emily is seated between two officers of Montoni's corps, dissolves into fighting when Montoni's

Figure 4. John Hamilton Mortimer, 'Banditti Returning' (pen and ink drawing); British Museum, Department of Prints and Drawings, London.

wine is found to be poisoned. Montoni's suspicion falls on Emily's aunt, Madame Montoni, and when Emily intervenes, he has them both incarcerated. 'Madame Montoni and herself were now prisoners; and she saw that his designs became more and more terrible.' Montoni's rage demonstrates how his masculine identity is immune to Emily's repertoire of sensibility, that his threat to these women might be physical (murder or rape), and that they are 'in danger of offending a man, who has unlimited power' over them.[40] The significance of this scene to contemporary readers is signalled by the fact that it was chosen by Henry Singleton as the subject of a painting, subsequently published as an engraving, in 1796.[41]

When Montoni, accompanied by 'three ruffian-like men', arrives at the room in which Emily and her aunt are imprisoned, her sensibility leads her to suspect that her sexual inviolability is directly threatened. While her aunt is carried out, Emily's response is literally pathetic: 'Emily sunk, senseless, on a couch, by which she had endeavoured to support herself.' When she recovers, so does her curiosity. The rest of the chapter details her travels around the darkened castle, past the dying bodies of wounded soldiers and her locked-up servant Annette, to the east turret where she supposes her aunt to be imprisoned. When she successfully passes this test of her courage by arriving at the room, she fails the next, by letting her fears get the better of her again. 'The image of her aunt murdered – murdered, perhaps, by the hand of Montoni, rose to her mind; she trembled, gasped for breath'. Although she 'dreaded to enquire further – dreaded to encounter some horrible spectacle' she 'could not . . . desist from them'.[42] Emily's curiosity is an active, and liberating, principle that here confronts and overwhelms her fear. Her subsequent encounter with the mysterious waxen corpse behind the curtain again epitomises the novel's narrative strategy (see Figure 2) Radcliffe's explanatory technique reveals that all these threats either come to nothing, or are a product of Emily's imagination. The nature of the threat to Emily remains vague and undefined in the novel: it remains anyway a threat that she passively reacts to, rather than an attempt on her person. The nature of the threat Emily perceives as being physical (forced marriage, rape, expropriation of estates) perhaps should be thought of as imaginative and sentimental. These threats she must learn to confront and command: she can only be alerted to them because of the refined delicacy of her emotions, yet this same sensibility is utterly inadequate to the task of dealing with them.

The final disclosure that Montoni's threat to Emily is against her property not her person exactly precedes her escape from his power (and, in a complex political resolution, the suppression of his power). Montoni's intimidating request for her to 'Sign the papers' resigning her estates to him, is followed by threats to her person (a 'terrible' fate, the same as her aunt's, is threatened 'this very night'). Emily's resistance to his coercion gives evidence of her self-command, strengthened by her memory of Valancourt. In fact, that night sees the destruction of Montoni's fugitive masculinity. The text explains that Montoni is not 'a captain of banditti' as Emily has surmised, even though the soldiers under his command had been employed in 'enterprises not less daring, or less atrocious, than such a character would have undertaken', such as pillaging helpless travellers and plundering the villas of the rich. Although it is not clearly stated, Montoni has been playing off the rival states of Venice and Rome. After Emily has escaped from the castle and resettled in Languedoc, his raids attract the attention of the Venetians. 'His depredations having exceeded their usual limits, and reached an extent, at which neither the timidity of the then commercial senate of Venice, nor their hope of his occasional assistance would permit them to connive, the same effort, it was resolved, should complete the suppression of his power and the correction of his outrages'.[43] Surprising Udolpho at night, Venetian forces have little difficulty in capturing Montoni, his officers, and the castle. In the end, Montoni's achievements do not quite add up to the threat Emily initially assumed. His military and political endeavours amount to little more than mercenary banditry. He is unable to force his wife's ward to give up her property to him. His physical threats, which Emily reads as essentially sexual, are shown to be impotent and powerless: Kenneth Graham thought that 'he lacks sexual drive'.[44] As an anti-hero and a demon-lover, Montoni is rather disappointing.

II. RADCLIFFE AND THE POLITICS OF MASCULINE SENSIBILITY

In pitting her heroines against tyrant males, Radcliffe proposes an analogy between the personal and the political. This extends to other codes of masculine manners that she considers, whose reformed masculinity successfully realises versions of sentimental revolution. The modern 'man of feeling', as he is sometimes called, can be seen in the examples of Arnand La Luc and Henry Montalt (Adeline's absent murdered father) in *The Romance of the Forest*, and Valancourt and St Aubert in *Udolpho*. The new sentimental model of femininity elaborated in the late eighteenth century also offered men an ideal of a revised and refined behaviour. Contemporaries argued that the manners of society had been civilised according to models that were explicitly gendered as feminine. Defending modern civility, *The Universal Magazine* argued in 1778 that by 'respectful attention to women' society 'refines the manners and softens the temper' and causes one to 'humanize the heart and refine the sentiment'.[45] In this way, manners of men were transformed alongside those of women; indeed, upon the model of women. Conduct books and novels recommended that men should become more gentle, graceful, and polite – more like women, in fact – to improve themselves and save the world from the corruptions of commerce and luxury. Some novelists spent considerable effort investigating varieties of feminised masculinity. In his novel *The Man of Feeling* (1771), Henry Mackenzie envisions a hero, Harley, who indulges emotional feelings and measures experiences by their ability to move him. In Radcliffe, the man of feeling proposes a reformed and enlightened political settlement, based on a benevolence and kindness envisaged as feminine.

Arnand La Luc offers the most fully realised rendering of the new man of feeling. Adeline, recovering from an illness initiated by her escape from Montalt, finds refuge in his peasant family in Savoy. La Luc's relative poverty is offset, she discovers, by his moral and intellectual wealth. He is a philosopher, a clergyman, a benevolist, and a scientist: a concatenation of discourses that he sees as unambiguous.

> His mind was penetrating; his views extensive; and his systems, like his religion, were simple, rational and sublime. . . . Philosophy had strengthened, not hardened, his heart. . . . Though he could not always relieve the necessities of the indigent, his tender pity and holy conversation seldom failed in administering consolation to the mental sufferer. On these occasions the sweet and exquisite emotions of his heart have often induced him to say, that . . . he would never after forego "the luxury of doing good".

La Luc's benevolence, described in the rhetoric of sensibility, unites clergyman with that of the enlightenment scientist: his study is 'fitted up with chymical apparatus, astronomical instruments, and other implements of science'. This peculiar mixture of rational deism makes his character distinctly anachronistic in a novel explicitly located in the 1650s, especially the recognisable influence of Rousseau's arguments about education and public virtue articulated in his philosophical novels *La Nouvelle Héloïse* (1760) and *Emile, ou De l'Education* (1761). La Luc's successfully realised rendition of a sentimentally engaged, reformed masculinity plays an important part in Adeline's education. Her experiences with the La Luc family teach Adeline as much about models of responsible and enlightened domesticity as about philosophy (or rather, how the one is the other). The society of La Luc at Leloncourt is a model of virtuous social harmony, organised under a feminine tutelary deity (the 'goodness of Madame La Luc', the deceased wife of La Luc):

> The chearfulness and harmony that reigned within the chateau was delightful; but the philanthropy which, flowing from the heart of the pastor, was diffused through the whole village, and united the inhabitants in the sweet and firm bonds of social compact, was divine.[46]

In this sentimental vision, the order of society flows outwards from the calm patriarchal heart through its splendid articulation in the domestic family, to the wider community.

Radcliffe explores the behaviour of men of sensibility, but while she invests their model with much moral significance, she also expresses anxiety about their power in the world. Henry Montalt was a benevolent and intelligent man, yet of course it is his powerlessness that leaves Adeline so precariously unprotected. St Aubert's early death leaves Emily in a similar predicament. La Luc battles with disabling disease through those periods when his strength is most needed. These examples of powerless fathers suggest that the sentimental man of feeling, though attractive, is dangerously frail, scarcely able to offer protection from the threats and plots of patriarchal tyrants. Oscillating ambiguously between these extremes, some male characters, such as La Motte and Valancourt, exhibit a pragmatic masculinity between sentimental and patriarchal codes of behaviour, establishing a weak and fragile masculine virtue. La Motte, compromised by debt, cowardice and his potentially sordid status as Montalt's pimp, is offered a kind of halfway reformation, learning the pleasure of virtuous action. La Motte's history, revealed in his confession to Montalt, shows that he 'dissipated the greater part of an affluent fortune in luxurious indulgences'.[47] Brought near to poverty by gambling and riotous living, La Motte is defrauded of his last money by card-sharks who introduce him to a life of crime. A weak man overwhelmed by the corruptions of the city, La Motte's fall is counterpoised with his hesitant attempts to restore his fortunes, and even act virtuously.

Valancourt, who initially appears in the guise of the man of feeling, succumbs to the temptation of corruption and luxury in the city, but is also offered reformation through following Emily's sentimentally valorised model. In Emily's first encounter with Valancourt, he is dressed as a huntsman and a peasant, but his 'manly grace', as Emily can intuitively see, has the bearing of noble status (although as a second son, under French law, he does not stand to inherit much). Wandering the Pyrenees to escape from the corruptions of the city, he takes delight in the 'simple people' who live contentedly 'without the luxuries of life'. Valancourt is not an outcast but a self-exile, one for whom rural retirement is a positively valued space for meditation and the cultivation of virtue. Valancourt's recapitulation of the discourse of retirement (familiar from Goldsmith's *Vicar of Wakefield* (1766) and Cowper's *The Task* (1782)) offers refined sensibility and delicate virtue as a counterpoint to the vices of city society. Nonetheless, Valancourt's sensibility also renders the corruptions of the city irresistible. With his hopes of marrying Emily dashed by Montoni's plotting, and Emily's departure to Venice and Udolpho, Valancourt journeys to Paris in despair, where he throws himself into a dissipated life. His experiences of male libertinism, involving both women and gambling, appear to debauch him. Eventually, when his money is exhausted, his incarceration in a debtors' prison allows him time for reflection and repentance. Emily (or her image and memory) have a significant role here:

> In the solitude of his prison, Valancourt had leisure for reflection, and cause for repentance; here too, the image of Emily, which, amidst the dissipation of the city had been obscured, but never obliterated from his heart, revived with all the charms of innocence and beauty, to reproach him for having sacrificed his happiness and debased his talents by pursuits, which his nobler faculties would formerly have taught him to consider were as tasteless as they were degrading.[48]

It seems that in the case of Valancourt, feminine sentimental virtues can reform masculine worldly energies. This is an important lesson for Emily and the reader, but it is one that the novel fails to pursue with complete attention.

Arguably, the novel's rigid scheme of the explained supernatural and its brutal assertion of closure, announces the vindication of sensibility, proposing that sensibility can control the passions as long as it is governed by stern moral principles. In order to ensure this victory for a morally proper sensibility, Radcliffe first abolishes those 'painful circumstances' that have been laying siege to Emily's virtue. Emily escapes from the prison-castle of Udolpho through the unmotivated agency of Du Pont; demonstrating that Montoni's absolute power is only absolute for as long as she believes in it (the model here being perhaps Clarissa, who escapes from the whorehouse within which Lovelace imprisoned her by literally walking out the front door). When Emily finally follows her father's advice by subduing her feeling for Valancourt, she demonstrates that she is in command of, rather than a victim of, her sensibility. The novel rewards her conversion to St Aubert's authorised moral sensibility by revealing the secret behind her father's apparent passion for another woman who is revealed as merely his sister. Emily, in this way, completes her long delayed marriage to Valancourt, and is rewarded with both the domestic happiness of the sentimental family and the restoration of her hereditary property. Furthermore, to emphasise that she is being rewarded, Valancourt inherits a substantial property himself, giving their union a sustaining equality. The language of this resolution stresses the similarity between Emily's situation at the beginning and end of the novel.

> O! how joyful it is to tell of happiness, such as that of Valancourt and Emily; to relate, that, after suffering under the oppression of the vicious and the disdain of the weak, they were, at length, restored to each other – to the beloved landscapes of their native country, – to the securest felicity of this life, that of aspiring to moral and labouring for intellectual improvement – to the pleasures of enlightened society, and to the exercise of benevolence, which had always animated their hearts; while the bowers of La Vallée became, once more, the retreat of goodness, wisdom and domestic blessedness![49]

Emily's return completes the circular structure of the narrative: as Hazlitt says, 'her story comes to nothing'.[50] The reader concludes, perhaps, that the novel denies the experience of the transformative power of education. At the beginning, Emily is presented as already a whole being, a complete woman of sensibility enjoying the protective nourishment of the domestic scene. When this domestic enclosure is torn apart by history, Emily is thrown into scenes of gothic horror. The novel tests Emily's response to the forces of gothic passion, a formation from which Emily has little to protect her but the fragile personal virtues established by sentimental domesticity. But in Radcliffe's account, these fragile virtues appear to be adequate, in as much as the conclusion seems to offer little more than a return to the stasis of the beginning, in which Emily is re-established at La Vallée in a broadly similar enclosure of sentimental domesticity. The apparent conservatism of this circular structure belies Radcliffe's historical argument, by which the tyrant's crumbling aristocratic order is remade and overcome by progressive, even radical, allegiances of sensibility with the middle station of life.[51]

THE 'SUPERNATURAL EXPLAINED' AND THE POLITICS OF GOTHIC FORM

The major technical signature of Ann Radcliffe is her domestication of the supernatural, that which she called the 'supernatural *explain'd*'. Sir Walter Scott defined her 'principal characteristic' as a 'rule' that 'the author imposed on herself, that all the circumstances of her narrative, however mysterious, and apparently superhuman, were to be accounted for on natural principles, at the winding-up of the story.'[52] Whilst the phenomenon remains unexplained, supernatural explanation is powerfully suggested. Contemporaries argued that she created an enchanting effect of terror. Thomas Green noted, in his *Diary* for 25 March 1797, that 'in the excitation of horror by physical and moral agency I know not that Mrs R. has any equal'.[53] Hazlitt remarked that her

> great power lies in describing the indefinable, and embodying a phantom. She makes her readers twice children: and from the dim and shadowy veil which she draws over the objects of her fancy, forces us to believe all that is strange, and next to impossible, of their mysterious agency.[54]

But while Radcliffe connives with her readers' desire to be enchanted, she is also careful to reserve the possibility of material cause. The narrator's manipulation of the reader's comprehension is a deliberate effect, explored for its creative potential. Nonetheless, deployed ubiquitously across her fiction, it disappointed some readers. Mary Wollstonecraft complained in her review of *The Italian* that 'her manner of accounting in a natural manner for supernatural appearances ... lessens the effect ... now the secret has gotten vent'.[55]

The perplexity suffered by Emily and Adeline mirrors their quest to discover their own secret history. Their state of incomprehension, coterminous with their fear, is central to the reader's experience of the novel. In a curious double bind, the reader wallows in Radcliffe's luxurious detail of scene and atmosphere, but central information is withheld. Emily and Adeline experience failure to understand as a breakdown in cognition: faced with a terrifying and incomprehensible experience, their characteristic response is to faint or swoon. The constraint on relevant information means that mysteries are experienced as epistemological blockage, not as transcendence. In Radcliffe, the inexplicable is not ineffable, and bathos rather than the sublime is the controlling aesthetic.

Radcliffe's explained supernatural is especially characteristic of the dominant mode of gothic writing in the 1790s. Other writers, such as Eliza Parsons, Regina Maria Roche, Eliza Fenwick and Elizabeth Bonhote, followed much the same rule. One example is Lawrence Flammenberg, whose gothic novel, translated from the German by Peter Teuthold, became well-known as *The Necromancer, or a Tale of the Black Forest* (1794). One of the 'horrid novels' mentioned by Isabella Thorpe in Austen's *Northanger Abbey* (1818), *The Necromancer* deploys an extreme version of the explained supernatural, in which the novel's anti-hero, Volkert, entices people into witnessing terrifying scenes in which he apparently conjures up ghosts from the dead in necromantic rituals. The reader, like the observer in the text, encounters these experiences as genuine, but in the end it is revealed that all the experiences were faked by Volkert as part of elaborate plots to defraud his spectators of their fortunes.[56] The supernatural is not only explained, but revealed to be a fraudulent deception. As Coleridge remarked in his review of *Udolpho*, 'Curiosity is raised oftener than it is gratified; or rather, it is raised so high that no adequate gratification can be given of it.'[57] As Radcliffe's narrator points out, Emily's life in the castle 'appeared like the dreams of a distempered imagination'. The novel as a whole proposes that the mind has an unlimited power over external reality. Many readers found this an intoxicating and revelatory experience. Amidst the social pleasures of Bath, Catherine Morland, the heroine of *Northanger Abbey* (1818), describes enjoying 'the luxury of a raised, restless, and frightened imagination over the pages of Udolpho'.[58] This unaccountable feeling aroused by the gothic novel was evidently deeply attractive to women readers. It ruffled emotions that otherwise remained unexercised in everyday life. The gothic thus made a tantalising suggestion of a psychological depth, and a sensual or sexual engagement with life, that was elsewhere proscribed.

The dynamic argument Radcliffe proposes in her fiction concerning sexuality and political morality found a ready response amongst writers and critics in the 1790s and beyond. While some replies concentrated on her aesthetic of supernatural explained, and others took on her argument about sensibility and sexuality, Jane Austen's *Northanger Abbey* does both. Although not published until December 1817 (title-page 1818), a note by Jane's sister Cassandra Austen claims it was written 'about the years 98 & 99'.[59] Its parody of Radcliffe's gothic strategies certainly suggests that its critical expectations are located in the late 1790s rather than two decades later, although later revisions are suggested in its satire on consumerism. The novel recapitulates the Radcliffe plot of female education, depicting the entry of a young woman, Catherine Morland, into fashionable society, a process that constitutes an entertaining dissection of social manners and concludes, upon the occasion of her marriage, with her arrival at adulthood and sexuality.[60] Although possessed of an innate sensitivity, Catherine Morland's plain looks and uneducated ignorance do not suggest her status as a sentimental heroine. Her misplaced trust in fiction as a guide to the world provides Austen with one vehicle for her satire on modern manners. When the ingénue first arrives in Bath, her reading comprises romances and Richardson's sentimental novels. More modish reading is directed her way by those around her:

the fashionable Isabella Thorpe introduces her to Radcliffe's gothic fiction, beginning with *The Mysteries of Udolpho* and *The Italian* before moving on to seven other 'Horrid' novels.[61] Although Henry Tilney tries and fails to teach her to see the world through the picturesque aesthetic, Catherine finds the seductions of gothic irresistible. The novel ironically entertains a long-running discourse against the morality of young women reading novels, subversively debating the late eighteenth century conduct book controversy about the propriety of fiction.

Spurred by reading Radcliffe, Catherine engineers conversations about the gothic novel with her friends. Taken together, these do not simply censure the gothic novel or novel reading. Rather, comparing the reading habits of Isabella Thorpe, Eleanor Tilney, John Thorpe and Henry Tilney, Catherine defines a set of distinctions about literature, organised around simple oppositions, such as masculine and feminine, refined and vulgar, libertine and sentimental.[62] Learning to be a critic (making judgements about books) prepares Catherine for subsequent decisions about her life (making judgements about morals). In the second volume, her insights are redeployed in a series of scenes in which Catherine allows herself to experience the gothic's terrible pleasures. The conscious self-indulgence of these gothic fantasies, in which Catherine wilfully takes pleasure from her feelings of distress, parodies Radcliffe both in mood and formal structure.[63] The atmospheric terror that envelops the scene when Catherine discovers a lost manuscript in a 'high old fashioned black cabinet' in her bedroom at Northanger Abbey explicitly recalls Radcliffe's *Romance of the Forest*.[64] However, the explanation, coming only three pages later, that it is not a suicide note but a misplaced laundry list, implicitly debunks Radcliffe's attenuated plots, the bathos of the supernatural explained and the embedded eroticism of pleasurable terror. But as readers and critics have long recognised, there is a residual quality of authentic terror in these scenes at the Abbey, through which Catherine learns to discriminate between self-authored delusion and worldly restraint. She fancies that her friends' tyrannical father, General Tilney, is a gothic monster, who has immured his wife in the walls of the house. Catherine declares his brooding malevolence 'the air and attitude of a Montoni! – What could more plainly speak the gloomy workings of a mind not wholly dead to every sense of humanity, in its fearful review of passed scenes of guilt? Unhappy man!'[65] In fact, the General's patriarchal cruelty and disagreeable temper, in such stark contrast to his son's reformed sentimentalism, have their own terrifying impact on Catherine's world when she is expelled from the house as a fraud.[66] Domestic tranquillity and fashionable modernity, Austen argues, are the true location of modern terror.

III. GOTHIC RADICALS: WOLLSTONECRAFT'S
THE WRONGS OF WOMAN

A different response to Radcliffe was proposed by Mary Wollstonecraft in her last novel, *The Wrongs of Woman* (1798), published posthumously after her death on 10 September 1797 (the result of puerperal fever following the birth of her daughter, Mary Wollstonecraft Godwin, the author of *Frankenstein*). Wollstonecraft's husband, the moral philosopher, political theorist and novelist, William Godwin, collected all her extant manuscripts into a publication entitled *Posthumous Works of the Author of A Vindication of the Rights of Woman* (1798).[67] At the same time, Godwin published his biography of his wife, a book called *Memoirs of the Author of a Vindication of the Rights of Woman*.[68] The *Memoirs* set out to relate the history of her life and work, relating especially the radical ideas that lay behind her most famous work, *A Vindication of the Rights of Woman*, published in 1792. The frank honesty with which Godwin related the events of Wollstonecraft's life – especially her unrequited romantic attachment to Henry Fuseli, her extramarital affair with Gilbert Imlay, and her two attempted suicides – secured her nothing but opprobrium, and clearly coloured the reception of the novel.[69] A contemporary critic in *The European Magazine* argued in 1798 that these ideas

> if followed, would be attended with the most pernicious consequences to society; a female who could brave the opinion of the world in the most delicate point, a philosophical wanton, breaking down the bars intended to restrain licentiousness; and a mother, deserting a helpless offspring, disgracefully brought into the world by herself, by an intended act of suicide.[70]

To her critics, her life, like a scandalous novel, offered a political homily that those who professed to belong to the 'new order' would end up similarly depraved.[71]

In the novel's 'Author's Preface', Wollstonecraft states that her 'main object' was 'the desire of exhibiting the misery and oppression, peculiar to women, that arise out of the partial laws and customs of society'. In delineating the 'Wrongs of Woman', she is turning upside down the radical defence of the rights of man. As the full title signals, *The Wrongs of Women, or Maria; a Fragment* is unfinished. Godwin's 'Preface' to the novel says, 'The public are here presented with the last literary attempt of an author, whose fame has been uncommonly extensive.' The novel was not fragmentary or unfinished on purpose, although its extant state recalls the ruined effects of sentimental novels like Mackenzie's *Man of Feeling* (1771). Indeed, no small part of the novel's power derives from this fragmentary unfinished structure, recollecting the ruined remains of a gothic abbey. The novel is by no means an orthodox gothic fiction, but it does have distinctly gothic elements such as its febrile, overheated tone, the sentimental theme of virtue in distress, and the prison setting. The first sentence of the novel, depicting Maria incarcerated in a private madhouse, establishes its allegiance to the gothic: 'Abodes of horror have frequently been described, and castles, filled with spectres and chimeras, conjured up by the magic spell of genius to harrow the soul, and absorb the wondering mind.'[72] But Wollstonecraft defines a distinct project by suggesting that gothic novels conform to the delusive expectations of the romance genre. Radcliffe's gothic castles, she declares, were (paraphrasing *The Tempest*) 'formed of such stuff as dreams are made of'. By contrast, Wollstonecraft's castle of terror has real horror: 'what were [the gothic castles] to the mansion of despair, in one corner of which Maria sat, endeavouring to recall her scattered thoughts!' The madhouse which imprisons Maria is not only a terrifying prospect to behold, it is also a terrible symbol of the system that imprisons her.

The madhouse, 'this most horrid of prisons', recalls Radcliffe's 'Silent, lonely, and sublime' description of Udolpho.[73] Through the 'small grated window of her chamber', Maria contemplates the walls of her prison:

a huge pile of buildings, that, after having been suffered, for half a century, to fall to decay, had undergone some clumsy repairs, merely to render it habitable. The ivy had been torn off the turrets, and the stones not wanted to patch up the breaches of time, and exclude the warring elements, left in heaps in the disordered court.[74]

Wollstonecraft's architectural imagination recalls Radcliffe's gothic tone, but also recapitulates the equation of castle as prison. As a political symbol of the *ancien régime*, Wollstonecraft has in mind Blackstone's picturesque image of the English constitution as 'an old Gothic castle' fitted up with 'chearful and commodious' apartments.[75] In contradistinction to Blackstone, Wollstonecraft's castle is gothicised into a lunatic asylum. As a symbol of that old order that oppresses, the interior of her castle does not have cheerful renovations, but rather, the prison cells of lunatics. In Wollstonecraft's sententious reformulation, Maria

turned her eyes from the gloomy walls, in which she pined life away, ... and contemplated the most terrific of ruins – that of a human soul. What is the view of the fallen column, the mouldering arch ... when compared with this living memento of the fragility, the instability, of reason.

Incarcerated in her gloomy cell, denied any visitors apart from the doctor and her warder, Maria's 'melancholy of indolence' has nearly overwhelmed her sense of injustice. 'The lamp of life seemed to be spending itself to chase the vapours of a dungeon which no art could dissipate – And to what purpose did she rally all her energy? – Was not the world a vast prison, and women born slaves?' Maria's condition interests her warder, a young woman called Jemima, who brings her some books and materials for writing. As Maria writes some 'rhapsodies descriptive of the state of her mind', they accumulate into a text that will 'instruct her [absent] daughter and shield her from the misery, the tyranny'.[76] The novel then, conceives of itself as a gothic conduct book (Pennington rewritten by Radcliffe).

The novel begins in the middle of the story, imparting an enigmatic obscurity maintained until the end. It is not until the middle of the novel that we establish that Maria has been imprisoned by her vicious and corrupt husband, Mr Venables. Having married her only for economic gain, Venables, absorbed in failed commercial schemes and debauched by secret vices, tries to prostitute his wife in payment for a debt. When she resists, he incarcerates her in a madhouse, and separates her from her child. Wollstonecraft conceives of character as argument, for, as she announced in the 'Author's Preface', 'The sentiments are all embodied', implying that she constructs argument by placing her philosophical ideas, enfleshed as characters, in relations of narrative organisation. In Maria's relationship with her husband Venables, we see a caustic critique of the poverty of female education, the delusions women suffer in courtship and the romantic-love complex, and the vicious treatment women receive in the courts and in the law. In Chapters 7 to 14, delineating her youth and education, Maria's history turns into narrative one of the key arguments of the *Vindication of the Rights of Woman*: that femininity is a social construct engineered by a debilitating system of education. She escapes her loveless and constrained youth by marriage with Venables, but there discovers not the emotional liberation promised by romances and novels, but a dangerous sexual persecution. In the *Vindication*, Wollstonecraft argued that the 'conduct and manners of women ... prove that their minds are not in a healthy state'.

> One cause of this barren blooming I attribute to a false system of education, gathered from the books written on this subject by men who, considering females rather as women than human creatures, have been more anxious to make them alluring mistresses than affectionate wives and rational mothers; and the understanding of the sex has been so bubbled by this specious homage, that the civilised women of the present century, with a few exceptions, are

only anxious to inspire love, when they ought to cherish a nobler ambition, and by their abilities and virtues exact respect.[77]

Imprisoned by their false consciousness, women come to believe that they are morally and intellectually weaker than men by a 'destructive process that renders women worthless creatures and then educates them accordingly'.[78] This inequality is maintained, elaborated and established by female education, which converts women into 'weak, artificial beings' whose lives are ruled by fashion, vanity and useless pursuits.

> I wish to persuade women to endeavour to acquire strength, both of mind and body, and to convince them that the soft phrases, susceptibility of heart, delicacy of sentiment, and refinement of taste, are almost synonymous with epithets of weakness, and that those beings who are only objects of pity and that kind of love, which has been termed its sister, will soon become objects of contempt.[79]

Maria's education has provided her with the sensibility of a refined woman, but in so doing, rendered her unfit for any purpose but marriage and motherhood.

The novel explores an alternative to the patriarchal marriage complex in the relationship between Maria and Darnford inaugurated in the madhouse. Driven almost insane by the terrors of the madhouse and separation from her child, Maria's emotional surrender to Darnford figures her return to society. As the two lovers embrace, 'Desire was lost in more ineffable emotions, and to protect her from insult and sorrow – to make her happy, seemed not only the first wish of his heart, but the most noble duty of his life.' Darnford's character suggests a philosophical man of feeling, a hero of sensibility, in contrast to Venables's patriarchal villainy. The physical love Maria feels for him is a transformative experience that banishes the gothic shadows.

> A despondent gloom had long obscured Maria's horizon – now the sun broke forth, the rainbow appeared, and every prospect was fair. Horror still reigned in the darkened cells, suspicion lurked in the passages, and whispered along the walls. [. . .] Still the world contained not three happier beings.[80]

The approving sentimental language with which the narrator constructs the love of Maria and Darnford does not prepare the reader for her subsequent betrayal. Despite their union remaining outside social norms of marriage, their self-conscious formulations cast it as based on love and equality. Their philosophical rejection of marriage turns on Darnford's libertine arguments that the passionate intensity of their love will give their union endurance. Their return to London and society proves the weakness of such utopian schemes.

In its unfinished state, the novel leaves the conclusion open-ended. Godwin collected a series of fragmentary 'minutes' comprising 'scattered heads for the continuation of the story', each of which set out from the same point in the narrative. Each alternative ending contributed a subtly different conclusion to the novel's argument. In some, Darnford's affection seems to wane, and in others, Maria effects a return to and reconciliation with her family. The fifth conclusion is the most pessimistic: 'Divorced by her husband – Her lover unfaithful – Pregnancy – Miscarriage – Suicide.'[81] In this tragic resolution, Wollstonecraft proposes an equivalence between Darnford and Venables: that is to say, she argues that both the patriarchal and the sentimental versions of masculinity oppress women. Both constructions assume the subservient status of women in institutions such as marriage and romantic love, by 'considering females rather as women than human creatures, [as] alluring mistresses than affectionate wives and rational mothers'.[82]

The history of Jemima, the warder in the madhouse whose benevolence does much to reform Maria, augments this counter-sentimental argument. Jemima's history begins by brutally domesticating the scene of sexual violation ('My father [. . .] seduced my mother'); and it continues with a narrative of incessant and repetitive victimisation that draws Jemima into a tragic downwards spiral: her childhood sees her persecuted as a bastard and a servant before she is raped by her master. Outside the domestic protection of the family, she is forced to have an abortion and coerced into prostitution, first on the street, then in a brothel, and finally as a kept mistress. Her story is relentlessly terrifying, but it is not the terror of the gothic novel. It is particularly moving because, as she describes it, she is unable to escape society's need to define her as a sexual being and commodity. She realises she must learn to be self-reliant if she is to survive: or rather she must learn not to rely on men. She learns this emotional resilience, crucially, by reading – and through her autodidactic intellectual awakening, she learns how to survive in society (even if only as a warder in a madhouse). Jemima's story has taught her to distrust men and the institutions of the patriarchal culture that have destroyed her (marriage, the family, love). Her coherent and self-conscious understanding of the bonds which define her make her a genuinely radical, even feminist, heroine.

Wollstonecraft's revision of Radcliffe's gothic scenario amends given properties such as the virtuous heroine, the crumbling castle, the vicious male villain in order to read them in a political framework, bringing the reader to an understanding that the real terrors of the world are polit-ical rather than imaginary. The gothicising elements of *The Wrongs of Woman* are not merely a fashionable supplement to her political and moral theory. Although her strategy in writing a Radcliffean novel may have been to cover the bitter pill of reform with the sugar coating of fiction, the novel's form resists fashionable and entertaining confection through its unfinished gothicism. The gothic allows her to extend the scope of the story from the domestic sphere of the family and the home into the world of prisons and courthouses, while retaining a form that is recognisable to female readers who have remained in the home. As well as the conventional gothic backdrop of the castle prison, the novel develops a distinctive melancholic sensibility to its narrative voice, whose allegiance to Maria is incompletely resolved. In this unsettling narrative tone, the gothic usurps the philosophical, fragmenting the ideological coherence of the argument.

Since the late nineteenth century, A *Vindication of the Rights of Woman* has been Wollstonecraft's most famous work, often hailed as the 'corner-stone of feminist thought'.[83] In the *Vindication*, Wollstonecraft argued that novels, especially the sentimental kind, educated women into a 'state of perpetual childhood', incapable of taking part in the cultural and polit-ical spheres of their own society. She placed the 'romantic twist of mind, which has been very properly termed *sentimental*' alongside the adverse influence of popular delusions such as magnetism, electricity and mesmerism; the effects of vanity, fashion, dress and ornament; and the excessive devotion to children and husbands. Novels disseminated meta-physical notions respecting the passion of sensual feeling caused by the happiness of love:

> These are the women who are amused by the reveries of the stupid novelists, who, knowing little of human nature, work up stale tales, and describe mere-tricious scenes, all retailed in a sentimental jargon, which equally tend to corrupt the taste, and draw the heart aside from its daily duties.[84]

Such novels were pernicious to female manners because they induced women to think their business is to 'please', rather than to enter 'into more important concerns'. Rather than these 'flimsy works', Wollstonecraft cautions, young women should read the superior works of history and moral essays, which will refine their rational powers. Wollstonecraft attacked the sentimental novel because of the moral impact of its over-refinement of the passions, whereby young women are led astray by an overdeveloped hunger for the happiness of love, into indiscriminate sensual feeling and unlicensed sexuality.

Her attack on the novel in *A Vindication of the Rights of Woman* nonethe-less recognised the power of fiction in circulating ideas. Its popularity amongst the young and women suggested that philosophy was best dissem-inated by fiction. Both Rousseau and Godwin provided examples in their *Emile* (1761) and *Caleb Williams* (1794). In *The Analytical Review*, Wollstonecraft stated that, 'It was said by Rousseau, that to a refined and sensible people instruction can only be offered in the form of a novel, and it is certain, that in the present age – "Sermons are less read than tales"'.[85] Wollstonecraft's decision to cast her philosophical argument into the form of a novel was a sophisticated conclusion. In this sense, the centrality of books and reading to the love affair between Maria and Darnford is revealing. Maria first comes to know Darnford through the books he lends her: both by his selection and by his marginal notations. Their subsequent communication by letters constitutes a courtship by ideas, only later confirmed by physical passion. Mary, Darnford and Jemima all achieve their self-enlightenment through reading, even though both women emphatically repudiate the lessons of novel reading. Jemima bitterly notes that, 'I have since read in novels of the blandishments of seduction, but I had not even the pleasure of being enticed into vice.'[86] So while Mary Wollstonecraft argues against sentimental novels as one of the foolish and fashionable delusions that corrupt the minds of women, she also consistently defends the political project of gothic fiction. She remains committed to the idea that moral argument, and politics may be successfully introduced into the narrative form of the gothic novel. Although Radcliffe and Wollstonecraft may have had significant disagree-ments about the status of women and the politics of reform, their notion of the politics of gothic fiction was arguably more in tune. The cautious liberalism of Radcliffe's equation of sensibility with reform meets a more caustic critique in Wollstonecraft's gothic sensibility.

— NOTES —

1. 'Mrs. Radcliffe's Posthumous Romance', *The New Monthly Magazine and Literary Journal*, 16, 1 (1826), pp. 532–6, p. 532.
2. Sylvia Harcstark Myers, *The Bluestocking Circle: Women, Friendship, and the Life of the Mind in Eighteenth-Century England* (Oxford: Clarendon Press, 1990).
3. *The Monthly Review*, 48 (1773), p. 154.
4. Jane Spencer, *The Rise of the Woman Novelist: From Aphra Behn to Jane Austen* (Oxford: Basil Blackwell, 1986), p. xi. See also Nancy Armstrong, *Desire and Domestic Fiction: A Political History of the Novel* (New York and Oxford: Oxford University Press, 1987), p. 7.

5. Rictor Norton, *Mistress of Udolpho: a Life of Ann Radcliffe* (Leicester: Leicester University Press, 1999), pp. 41–53. See also Deborah D. Rogers, *Ann Radcliffe: a bio-bibliography* (Westport, CT and London: Greenwood Press, 1996).

6. T. N. Talfourd, 'Memoir of the Life and Writings of Mrs. Radcliffe', in Ann Radcliffe, *Gaston de Blondeville, or The Court of Henry III. Keeping Festival in Ardenne, A Romance* (London: Henry Colburn, 1826), pp. 7, 13.

7. William Hazlitt, 'On the English Novelists', *Lectures on the English Comic Writers* (London: Taylor and Hessey, 1819), pp. 250–1.

8. 'Mrs. Radcliffe's Posthumous Romance', *The New Monthly Magazine and Literary Journal*, 16, 1 (1826), p. 533.

9. Nathan Drake, *Literary Hours: or Sketches Critical and Narrative*, 2 vols, 2nd ed. (Sudbury: T. Cadell & W. Davies, 1800), I, p. 359.

10. Talfourd, 'Memoir', p. 106.

11. *The New Monthly Magazine and Literary Journal*, 16, 1 (1826), p. 533.

12. Ann Radcliffe, *The Romance of the Forest*, ed. Chloe Chard (Oxford: Oxford University Press, 1986). All references to this edition.

13. *Critical Review*, 4 (1792), p. 458.

14. Deborah Rogers (ed.), *The Critical Response to Ann Radcliffe* (Westport, CT and London: Greenwood Press, 1994).

15. S.T. Coleridge, *The Critical Review*, 9 (1794), pp. 361–72, p. 362.

16. Radcliffe has been cast as the progenitor of the 'female gothic' in Ellen Moers, *Literary Women* (London: W. H. Allen, 1977); and C. G. Wolff, 'The Radcliffean Gothic Model: A Form for Feminine Sexuality', in J. E. Fleenor (ed.), *The Female Gothic* (Montreal: Eden Press, 1983), pp. 207–33. In reply see Jacqueline Howard, *Reading Gothic Fiction: a Bakhtinian Approach* (Oxford: Clarendon Press, 1994), p. 64.

17. Radcliffe, *Romance*, p. 29.

18. Lawrence Stone, *The Family, Sex and Marriage in England, 1500–1800* (London: Weidenfeld and Nicolson, 1977), pp. 239–40.

19. Ann Radcliffe, *The Mysteries of Udolpho*, ed. Terry Castle and Bonamy Dobrée (Oxford: Oxford University Press, 1998), pp. 5, 79–80.

20. Claudia Johnson, *Equivocal Beings: Politics, Gender and Sentimentality in the 1790s* (Chicago and London: The University of Chicago Press, 1995).

21. Paul Langford, *A Polite and Commercial People: England 1727–1783* (Oxford: Oxford University Press, 1989), p. 461.

22. John Mullan, *Sentiment and Sociability: The Language of Feeling in the Eighteenth Century* (Oxford: Clarendon Press, 1988); Graham Barker-Benfield, *Culture of Sensibility: Sex and Society in Eighteenth-Century Britain* (Chicago: University of Chicago Press, 1992); Markman Ellis, *The Politics of Sensibility: Race, Gender and Commerce in the Sentimental Novel* (Cambridge: Cambridge University Press, 1996).

23. Mary Poovey, 'Ideology and *The Mysteries of Udolpho*', *Criticism*, 21 (1979), p. 321.

24. Clara Reeve, *The Progress of Romance, Through Times, Countries, and Manners*, 2 vols (London: the Author, 1785), II, pp. 77–8.
25. Sarah Pennington, *An Unfortunate Mother's Advice to her Absent Daughters* (London: S. Chandler and W. Bristow; York: C. Ethrington, 1761), pp. 39, 40.
26. Rev. Edward Barry, *Essays, on the Following Subjects: Celibacy, Wedlock, Seduction, Pride, Duelling, Self-Murder, Lying, Detraction, Avarice, Justice, Generosity, Temperance, Excess, Death* (1791; Reading: Smart and Cowslade, 1806), pp. 56–7.
27. *The Analytical Review*, XIV (September 1792), p. 101.
28. 'Terrorist Novel Writing', *The Spirit of the Public Journals for 1797* (London: R. Phillips, 1798), pp. 223–5.
29. Radcliffe, *Udolpho*, pp. 23, 122.
30. Radcliffe, *Udolpho*, pp. 226–7.
31. Radcliffe, *Udolpho*, pp. 2–3, 227–8.
32. Radcliffe, *Udolpho*, pp. 312–13.
33. Thomas Coryate, *Coryats Crudities* (London: W. S., 1611), p. 117.
34. Eric Hobsbawm, *Bandits* (London: Weidenfeld and Nicolson, 1969), p. 62.
35. M. Archenholtz, 'Curious Account of the Banditti of Naples', *The Lady's Magazine*, 22 (April 1791), pp. 197–8.
36. Johann Christoph Friedrich von Schiller, *Die Räuber* (Frankfurt and Leipzig: n.p., 1781), *The Robbers*, trans. A. F. Tytler (London: G. G. & J. Robinson, 1792).
37. John Hamilton Mortimer, 'Banditti Returning' (pen and ink drawing, 35.2 × 41 cm, 1775) London: British Museum, Department of Prints and Drawings (L. B. 25.Oo.5.9). Boydell published this as a mezzotint by J. B. Smith, after the oil painting, on 14 February 1780.
38. Benedict Nicolson, 'Introduction', *John Hamilton Mortimer, 1740–1779: Paintings, Drawings and Prints* (Eastbourne: Towner Art Gallery; London: Iveagh Bequest Kenwood, 1968), p. 11.
39. John Sunderland, *John Hamilton Mortimer: his Life and Works* (Leeds: W. S. Maney for the Walpole Society, 1986), pp. 54–62.
40. Radcliffe, *Udolpho*, pp. 311, 314–15, 305.
41. Henry Singleton, *The Mysteries of Udolpho*, colour-printed stipple engraved by William Bond, 1796; in David Alexander, *Affecting Moments: Prints of English Literature made in the Age of Romantic Sensibility, 1775–1800* (York: University of York, 1993), pp. 60–2.
42. Radcliffe, *Udolpho*, pp. 316–17, 323.
43. Radcliffe, *Udolpho*, pp. 394, 397, 521.
44. Kenneth W. Graham, 'Emily's Demon-Lover: The Gothic Revolution and *The Mysteries of Udolpho*', in *Gothic Fictions: Prohibition/Transgression*, ed. Kenneth W. Graham (New York: AMS Press, 1989), p. 167.
45. 'On Delicacy of Sentiment', *Universal Magazine*, LXII (April 1778), pp. 172–3.

46. Radcliffe, *Romance*, pp. 245–6, 248, 277.
47. Radcliffe, *Romance*, p. 218.
48. Radcliffe, *Udolpho*, pp. 31–2, 652
49. Radcliffe, *Udolpho*, p. 672.
50. Hazlitt, 'English Novelists', p. 250.
51. See also Robert Miles, *Ann Radcliffe: The Great Enchantress* (Manchester: Manchester University Press, 1995), pp. 76–7. Compare with David Durant, 'Ann Radcliffe and the Conservative Gothic', *Studies in English Literature, 1500–1900*, 22, 3 (1982), pp. 519–30; and James Watt, *Contesting the Gothic* (Cambridge: Cambridge University Press, 1999), pp. 108–12.
52. Walter Scott, *The Lives of the Novelists*, 2 vols (Paris: A. and W. Galignani, 1825), p. 245.
53. Thomas Green, *Extracts from the Diary of a Lover of Literature* (Ipswich: John Raw, 1810), p. 28.
54. Hazlitt, 'English Novelists', p. 251.
55. *The Analytical Review*, 25 (May 1797), p. 516.
56. Lawrence Flammenberg, *The Necromancer, or a Tale of the Black Forest*, trans. Peter Teuthold (1794; London: Skoob Books, 1992).
57. *The Critical Review*, ser. 2, 2, 11 (August 1794), pp. 361–72.
58. Jane Austen, *Northanger Abbey*, ed. Terry Castle (1818; Oxford: Oxford University Press, 1990), I, vii, p. 34.
59. Cecil S. Emden, 'The Composition of Northanger Abbey', *Review of English Studies*, 19 (1968), pp. 279–87.
60. Marilyn Butler, *Jane Austen and the War of Ideas* (1975, Oxford: Oxford University Press, rev. edn 1987); Tony Tanner, *Jane Austen* (London and Cambridge, MA: Macmillan, 1986); Claudia Johnson, 'A "Sweet Face as White as Death": Jane Austen and the Politics of Female Sensibility', *Novel*, 22 (1988), pp. 159–74; Claudia Johnson, *Jane Austen: Women, Politics and the Novel* (Chicago and London: University of Chicago Press, 1988).
61. Eliza Parsons, *The Castle of Wolfenbach* (1793) and *Mysterious Warnings* (1796); Regina Maria Roche, *Clermont* (1798); Lawrence Flammenberg, *The Necromancer* (1794); Francis Lathom, *The Midnight Bell* (1798); Eleanor Sleath, *The Orphan of the Rhine* (1798); and Peter Will, *Horrid Mysteries* (1796).
62. Austen, *Northanger Abbey*, I, vi, pp. 23–6; I, vii, pp. 31–2; I, xiv, pp. 83–4.
63. Eve Kosofsky Sedgwick, 'Jane Austen and the Masturbating Girl', *Critical Inquiry*, 17, 4 (1991), pp. 818–37.
64. Austen, *Northanger Abbey*, II, vi, pp. 133–4.
65. Austen, *Northanger Abbey*, II, viii, p. 150.
66. Robert Hopkins, 'General Tilney and Affairs of State: The Political Gothic of *Northanger Abbey*', *Philological Quarterly*, 57 (1978), pp. 213–24; Nancy Armstrong, 'The Nineteenth-Century Jane Austen: A Turning Point in the History of Fear', *Genre*, 23 (1990), pp. 227–46.

67. Mary Wollstonecraft, *Posthumous Works of the Author of A Vindication of the Rights of Woman*, ed. William Godwin, 4 vols (London: J. Johnson and G. G. and J. Robinson, 1798).

68. William Godwin, *Memoirs of Mary Wollstonecraft*, ed. Richard Holmes (1798; Harmondsworth: Penguin, 1987).

69. Claire Tomalin, *The Life and Death of Mary Wollstonecraft* (London: Weidenfeld and Nicolson, 1974).

70. *The European Magazine*, 33 (1798), pp. 246–51.

71. Regina M. Janes, 'On the Reception of the Mary Wollstonecraft's *A Vindication of the Rights of Woman*', *Journal of the History of Ideas*, 39 (1978), pp. 293–303, p. 303.

72. Mary Wollstonecraft, *The Wrongs of Woman*, in *Mary and The Wrongs of Woman*, ed. Gary Kelly (Oxford: Oxford University Press, 1976), pp. 73, 71, 75.

73. Radcliffe, *Udolpho*, p. 227.

74. Wollstonecraft, *Wrongs*, pp. 76–7.

75. William Blackstone, *Commentaries on the Laws of England*, 4 vols (Oxford: Clarendon Press, 1765–1769), III, 17, p. 268.

76. Wollstonecraft, *Wrongs*, pp. 83, 79, 82

77. Mary Wollstonecraft, *A Vindication of the Rights of Woman*, ed. Carol H. Poston, 2nd edn (New York: W.W. Norton, 1988), p. 7.

78. Moira Ferguson and Janet Todd, *Mary Wollstonecraft* (Boston: Twayne Press, 1984), p. 68. See also Mary Poovey, 'Mary Wollstonecraft: The Gender of Genres in Late-Eighteenth-Century England', *Novel*, 15, 2 (Winter 1982), pp. 111–26.

79. Wollstonecraft, *Vindication*, p. 9.

80. Wollstonecraft, *Wrongs*, pp. 100, 101

81. Wollstonecraft, *Wrongs*, pp. 201–2.

82. Wollstonecraft, *Vindication*, p. 7.

83. Harriet Devine Jump, *Mary Wollstonecraft: Writer* (Hemel Hempstead: Harvester Wheatsheaf, 1994), p. 67; Moira Ferguson, *First Feminists: British Women Writers 1578–1799* (Bloomington, IN: Indiana University Press, 1985).

84. Wollstonecraft, *Vindication*, p. 183.

85. *Analytical Review*, 24 (September 1796), p. 315.

86. Wollstonecraft, *Wrongs*, p. 109.

CHAPTER THREE

Revolution and libertinism in the gothic novel

Matthew Lewis, The Monk (1796);
Charlotte Dacre, Zofloya; or, The Moor (1806)

The conjunction in the 1790s of the rise to prominence of the gothic novel and the profound political upheaval of the French Revolution has long been contemplated by critics, readers and historians. Analysing these 'new novels' dealing in 'sorcery and phantasmagoria', the Marquis de Sade in 1800 proposed that the foremost amongst them was Matthew Lewis's The Monk (1796), 'superior in all respects to the strange flights of Mrs Radcliffe's brilliant imagination'. Such gothic novels, he continued, were 'the inevitable result of the revolutionary shocks which all of Europe has suffered'. Against such events, Sade asserts, the old domestic novel 'became as difficult to write as monotonous to read', and 'to compose works of interest, one had to call upon the aid of hell itself'. In Sade's estimation, the gothic novel's strategies of wizardry and secrecy – the supernatural and terror – are alone adequate to the bloody terrors of recent history.[1] Sade's insight, albeit without much immediate influence, suggestively read The Monk as the product of revolutionary commotion, even though it is not in any conventional historical or geographical sense located in France in the 1790s. Despite the search for 'a direct political-fictional correspondence', as Emma Clery phrases it, between the French Revolution and the gothic novel, there can be no straightforward account of the interaction of novel and history.[2] Literary critics of The Monk have repeatedly sought to draw connections between it and the events of the 1790s in France and in Britain. For example, Ronald Paulson argues that 'the popularity of gothic fiction in the 1790s and well into the nineteenth century was due in part to the widespread anxieties and fears in Europe aroused by the turmoil in France finding a kind of horror or catharsis in tales of darkness, confusion, blood, and terror.'[3] The historian Emmet Kennedy argues that The Monk while 'still moral in its message' offered a 'parable' of the 'French Revolution's atrocity and violence.'[4]

The destruction of the Convent of St Clare in *The Monk*, a much discussed example, has often been read as an analogy for the popular violence of the Revolutionary '*journées*' (revolutionary intervention by the crowd). The revelation that the prioress of the Convent of St Clare has imprisoned and put to death nuns who have succumbed to sexual temptation incites the violence of the crowd. Incensed by despotism, the people rise up *en masse*, destroying the convent and lynching the prioress. Nothing remains of her corpse but a bloody pulp: 'They beat it, trod upon it, and ill-used it, till it became no more than a mass of flesh, unsightly, shapeless, and disgusting.' Both in England and France, the collective expression of popular political will by the mob appeared to conservative commentators to signal the release of darker, irrational, savage forces in the body politic. These notions are coloured by a gothic language, as *The Monk* testifies: 'The Rioters heeded nothing but the gratification of their barbarous vengeance.'[5] Lewis's representation of the crowd, the most notorious phenomenon of popular revolution, invites readers to compare text and event, fictional and historical narrative. But critics have been unable to agree upon which event is recalled here: André Parreaux suggests that the destruction of the convent 'gives an echo of the French September Massacres' of 1792, while Paulson suggests as well the 'Revolutionary emblem' of the castle-prison, specifically the fall of the Bastille in 1789.[6]

Although Lewis had direct experience of the French revolution, both as a witness in Paris in 1791 and as a diplomat in The Hague in 1794, his view of these events is that of a loyal Briton, to some extent distanced from, and critical of, the unfolding events. Lewis was not simply writing an allegory of revolution, nor propaganda for one of its factions. However, the confusion engendered by his novel's representation of revolutionary events suggests deliberate obfuscation. The recent historiography of the French Revolution has highlighted its political character, arguing that rather than being a social transformation, it should be considered 'a contest for power through the appropriation of the symbols of revolutionary legitimacy'.[7] The French historian, François Furet, argues that the revolutionaries commanded a 'network of signs' that dominated political culture by 'establishing just who represented the people, or equality, or the nation: victory was in the hands of those who were capable of occupying and keeping that symbolic position'.[8] Lewis's engagement with revolution might better be understood at the level of language and tone in the deployment of key revolutionary symbols. This chapter charts this engagement by exploring how Lewis's contemporaries understood *The Monk*. In their readings, Lewis's novel explores cultural fissures opened in British political culture by the revolution in France. The novel's deliberate confusion of its ideological commentary, which illuminates British opinion on the revolution in the period up to 1794, was itself readable as a political intervention during its critical reception in 1797. As a result, *The Monk* became one of the most celebrated, and notorious, novels in English.

— I. COMPOSITIONAL POLITICS OF *THE MONK* —

Lewis proudly declared that he wrote *The Monk* 'in the space of ten weeks', although evidence indicates that the book's gestation was a longer affair.[9] He had toyed, in a desultory fashion, with the idea of writing a romance for some years. He had already abandoned a burlesque satire on the sentimental novel of manners, called *The Effusions of Sensibility*;[10] and whilst still at university in Oxford, he had secretly begun 'a Romance in the style of [Walpole's] *Castle of Otranto*'.[11] The hesitant novelist remarked that he was 'induced' to go back to prose fiction 'by reading "The Mysteries of Udolpho", which is in my opinion one of the most interesting Books that ever have been published.'[12] The novel certainly bears signs of this and other influences. In the prefatory 'Advertisement' to *The Monk*, Lewis declares that the book has borrowed elements, some of which he confesses he might not be aware of. 'I doubt not [that] many more [plagiarisms] may be found, of which I am at present totally unconscious.'[13] A great deal of critical attention has focussed on these borrowings, beginning with the sources he himself admits to in the advertisement, and going on to identify more than fifty works that might have contributed a character, scene or theme.[14] Although Lewis was unusually well read in little-known recent German and French literature, the most important influence was Radcliffe. However, Lewis's interest in Radcliffe's work is distinctly hostile, exploring some of the consequences or implications of Radcliffe's argument about the moral status of contemporary notions of femininity. In a way, then, *The Monk* might usefully be read as a satiric attack on the moral tendencies of Radcliffe's fiction. This was so effective – in particular the scandalously obscene clarity that Lewis brings to Radcliffe's emotional intensity – that Radcliffe was prompted to write a reply to his criticism in the form of her last gothic novel, *The Italian* (1797).

The Monk borrows its gothic *mise en scène* from Radcliffe's fictions, especially *The Mysteries of Udolpho*. The exotic and medieval location of Radcliffe's castle and secret chambers is transformed into Lewis's cloister and dungeon. Radcliffe's renowned techniques, such as her prolongation of terror, are also examined, although Lewis gleefully abandons the explained supernatural in favour of unrestrained use of necromancy and diabolic powers. Lewis also takes considerable interest in the febrile, emotional tone of Radcliffe's fiction, which, his novel suggests, he understands both as a mode of writing (intense, passionate and over-heated) and as a discourse on the passions itself. The prime connection between the novels, then, is their shared interest in the motivating power of desire. Radcliffe's novels consistently structure themselves around a romantic-love plot, in which feminine innocence is confronted and tested by experience of the wider world of sexuality. The struggle between innocence and experience is resolved by marriage, transforming private female virtue into a public standard upon which order is securely re-established. Lewis works from a contrary impetus: the paranoid fears of a Radcliffe heroine are made the real exploits of diabolical protagonists. His plot follows a trajectory that leads away from innocence, the family and the established order towards a morally chaotic conclusion in rebellion and punishment. Lewis's plot hinges on the contamination of innocence, not its endurance or restoration.

Little of this is immediately apparent. The novel opens in the exotic environment of the Church of the Capuchins in Madrid, at an unspecified historical period, arguably the seventeenth century. The setting in the Catholic environment of monastery and convent locates the novel amongst that patriotic English mode of anti-Catholic gothicism. The novel's protest against the hypocrisy of Catholic 'superstition' is immediately apparent in the opening scene in the church, which it depicts as a place of lecherous flirtation rather than pious religious observance. Two cavaliers (gentlemen) vie for the attention of a young woman, Antonia, who has come to the city to seek the aid of a distant rich relative (the Marquis de las Cisternas). Their gaze is attracted as much by Antonia's innocent demeanour of 'sweetness and sensibility' as well as the 'dazzling whiteness' of her complexion, 'carefully veiled' bosom and 'long fair hair'. Despite her bashful attempts to remain veiled, the men notice her sparkling eyes and arch smile, which 'declared her to be possessed of liveliness, which excess of timidity at present represt'.[15] The narrator explains that the Church of the Capuchins has become the resort of flirtatious and fashionable society through the influence of a compelling priest, the Abbot of the Capuchins, Ambrosio.

Known throughout the city as the 'Man of Holiness', as the most eloquent orator in the city, esteemed by the 'common People' as a 'Saint', the novel proposes Ambrosio as the centre of moral order. A foundling left at the Abbey door, he was raised by the Capuchins in 'singular austerity' and 'total seclusion from the world', never going outside the Abbey walls. He is a man of untrammelled virtue:

> In the whole course of his life. He has never been known to transgress a single rule of his order; The smallest stain is not to be discovered upon his character; and He is reported to be so strict an observer of Chastity, that He knows not in what consists the difference of Man and Woman. The common People therefore esteem him to be a Saint.

At the beginning of the novel Ambrosio appears to be the very model of sentimental virtue and propriety, so much so that gender has no meaning. Occupying the extreme wing of the virgin-innocence-chastity faction, Ambrosio begins the novel like one of Radcliffe's befuddled but virtuous heroines. Ambrosio's sermon, delivered with captivating eloquence, casts a spell over his congregation, even the non-believers. Lewis makes it clear that it is not what Ambrosio says, but rather, the manner in which he says it. His 'distinct and deep' voice, from which the 'Thunder seemed to roll', transports those who hear it 'to those happy regions which He painted to their imaginations in colours so brilliant and glowing'.[16]

Antonia's chaste virtue is founded on ignorance of human sexuality: an ignorance, like Ambrosio's, so profound she imagines 'every body to be of the same sex' as herself. Unlike Radcliffe's heroines, however, her ignorance is no preservative of her chastity, because at her first sight of Ambrosio's noble and commanding features, she felt 'a pleasure fluttering in her bosom which till then had been unknown to her'. Ambrosio's oratory moves the pious and chaste Antonia to admire his person rather than his argument. She declares with wonder that, 'his voice inspired me with such interest, such esteem, I might almost say such affection for him, that I am myself astonished at the acuteness of my feelings.'[17] Antonia's reaction, driven by affection for his person (lust) rather than affection for his message (piety), is improper in the context of the church, and signals in its language the libertine interest of the novel. When Ambrosio returns to his cell in the monastery, he is depicted as giving 'free loose to the indulgence of his vanity', as he excitedly reviews the 'Enthusiasm' his sermon had aroused. 'Enthusiasm' was a key word for the eighteenth century, where it was used to refer to the uncontrolled encouragement of feelings and sentiments. He also celebrates how he has subdued all 'strong passions' and regards himself as 'the sole uncorrupted Pillar of the Church!' Ambrosio declares that as 'the passions are dead in my bosom', he would resist 'Objects of temptation' and 'the seduction of luxury and desire'.[18] However, the adoration he expresses for a portrait of the Madonna, which dwells on her bodily charms and especially her 'snowy bosom', suggests his resolutions are in vain. The novel revels in the scandalous disparity between the supposedly holy locations of the story (church, monastery, convent), the modes of behaviour exhibited by the religious inhabitants (flirtation, modishness, vanity), and the passions depicted in the characters (jealousy, pride and, most of all, lust).

Ambrosio's first test is offered, bizarrely, by a mysterious young novice of the monastery, Rosario, who has established himself as Ambrosio's favourite by 'performing numerous little tasks and offices'. Veiled by his cowl at all times, Rosario's air of melancholy excites in Ambrosio a desire to know his secret. In the picturesque grotto of the Abbey garden, Rosario eventually reveals his long-nurtured passion for Ambrosio. His secret is not simply his love for Ambrosio, but rather, that 'I am a Woman!'[19] Lewis makes the scene turn on a double perversity of homosexuality and transvestism (to use the language adopted in the nineteenth century for this behaviour). The novel expresses the emergent love between Ambrosio and Rosario (or Matilda) as a powerful sexual desire, and as a diabolic aberration. Proscriptions about same-sex homosexual acts between men, historians argue, were relatively new in the eighteenth century, concomitant with the emergence of the ideals of love and marriage. The novel then 'rescues' this perversity by Matilda's declaration: Ambrosio feels heterosexual not homosexual desire, a cross-dressing woman invading the masculine institution of the monastery, intensified after the couple proceed to a passionate sexual affair. Ambrosio's desire for Matilda is both normative (responding to passions allowed by the new language of marital friendship) and transgressive (as it occurs in a supposedly chaste environment and expresses itself in uncontrolled extramarital sexuality). Matilda's subsequent revelation as a witch of Satan indicates how her sexual desire remains problematic within the new constructions of gender that emerge in the eighteenth century.[20] Equally, a transvestite woman entering the homosocial world of a monastery to pursue her erotic desires for an abbot engenders even more scandal.

Matilda, as this gender-shifting demon can be called, is a powerful character. As a 'woman', as she sometimes is, she quickly moves away, permanently and radically, from the sentimental construction of femininity familiar from Radcliffe. Rosario is at first a delicate, graceful, demure and deeply effeminate novice; a set of characteristics that survive, initially, his revelation as a woman. This is a revelation rather than a transformation. But the sudden external unveiling of her gender signals the beginning of a breakdown of the conventional constructions of gender (destabilising a simple opposition between a strong, patriarchal masculinity and a weak, domestic, submissive femininity). Certainly, she remains woman: arousing in Ambrosio 'lust-exciting visions', Matilda appeared 'in all the pomp of beauty, warm, tender and luxurious'. Matilda, the revealed woman, soon surpasses the sentimental construction of femininity which she obeyed as a man, as if her change was designed to expose the constructedness of gender identity. Matilda soon becomes like a man, in fact.

> But a few days had past, since She appeared the mildest and softest of her sex, devoted to his will, and looking up to him as to a superior Being. Now She assumed a sort of courage and manliness in her manners and discourse but ill calculated to please him. She spoke no longer to insinuate, but command.[21]

The strong, even monstrous figure Matilda becomes is reminiscent of misogynist constructions of femininity.

Although Matilda was a demon, her seduction of Ambrosio was conducted through the vehicle of her beautiful body. *The Analytical Review* argued in 1796 that, 'The monk, in fact, inspires sympathy, because soiled by more than mortal weapons; yet nothing was done by Matilda, which could not have been achieved by female wiles – the monk's pride was the arch devil that betrayed him.'[22] In the sense that Matilda's seductive power derives from her femininity, the novel invokes the misogynist ideology of women's rapacious sexuality and propensity for pleasure. It is as a woman, then, rather than a demon, that Matilda is simply irresistible, despite all Ambrosio's resolutions. When Matilda reveals her true sexuality to Ambrosio in the garden, by accidentally exposing her breast through her torn habit, Ambrosio is transfixed, and then transmogrified, by his passion.

> Oh! that was such a breast! The Moon-beams darting full upon it, enabled the Monk to observe its dazzling whiteness. His eye dwelt with insatiable avidity upon the beauteous Orb. A sensation till then unknown filled his heart with a mixture of anxiety and delight: A raging fire shot through every limb; The blood boiled in his veins, and a thousand wild wishes bewildered his imagination.[23]

This is only one of many powerful and eloquent female breasts in the novel. That Matilda's unveiling reveals both her secret and her bosom, is an unsubtle satirical jibe at Radcliffe's veiled mysteries. But in fact Matilda's secret is her femininity, and to Ambrosio, her body is incontrovertible proof of her femaleness, a state he equates with sexual availability. Ambrosio's discovery of carnal desire is represented as a physiological effect, even as it has its origin in his imagination. Eighteenth-century constructions of femininity indicated that potentially limitless desire was the essential condition of femininity (all other aspects of femininity were directed to control and suppress this lustfulness). Ambrosio's inability to resist his desire is the cause of his fall, and as such, Lewis has him occupy a position traditionally accorded to women. The novel offers further examples of the desiring woman in Agnes and the Bleeding Nun. Female sexual monstrosity is confirmed in Matilda by her revelation as a sorcerer and devil-woman.

Each of the crimes and outrages that Matilda entices Ambrosio to perpetrate is greater than the last: first he permits her to remain in the abbey; then he fornicates with her against the vows of chastity; then he murders Elvira, his mother; then he rapes and murders Antonia his sister; and finally he signs a pact with the devil. Matilda's transformations give Ambrosio the ability to achieve the next outrage: their plots are inter-twined. As his crimes grow worse, Ambrosio's sense of remorse grows more and more acute, but he never repents and never returns to virtue. Rather, a deeper sense of sin drives him to commit even greater sin. After he has murdered Elvira, he finds that the remorse he feels 'served but to strengthen his resolution to destroy Antonia's honour'. Desire leads Ambrosio to commit crime, but the desire is always in excess of the crime, and so the crime does not satisfy him. This dissatisfaction, this sublime lust, spurs him to still greater sin. As D. L. MacDonald has argued, the novel's powerful forward momentum derives from the char-acteristic pattern whereby each outrage satiates one passion but excites the next.[24] This progression might be compared with the consistently circular repetitions of The Mysteries of Udolpho in which the unnaturally horrible fancies of Emily's imagination are shown to have material, even everyday, causes. Having committed one 'enormous crime', Ambrosio is filled with 'real horror' and reflects on his 'rapid advances in iniquity', as if damnation for him has supplanted the state of grace as the destination of his life.[25] Ambrosio's sinner's progress has echoes of seventeenth-century spiritual biography (such as that of John Bunyan), a form revived by the Evangelical churches in the late eighteenth century. The formal conventions of the spiritual biography depict life as a series of stages, starting with the depiction of the penitent's initial sin, followed by recog-nition of sinfulness, repentance and eventually, after much backsliding, internal heart-searching and repentance, the attainment of a state of grace. In Lewis's black-magic revision of the spiritual autobiography, Ambrosio moves from initial innocence and virtue, to the experience of sin. Through a gradual process of self-vilification, remorse and sin, he finally achieves damnation by selling his soul to the devil.

The Monk's most significant revision of its chosen model, the Radcliffe gothic novel, is its deployment of a libertine descriptive language in moments of sexual encounter. Where Radcliffe coyly but deliberately leaves erotic engagement at the level of suggestive hints, or draws a veil over sexual encounters through her heroines' propensity for fainting, Lewis revels in explicit detail. Radcliffe's decorous evasion of sexual material is of course determined by her sentimental agenda: she omits matter that is inappropriate for her implied female readers. Lewis, who deliberately courts both the horizon of expectations of Radcliffe's novel form and her audience, mounts a wounding satiric attack in his explicit obscenity. In this way, *The Monk* is a satire on, not a homage to, *The Mysteries of Udolpho*, designed to expose the folly and hypocrisy of its ostensibly demure sexual agenda.

Ambrosio's progress towards sin is driven by his desire to be free from the restraints of his monastic society. His liberty, when he finds it, gives free reign to his desires and lusts, rather than those moral capacities he thought he represented (chastity, virtue, propriety, generosity, faith). Ambrosio's desire for the liberty to pursue erotic desires articulates an idea at the centre of revisionist enlightenment constructions of sexuality. Here *The Monk* appeals to an historically enduring literary and philo-sophic discourse on sexuality, known as libertinism, imbricated in classical scholarship, enlightenment science and radical political culture. 'Manly' libertinism associated a construction of masculinity with a particular philo-sophical and political platform. The 'libertine', derived from the Latin for 'free', came to mean, in the early seventeenth century, 'free or loose opinions about religion', and later the 'habitual disregard of the moral law, especially with regard to the relation of the sexes' (*OED*). The libertine, like the rake, was characterised by dissolute licentiousness. As the sentimental novelist Samuel Richardson observed in *Sir Charles Grandison* (1753–4), this 'narrow-hearted race of men, . . . live only for the gratifi-cation of their own lawless appetites'. The discourse of libertinism, it may be concluded, is essentially masculine in its nature, and closely allied to misogyny.[26]

Alongside this conception of male behaviour (akin to the rake's 'phallic adventuring'), libertinism offered a mode of philosophical enquiry and political engagement. Kathleen Wilson has argued that in the late eighteenth century, libertinism was both a mode of personal behaviour and as expression of radical politics particularly associated with the populist patriot Whigs John Wilkes and Charles James Fox.[27] Although the alliance of libertinism and radical Whiggism was challenged during the Revolution controversy, the personal behaviour of Fox and his associates, amongst whom Lewis can be numbered, can be described by this discourse. In *The Monk*, Lewis appropriates the discourse of libertinism to his contestation of orthodox manners and morals: in this sense libertinism is a critique of the sentimental transformation of the patriarchal model of female domesticity examined in the previous chapter. The distinctive innovation of the new libertine discourse of the late-eighteenth century, as Roy Porter and Randolph Trumbach have argued, was its central assumption, in contradistinction to Christian orthodoxy, that the pursuit of sexual pleasure was good and natural.[28] Porter observes that the Scottish moral philosopher David Hume, in his *Treatise on Human Nature* (1739–40), locates erotic attraction, or the 'natural appetite betwixt the sexes', as the 'first and original principle of human society'.[29] Porter concludes that, 'These naturalistic and hedonistic assumptions – that Nature had made men to follow pleasure, that sex was pleasurable, and that it was natural to follow one's sexual urges – underpinned much enlightenment thought about sexuality.'[30] The libertine equation of sexual gratification with pleasure and felicity was consistently constructed in the emancipatory discourse of liberty.

Libertine notions of sexuality proposed that sexual behaviour, like all natural phenomena, could be understood by rational and empirical analysis, accounting for desire and pleasure according to a mechanistic treatment underpinned by medical science. As Ambrosio's responses to Matilda's body suggest, Lewis proposes sexual pleasure as an instinctual urge, and as such, not subject to the force of the will; yet this same sexual desire is mastered by narrative through an empirical mode of description that describes sexual desire through its physiological effects on the body (sensibility). Despite the sometimes overheated rhetoric, Lewis's slow and detailed examination of Ambrosio's (or Matilda's) physiological response to erotic excitement demonstrates that his manner of representation of the sexual is materialist and empirical. Ambrosio, from his first encounters with Matilda, recognises that like St Anthony he must vanquish, not merely avoid, the temptation of lust. His dreams, dominated by 'sensations of voluptuousness' and 'lust-exciting visions', lead him to a language of liberty to describe his position: considering the foregone pleasures of sexuality, he complains that he is 'restrained by monastic fetters', and 'breathed a sigh' of regret when he looks towards the freedom of the wider world. The language of liberty is also close to that of libertinism when Matilda declares her irrepressible desire for Ambrosio: 'I lust for the enjoyment of your person. The Woman reigns in my bosom [an abstraction signifying an unlimited and unregulated desire], and I am become a prey to the wildest of passions. . . . My bosom burns with love, with unutterable love, and love must be its return.'[31]

The particular focus of Lewis's libertine imagination is the female breast. Ambrosio's seduction in the garden of the monastery is initiated by Matilda's exposed bosom. Having already dwelt on Ambrosio's fascination with the 'treasures' of the Madonna's 'snowy bosom', the novel depicts the sudden, accidental, revelation of Matilda's 'beauteous Orb' as the irresistible temptation. The breast is a powerfully seductive force: Matilda seduces Ambrosio by placing his hand on her heart, and his hand, having 'rested on her bosom' excites the 'full vigour of Manhood' and causes him to yield to temptation.[32] In *The Monk*, the bosom is not only the repository of the heart and its secrets (invoking the historically enduring language of piety and romantic love), but also a more erotic quantity (derived from the new materialist libertine discourse which used physiological phenomena to trace erotic excitement). The contest between these languages of the breast can be observed in the perversely picturesque scene when Matilda enables Ambrosio to peer into Antonia's bath closet through the magic Mirror. Like the Venus de Medici, with whom Lewis draws an explicit connection, Antonia seems possessed of both virtuous innocence and an innate erotic knowledge. In a scene excised from the abridged version, Lewis depicts Antonia 'undressing to bathe herself':

> She threw off her last garment . . . Though unconscious of being observed, an in-bred sense of modesty induced her to veil her charms; and She stood hesitating upon the brink, in the attitude of the Venus de Medicis. At this moment a tame Linnet flew towards her, nestled its head between her breasts, and nibbled them in wanton play. The smiling Antonia strove in vain to shake off the Bird, and at length raised her hands to drive it from its delightful harbour. Ambrosio could bear no more: His desires were worked up to phrenzy.[33]

Ambrosio's response to her coyly exposed breasts – the 'phrenzy' of the nymphomaniac male – seems to suggest that this scene, inherently absurd, can be read as a variety of that distinctly 'modern', post-Cleland pornography defined by Lynn Hunt as 'the explicit description of sexual organs or activities with the sole aim of producing sexual arousal in the reader or viewer', typically through the structure of voyeurism.[34] It is also part of a consistent attitudinal pattern in the novel, in which Ambrosio's heart's desire is keyed by the exposure of female breasts. Antonia unveiling in the bath reveals again that her body has the incendiary effect, and not merely Matilda's demonic skills. In the revised and expurgated fourth edition, Lewis replaced the entire scene with the sentence 'Ambrosio gazed upon it for a few minutes; those few were sufficient to fix his irresolution.'[35]

Ambrosio's curious inability to control his passions recalls the contemporary debate on the nymphomaniac, a woman whose desire for carnal encounters is insatiable. A popular treatise by the French physician de Bienville, translated as *Nymphomania, or, a Dissertation on the Furor Uterinus* (1775), described the symptoms of a compulsive nymphomaniac: 'At the mere sight of a handsome man or beautiful woman, my body became restless, an expression of pleasurable possession spread over my face; I could scarcely conceal the violence of my desires.'[36] Gazing at Antonia's drugged and naked body, the narrator describes how Ambrosio's 'desires were raised to that frantic height, by which Brutes are agitated.'[37] Ambrosio's irresistible libertine curiosity, both in language and symptoms, reveals him as a kind of nymphomaniac: a victim rather than master of desires akin to rage or madness.

The commitment of enlightenment libertinism to the empirical method and materialist understanding of the body underlined its critical subversion of orthodox Christianity and reaffirmed its alliance with political radicalism. Recent research has shown that the allegiance between radical politics, philosophy and obscene writing was underlined in France, and perhaps in Britain, by the booksellers. In France, in the *ancien régime* and after, in a modified form, as Robert Darnton has shown, libertine works that would now be classified as pornographic circulated as part of a clandestine literature identified as 'philosophical'.[38] Although the English book trade followed a different pattern, Iain MacCalman's research has shown the cohabitation of pornography and political radicalism amongst the publications of the *ultras* of the Spencean underground. Libertine satire on the Church and aristocratic morality, dependent on enlightenment materialist ideals, had emerged as a significant theme in the eighteenth century. The recurrence of anti-clerical and anti-aristocratic sentiment in libertine writing led Peter Wagner to define it generally as 'a vehicle of protest against the authority of Church and State'.[39]

By the late eighteenth century, the figure of the lascivious monk and the desiring nun had entered the commonplace book of satire. Narratives of amorous monks and nuns, revealed lecherous practices amongst the supposedly celibate and chaste, were a powerful convention of the anti-clerical pornography.[40] Monasteries and convents, where the moral law was supposedly absolute, offered the libertine text a potent transgressive effect. Early French anti-clerical libertine texts like Jean Barrin's *Venus in the Cloister or the Nun in her Smock* (1683), which offered tales of nuns engaged in masturbation, voyeurism and lesbianism, had appeared in English throughout the eighteenth century. Texts retailing the sensational Catherine Cadiere case of 1732, bearing some similarities with Antonia's narrative in *The Monk*, offered a salacious story in which a Jesuit priest, Father Girard, attracted by the nun's unusual chastity and piety, had raped her during a visionary fit of ecstatic possession.[41] The Marquis D'Argens' adaptation of the story in *Thérèse philosophe* (1748) exploited the supposed discrepancy of desire in the cloister, deploying the young nun's innocence to comically defamiliarise the voyeuristic depiction of sexual pleasure. Such texts were enthusiastically received in England as evidence of the depravity of the Catholic Church. Anti-catholic sentiment thus focussed not merely on clerical life but on its most spectacular manifestation, the monastery, unknown in England since the Reformation. While English anti-aristocratic erotica, as Peter Wagner observes, satirically exposed the debauchery and hypocrisy of the upper stations of life, French obscene libels (*libelles*), on the other hand, offered a merciless attack not only on the person and politics of the King and Queen but also any person who came into a position of power, such as the radical leaders Lafayette, Marat or Danton.[42] As Lynn Hunt has argued, during the Revolution, 'political pornography', through its delineation of a 'self-consciously vulgar popular politics', played an important role in the political attack on the monarchy.[43] The libertine *libelles* constructed the aristocracy and the royal family as sexually depraved, and argued that this was a signal of their political impropriety.

In the 1790s, British readers, critics and moralists, understood that libertinism – especially in its anti-clerical form – was closely allied with revolutionary radicalism, and as such, a dangerous species of sedition. *The Monk*, both in the libertine scenic language it uses to depict the libertine encounters (such as Matilda's bared breast and the sexual encounter between Matilda and Ambrosio), and in the representation of Ambrosio's uncontrollable and nymphomaniac desires, recalls French revolutionary pornography, in particular its representation of the royal court and the dispossessed clergy. Lewis's libertine language invites a reading as revolutionary iconography. The consistent focus on the breast in *The Monk* recalls the depictions of the bared breast of revolutionary 'virtue' in the iconology of the French revolution. The French republic identified itself through female representations which routinely and not coincidentally exposed a bare breast – an allegory derived from the Roman goddess of liberty.[44] As Simon Schama has observed, revolutionary representations of state virtue made 'an icon out of the republican breast: fecund, innocent, and generous'.[45] As well as fruitfulness, however, the revolutionary exposed breast of liberty was deliberately erotic (like liberty, worth pursuing).[46] In revolutionary allegory, the exposed breast establishes a discursive connection between femininity and love or desire (in the sense that the revolutionaries' heart's desire is liberty). In *The Monk*, the woman's breast is what Ambrosio wants: it signals for him, as it inaugurates, the liberty to indulge his desires. The novel again deliberately conflates (or confuses) the language of libertinism with that of revolutionary liberty.

As Lewis was no doubt aware, *The Monk*'s libertinism was a contentious strategy, that was always likely to – and in fact did – arouse the anger of readers and critics. *The Monk* aroused moral outrage not only for its libertine narrative strategies but also because of its generic status. As a novel, or rather a gothic romance, it was understood to be material suitable for women and the young. Despite its gentlemanly concerns, the form and gothic mode of *The Monk* earned it a female readership. The form of the novel was widely understood to have a special role in the formation of female moral judgements. In his conduct book *An Enquiry into the Duties of the Female Sex* (1797), the moralist Thomas Gisborne noted that the romance (or novel) 'obtains from a considerable proportion of the female sex a reception much more favourable than is accorded to other kinds of composition more worthy of encouragement'. But, Gisborne warned, 'To indulge in a practice of reading novels is, . . . liable to produce mischievous effects.' Novels were a kind of drug, by which 'the palate is vitiated or made dull'. Reading novels exposed women to seduction by creating 'a susceptibility of impression and a premature warmth of tender emotions'.[47]

Lewis's contemporaries certainly thought that *The Monk* was consumed by women. One woman reader told Lewis that 'I know those who have read "The Monk", and have been so horrified and so – enchained!'[48] The fascination the book held for women was satirised in James Gillray's engraving, *Tales of Wonder!* (1802) (see Figure 5). In his estimation, the audience for *The Monk* was women in the middle station of life. Assembling in a fashionably decorated and candle-lit room, a group listen as a young woman reads aloud from the novel. Their responses display a mixture of moral outrage and prurient titillation: the young women signal their arousal with heaving breasts and expressions of rapt interest, while an older woman, perhaps acting as chaperone, expresses the horror of moral outrage. Their licentious curiosity is confirmed by the interior decoration of the room: the burning fire, the mantle ornaments, and the painting of a ravishment reflects an interest in the bestial, the monstrous and the libertine.[49] An early review of the novel argued that:

Figure 5. James Gillray, Tales of Wonder! (London: H. Humphrey, 1 February 1802); British Museum, Department of Prints and Drawings, London.

A vein of obscenity, however, pervades and deforms the whole organisation
of this novel, which must ever blast, in a moral view, the *fair* fame that, in
point of ability, it would have gained for the author; and which renders the
work totally unfit for general circulation.[50]

Other satirists argued that *The Monk* could have a direct effect on a
passions of a woman reader. The engraving, caricaturing a woman reader
entitled 'Luxury' (1801), perhaps by Williams, (see Figure 6), depicts an
attractive young woman reading in a luxuriously furnished boudoir, dressed
in modish décolletage, warming herself in front of a roaring fire, while
her kitten writhes in ecstasy at her feet. On the mantlepiece, the clock
features kissing cupids; on a nearby wall hangs a lubricious painting,
partially veiled, of Danaë receiving the golden shower. The subtitle, 'the
Comforts of a Rum p ford', puns her naked posterior with the modish
fireplace designed by Benjamin Thompson, Count Rumford, who had in
1796 redesigned chimneys so as to lessen their smokiness and increase
the fire's heat. Opened volumes of libertine texts litter the room: on the
floor is a copy of John Armstrong's *Oeconomy of Love* (1736); while the
side table has a copy of an untraced book called *The Kisses* next to a
decanter of *Crème de Noyau* liqueur. In one hand the woman holds a
novel, whose title page clearly identifies it as *The Monk, a Novel by* M.
G., while her other hand is slipped inside her raised dress. While the
fire warms her exposed backside, the novel warms her passions, and she
has begun to masturbate.[51] To contemporaries, Lewis's decision to write
a gothic novel in a libertine mode was a kind of category error that
contemporaries derided as subversive to morals and the state. The categorical instability of the libertine gothic, then, is a powerful generator of
the novel's peculiar and disturbing rhetorical effect, outlined above,
of seeming to deploy antithetical languages of liberty and piety, libertinism and moral propriety, irony and sincerity. *The Monk's* weird
ambiguity stems from its confusion of genres: a gothic libertine novel for
young ladies. This hybrid ambiguity was scandalously obscene, and caused
the novel to be prosecuted and repressed by the authorities.

II. LEWIS AND THE FRENCH REVOLUTIONARY WARS

During a sojourn in Paris in the summer of 1791, Matthew Lewis was an
eyewitness to the French Revolution, just as later he heard hair-raising
stories from its victims, the émigré aristocratic refugees in Weimar in
1792 and The Hague in 1794. The events to which he was an eyewitness and those which he learned at second hand from the émigrés had

Figure 6. [Williams], 'Luxury or the Comforts of a Rum p ford' (London: S. W. Fores, 26 February 1801); British Museum, Department of Prints and Drawings, London.

an important impact upon *The Monk*, although his own letters from this period, addressed to his mother, carefully conceal how close he was to the action. The seventeen-year-old Lewis was one of a substantial body of British visitors to revolutionary Paris during his Oxford University summer vacation of 1791. The revolution was in its constitutional mode, nursing a republicanism in the face of increasingly active counter-revolutionary activity. Whilst Lewis was there, the King and Queen made their ill-fated attempt to join the counter-revolutionary forces in Germany; and after their ignominious arrest at Varennes on 22 June and return under guard to Paris, it no longer seemed possible to reconcile the monarchy with the constitutional gains made since 1789. The monarch had renounced the revolution, and in June and July, while Lewis was in Paris, the political clubs debated how the King could remain head of state. Lafayette and the constitutional monarchists seceded from the increasingly radical Jacobin Club dominated by Robespierre. The Constituent Assembly promulgated a new constitution, accepted without much sincerity by the King on 14 September, that further alienated the clergy from the republicans.

Although there is little evidence either way in his correspondence from Paris in the summer of 1791, it would seem that Lewis greeted the revolution with equanimity. Engaged in various writing projects, including a farce and a burlesque sentimental novel, Lewis spent his weeks reading widely in recent French drama and translations of German literature. He found Parisian society remained pleasingly sybaritic and luxurious despite the upheavals. His letters to his mother ignore the political crisis around him, in itself a kind of tacit approval; certainly Lewis did not reject the revolution in the manner of Edmund Burke, who described the new constitution in France as a 'monster'.[52] Lewis's opinion on these early stages of the revolution reflects his allegiance to the loyal opposition Whigs in England, who welcomed the revolution's constitutional reform of the Bourbon tyranny. In Paris, Lewis renewed his friendship with a fellow student from Christchurch College, Oxford, Henry Richard, Lord Holland (1773–1840), the orphaned nephew and ward of Charles James Fox, the celebrated Whig politician and the most powerful British supporter of the French revolution in this period.[53] Through his uncle's connections, Holland's guides to Paris included prominent constitutional reformers, such as Lafayette and Talleyrand.[54] Fox, Holland and Lewis all professed to love French culture just as they detested the autocratic French monarchy. Fox himself likened the revolution to the events in Britain in 1688, arguing that the 'most extensive good consequences' would follow the new French constitution, which he argued was based on Whig principles of a property franchise and religious toleration.[55] Lewis's knowledge of French revolutionary politics may have been more substantial than his correspondence to his mother reveals.

On the advice of his father, who wished him to pursue a diplomatic career, Lewis spent the period from July 1792 until early 1793 in Weimar, the capital of the Duchy of Weimar in Germany. A major cultural centre, Weimar allowed Lewis to meet notable writers of the German enlightenment, Goethe and Wieland included, and to gain a thorough knowledge of recent German literature, especially the fashionable *Sturm und Drang* movement. Lewis was influenced by the heightened emotional intensity of these works, and he saw how they adopted supernatural material derived from popular culture (in stories of elves, ghosts, and the wandering Jew). Lewis began a translation of Schiller's play *Kabale und Liebe*, later published as *The Minister* in 1799. But although he wrote to his mother that 'we have nothing but Ball, Suppers, and Concerts',[56] Weimar was not immune to the turmoil caused by the French Revolution. When Lewis arrived in July, the Duke, Karl August, had left for Coblenz in the Rhine, where the Prussian army was making preparations for war.[57] Weimar itself was packed with French émigrés, full of gloomy gossip from Paris. Against a worsening military situation with France, Lewis returned to Oxford early in 1793.

Lewis's ability in languages, his sociable nature, and his general aversion to work suggested to his father that a diplomatic career beckoned. After his graduation in spring 1794, his father's influence secured him a place in the embassy to the United Provinces of the Netherlands, lead by Alleyne Fitzherbert, Baron St Helens. As an attaché to the embassy, Lewis was unpaid (his father allowed him an allowance of £400 per annum), but such a post would have offered meaningful training in diplomatic methods. The purpose of the St Helens embassy was to liaise between the British and Dutch governments on the projected counter-revolutionary invasion of France, and to secure Dutch agreement to a loan to subsidise the Prussian army. As the military situation in the Netherlands worsened, and the war moved from being an attack on France to a desperate defence, the nature of the embassy changed. After the French revolutionary army invaded first the Austrian Netherlands in Flanders (Belgium), and later, Holland itself, St Helens's embassy became part of a struggle to shore up crumbling Dutch resistance to the French.[58]

Lewis was no doubt a junior member of the embassy: one critic has been moved to describe him as a 'cultural attaché', though no such position existed at this period.[59] His four surviving letters from The Hague to his mother detail his progress with writing and his attempts to ingratiate himself into society. On 22 July 1794, he complained that the Dutch court was dull: 'I am certain the Devil Ennui has made the Hague his favourite abode', as there is 'hardly any society of any sort or kind'. However, his letters also display an interest in the deteriorating political and military situation in Holland. During the summer drought, a lack of water made the canals impassable, which posed, he commented, a serious security risk, since 'the security of Holland depends in a great measure upon the Canals, which resource it is impossible to make use of'. He notes with alarm 'the progress of the French' and 'the bad success of the combined Armies' of the counter-revolution, but assures his mother that 'at the Hague there is no possible danger of our being visited by the Carmagnols' (the army of the republic).[60] Since the beginning of the military campaign in May, however, things had gone badly. On 18 May, at Turcoing (near Lille), the French defeated the combined forces of Austria and Britain: the British commander, the Duke of York, recognised by the star on the breast of his uniform, was humiliatingly chased about the countryside by the French dragoons. Initial confidence gave way to pessimism, and despite some victories, the coalition forces retreated in disarray, abandoning Brussels on 11 July and Antwerp on 24 July. Holland was now on the front line.[61]

Lewis's next letter to his mother (23 September 1794) complained anew about 'insufferable' Dutch company, but declared that he had found society amongst the French émigrés: 'a very agreeable Coterie which assembles every other night at the House of one of the cleverest Women I ever met with, a Madame de Matignon. She is the daughter of the celebrated Baron de Breteuil, who lives with her.' The nobility, princesses, and army officers who had fled the revolution to await the restoration of the ancien régime were, Lewis remarked, 'the very best society of Paris'. Befriending royalist French émigrés was both socialising and a species of covert information gathering. Madame de Matignon's circle included significant counter-revolutionary leaders, such as the Vicomte de Bouillé and the Duc de Polignac, both senior Royalist army officers who had raised corps for the counter-revolutionary army of the Prince de Condé. Others were closely associated with the French court, such as Edward 'Beau' Dillon (a handsome Irish Catholic rumoured to be the lover of Marie Antoinette).[62] St Helens' mission to The Hague was recognised in London as the most important source of military and political intelligence on events in France and enemy troop movements, much of which was gleaned from or supplied by the émigrés and their agents.[63] Lewis's duties took him to the front line at Osterhout, where he dined with the Duke of York, the commander of the British army. Lewis reassured his mother he was safe from the approaching French army (the Carmagnols), ironically commenting that 'to avoid a disagreeable visit . . ., I shall take care . . . not to receive them'. The domesticating irony of Lewis's representation of the revolutionary army as an unwelcome guest has a fragile and not wholly convincing courage. Certainly, the campaign had gone from bad to worse: by the end of July, the Austrians were defeated at Fleurus, and the coastal ports of Flanders, which supplied the British army, was lost. The French entered Holland in early September, driving the Duke of York's army across the River Maas. Back in London, Pitt was already describing the campaign as a 'Calamity' and an 'Embarrassment'.[64]

Lewis's final letter from The Hague (22 November 1794), was written two days after the recall of the Duke of York's army from the Continent.[65] Lewis too was to return, accompanying the émigrés fearful of massacre by the approaching revolutionary army. Another visit to York's headquarters at Arnheim (on or around 7 November) had convinced him of the British army's desperate situation, retreating in disarray, plagued by indiscipline, and without the support of the republican-leaning Dutch populace. Lewis commented, 'I did not despair that our affairs upon the continent would take a better turn, till I was a witness myself of the disorders of the soldiers and discontents of the officers.' Lewis recognised that Holland was lost, and the counter-revolution must regroup elsewhere. Whilst in Arnheim, he was once so close to the front line that he came under fire from the French artillery near Nijmagen.

> I saw two cannon balls pass through the roof of the house about ten yards distant, one after another, and at length a ball passed through the house under the shelter of whose roof I was standing, and knocked all the tiles about my ears [. . .]. As I was coming away from the village, I was much shocked at seeing a countryman whose leg had been shot away at that moment, as he was sitting at his cottage-door, and the same ball carried off the arm of his child, an infant of three years old, which he held upon his knee.[66]

The sentimental tableau of the wounded civilian, which shapes this battlefield reminiscence into a satisfying portrait, also demonstrates how close Lewis came to the action. The situation in Arnheim was serious: 'The British troops now stationed at Arnheim and its vicinity, were, from incessant fatigue, the inclemency of the season, and the difficulty of procuring supplies, in the most deplorable state of ill health, and almost in want of all necessaries.'[67] The River Waal provided some defensive cover, but by 27 December the canals were 'sufficiently frozen to bear armies with their cannon'.[68] Holland was lost and Lewis, now in personal danger, made haste to retreat to England.

— LEWIS AND THE TERROR —

In the period Lewis was employed by the mission to The Hague, the French Revolution was undergoing its most bloody and autocratic phase. With the government effectively commanded by the twelve-man Committee of Public Safety, France was ruled with a violence unlike anything seen hitherto. Spurred by the incursions of foreign armies and a severe economic crisis, the state undertook to 'neutralise centres of opposition', in the words of Simon Schama, by the liquidation of all who expressed opinions contrary to those in power.[69] At the *journée* of 5 September 1793, the Convention, pressurised by an immense crowd, called for the establishment of an *armée revolutionnaire* to wage war upon the enemies of the revolution. Their target was especially the rich, who were widely suspected of hoarding food; the nobility, who were suspected of plotting for the restoration of the monarchy; and the clergy, who were suspected of conspiring to re-establish the Catholic faith. This internal enemy was to be sought out and destroyed: the Convention decreed that 'terror will be the order of the day'. In the eleven months between September 1793 and July 1794, it is estimated that somewhere between 40,000 and 250,000 individuals were killed. As well as those executed without trial in civil war conditions, this total includes 16,594 people sentenced to death by special criminal courts called revolutionary tribunals, whose judgements were without appeal, and whose punishments were carried out within twenty-four hours.[70] Those executed were found guilty of counter-revolutionary offences, but this was interpreted unusually broadly, as the tribunal considered 'moral' as well as material evidence, frequently identified by popular denunciation. The terror worked with impressive efficiency through the work of the 'national razor', as the guillotine was affectionately known. When the guillotine could not work fast enough, other means were found: in notorious cases the condemned were shot in groups by cannon fire, or tied naked together in so-called 'republican marriages' and drowned in rivers.[71] The lists of those executed abounded with nobility, the rich, merchants, the clergy, monks and nuns, and with members of the revolutionary parties whose moment had passed. An early victim was Marie-Antoinette, guillotined on 16 October 1793. The period of greatest bloodshed, the so-called 'Great Terror', was initiated by the law of 22 Prairial (10 June 1794), which refocussed the tribunal's work to 'punish the enemies of the people', by speeding up the rate of convictions. Henceforward, the work of investigation was suppressed; indictment was based on accusation; the accused were denied the aid of a lawyer for their defence; and judges were authorised not to hear witnesses. In the seven weeks between 10 June and 27 July, nearly

1,500 individuals were guillotined in Paris. At a rate of twenty-six executions a day, the ditches surrounding the scaffold overflowed with blood,
leading local residents to complain of the stench. As one radical
complained bitterly (only weeks before he was himself guillotined),
'Liberty is a bitch who likes to be bedded on a mattress of cadavers.'[72]

Literary critics, in dealing with Lewis's engagement with the revolution, have acknowledged his reading amongst revolutionary plays set in
the cloister and prison. Lewis had become acquainted with this anti-
clerical 'claustral literature' in Paris in 1791, and he later translated
Jacques Marie Boutet de Monvel's *Les Victimes Cloitrées* (1791) as *Venoni;
or, The Novice of St Marks* (1809).[73] However, critics have not allowed
him an engagement with the political culture of the Terror itself. Yet in
Holland, in 1794, he had read the stream of texts that poured from the
émigré press bearing witness to Revolutionary atrocities. These Terror
narratives – whose ideological purpose was to render the revolution
monstrous – focus as much on the prison histories of the condemned as
on their spectacular execution: detailing the harsh conditions of the
dungeons (often located in the crypts and cloisters of monasteries),
numerous claustral humiliations and last-minute reprieves. Like the narrative of the Inquisition in *The Monk*, the accounts of the Revolutionary
Tribunals advertised the injustice of their summary proceedings. Reports
of carceral humiliations, the bloody work of the guillotine and sinister
mass executions circulated around Europe. Employed in gathering information on French affairs in The Hague between May and December
1794, Lewis would have systematic access to these accounts.

In his letters, Lewis related one anecdote about the sensational aspects
of the revolutionary news. It concerned an aristocratic refugee, the
Duchesse de la Force, he encountered in The Hague in 1794, whose tedious
conversation, he reports, was 'composed of the same set of phrases, which
She vents upon all occasions'. One of her banalities, Lewis explains, was
to ask after the latest news, and being told the headline, to ask for the
details. 'When they told her that the Queen of France was dead, She asked
for the "détails".'[74] The joke here turns on what those details may have
included: at the trial of the Queen by the Revolutionary Criminal Tribunal
in October 1793, the public prosecutor Antoine-Quentin Fouquier-
Tinville made much of the extensive obscene literature which made the
Queen its subject. The Queen had been the subject of a substantial pornographic literature during the *ancien régime* and during the Revolution itself:
she was explicitly depicted in sexual liaisons with her ministers, her friend
Madame de Lamballe, and her brother, the Emperor of Austria. At her
trial, which culminated in her execution by guillotine, the prosecution

made a connection between her counter-revolutionary subversion of the new government and her obscene pleasures, which were in themselves raised as indictable offences.[75] Jacques-René Hérbert, in the radical journal *Père Duchesne* (No. 299, 1793), announced her decapitation as 'the greatest of all the joys . . . having seen . . . the head of the female veto separated from her fucking tart's neck.'[76] The details of revolutionary news, whether radical or reactionary in mode, were imbrued with a bloody and lecherous spirit, fusing libertinism with revolutionary politics.

Historians of the French revolution long argued that the Terror was an 'aberration' from the rational course of the revolution, engendered by pressures fuelled by the counter-revolutionary wars. In recent years, historians have argued that the Terror was an integral part of the revolution's ideology – 'a characteristic feature of the mentality of revolutionary activism' – and as such, can be traced back to the events of 1789.[77] Furet's analysis of the logic of the Terror in the revolutionary narrative hinges on the role of conspiracy in political culture. He argues that 'the French Revolution could envisage resistance – real or imaginary – only as a gigantic and permanent conspiracy, which it must ceaselessly crush, by means of a people constituted as a single body, in the name of its indivisible sovereignty.' The conspiracy was a consequence, therefore, of the *journée*, those days when the people acted as one, as a crowd. The enemy within could not be allowed to express, or even be represented as expressing, their opposition by legitimate means: after the flight to Varennes, the opposition was repeatedly exposed as attempting to mount a coup against the revolution. In the face of the unity of the people, the enemies of the revolution could only be engaged in subversion. 'Conspiracy was the other face of that vision, a counter-revolution that was concealed and evil, in contrast with the people, who were public and good, and nearly as powerful as they, for it had to be overcome again and again.'[78] The counter-revolution, in this estimation, is sublimed beyond the machinations of men into a shape-changing force of diabolical proportions.

In *The Monk*, within the closed system of the monastery, Lewis depicts the disruptive forces personified by Ambrosio and Matilda as the work of the devil, and having identified them beyond doubt, causes their extirpation in an orgy of violence. *The Monk*'s reliance on diabolic conspiracy reaffirms its location within the logic of Terror. There is, however, no simple correlation between the novel's plot and the narrative of the revolution: *The Monk* is not simply a romance of the Terror. Instead, multiple zones of overlap are located and explored. The novel reinvents the absolutist tyranny of the *ancien régime* in the closed system of the monastery: the revolution reinvents the absolutist tyranny of the *ancien régime* in the Committee of Public Safety; the novel judiciously feeds on the absolutist principles of both revolutionary and Bourbon tyrannies. Acts of 'terror' are first perpetrated by the conspirators (Matilda and Ambrosio). Their atrocities are spectacularly repressed by the forces of established order – which are ironically imaged not only as the Inquisition and the Devil himself, but also the people as revolutionary mass.

Lewis's novel also preys on another aspect of the political culture of the French Revolution in the Terror, that of its libertine anti-clericalism. The revolution had long articulated anti-clerical arguments. On 13 February 1790, all religious orders were dissolved, as a violation of inalienable rights of liberty. Monasteries and nunneries were closed, and their occupants forced to leave. Despite the obvious hardship this imposed on many individuals, these expulsions were depicted in popular prints as emancipation and salvation. Libertine prints depicted celibate but lascivious nuns moving straight from the cloister to the brothel.[79] In Year II, with the onset of the Terror, outbreaks of anti-clerical violence became frequent. Churches were looted, their silver melted down, icons smashed and cassocks burnt. In many cases, the iconoclasm extended to the clergy too. Priests were treated to ritual humiliation (being made to ride asses backwards); monks and nuns were forced to marry and in some cases forced to consummate their marriage in public. As the Terror progressed, the remaining refractory clergy (who had not emigrated) came under intense scrutiny by the Revolutionary Tribunals. Identifying religion as the heart of the counter-revolution, a militant de-Christianisation campaign was initiated, led in Paris by Hérbert. Elaborate pagan ceremonies were staged in the nationalised buildings of former churches and cathedrals, until, following Robespierre's lead, the report of 18 Floréal established a *rapprochement* between republican and religious sentiment in the notion of the 'Supreme Being'.

This anti-clerical agitation included the publication of obscene libertine texts detailing the scandalous promiscuity concealed behind vows of celibacy. By extension, the homosocial society of the monastic orders made them the natural home of sodomy and sapphism. Like the anti-royal pornography that attacked Marie-Antoinette by making her body scandalously visible to all, the revolutionary pornography about monks and nuns had a profoundly levelling effect. These texts attacked what many saw as the moral hypocrisy of the religious orders, especially those which flaunted their opulence and luxury. The Abbé Augustin Barruel argued in *The History of the Clergy during the French Revolution* (1794) that this anti-clerical writing played an significant part in the resolution of the National Assembly to nationalise the property of the Church in October 1789. Through these 'calumnious accusations swelled against the priests', they were 'represented as objects of hatred and contempt'. To destroy the 'respect and esteem' the people felt for the clergy, the revolutionaries 'filled the windows of every shop ... with caricatures, expressive of every vice in the priesthood ... Lascivious and obscene prints every where exhibited the lubricity, the incontinence of priests squandering the patrimony of the poor, in the company of the most abandoned prostitutes.' Barruel alerts readers to the political resonances of Lewis's representation of Catholic monastic orders as locations of vice and hypocrisy. Like the radical anti-clerical writings of the revolution, the construction of the monk in Lewis's character of Ambrosio reveals his piety and virtue as a fraud. 'They insinuated to the people that the most infamous vices were concealed under the mask of hypocrisy, and that they had granted their esteem only to the semblance of virtue.'[80] To Barruel, and the conservative interpretation of the revolution, Lewis's anti-Catholic libertinism was the equivalent of revolutionary Jacobinism.

III. PUBLICATION AND THE POLITICS OF CENSORSHIP

Lewis had returned from The Hague in early December 1794, bearing the manuscript of the novel, which 'The Preface' records was completed on 28 October 1794. Joseph Bell agreed to publish the novel in 1795, and some copies may have circulated then. However, for some reason, the edition was postponed until 9 March 1796, when the *Morning Herald* announced that 'on Saturday next' (12 March), *The Monk, A Romance* would be published in three volumes.[81] Reviewing novels, like writing them, was not perceived to be intellectually demanding or stimulating in this period. As a result, critical notices were generally brief, bland and descriptive: the reception of *The Monk*, which became extensive, heated and detailed over the following years, was most unusual. But the first anonymous edition received polite and unsensational notice in June 1796. *The Monthly Mirror*, a journal noted for its mercy to writers, praised it as 'most masterly and impressive' and declared it a 'most interesting production. The stronger passions are finely delineated and exemplified in the progress of artful temptation working on self-sufficient pride, superstition and lasciviousness.'[82] *The British Critic*, which prided itself on its pious morality, felt that the writer's 'good talents' had been wasted on 'this monster', wherein the general moral improbably countermands the description of 'lust, murder, incest, and every atrocity that can disgrace human nature'.[83] Early criticism, then, found literary merit in *The Monk*, but signalled the libertine nature of Lewis's method.

Following his return from Holland in December 1794, Lewis seemed destined for another diplomatic mission. In early 1795, his father wrote to the minister heading his department, William Windham, the Secretary-at-War, 'asking whether it would be agreeable to you to introduce my Son into the War Office in a respectable situation'. Even as he asked for one position, however, he held hopes of another: 'it may be possible, by addressing Mr Pitt, to get my Son placed in some situation better suited to his ambition'.[84] Such nepotism would have been uncontroversial and even expected in this period, and Pitt's influence secured Matthew Lewis a parliamentary seat in Pitt's gift. Lewis turned 21 on 9 July 1796 and, as such, was eligible to vote and to hold office. He was elected to Parliament in the representation of Hindon, Wiltshire in July 1796. This seat, previously held by William Beckford, gothic novelist and eccentric, had only 120 electors, and was one of the 56 'rotten boroughs' abolished in the Reform of 1832. Like the Lewis family, the Beckfords owned extensive sugar plantations in Jamaica. The member for Hindon would be expected to defend the West India interest (the trade in slaves and sugar).

Lewis's first biographer, Baron-Wilson, observes that he was an undistinguished MP: 'The senate had no charms for the young poet. His parliamentary career was brief and inglorious; he never once attempted to address the house; his attendance became extremely irregular; and in a few years he retired from it altogether.'[85] Baron-Wilson, however, overstates his lack of engagement with parliamentary politics: Peck notes that he not only served on four select committees of the House, but also once addressed the House, in 1802, in support of a bill designed to relieve the suffering of prisoners committed for debt.[86] He also voted on 4 January 1798 for Pitt's assessed taxes. But Lewis's politics were rather ambiguous. His friend Lord Holland later wrote that Lewis 'supported the Minister [Pitt] and the French war. He inculcated in his writings opinions which led to a directly opposite conclusion.'[87] As his father's son, Lewis was expected to be of Pitt's party (Lewis senior regarded his son's seat as a reward for twenty-five years' service to Pitt).[88] His father was Deputy Secretary-at-War in Pitt's administration, responsible for granting contracts for the supply of the army, a demanding position that became very lucrative in times of war. Inserted into Pitt's ministry, young Lewis would have been expected to return his patron's favour by his vote in Parliament. But as Walter Scott observed in 1830, Matthew Lewis's politics 'were not of the complexion which his father, attached to Mr Pitt's administration, would have approved'.[89]

Evidence suggests that, in his opinions and society, Lewis continued to associate with the radical Whig faction lead by Charles James Fox. As the Foxites, known as the 'wicked and witty',[90] led the parliamentary opposition to Pitt's repressive counter-revolutionary legislation, they seemed to many the constitutional wing of the Jacobin reformers. Fox was also a notorious libertine who 'revelled in sexual license', and whose defence of sexual liberty was mirrored by his lifelong defence of political liberty. This mixture of the language of liberty and sexual freedom found a ready mirror in *The Monk*. On taking up his seat in Parliament, Lewis received the congratulations of Charles James Fox in the chamber of the House of Commons. According to Walter Scott, Fox 'paid the unusual compliment of crossing the House of Commons that he might congratulate the young author, whose work obtained high praise from many other able men of that able time'.[91] Outside the House, Lewis frequented the influential Whig social and literary circles of Fox and his nephew Lord Holland, whom Lewis knew at university and in Paris. In 1793, Lewis had defended Fox in an unpublished satirical poem written for the newspapers.[92] In 1799, he dedicated *The Love of Gain*, an imitation of Juvenal's thirteenth satire to Fox, and the inscription stated that it was 'a trifling Mark of the veneration in which I hold his Talents and Character'.[93] In 1806, Lewis published an elegy on Fox which imagined the globe weeping at Fox's death: India for his work in the trial of Warren Hastings; America for his support for the rebellious colonists; Africa for his anti-slavery eloquence; and Europe for his support for an early negotiated peace. In the last years of the eighteenth century, Lewis was on such good terms with Fox that on several occasions Lewis asked the great politician to translate Italian literature for him.[94]

— *THE MONK*: CRITICISM AND CENSORSHIP —

The commercial success of the first edition of *The Monk*, which appeared in March 1796, was followed by a second edition in October and a third in April 1797.[95] Although the first was anonymous, subsequent editions attributed the work to 'M.G. Lewis, Esq. M.P.' In celebration, *The Monthly Mirror* for October 1796 printed a short biography, together with a portrait, of the newly elected MP, 'of late so much the subject of public conversation and eulogium'.[96] Lewis's near-simultaneous acknowledgement of his authorship of the book and his election to the House of Commons polarised the initially uncontroversial reception. As a consequence, it received more critical attention than is usual: Parreaux notes twenty-four notices, extracts and reviews before 1799.[97] The scandal that erupted about the public morality of Lewis's novel extended to the gothic in general. The 'terror novel' controversy intensified the ongoing debate about the public morality of fiction-writing and the status of women's reading. In the process, it made explicit a political reading of the gothic in the 1790s, and for that reason, it is useful to follow the debate closely. The result was that, having been threatened with prosecution, Lewis backed down and edited the novel. The fourth edition, issued on February 28 1798 with a new title, *Ambrosio, or the Monk*, was advertised as having 'considerable additions and alterations', which Lewis undertook in order to dispel the intense criticism. The unexpurgated version, however, remained available to callers at the shop of the publisher Joseph Bell. This under-the-counter trade, which confirmed the novel's claim to libertine status, was pursued by him as late as 1801.[98]

The novel received enthusiastic praise in *The Morning Chronicle* (Tuesday 26 July 1796), a daily newspaper closely associated with the Foxite Whigs and hence more sympathetic to the activities of the English radicals. *The Analytical Review* (October 1796), a journal closely associated with the group of English intellectual radicals around Godwin and Wollstonecraft, found Lewis's libertine style alluring. The reviewer suggested that the author 'displays no common powers' and 'has introduced some scenes to mark the progress of passion very happily imagined'. Recognising its controversial libertinism, the reviewer observed that 'the gradual discovery of Matilda's sex and person' was 'very finely conceived, and truly picturesque' (that is, depicted like contemporary pornographic images).

> Indeed the whole temptation is so artfully contrived, that a man, it should seem, were he made as other men are, would deserve to be d–ned who could resist even devilish spells, conducted with such address, and assuming such a heavenly form.[99]

Approving reviews from these papers helped to identify the novel as being of the radical party, and ensured a hostile reception from more conservative organs. By 1797, the Pitt ministry perceived *The Morning Chronicle* as an organ of sedition employed 'to promote the Principles of Jacobinism',[100] and moved to police it in 1798 (38 Geo. III, c78).

Critics found *The Monk* a useful place to articulate a moral argument about the propriety of fiction, and to exercise their counter-revolutionary credentials. Samuel Taylor Coleridge's long and demanding examination in *The Critical Review* of February 1797 begins with a survey of the state of gothic fiction writing, which he supposes to be a kind of cheapening narcotic that debauches taste and judgement: 'powerful stimulants' that 'can never be required except by the torpor of an exhausted appetite'.

The Monk, however, he supposed an exception, as it was 'the offspring of no common genius'. Coleridge found scattered 'excellencie': the tale of 'The Bleeding Nun' was 'truly terrific'; the character of Matilda was 'the author's masterpiece'. The novel, he said, 'discovers an imagination rich, powerful, and fervid'. But there were also serious 'errors and defects'. Coleridge complained that the romance elements of the story, that which is marvellous, anti-naturalistic, supernatural, made the novel improbable: that anything may happen. This formal problem, Coleridge said, over-flowed into the moral problem that Ambrosio's punishment taught no moral truth. A still 'more grievous fault' was that the work's minute and explicit depiction of sexual events was morally corrupting. 'The temptations of Ambrosio are described with a libidinous minuteness . . . The shameful harlotry of Matilda, and the trembling innocence of Antonia, are seized with equal avidity, as vehicles of the most voluptuous images.' The result, in Coleridge's view, made the novel entirely unsuited for a general readership: it is a 'poison for youth and a provocative for the debauchee'. He warned that if a parent saw *The Monk* in 'the hands of a son or daughter, he might reasonably turn pale'.[101] Such innocent readers, he suggested, should be proscribed the novel. As if for confirmation, Coleridge asserted that the scene where Antonia is found reading a Bible from which scenes of vice have been expurgated was blasphemous. He concluded that *The Monk* 'certainly possesses much real merit, in addition to its meretricious attractions. Nor must it be forgotten that the author is a man of rank and fortune. – Yes! the author of the Monk signs himself a LEGISLATOR! – We stare and tremble.'

Other commentators agreed with Coleridge's political reading that the novel was morally unacceptable. In September 1796, a little-known Dublin essay-periodical called *The Flapper*, had suggested that the novel abounded 'with passages plainly and unequivocally *immoral*', a libertinism producing 'scenes of the most wanton and immodest nature, described in terms scarcely decent'.[102] In August 1797, *The Monthly Review*, concluded that 'A vein of obscenity . . . pervades and deforms the whole organisation of this novel, which must ever blast, in a moral view, the *fair* fame that, in point of ability, it would have gained for the author; and which renders the work totally unfit for general circulation.'[103] The review in *The European Magazine* (February 1797) likened Lewis's '*oblique attack on venerable establishments*' to the 'compositions' that 'the presses of the Continent teemed with . . . while the Revolution was preparing in France' produced by '*democratic enthusiasts and atheistical devotees*'.[104] Lewis's compelling writing made his obscenity even more dangerous to morals and religion. Reviewers felt obliged by the novel's combination of literary skill and popular success to treat it seriously. Lewis's ambitions to high-status literary allusion and irony were not incompatible with his gentlemanly libertinism, whereas his gothic medium gestured towards the radical agitation of unruly popular culture, thus confusing two categories convention deemed separate. Invoking the example of Richardson, critics declared that fiction must maintain propriety and piety to be acceptable. *The Monk* quite clearly did not: as a burlesque poem opined in 1800, the novel 'fills a giddy female brain/ With vice, romance, lust, terror, pain'.[105]

The most rancorous, illiberal and dangerous attack on Lewis came in July 1797, in an anonymous satirical poem called *The Pursuits of Literature*, serially published between 1794 and 1797. Later revealed to be the work of Rev. Thomas Mathias, a fervently anti-Jacobin Tory polemicist, this scholarly four-book verse satire, armed with extensive prose introductions and notes, stretched to over 380 pages. His poem, he adds, 'was not intended merely to raise a smile at folly or conceit' like the satires of Horace, but rather, was conceived in the mode of Juvenal, 'written with indignation against wickedness, against the prostitution of superior talents, and the profane violence of bad men'.[106] *The Pursuits of Literature* offered a survey of the state of writing in the 1790s, and, believing that 'Good books are the mind's bread' because 'They give the life-blood, nutriment and health', it treated the topic with all the seriousness of Juvenal's satire. To Mathias, all writing, even novels, were acts of considered political intent, and the literary events of the 1790s gave Mathias serious cause for concern. Italicising and capitalising in a manic attempt to gain credence, he proclaimed that 'LITERATURE, *well or ill conducted*, IS THE GREAT ENGINE *by which, I am fully persuaded, all* civilised *states must ultimately be supported or overthrown.*'[107]

The criticism of Lewis appeared in Book IV, first published in July 1797, and augmented for the fifth edition of 1798. Mathias claimed that Lewis's status as parliamentarian demands the critic's intervention.

> A legislator in our own parliament, a member of the House of Commons of Great Britain, an elected guardian and defender of the laws, the religion, and the good manners of the country, as neither scrupled nor blushed to depict and to publish to the world the arts of lewd and systematic seduction, and to thrust upon the nation the most open and unqualified blasphemy against the very code and volume of our religion.

He concluded that 'I consider this as a new species of legislative or state-parricide' – subversion of the state by one charged with defending it.[108] In the poem's extensive prose footnotes, fizzling with cantankerous censure, Mathias located Lewis's work within a tradition of libertine literature, alongside Richard Payne Knight's scholarship on ancient phallic worship and Cleland's *Memoirs of a Woman of Pleasure* (1748). He asked, why the 'state' does not move to suppress the 'madd'ning orgies' of these 'Pandars to lust and licens'd blasphemy', and maintained that, 'The publication of this novel by *a Member of Parliament* is in itself *so serious an offence to the public*, that I know not how the author can repair this breach of public decency, but by suppressing it himself.' Elsewhere, however, Mathias suggested that action might be taken by the law.

> It is sufficient for me to point out Chap. 7 of Vol. 2. As a composition the work would have been better, if the offensive and scandalous passages had been omitted, and it is disgraced by a diableries and nonsense fitted only to frighten children in the nursery. I believe this 7th Chap. of Vol. 2. *is actionable at Common Law.*[109]

The section identified (Chapter IV, Volume II) contains both the blasphemous description of the expurgated bible prepared by Elvira for Antonia, and the libertine description of Ambrosio's supernatural and voyeuristic spying on Antonia in the bath. To aid his argument, Mathias drew attention to the most important cases in English law of obscenity, that of the trials of Edmund Curll and John Cleland. This was a serious and weighty accusation. If Lewis had been prosecuted, he would have been the second radical so assailed (after Thomas Williams, the printer of Paine's *Age of Reason* (1794), indicted for seditious and blasphemous libel in 1796). Although this would have severely embarrassed Lewis's political career, and exposed him to his father's wrath, some commentators have suggested that Lewis's private life – notorious for what Thomas Medwin later called 'male-love' – would not stand the public scrutiny of a scandal.[110]

Official moves to suppress *The Monk* were instigated. Lewis's recognition of the book created a stir in the highest echelons of Pitt's ministry: William Wilberforce noted *The Monk* had raised 'much talk' of a 'rather loose' nature at a dinner at the Lord Chancellor's in November 1796, attended by virtually the entire cabinet, including Loughborough (Lord Chancellor), Windham (Secretary at War), Pitt (Prime Minister), Lord Chatham (President of the Privy Council), and Westmoreland (Lord Privy Seal).[111] Lewis's obituary in *The Gentleman's Magazine* (August 1818) states that 'a prosecution was talked of, and we believe commenced; but on a pledge to recall copies, and to recast the Work in another edition, legal proceedings were stopped'.[112] Such actions were promoted by public charities who took upon themselves the task of policing morals. The name of the most active charity in this period reveals some of its interests: The Committee for the Carrying into Effect His Majesty's

Proclamation against Vice and Immorality, and for the Encouragement of Piety and Virtue. The Proclamation Society, as it was known, had been set in action by the evangelical Anglican parliamentarian William Wilberforce in 1787, to press for the moral reform of his countrymen, especially 'excessive drinking, blasphemy, profane swearing and cursing, lewdness, profanation of the Lord's Day, or other dissolute immoral or disorderly practices'.[113] Libertine publication was a particular focus of the Society, which sought 'to suppress all loose and licentious Prints, Books and Publications, dispersing Poison to the Minds of the Young and Unwary, and to punish the Publishers and Vendors thereof.'[114] Bishop Porteus, president of the Society from 1793, wrote of their object 'to give support, and activity to the magistrates in the prosecution and punishment of offenders against good manners and public decency.'[115] As Pitt's counter-seditionary measures unrolled in the 1790s, this brief was expanded to include the prosecution of works for seditious and blasphemous libel. Late in 1796, the Society successfully sought the prosecution of Thomas Williams, a printer, who had republished a cheap edition of Thomas Paine's radical tract, *The Age of Reason*. In the language of the ministry's report on sedition, the publication of books was in itself seditious. The loyalist polemicist John Reeves, in his 'Report on Sedition' in 1794, argued that, 'The people have carried to the utmost extent the abuse that may be made of the Press. They print the most licentious libels against every branch of the established government.'[116] The Proclamation Society might have objected to *The Monk* for both its obscenity and blasphemy: the *Report of the Committee for the year 1799* states that, 'The publication of obscene books and prints is an offence which has attracted the Society's . . . regard'.[117] Lewis's calculated insult to the prevailing moral climate transgressed both the counter-libertine measures of anti-vice societies and the anti-sedition measures of the ministry.

In response to this criticism and investigation, Lewis found it prudent to revise his novel, editing out the most objectionable sections of obscenity and blasphemy. Critics and biographers have long ascribed this to Mathias's anonymous threat, although Lewis was also sensitive to the criticism about his radical libertinism aroused by his entry into Parliament. Contemporaries found his discomfort amusing. Lewis's emasculation of the novel was parodied in the Minerva Press's *The New Monk* (1798), perhaps by Richard Sickelmore. Published after Lewis's abridgement, *The New Monk* relocated the story to London, where a Methodist preacher, Joshua Pentateuch, is seduced by a female demon to indulge his passion not for carnal pleasures but for gluttony and avarice. Joshua discovers Ann Maria, the Antonia figure, reading *The Monk*, a book whose 'indecent scenes' – akin to 'the ocular observations of a brothel' – are 'the worst calculated for a youthful mind ... as they inflame dangerous passions'. The book which Ann Maria is reading with 'so much pleasure', however, has been edited, so as to leave only the 'beauties' of this 'master piece of writing'.[118]

The suppression of *The Monk* suggested to imitators the perilous climate for libertine gothic. Eschewing libertinism in favour of her scheme of picturesque terror and explained supernatural, Radcliffe in *The Italian, or the Confessional of the Black Penitents* (1797) depicts the sentimental virtues of Ellena as being sufficiently resourceful to resist the murderous brutality of the monk Schedoni.[119] However, the radical novelist Charlotte Dacre, daughter of a noted Jewish money-lender and 'Jacobin' pornographer, engaged fruitfully with Lewis's combination of revolutionary and libertine terror in *Zofloya, or The Moor* (1806). Byron signalled her inheritance of libertine interests when he attacked Dacre's Della Cruscan influences in *English Bards and Scotch Reviewers* (1809), suggesting that her novels were 'in the style of the first edition of the Monk'. Certainly, the lust between Victoria Loridani and her mysterious and demonic Moorish servant Zofloya uses the highly-charged language of the passions – hyperbolic rage, lust, madness and despair – to celebrate its transgressive elements. Similarly, the novel's cycles of punishment are structured like Lewis's in scenes voyeuristicly exposing innocence to violence, as when the defenceless virgin Lilla is chained almost naked in a cave, before being killed by the lust-inspired frenzy of her persecutor Victoria.[120] *The General Review* recognised the force of her 'tales of indiscriminate horror', but *The Literary Journal* suggested that Dacre was 'afflicted with the dismal maggots of the brain.' Dacre's novels did not have the popular success of *The Monk*, but their notoriety attracted the attention of Percy Bysshe Shelley, whose *Zastrozzi* (1810) was written in imitative awe of Dacre's (and by extension Lewis's) revolutionary terrors.

The novel which Lewis found so easy to author as a private gentleman of fortune in Holland in 1794, seemed less easy to authorise three years later as an MP. It is hard to imagine that Lewis thought his book would escape the censors if their attention was drawn to it. The book engages with the discourse of censorship in Ambrosio's self-analytic soliloquies, which deliberately court a moral reading, even as he repeatedly violates his repentance. Ambrosio confesses that each of his crimes had been accompanied by comprehension and remorse:

> He had not been deceived into error: Ignorance could furnish him with no excuse. He had seen vice in her true colours; Before He committed his

crimes, He had computed every scruple of their weight; and yet he had committed them.[121]

Lewis perhaps assumed the book, like Beckford's *Vathek*, would be tolerated as the product of a gentleman. The libertine sections (sexual and blasphemous) were little more than conventional for an under-the-counter publication for gentlemen's interest only. He may also have wagered that the exotic setting, the extravagantly fictional status of his fiction, and the inconsequentiality of the gothic novel would protect it from prosecution. But these prophylactic gambits failed in the highly-charged political climate of 1797. The problem of *The Monk*'s libertinism is not that Lewis wrote it – such attitudes were entirely appropriate for a gentleman of his means and interests – but in the form of the novel, especially in its sensationalist gothic mode, such libertine discourse was scandalous, because it addressed a wide and indiscriminate audience, including many young women. Crossing such boundaries made the novel suddenly and seriously obscene.

— NOTES —

1. Donatien Alphonse Françoise de Sade, 'Reflections on the Novel' (1800), in *The 120 Days of Sodom and Other Writings*, trans. Austryn Wainhouse and Richard Weaver (London: Arrow Books, 1991), pp. 108–9.
2. Emma Clery, *The Rise of Supernatural Fiction, 1762–1800* (Cambridge: Cambridge University Press, 1995), p. 156.
3. Ronald Paulson, *Representations of Revolution (1789–1820)* (New Haven and London: Yale University Press, 1983), pp. 220–1.
4. Emmet Kennedy, *A Cultural History of the French Revolution* (New Haven and London: Yale University Press, 1989), p. 137.
5. Matthew Lewis, *The Monk*, ed. Emma McEvoy (Oxford: Oxford University Press, 1995), p. 356. All further references to this edition unless otherwise stated.
6. André Parreaux, *The Publication of 'The Monk': a literary event 1796–1798* (Paris: Didier, 1960), p. 132; Paulson, *Representations of Revolution*, pp. 217–18.
7. T. C. W. Blanning, *The Rise and Fall of the French Revolution* (Chicago and London: University of Chicago Press, 1996), p. 11.
8. François Furet, *Interpreting the French Revolution*, trans. Elborg Forster (Cambridge: Cambridge University Press, 1981), pp. 48–9. See also Keith Michael Baker, *Inventing the French Revolution* (Cambridge: Cambridge University Press, 1990); Lynn Hunt, *Politics, Culture and Class in the French Revolution* (Berkeley: University of California Press, 1986); and Colin Lucas, *The Political Culture of the French Revolution* (Oxford: Pergamon, 1988).

9. Lewis to his mother, The Hague, 23 September 1794, in Louis F. Peck, *A Life of Matthew G. Lewis* (Cambridge, MA: Harvard University Press, 1961), p. 213; see also pp. 19–20.

10. Margaret Harries Baron-Wilson, *The Life and Correspondence of M. G. Lewis*, 2 vols (London: Henry Colburn, 1839), II, pp. 241–70.

11. Lewis to his mother, Oxford, 25 March 1792, in Peck, *Life*, p. 189.

12. Lewis to his mother, The Hague, 18 May 1794, in Peck, *Life*, p. 208.

13. Lewis, *Monk*, p. 6.

14. Peck, *Life*, pp. 21–3. On Lewis's German sources see: Karl S. Guthke, 'C. M. Wieland and M. G. Lewis', *Neophilologus*, 40 (1956), pp. 231–3.

15. Lewis, *Monk*, pp. 9, 11–12.

16. Lewis, *Monk*, pp. 17, 18, 19.

17. Lewis, *Monk*, pp. 18, 20.

18. Lewis, *Monk*, pp. 39–40.

19. Lewis, *Monk*, p. 58.

20. Randolph Trumbach, 'Erotic Fantasy and Male Libertinism in Enlightenment England' in *The Invention of Pornography*, ed. Lynn Hunt (New York: Zone Books, 1993), pp. 257–58. See also Clara Tuite, 'Cloistered Closets: Enlightenment Pornography, the Confessional State, Homosexual Persecution and *The Monk*', *Romanticism on the Net* 8 (November 1997): (Online: Internet, 2.8.98 <http://users.ox.ac.uk/~scat 0385/closet.html>).

21. Lewis, *Monk*, pp. 84, 231

22. *The Analytical Review*, XXIV (October 1796), p. 403.

23. Lewis, *Monk*, p. 65.

24. D. L. MacDonald, 'The Erotic Sublime: The Marvellous in *The Monk*', *English Studies in Canada*, 18, 3 (1992), pp. 273–85. See also Wendy Jones, 'Stories of Desire in *The Monk*', *ELH*, 57, 1 (1990), pp. 129–50.

25. Lewis, *Monk*, p. 305

26. Samuel Richardson, *The History of Sir Charles Grandison*, ed. Jocelyn Harris, 3 vols (1753–54; Oxford: Oxford University Press, 1986), I, xvii, pp. 348–9.

27. Kathleen Wilson, *The Sense of the People: Politics, Culture and Imperialism in England, 1715–1785* (Cambridge: Cambridge University Press, 1995), p. 219. See also John Sainsbury, 'John Wilkes, Debt, and Patriotism', *Journal of British Studies*, 34 (April 1995), pp. 165–96; James G. Turner, 'The Properties Of Libertinism', *Eighteenth-Century Life*, 9, 3 (1985), pp. 75–87.

28. Roy Porter, 'Mixed Feelings: the Enlightenment and Sexuality in Eighteenth-Century Britain', in *Sexuality in Eighteenth-century Britain*, ed. Paul-Gabriel Boucé (Manchester: Manchester University Press, 1982), pp. 4–5.

29. David Hume, *A Treatise of Human Nature*, ed. L. A. Selby-Bigge (Oxford: Clarendon Press, 1978), p. 486.

30. Porter, 'Mixed Feelings', p. 4.

31. Lewis, *Monk*, pp. 83, 84, 86, 89.
32. Lewis, *Monk*, pp. 41, 65, 90.
33. Lewis, *Monk*, p. 271.
34. Lynn Hunt, 'Pornography and the French Revolution' in Hunt, *Invention of Pornography*, pp. 301–39, p. 305.
35. Matthew Lewis, *Ambrosio, or The Monk: A Romance*, 4th edn, 3 vols (London: J. Bell, 1798), II, p. 265.
36. J. D. T. de Bienville, *Nymphomania, or, a Dissertation on the Furor Uterinus*, trans. Edward Sloane Wilmot (London: Bew, 1775).
37. Lewis, *Monk*, pp. 300–1.
38. Robert Darnton, *The Literary Underground of the Old Regime* (Cambridge, MA and London: Harvard University Press, 1982).
39. Peter Wagner, *Eros Revived: Erotica of the Enlightenment in England and America* (London: Secker & Warburg, 1988), p. 6.
40. Wagner, *Eros Revived*, pp. 47–86.
41. *A Compleat Translation of the Whole Case of Mary Catherine Cadiere, against the Jesuite Father John Baptist Girard* (London: J. Millan, 1732), pp. 24–5.
42. Wagner, *Eros Revived*, pp. 88–112.
43. Hunt, 'Pornography and the French Revolution', p. 302.
44. Lynn Hunt, 'The Political Psychology of Revolutionary Caricatures', in *French Caricature and the French Revolution, 1789–1799* (Los Angeles, CA: Wright Art Gallery, University of California, Los Angeles, 1988), pp. 33–40, p. 38.
45. Simon Schama, *Citizens* (London: Viking, 1989), p. 768.
46. Madelyn Gutwirth, *The Twilight of the Goddesses: Women and Representation in the French Revolutionary Era* (New Brunswick, NJ: Rutgers University Press, 1992), pp. 258–73, 359–67.
47. Thomas Gisborne, *An Enquiry into the Duties of the Female Sex* (London: T. Cadell, and W. Davies, 1797), pp. 214–16.
48. Baron-Wilson, *Life and Correspondence*, p. 180.
49. James Gillray, 'Tales of Wonder!' (London: H. Humphrey, 1 February 1802). See M. D. George, *Catalogue of the Political and Personal Satires Preserved in the Department of Prints and Drawings in the British Museum* (London: British Museum Publications, 1870–1954), VIII, pp. 118–19.
50. *The Monthly Review*, New ser., 23 (August 1797), p. 451.
51. [Williams], 'Luxury or the Comforts of a Rum p ford' (London: S. W. Fores, 26 February 1801). See George, *Political and Personal Satires*, VIII, p. 57.
52. Edmund Burke, *Reflections on the Revolution in France*, ed. Conor Cruise O'Brien (Harmondsworth: Penguin, 1976), pp. 313, 333.
53. Peck, *Life*, p. 49.
54. Henry Richard, Lord Holland, *Foreign Reminiscences* (London: Longman, Brown, Green, and Longmans, 1850), pp. 2–21.
55. Fox to Thomas Grenville, August 1789; quoted in L. G. Mitchell, *Charles James Fox* (Oxford: Oxford University Press, 1991), p. 110.

56. Lewis to his mother, Weimar, 17 September 1792, in Peck, *Life*, p. 192.
57. Frances Gerard, *A Grand Duchess: the Life of Anna Amalia, Duchess of Saxe-Weimar-Eisenach and the Classical Circle of Weimar* (London: Hutchinson, 1902), II, pp. 511–21.
58. A. W. Ward and G. P. Gooch, *The Cambridge History of British Foreign Policy, 1783–1919; Volume I: 1783–1815* (Cambridge: Cambridge University Press, 1922), pp. 216–56.
59. Tuite, 'Cloistered Closets', unpaginated.
60. Lewis to his Mother, 22 July 1794, The Hague, in Peck, *Life*, pp. 210–11.
61. J.W. Fortescue, *A History of the British Army* (London: Macmillan, 1906), IV (1789–1801), p. 269.
62. James Roche, *Critical and Miscellaneous Essays*, 2 vols (Cork: G. Nash, 1850), II, pp. 142–3.
63. Ward and Gooch, *British Foreign Policy*, p. 221; Jacques Godechot, *The Counter-Revolution: Doctrine and Action 1789–1804*, trans. Salvator Attanasio (1961; Princeton, NJ: Princeton University Press, 1971), pp. 173–200; Hugues Marquis, 'Espions et agents secrets pendant la campagne des Flandres (1793–1794)', *Revue du Nord*, 75, 229 (1993), pp. 121–32.
64. Pitt to Windham, 19 September 1794; 21 September 1794, quoted in John Ehrman, *The Younger Pitt: The Reluctant Transition* (London: Constable, 1983), p. 374.
65. Jennifer Mori, *William Pitt and the French Revolution, 1785–1795* (Edinburgh: Keele University Press, 1997), p. 213.
66. Lewis to his mother, The Hague, 22 November 1794, in Baron-Wilson, *Life and Correspondence*, I, pp. 140–2.
67. *The Annual Register, or a View of the History, Politics, and Literature, for the Year 1795* (2nd edn: London, 1806), p. 45.
68. *Annual Register for 1795*, p. 45.
69. Schama, *Citizens*, p. 756. See also François Furet, *The French Revolution, 1770–1814* (1st French edn 1988; Oxford: Blackwell, 1996), pp. 134–42.
70. Donald Greer, *The Incidence of the Terror in the French Revolution: a statistical interpretation* (Cambridge, MA: Harvard University Press, 1935); and Schama, *Citizens*, pp. 791–2.
71. Schama, *Citizens*, pp. 788–9.
72. Camille Desmoulins, No. VI, 30 December 1793, *Le Vieux Cordelier, Journal Politique, rédigé en l'an II* (Paris: Baudouin Frères, 1825), p. 119.
73. Peter Brooks, 'Virtue and Terror: *The Monk*', *ELH*, 40 (1973), pp. 249–63, p. 258; Peck, *Life*, pp. 20–3, and Christopher Rivers, 'Safe Sex: The Prophylactic Walls of the Cloister in the French Libertine Convent Novel of the Eighteenth Century', *Journal of the History of Sexuality*, 5, 3 (1995), pp. 381–402.
74. Lewis to his mother, 23 September 1794, in Peck, *Life*, p. 212.
75. Lynn Hunt, 'The many bodies of Marie Antoinette: political pornography and the problem of the feminine in the French Revolution', in *Eroticism*

and the Body Politic, ed. Lynn Hunt (Baltimore and London: Johns Hopkins University Press, 1991), pp. 108–30.

76. Schama, Citizens, p. 800.

77. T. C. W. Blanning, The origins of the French Revolutionary Wars 1787–1802 (London: Arnold, 1996), p. 139.

78. Furet, Revolutionary France, p. 140.

79. Gilles Nerét, Erotica Universalis (Köln: Benedikt Taschen, 1994), pp. 360–4.

80. Augustin Barruel, The History of the Clergy during the French Revolution (London: J. P. Coghlan, 1794), I, pp. 18–21.

81. William B. Todd, 'The Early Editions and Issues of The Monk, with a Bibliography', Studies in Bibliography, II (1949–50), pp. 3–24.

82. The Monthly Mirror, 2 (June 1796), p. 98.

83. The British Critic, 7 (June 1796), p. 677.

84. Matthew Lewis Snr to William Windham, Secretary at War, undated letter [1795?]; quoted in Peck, Life, p. 17.

85. Baron-Wilson, Life and Correspondence, p. 181.

86. Peck, Life, pp. 43–4.

87. Henry Vassall, Lord Holland, Further Memoirs of the Whig Party 1807–1821 (London: John Murray, 1905), p. 379.

88. 'Matthew Gregory Lewis', The History of Parliament: The House of Commons, 1790–1820, IV, Members, ed. R. G. Thorne (London: Secker & Warburg, 1986), pp. 432–3. See also Peck, Life, p. 17.

89. Walter Scott, 'Essay on Imitations of the Ancient Ballad' (1830), Minstrelsy of the Scottish Border, ed. Thomas Henderson, 4 vols (Edinburgh and London: William Blackwood, 1902), p. 30.

90. Sylvester Douglas, Lord Glenbervie, The Diaries, ed. Francis Bickley, 2 vols (London: Constable, 1928), II, p. 231.

91. Scott, 'Ancient Ballad', p. 31.

92. 'To C. J. F-. Esqre on the mention made of the Empress of Russia, in the House of Commons, by Mr. Sheridan, on Thursday, April 25th [1793]', in Peck, Life, pp. 197–9.

93. Matthew Lewis, The Love of Gain: a poem. Imitated from the Thirteenth Satire of Juvenal (London: J. Bell, 1799).

94. Mitchell, Fox, p. 187.

95. In addition, two piratical editions were published in Dublin in 1796 and 1797 in two volumes.

96. 'M. G. Lewis, Esq. M.P.', The Monthly Mirror, 2 (October 1796), pp. 323–8.

97. Parreaux, Publication, pp. 183–7.

98. Todd, 'Early Editions', pp. 19–20.

99. The Analytical Review, XXIV (October 1796), p. 403.

100. Auckland to Wickham, 24 December 1798; quoted in Mori, Pitt, p. 274.

101. S. T. Coleridge, The Critical Review, series II, 19 (February 1797), pp. 194–200; in Coleridge's Miscellaneous Criticism, ed. T. M. Raysor (London: Constable & Co., 1936), pp. 370, 371, 373–4.

102. 'Aurelius', *The Flapper* [Dublin], LV, 1796 September 17, pp. 3–4.
103. *The Monthly Review*, New ser., 23 (August 1797), p. 451.
104. R.R., *The European Magazine*, 31 (February 1797), p. 114.
105. 'Modern Novels: inscribed to the Author of The Monk', *The Spirit of the Public Journals for 1800*, IV (London: James Ridgway, 1801), p. 259.
106. Thomas Mathias, *The Pursuits of Literature. A satirical poem in four dialogues. With notes*, 5th edn rev. (London: T. Becket, 1798), IV, pp. 213–14.
107. Mathias, *Pursuits*, IV, ll. 605, 607, pp. 365–6; II, p. 120
108. Mathias, *Pursuits*, IV, pp. 194–5.
109. Mathias, *Pursuits*, IV, ll. 309–24, pp. 291–6; IV, pp. 293–4n.
110. Parreaux, *Publication*, p. 119; Thomas Medwin, *Journal of the Conversations of Lord Byron* (London: Henry Colburn, 1824), pp. 190–1.
111. Robert Isaac Wilberforce and Samuel Wilberforce, *The Life of William Wilberforce*, 5 vols (London: John Murray, 1839), II, pp. 183–4.
112. *Gentleman's Magazine*, LXXXVIII, [New series 11] (August 1818), p. 183.
113. *Life of Wilberforce*, I, pp. 129–38; John Pollock, *Wilberforce* (London: Constable, 1977), pp. 59–66.
114. *By the King, A Proclamation, for the Encouragement of Piety and Virtue, and for the Preventing and Punishing of Vice, Profaneness and Immorality . . . Given at . . . the First Day of June, 1787* (London: no publisher, 1787).
115. Beilby Porteus, Bishop of London, 'Occasional Memorandum and Reflexions', quoted in Pollock, *Wilberforce*, p. 60.
116. 'Mr Reeve's Report on Sedition &c.', 29 April 1794, quoted in David Worrall, *Radical Culture: discourse, resistance and surveillance, 1790–1820* (London: Harvester Wheatsheaf, 1992), p. 19.
117. *Report of the Committee for the Carrying into Effect His Majesty's Proclamation against Vice and Immorality, for the year 1799* (London: J. Hatchard, 1800), pp. 15–16
118. *The New Monk, a romance, in three volumes, by R. S. Esq.* (London: Minerva Press for William Lane, 1798), II, pp. 167–8.
119. Ann Radcliffe, *The Italian, or the Confessional of the Black Penitents*, ed. Frederick Garber (Oxford: Oxford University Press, 1968).
120. Charlotte Dacre, *Zofloya, or The Moor*, ed. Kim Ian Michasiw (Oxford: Oxford University Press, 1997), pp. 222–5.
121. Lewis, *Monk*, p. 426.

CHAPTER FOUR

Science, conspiracy and the gothic enlightenment
Charles Brockden Brown, Wieland (1798); Mary Shelley, Frankenstein (1818)

It seemed to many contemporary commentators that if the late eighteenth century was to be known as an age of reason, then the rejection of magic and the supernatural, seemingly the origin of the contemporary cult of gothic terror, would be central to such claims. The scientist and poet Erasmus Darwin, in his *Zoonomia; or, the laws of Organic Life* (1801) scathingly noted that:

> In this age of reason, it is not the opinions of others, but the natural phænomena, on which those opinions are founded, which deserve to be canvassed. And with the supposed existence of ghosts or apparitions, witch-craft, vampyrism, astrology, animal magnetism, and American tractors, such theories as the above must vanish like the scenery of a dream; as they consist of such combinations of ideas, as have no prototype or correspondent combinations of material objects existing in nature.[1]

Science, or natural philosophy as it was more often called, was the preferred model of enlightenment progress. Science, its rational method and public verifiability, represented the highest expression of modernity. Enlightenment science was progressively revealing the essential laws of nature, offering ever more accurate and convincing rational explanations of nature's variety. Each of the emerging disciplines of the new science – from mechanics, electricity, natural history (botany and zoology), and meteorology, to chemistry, physics and mathematics – searched for materialist explanation, adopted classificatory methods, and reformed scientific language. The scientific enlightenment reflected a profound cultural transformation, in its belief in the power of human enquiry to solve the problems of existence and its rejection of received ideas of orthodox religion. Enlightenment science had its own politics, explicitly identified with its cultural context in society, urban life and the city, and implicitly allied with radical political philosophy elsewhere concerned with anti-clericalism, utopianism and human perfectibility.[2]

Science was not included in the common syllabus of education: or at least, English universities did not teach it. Instead it was taught largely by a process of emulation and repetition. In its philosophy, empirical science, with its practical experiments, was essentially autodidactic: each enquirer ought to be able to repeat each experiment, and so learn by eyewitness demonstration. The results and methods of these experiments, and the ideas they generated, were disseminated through a culture of scientific enquiry, especially in print and in lecture demonstrations. Science did not only happen in scientific treatises and specialist journals such as the *Philosophical Transactions* of the Royal Society, but also in general magazines and literary reviews, such as *The Edinburgh Review* and *The Quarterly Review*. Demonstrations were held not in academic environments but in public locations, such as the upstairs rooms of coffee-houses or in specially constructed lecture halls. As a child, Mary Shelley attended the public lectures of Humphry Davy at the Royal Institution in London. Addressing a fashionable audience, his demonstrations of his newly discovered gas, nitrous oxide or laughing gas, were particularly compelling.[3] Scientific discovery was popular culture in a way that students of literature might now find surprising.

In *The Dialectic of Enlightenment* (1944), Horkheimer and Adorno defined the aims of the enlightenment as a programme of 'disenchantment' 'aimed at liberating men from fear.'[4] Despite the categorical counter-gothicism of much enlightenment science, substituting knowledge for superstition, writers of fiction in the gothic mode found a creative opportunity in science. As they attempted to insinuate their fiction into the place of popular scientific culture, such a project seemed fraught with serious difficulties, for the reason that by convention, gothic novels rejected rational cause – 'events which flow from causes well known and constantly in operation among men in society' – in favour of convention and supernaturalism, 'the hacknied machinery of castles, banditti and ghosts'.[5] Readers tolerate the gothic novel's indulgence of the supernatural by wilful suspension of disbelief. Despite the coherence and mastery of the rational materialist world view, in the gothic mode the reader may suffer an alternative in order to have life and cogency (recapitulating the divergence between the discourses of history and romance). This enchantment occurs within the happy confines of fiction, where anything may happen, without mattering if it does. Some gothic writers recognised in the supernatural a creative potential to engage the emotional interest (curiosity or fancy) of their readers, and exploited them in a way that toyed with credulity as much as scepticism. Both Charles Brockden Brown and Mary Shelley, writing two decades apart (1798–1818), located gothic themes within material that skirted the edges of reason and irrationality, nature and magic, scepticism and credulity.

I. CHARLES BROCKDEN BROWN:
— CONSPIRACY, ENLIGHTENMENT AND —
THE SUPERNATURAL EXPLAINED

One of the first professional novelists active in the United States, Charles Brockden Brown (1771–1810) wrote four gothic novels in the space of four years: *Wieland* (1798), *Ormond* (1799), *Arthur Mervyn* (1799–1800), and *Edgar Huntly* (1799). A Quaker by birth and upbringing, Brown continued his education beyond school by reading extensively in the latest European philosophy of Rousseau, Godwin, Bage and Wollstonecraft. His reading in the novel, especially Richardson and Johnson, confirmed his conclusion that the novel must entertain, but must also serve a moral purpose. It was not clear, he later argued, that the gothic novel, which enlivened its narratives with 'murders, ghosts, clanking chains, dead bodies, skeletons, old castles, and damp dungeons' could be said to instruct.[6] His own novels, though replete with murders, also reflected a studied, intellectual, approach to fiction. In the 'Advertisement' prefixed to *Wieland*, Brown stressed the moral dimension of his project, stating that his aim was 'the illustration of some important branches of the moral constitution of man'.[7] Similarly, the female narrator, Clara Wieland, places her story in a moral framework: explaining that it 'will exemplify the force of early impressions, and show the immeasurable evils that flow from an erroneous or imperfect discipline'.[8] Like Wollstonecraft and Godwin, Brown argued that the novel was a philosophical medium as much as an entertainment: that the novel had intellectual weight, and, by addressing a wide audience, was an important vehicle for political critique. Moreover, the emotional power of the novel, its ability to transform readers' opinions by seducing them into the writer's point of view, through the occultations of sympathy and character, meant that the novel was the most powerful form of writing available to the philosopher. The novel's political and philosophical dimension, signalled in its subtitle '*An American Tale*', was underlined when Brown sent a copy to the vice-president of the United States, Thomas Jefferson (although to what end is not clear).

Brown's animadversions on the novel's function aimed at the reformation of the 'the ordinary or frivolous sources of amusement' such as the gothic novel. Like Wollstonecraft, he offers this revision in the form of a gothic novel, co-opting many of the methods and resources of the Radcliffe school, such as the use of the pathetic fallacy in representing the emotional force of nature, and also the exploration of emotion in moments of terror. Most significantly, however, *Wieland* repeats and revises Radcliffe's project of the 'explain'd supernatural'. In Brown's mode of explanation, the cases of the supernatural are deliberately difficult to explain, and the clarification, when it comes, all the more ingenious. Unlike Radcliffe, whose terrors were sometimes incredible or deflating, Brown strove to overturn the incredulity aroused by the 'extraordinary and rare' incidents related in the narrative. Despite their approach 'nearly to the nature of miracles', Brown asserted that all conform to scientific rationalism:

> It is hoped that intelligent readers will not disapprove of the manner in which appearances are solved, but that the solution will be found to correspond with the known principles of human nature. The power which the principal person is said to possess can scarcely be denied to be real.[9]

While Radcliffe's explanations flirt with the ridiculous, Brown asserts his terrors deal with powers that are real, 'supported by . . . historical evidence' even though 'extremely rare'. Brown's gothic vanquishes supernaturalism as superstition, but reasserts terror as a real category of human experience.

A test case is introduced in the second chapter, a prologue to the main narrative concerning a most unusual experience of spontaneous combustion. The father of the narrator Clara, the elder Wieland, was a fanatical religious autodidact who professed a strangely archaic Protestant theology which viewed the world as a direct conflict between the forces of God and the Devil. In his manner he was austere and stern, enforcing a strict morality based on the denial of worldly pleasures. Wieland's Calvinism is a survival of archaic thought into a more enlightened age, and a form of gothicism. However, despite his pious devotions, Wieland believes that he has failed his duty to God, and is filled with foreboding and dread at his approaching death. The event of his death, related in the second chapter of the novel, adopts a mode of radical formal realism, deploying well-known strategies of empirical authentication to an unusual extent: reciting circumstantial evidence, providing extensive spatial and chronological detail, and itemising the physiological and mental condition of each of the players. At midnight on a sultry August night, Wieland attended his customary solitary worship in his private chapel (known as the Temple), despite alarming premonitions. Half an hour later, his wife notices a strange gleam of light from the chapel, followed by a loud report, similar to an explosion, and the sound of piercing shrieks for help. The building does not burn, but it is enveloped by a cloud impregnated with light. Brought to his bed, naked and scorched, the elder Wieland reports that a strange faint light like that cast by a lamp had approached him, and that as he turned towards it, he was struck on the arm as if by a club. Immediately afterwards, a spark ignited his clothes.

Despite the accumulated evidence, Wieland's death remains clothed in mystery. To Clara's wondering mind, the mysterious events have either a rational or a supernatural explanation:

> Is it a fresh proof that the Divine Ruler interferes in human affairs, meditates an end, selects, and commissions his agents, and enforces by unequivocal sanc-tions, submissions to his will? Or, was it merely the irregular expansion of the fluid that imparts warmth to our heart and our blood, caused by the fatigue of the preceding day, or flowing, by established laws, from the condition of his thoughts?

The reader too is offered no clarification: events imply a supernatural cause, but the formal method suggests an earthly one. This is reiterated by Brown's insertion of an explanatory footnote. Within the purview of the novel, it is not clear who writes the footnote, although convention implies it is the editor, 'C. B. B.', signed at the foot of the 'Advertisement'.

> A case, in its symptoms exactly parallel to this, is published in one of the Journals of Florence. See, likewise, similar cases reported by Messrs. Merille and Muraire, in the 'Journal de Medicine,' for February and May, 1783. The researches of Maffei and Fontana have thrown light upon this subject.[10]

The scholarly method of the footnote – masculine and authoritative – reasserts the hegemony of the scientific discourse over the fluid specula-tions of Clara's feminine mind, ranging between theology and physiology. Nonetheless, the presence of the scholarly apparatus suggests a certain lack of faith in the resources of the novel medium. To Brown's mind, perhaps, the fictional magic of the novel as a genre (where anything might happen) could legitimate the act of spontaneous combustion as a metaphysical or supernatural event, rather than a materialist and rational one. Brown's contemporaries, such as his friend and critic William Dunlap, argued that Brown's scientific wonders were less credible, to most readers, than supernatural causes. 'The instances of self-combustion . . . are so rare, that a work, whose events are founded on such materials, accords less with popular feelings and credulity, than if supernatural agency had been employed.' The discovery of an empirical explanation for the mysterious events, Dunlap argues, is diminishing and bathetic:

> It is perhaps always unsatisfactory, to find that causes which had purposefully been made to convey an idea of more than mortal agency, are merely natural. The reader will remember ... the waxen doll which inspires such high and mysterious ideas in Mrs Radcliffe's "Mysteries of Udolpho".[11]

The contest initiated here between formal realism and gothic supernaturalism, between science and metaphysics, is enacted throughout the novel.

Reports of spontaneous combustion in the eighteenth century were not unknown. Dunlap asserts that, 'Self-combustion is an awful and mysterious phenomenon of nature' which 'though known and established' was 'still mysterious and undefined'.[12] Spontaneous human combustion – of which Wieland's case is an irregular example – has even to this day at best quasi-scientific status, hovering on the edge of empirical verifiability and sensational anecdote. Late eighteenth century research accepted that in certain conditions, such as excessive consumption of alcohol, human flammability might occur. The Florentine journal report, noted by Brown in his footnote, had been analysed in the *The Literary Magazine and British Review* of London in 1790, and reprinted in a Philadelphia journal in 1792. Entitled 'Letter respecting an Italian Priest, killed by an Electric Commotion, the cause of which resided in his own body', it reported the strange death of Don G. Maria Bertholi, a priest of Livizzano in northern Italy. Whilst he was at prayer one evening,

> a loud noise was heard in Mr Bertholi's chamber, and his cries having alarmed the family, they hastened to the spot, where they found him extended on the floor, and surrounded by a faint flame, which retired to a greater distance in proportion as it was approached, and at length disappeared entirely.

Battaglia, the surgeon who narrates the account, details his strange burns and slow death over four days.

> During my last visit, which he was sunk in a lethargic sleep ..., I observed with astonishment, that putrefaction had already made so great progress, that his body exhaled an insupportable smell. I saw the worms which issued from it crawling on the bed, and the nails of his fingers drop of themselves.

Before he died, Bertholi had related that 'he had felt a stroke, as if somebody had given him a blow over the right arm with a large club, and that at the same time, he had seen a spark of fire attach itself to his shirt, which in a moment was reduced to ashes'. This 'form of elementary fire', the surgeon concludes, was particularly susceptible for those 'advanced in years, remarkably fat, and had been much addicted to the use of spiritous liquors'. Such people might indeed perish 'by their whole substance spontaneously taking fire', catalysed by an 'Electric Commotion'.[13] Spontaneous human combustion, of the kind evidenced by Battaglia and Merille, became a favourite trope of the temperance movement, as one of the detrimental effects of imbibing alcohol.[14] In Wieland's case, the catalyst of his flammability is imputed to theological, rather than alcoholic, spirits. His faith is intensely private and internal: 'Social worship [. . .] found no place in his creed. [. . .] His own belief of rectitude was the foundation of his happiness.' He relies on his own internal enlightenment unmediated by any sect or ecclesiastical institution. It is something of a black joke then that this reliance on inner light leads to his literal illumination when he burns to death. Her father's death provokes Clara's prolonged and sententious debate between a providential and theological account, or a physiological and scientific one.[15] The reader's credulity, stretched by the father's highly unusual death, is not offered a secure explanation, not even in gothic diablerie. This debate, produced by Clara and enacted in the reader, establishes fictional epistemology as a central concern of the novel.

— A 'SINGLE FAMILY' AND 'THE CONDITION OF A NATION' —

Raised by a maiden aunt, Clara and her brother form an idyllic and retired community – a model of enlightened reform – on the banks of the Schuylkill River in Pennsylvania. Their extended family community embodies the domestic sentimental family, but recast in a classical mode derived from the Hellenic aesthetic of the Scottish enlightenment. Their father's austere Temple is renovated as a summer house for entertaining, with a harpsichord and a bust of Cicero (politely reforming history's burden). Unlike their father, Clara and her brother, Theodore, have a measured and enlightened understanding, 'enriched by science, and embellished with literature'.[16] Theodore Wieland, a studious young man, with a serious demeanour and a melancholic disposition, is given to Calvinist speculation, but tempers this with enlightenment philosophy. To their circle is added Theodore's wife, Catherine, and her brother, Henry Pleyel, a sociable rationalist drawn by Clara's charms. The Wielands are thoroughly modern about their neoclassicism: they emphasise reason as the cornerstone of their society, and value leisure as the opportunity to develop their intellect, and hence, their civic virtues. They believe that reason guides their study, and can also account for all natural phenomena. Truth can be deduced from sensory experience: obscure sensations must be interrogated by introspective analysis and research, but nonetheless, any obscurity can be understood upon examination.

Their ideal community, modelled on these classical virtues and values, not only recalls the speculations of utopian philosophers of the 1790s but also forges an analogy with the neoclassical rhetoric of the American republic.

Their calm is disturbed, however, by a series of mysterious events that serve to test the strength of their morality. One evening, when Theodore Wieland had returned to the Temple to retrieve a lost letter, he hears the voice of his wife telling him he is in danger, and that he must return to the house. Examining his experience, Wieland and Pleyel sceptically ascertain that it cannot have a natural cause, and thus belongs to the supernatural. The recurrent voices focus especially on Clara, who even hears inexplicable and mysterious voices apparently plotting her murder in the female privacy of her own bedroom.[17] Clara, Wieland and Pleyel cannot discern whether these mysterious incidents are illusions of the senses (a dream or hallucination) or imperfect signs of the existence of superior beings engaged in their lives (supernatural), perhaps to malevolent purpose. The novel's tone of febrile intensity initiates an epistemological insecurity approaching paranoia. Brown again expends considerable energy detailing spatial and chronological relations within the text, asking the reader to imagine the house and its rooms as a real three-dimensional space. The novel's reliance on the genre's classical resources of formal realism is revealed as a kind of rationalising strategy that can be juxtaposed to descriptions of Clara's terror. The reader, in short, is positioned as a player within the text.

The arrival of a new character, Francis Carwin, both intensifies and, eventually, resolves this enigma. Despite Carwin's unprepossessing appearance ('rustic and aukward', 'ungainly and disproportioned') he exercises a powerful, almost erotic, fascination for Clara. His voice, in particular, with its curiously antiquated cadences, imparted to her 'an emotion altogether involuntary and incontroulable'. Unusual and supernatural powers are suggested by the 'vivid and indelible' countenance of this strangely compelling man.[18] Carwin, on the strength of an old acquaintance with Pleyel, insinuates himself into their circle. One night, after Clara has again heard the voice, he appears in her room, threateningly observing that but for the supernatural intercession of the voice, he would have seduced or, rather, raped, her. Although he leaves without touching her, his exit is observed by Pleyel, who turns against Clara because he assumes she has been unchaste. It becomes clear that in fact Carwin has arranged matters in such a way that Pleyel will conclude that Clara and Carwin have been alone together in her bedroom, and will suspect that she has been seduced by him. Carwin has destroyed her reputation, not in reality but by report.

Figure 7. 'Passions: Plate CCCLXXIX', illustration to Johann Caspar Lavater, 'Passion', Encyclopaedia Britannica; or, a Dictionary of Arts, Sciences, and Miscellaneous Literature, 3rd edn (Edinburgh: A. Bell and C. Macfarquhar, 1797), XIV, opp. p. 379. Reproduced with permission of University of Sydney Library.

Carwin's history reinforces his rootless, masterless quality. He has the ability to change – seemingly at will – faith, nation, class and even appearance. When Clara first encounters him, he appears as a poor wanderer, but Pleyel recounts his prior appearance as a man of consequence in Spain, where he had undergone a '*transformation* into a Spaniard' and assumed the Catholic faith. 'His garb, aspect and deportment, were wholly Spanish'. Although Carwin was 'indistinguishable from a native', Pleyel had found him a communicative interlocutor on all topics but his prior life, arousing suspicions that his Catholicism was 'counterfeited for some political purpose'.[19] A newspaper account discovered later appears to relate that Carwin was a fugitive criminal, having been found guilty of murder and robbery in Dublin. According to the testimony of 'the honourable Mr Ludloe', Carwin was:

> the most incomprehensible and formidable among men [. . .] engaged in schemes, reasonably suspected to be, in the highest degree, criminal, but such as no human intelligence is able to unravel: that his ends are pursued by means which leave it in doubt whether he be not in league with some infernal spirit: that his crimes have hitherto been perpetrated with the aid of some unknown but desperate accomplices: that he wages a perpetual war against the happiness of mankind, and sets his engines of destruction at work against every object that presents itself.[20]

Ludloe reports that Carwin was a dangerous enemy agent, bent on the destruction of domestic happiness, and in league with powerful, even diabolic, forces. Carwin's machinations against the Wieland family circle (his plot) disseminate suspicion in the community, creating faction and dissension where previously all was open and reasonable. His secret plot (the plot of secrecy), then, is against the public rationality of the ideal community. Within the commonwealth of the family, Carwin is figured as a revolutionary subversive (a secret plotter, possessed of secret motives and secret powers).

The novel's resolution depends on the eventual exposure of Carwin's 'invisible' powers, but it mediates this through a violent sanguinary catharsis. The novel explains Carwin's plot through a work of detection, undertaken by Clara, in which the reader is positioned as arbiter or judge. When Clara discovers the murdered body of Wieland's wife Catherine, she suspects Carwin, especially after Pleyel's discovery of Carwin's criminal past. However, Theodore Wieland himself confesses to the murder of his wife, along with that of his children and his young ward, Louisa Stuart, acting under the command of a voice whose origin he believed to be divine. Experiencing a religious mania, Wieland demonstrates his supreme obedience to God's will through murder. Clara detects not diabolical or divine intervention, but rather the malevolent genius of Carwin. Her powerful rejection of the supernatural reduces it to showmanship: 'The dreams of superstition are worthy of contempt. Witchcraft, its instruments and miracles, the compact ratified by a bloody signature, the apparatus of sulpherous smells and thundering explosions, are monstrous and chimerical.'[21] The modernity of Clara's investigative procedures contests and overwhelms Wieland's atavistic and gothic primitive religious enthusiasm.

— SUPERSTITION AND MADNESS, REASON AND WONDER —

Wieland's actions are categorised as a kind of insanity. Accounting for his madness in medical language, as a *Mania Mutabilis*, Clara (and the novel) seeks to eviscerate the explanatory power of Theodore's religious understanding. Clara and her recently arrived uncle Thomas Cambridge discover other 'remarkable cases' of maniacal illusions which end in bloody murders and strange suicides. Their research, and another footnote, seeks to use the rational language of science to render the gothic wonder of infanticide and wife-murder into another, merely credible, news report. The editor's footnote (hovering on the bounds of bathos) underlines the link to recent researches in sensationist psychology. 'Similar cases' of temporary insanity, the footnote states, can be found in Erasmus Darwin's poem *Zoonomia* – reinforcing Clara's determination to establish a rational and empirical account of events that appear wonderful or diabolical.[22] Wieland's multiple murder had similarities to the account of a religious maniac's murder of his family related in the *New York Weekly Magazine* of 20 and 28 July 1796.[23] Sensational stories of vicious domestic murder were the object of public fascination in late eighteenth-century America. Rather than manifestations of evil, they were increasingly subject to rational explanation, using narratives of detection to understand experiences of madness and frenzy.[24]

The novel both celebrates and avoids gothicising Wieland's murderous exploits through Brown's most significant device of rational wonder, Carwin's power of ventriloquism, or '*Biloquium*', as Brown calls it. In his lengthy confession to Clara, Carwin reveals that he is an adept of the art of ventriloquy, and that he has used this skill to his own ends, although he denies that he has thus caused the terrible crimes. Carwin says to Clara that she is 'not apprized of the existence of a power which I possess. I know not what to call it. It enables me to mimic exactly the voice of another, and to modify the sound so that it shall appear to come from what quarter, and be uttered at what distance I please'.[25] The aural incidents experienced by Clara and her brother are revealed to be the product of Carwin's capacity for throwing his voice. Alerted by reports of Clara as a woman both beautiful and rational, who 'held apparitions and goblins in contempt', he wished to put her 'courage to the test'.[26] Clara's later misfortunes, with Carwin and Pleyel, are similarly explained as the product of his corrupt machinations. The family is the victim of a plot, a conspiracy against their felicity, which has a rational and material cause.

Exposing gothic superstition, the secret arts of ventriloquism, redolent of magic and demonism, are refigured scientifically as a rational event. Brown's scholarly footnote again reinforces a rational hegemony: defining 'Biloquium, or ventrilocution' as: 'Sound is varied according to the variations of direction and distance. The art of the ventriloquist consists in modifying his voice according to all these variations, without changing his place.'[27] The footnote reveals the 'ingenious but unsatisfactory speculations' on the phenomenon published by Joannes Baptista de La Chapelle in a tract entitled *Le Ventriloque ou L'Engastrimythe* (1772).[28] Brockden Brown knew of La Chapelle's dissertation through a lengthy essay on 'Ventriloquism' in the 1797 edition of the *Encyclopaedia Britannica*. As Brown remarked, in his review of the edition published in Philadelphia in 1798, this 'epitome of knowledge' not only condensed the 'vast and cumbrous mass' of the wisdom of the ages, but also offered 'an account of recent improvements' in 'the rapid fluctuations and progress of physical sciences'.[29] In the *Encyclopaedia*, 'Ventriloquism' was defined as 'an art by which certain persons can so modify their voice, as to make it appear to the audience to proceed from any distance, and in any direction'.[30]

Scientific discourse on ventriloquism first identified it as a type of acoustic deception in the late eighteenth century. As such, the theory of ventriloquism explained a series of theological experiences associated with demonology.[31] Amongst such wonders were enumerated the voices of demonic possession; necromantic ritual; the speaking prophetic voices of oracles; and pagan idolatry (shamanism). The term, derived from Latin and Greek origins, literally meant one who speaks from his belly. Thomas Blount defined 'Ventriloquist' in his *Glossographia* (1656) as 'one that hath the evil spirit speaking in his belly, or one that by use and practice can speake as it were out of his belly, not moving his lips.'[32] Sixteenth-century scriptural debate, especially around the story of the Witch of Endor (recounted in 1 *Samuel* 28) who summoned up the ghost of the prophet Samuel, increasingly proposed that the event was a deception. Sceptics linked such accounts with other aural wonders, under the rubric of witchcraft. Thomas Hobbes, in *Leviathan* (1651), explaining that men were 'apt to be deceived by false Miracles', included the '*Ventriloqui*' amongst the 'innumerable and easie tricks' by which 'crafty men' were 'able to make very many men beleeve it is a voice from Heaven'.[33] Eighteenth-century rationalists were even more categorical. The Scottish enlightenment philosopher Bishop Francis Hutchinson remarked that:

> Some Counterfeits can speak out of their Bellies with little or no Motion of their lips. They can change their Voices, that they shall be not like their own. They can make, that what they shall say be heard, as if it was from a different part of the Room, or as if it came from their own Fundament.[34]

Such persons, Hutchinson concludes, are called 'Engastriloques' or 'Ventriloquists'. In short, enlightenment attacks on the false miracles of demonic prophecy identify certain vocal deceptions under the name ventriloquism.

According to the new empirical explanation, such sounds had their origin not in supernatural demonology but in vocal deception. La Chapelle concluded that ventriloquism 'was an art, a practised technique of modulation, misdirection, and muscular control, which required neither supernatural assistance nor any special endowments of nature'. Although he revisited the renaissance and biblical debates on aural wonders and witchcraft, his decisive shift was to offer an empirical analysis of two magical performers who were able to perpetrate such religious impostures, locating a material cause for their magical wonders. As Schmidt argues, La Chapelle's point was 'that he had found one of the originating causes of religious phantasms and that now, so identified, ventriloquism could be turned with delicious irony from being a buttress of superstition to a tool of the enlightenment'.[35] In this way, the enlightenment method is used to explore supernatural events or miraculous wonders, so as to expose them as versions of superstition. As the *Encyclopaedia* essay on 'Ventriloquism' explains, 'the responses of many of the oracles were delivered by persons thus qualified to serve the purposes of priestcraft and delusion'. Rational explanation subverts magical or supernatural explanation by confirming the truth of its effects, and demonstrating their origin in illusion or deception. Nonetheless, despite examining several empirical examples, La Chapelle and the *Encyclopaedia* essay are unable to describe how the deception is achieved. The 'manner' in which these 'acoustic deceptions' are produced cannot be revealed, the *Encyclopaedia* coyly remarks, for 'the practical rules of the art' would be dangerous to the public good, as unscrupulous people would use it for 'the purposes of knavery and deception'.[36] Carwin's confession reveals his power is not unearthly and supernatural, but is a deception produced by human art. As Brown says in the Advertisement, 'The power which the principal person is said to possess can scarcely be denied to be real. It must be acknowledged to be extremely rare; but no fact, equally uncommon, is supported by the same strength of historical evidence.'[37] *Wieland* takes this unprepossessing material and weaves it into the fabric of the novel, although the result is not a novel about ventriloquy, but about credulity and deception.

Carwin's ventriloquism is an expression of his power, not its source, exploited to further his fascination with Clara. Brown's attack on his talent focuses on the misappropriation of scientific knowledge for personal gratification. By misconstruing Carwin's ventriloquised utterances as signs of divine approval, Theodore Wieland becomes convinced of his own election, of his special place in God's plan, and he believes himself above the normal, mortal, scheme of morality. In murdering his wife, children and servant, and attempting the life of his sister, he is making a 'sacrifice' 'demanded' by a vengeful, persecuting God. Carwin's ventriloquised voices convinced Wieland of his state of grace, but it is his own self-authorising decision that commands him to murder. Although Clara initially suggests Theodore has a sceptical reliance on 'moral necessity and calvinistic inspiration', the novel betrays Wieland's reversion to an internal method for seeking after truth. In his confessional document, Theodore explains that, 'I have thirsted for the knowledge of his [God's] will'. In such a state, he eventually comes to believe he has found the 'blissful privilege of direct communication' with God through 'listening to the audible enunciation of [God's] pleasure' – the voices that later prove to be Carwin's ventriloquy. This is figured as enlightenment, an illumination in the literal dark of the night. Theodore is 'dazzled' by 'the lustre, which, at that moment, burst upon my vision!'[38] He piously obeys the Deity's instruction to prove his faith by sacrificing his family.

GOTHIC REVOLUTIONARIES AND THE SECRET ENLIGHTENMENT

In Theodore, and his father before him, Brown volunteers a portrait of the deviations of fanaticism. In the context of the 1790s, such religious fanaticism was known as 'enthusiasm', a state of mind which rigidly follows a strict set of doctrines. As Pamela Clemit and others have observed, Wieland's portrait of religious enthusiasm points not only to theological mania but also to radical Godwinian philosophers. 'In his analysis of the disintegration of the Wieland family, Brown presents an imaginitive reworking of conservative attacks on revolutionary philosophers as destructive of family ties in the name of universal philanthropy.'[39] Conservatives argued that revolutionary fervour amounted to a kind of mania, an irrational and directionless furore. In Edward Burke's polemic attack on its principles in *Reflections on the Revolution in France* (1790), revolution was a kind of madness, an 'epidemical fanaticism' communicated like a disease to the minds of men. Burke proposed a rational cause for revolutionary feeling in conspiracy: 'The spirit of proselytism attends this spirit of fanaticism. They have societies to cabal and correspond at home and abroad for the propagation of their tenets [that] have in some measure succeeded in sowing there the seeds of destruction.'[40]

The fierce factional disputes of American politics in the late 1790s were of serious concern to Brown. Initial admiration for the French Revolution in America, lauding its anti-clerical measures and republican rhetoric, had given way to alarm at the extremism of Jacobin revolutionary principles of liberty and equality. As the events of the Terror unfolded, American observers repeated British concerns that the revolution would destroy all religious and social order. The factional divisions in American politics of the late 1790s suggested that the United States was about to descend into a civil war between radical republicans and a Federalist reaction, especially as republican popular agitation seemed modelled on Jacobin-inspired modes of political violence. Federalist leaders, such as George Washington, denounced the activities of radical debating societies and advertised the threat of Napoleonic invasion. The threat of internal subversion, civil war, and foreign invasion excited Brown to write in 1803 that 'intestine disputes', the 'national preference' of 'popular forms of government', were 'favourable to the arts of intriguers . . .; spreading among us, with fatal diligence, the seeds of faction and rebellion'.[41] In 1798, the Federalists succeeded in passing the Alien and Sedition Laws to allow the full power of government to be used to suppress those of their opponents they identified as subversive.[42]

Brown invites the reader to consider the analogy between the Wieland family and the young republic, in which Carwin's secret and seemingly diabolic plot replicates the perceived threat of foreign subversion. As Clara states, she is 'to make the picture of a single family a model from which to sketch the condition of a nation'.[43] In 1798, the American polity was widely perceived as being under threat from a foreign conspiracy. While writing *Wieland* in New York in 1798, Brown associated with a group of intellectuals, such as Jedidiah Morse, an influential Calvinist preacher and geographer, who were persuaded of the existence of a worldwide conspiracy against religion and government. These men were influenced by two tracts from Britain by the Scottish scientist, John

Robison, and an émigré French clergyman, Abbé Augustin Barruel. Their works, derived independently but published almost simultaneously, claimed that a secret society of enlightened radicals, called the *Illuminati* was engaged in fomenting rebellion, and had already caused the French Revolution. In Bavaria in 1776, a party of reformers, styling themselves the *Illuminati*, had been founded by Adam Weishaupt, a professor of canon law at the University of Ingolstadt. Their name revealed their self-conscious state of enlightenment, which they pursued through a secret society modelled on that of the Freemasons, with whom they had formal relations. The *Illuminati* were committed to an enlightenment programme of utopian political, social and educational reform derived from Adam Smith, Lessing, Rousseau, Holbach, and Helvetius. To protect their identity and their plan, they adopted secret names derived from classical and alchemical sources: Weishaupt was Spartacus, after the rebel Roman slave, while Munich was known as Athens. Their ideas gained some influence amongst intellectuals in Germany, including Goethe, Herder and perhaps the poet Wieland. Nonetheless, their anticlericalism led to their exposure, and suppression, in 1784 and 1785, by the Jesuit-influenced Elector Karl Theodore, who branded them subversive revolutionaries. The celebrity of the society was insured by the publication of hitherto secret documents detailing their plans and rituals; and while their direct influence soon faded, their legacy took on new force as a spectre of revolutionary subversion.

Against the turbulent politics of the 1790s, the spectre of the *Illuminati* haunted Europe. In 1790, Edmund Burke, observing the 'open disorder' in France, opined that in many parts of Europe 'there is a hollow murmuring under ground; a confused movement is felt, that threatens a general earthquake in the political world. Already confederacies and correspondences of the most extraordinary nature are forming, in several countries.' As evidence, he footnoted the Munich-published *Illuminati* texts.[44] Such conspiracies became the subject of ever more elaborate theorisation. As Gordon S. Wood has argued, the idea of a conspiracy by secret hands has a powerful historiographical force in this period: rather than events being the result of 'social forces' or 'the stream of history', they can be seen to be the result of 'the concerted designs of individuals'. As such, apparently meaningless acts of destruction can be understood as rational and personal, the consequences of human will and agency.[45] The *Illuminati* conspiracy, then, makes sense of the dreadful confusions of Revolutionary history, providing a single orchestrating villain behind the varied scene of declarations, insurrections and atrocities.

The first significant statement of the Illuminati conspiracy was John Robison's *Proofs of a Conspiracy Against all the religions and governments of Europe, carried on in the secret meetings of Free Masons, Illuminati, and Reading Societies*, published in September 1797. The serious purpose of the Proofs was underlined by its dedication to William Windham, Secretary-at-War, the minister responsible for domestic counter-subversion measures. Robison's research, undertaken over many years, detected a group acting under 'the covert of a Mason Lodge' for the purpose of 'venting and propagating sentiments in religion and politics' that were contrary to the public good. Robison identified 'men of licentious principles' who taught 'doctrines subversive of all notions of morality'.

> I have been able to trace these attempts, under the specious pretext of enlightening the world by the torch of philosophy, and of dispelling the clouds of civil and religious superstition which keep the nations of Europe in darkness and slavery. I have observed these doctrines gradually diffusing and mixing with all the different systems of Free Masonry; till, at last, AN ASSOCIATION HAS BEEN FORMED for the express purpose of ROOTING OUT ALL THE RELIGIOUS ESTABLISHMENTS, AND OVERTURNING ALL THE EXISTING GOVERNMENTS OF EUROPE.

Robison identifies 'the most active leaders in the French Revolution' in a subversive cabal of libertines, enlightenment philosophers and Freemasons. The book is thus intended as a memorandum to authority and a warning, for as Robison declares, 'I have seen that this Association still exists, still works in secret, and that not only several appearances among ourselves show that its emissaries are endeavouring to propagate their detestable doctrines among us.'[46] Abbé Barruel's *Memoirs, Illustrating the History of Jacobinism* (1797–8), had a similar prophylactic intention, but with a wider cast of villains, Barruel exposed the emergence 'at an early period of the French Revolution' of 'a Sect calling itself Jacobin, and teaching *that all men were equal and free!*' Under the 'auspices of this Sect, and by their intrigue, influence, and impulse', the French Revolution destroyed church and monarchy. The Jacobin plot, Barruel continues, even 'to the most horrid deeds', 'was foreseen and resolved on, was premeditated and combined' as 'the offspring of deep-thought villainy'. 'Though the events of each day may not appear to have been combined, there nevertheless existed a secret agent and a secret cause, giving rise to each event, and turning each circumstance to the long-desired end.'[47]

Robison and Barruel derived their theories independently and published them almost simultaneously: a coincidence, both claimed, that lent credulity to their arguments. In the 'Postscript' appended to his fourth edition (1798), Robison stressed that the kinds of subversion he imputed to the *Illuminati* were at the level of ideas, rather than events: 'I meant to prove that the machinations of the Illuminati, whether associated under that denomination or not, had contributed to the revolution, by making a revolution, unfavourable to virtue and good order, in the public mind.' Nonetheless, the secret plots of the 'Enlighteners' (Robison's English for Barruel's '*Philosophists*'), even if 'not the *sole*, nor perhaps the *chief*, cause of that extraordinary event', the French Revolution, still posed a considerable threat to British and American society. The popular success of Robison's book, which sold its entire first impression in days, demonstrated to him a timeliness that justified his claim that '*this detestable Association exists, and its emissaries are busy amongst ourselves*'.[48]

American controversialists were quick to seize upon the British exposure of the *Illuminati* conspiracy, following the publication of Robison in Philadelphia in 1798. Demonised in Britain for their republicanism, in America the *Illuminati*'s anticlericalism and secrecy suggested a major threat to public order.[49] Brockden Brown's friend Jedidiah Morse discerned their subversions in local politics, both by influence and the work of emigrant agents. Morse's Fast Day sermon, preached on 9 May 1798, exposed the *Illuminati* conspiracy, which, he claimed, threatened America through 'Jacobin clubs' and debating societies.[50] Timothy Dwight, the president of Yale College, argued that Voltaire himself was the 'standing President' of this 'secret Academy' of '*Philosophists*' conspiring against American society.[51] Whilst Brown was composing and revising *Wieland*, in July and August 1798, his friends in New York, the physician Elihu Hubbard Smith and dramatist William Dunlap record both reading and discussing with Brown, American counter-conspiracy accounts and Robison's *Proofs of a Conspiracy*.[52]

In *Wieland*, Brown identified a common purpose between conspiracy theory and the gothic narrative strategy of the supernatural explained. In the course of Radcliffe's novels, incomprehensible and supernatural events are subsequently exposed to a material cause. Brown had further experience of such structures in German fictions exposing necromantic magic as elaborate sleight of hand, such as Schiller's *The Ghost-seer* ('The Apparitionist') and Cajetan Tschink's *The Victim of Magical Delusion* (1795), both of which were serialised in an abridged form in the *New York Weekly Magazine* in 1795–7.[53] As Schiller's translator opined, 'the sect of the *Illuminated* . . . were accustomed to seduce the ignorant and the superstitious, by extravagant and incredible powers and appearances.'[54] *Wieland* borrows the structure of conspiracy, in that all the wondrous and seemingly supernatural events are shown to be the result of intention and premeditation on the part of Carwin. The text emplots his plot; and like the detective story, of which *Wieland* is a forerunner, the narrative is heavily impressed by Carwin's criminal plot.

CONSPIRACY AND ENLIGHTENMENT IN CARWIN'S 'MEMOIRS'

The secret of Carwin's ventriloqual plot against the Wieland's domestic republic is revealed at the end of the novel. The motive behind such a conspiracy, however, was only answered in Brown's prequel to the novel, entitled *Memoirs of Carwin the Biloquist*. Written soon after publication of *Wieland* in 1798, this novel remained unfinished and unpublished until 1803, when it appeared serially in ten short instalments in the *Literary Magazine and American Register*, edited by Brown. The picture of Carwin that emerges is deliberately confused and enigmatic, as he is in both texts possessed of an uncanny ability to mutate identity, appearance, religion and even nationality. As a child, Carwin discovers the ability to ventriloquise through his study of such natural phenomena as a remarkable natural echo and endemic animal mimicry.

Carwin's education, and enlightenment, is undertaken by a mysterious, wealthy, Irishman named Ludloe, who takes him to Dublin and allows him unlimited access to his library. As Carwin slowly comes to realise, his education is also an initiation, each step of which was 'suggested by my own reflections': a process of initiation that in hindsight appears as a plot orchestrated by Ludloe 'to fit me to his purpose'. In its structure of enlightenment through initiation, Carwin's education recalls Robison's description of the relationship between the Novice and his Mentor in the *Illuminati*. The Mentor instructs the novice by bringing him through commonplace learning to a realisation that a higher knowledge awaits within himself. Subsequently, this 'speculative' (or abstract) information is shown to have an 'active' quality, 'engaged in doing good to others', and the novice is initiated into the 'hidden science' of the higher echelons, the Minervals and Illuminatus Minor.[55] Carwin's noviciate is spent in Barcelona, where he undergoes a transformation into a Spaniard: not only learning the language, and adopting the dress and manners of the country, but undergoing a conversion to the Catholic faith. His success in these remarkable alterations convinces Ludloe to outline more of his scheme:

> He taught me to ascribe the evils that infest society to the errors of opinion. The absurd and unequal distribution of power and property gave birth to poverty and riches, and these were the sources of luxury and crimes. ... We

have been inclined to impute [these errors] to inherent defects in the moral constitution of men: that oppression and tyranny grow up by a sort of natural necessity, and that they will perish only when the human species is extinct. Ludloe laboured to prove that this was, by no means, the case: that man is the creature of circumstances: that he is capable of endless improvement: that his progress has been stopped by the artificial impediment of government: that by the removal of this, the fondest dreams of imagination will be realized.[56]

Brown's depiction of Ludloe constructs him as a radical revolutionary villain: wealthy, given to abstract reasoning, committed to terror, and cloaked in self-absorbed mystery. Ludloe's anarchist radicalism refers the reader to radical political economy in the 1790s, especially that of the 'English Jacobins' such as William Godwin, Thomas Paine and Joseph Priestley. Ludloe's plans include a 'scheme of Utopian felicity, where the empire of reason should supplant that of force; where justice should be universally understood and practised; where the interest of the whole and of the individual should be seen by all to be the same'.[57] Ludloe's utopian project for a colony of the 'enlightened and disinterested' bears many allegiances to the radical speculations entertained by Godwin and his circle in the 1790s. Schemes for utopian colonies were widely circulated, and some even enacted: the poets Coleridge and Southey, for example, proposed in 1794 a colony in Pennsylvania on a scheme of 'Pantisocracy', a word they invented 'signifying the equal government of all'.[58]

Carwin comprehends that Ludloe is preparing him for some secret station in life above that of his present state. 'He had entertained a faint hope that I would one day be qualified for a station like that to which he himself had been advanced.'[59] Carwin slowly realises (a dawning recognition shared by the reader) that the station Ludloe hints at is not higher in status, but rather, a metaphysically advanced level. Upon his return to Ireland, Ludloe satiates Carwin's curiosity about the next 'stage' of his education by revealing the existence of a fraternity dedicated to the prosecution of his utopian ideas. 'A number of persons are leagued together for an end of some moment. To make yourself one of these is submitted to your choice. Among the conditions of their alliance are mutual fidelity and secrecy.'[60] Ludloe is the representative of a secret society not only modelled on the *Illuminati* but modelled on the account of the *Illuminati* detailed in the conspiracy theories of Robison and Barruel. Indeed, Brown's friend, William Dunlap, who read the beginning of the 'life of Carwin' in manuscript in September 1798 commented that 'he has taken up the schemes of the Illuminati'.[61] Carwin's initiation into the secret fraternity is offered to the reader as an explanation of his subsequent actions in the incidents related in both *Carwin* and *Wieland*.

It remains unclear how the proof of Ludloe's conspiracy explains Carwin's diabolic plots against the Wieland family. The novel itself, *The Memoirs of Carwin the Biloquist*, functions as a kind of conspiracy theory, in which Carwin is the key to unlock the mystery of *Wieland*, itself a conspiratorial structure. Such involutions of theme into form, as secrecy becomes both matter and medium of the novel, produces a climate of secrecy that lends itself to paradox, as when Carwin refers to 'the certainty of that suspicion'.[62] The signal tone of Brown's two novels remains one of conspiratorial enigma. The enigmatic ambiguity of Brown's depiction of the menace of foreign agents suggests that in his view the United States was threatened as much by the conspiracy theory as by the conspiracy itself – by oppressive Federalist reaction to legitimate republican agitation. By refusing to resolve the nature of Wieland's crisis (and moreover noting that the bloodthirsty result remains the same whether prompted by religious mania, physiological breakdown or malevolent conspiracy), the reader is not offered any safe place to expel revolutionary crisis.

II. Fictions of science in Mary Shelley's *Frankenstein*

The debate in Mary Shelley's *Frankenstein* (1818) on the history, character and language of science likewise raises the political spectre of revolution.[63] In Victor's education as a man of science, and his experimental creation of a synthetic human creature through the reanimation of disparate dead body parts, the novel establishes and assesses several distinct kinds of experimental investigation into the meaning of life, some associated with modern science, others with Renaissance alchemy and the occult. Such concerns reflect Shelley's interest in the radical political culture of her time and the recent past. Over the last decade, *Frankenstein* criticism has been much interested in the status of Shelley's science. In 1990, for example, Maurice Hindle remarked that 'early-nineteenth century science had much more of an impact on the genesis and substance of Frankenstein than is normally noticed, or even allowed, by literary critics.'[64] Since that time some excellent work by scholars, such as Marilyn Butler, Anne Mellor, and Samuel Vasbinder, has broadened an understanding of how Shelley had an active interest in, and a sophisticated understanding of, some important scientific debates of her time concerning electricity and the origin of life.[65] Other critics have suggested that though Shelley was curious about it, her science is indistinctly represented and technologically improbable: as James Reiger declared, 'she skips the science.'[66] There is reason to admit a more complex view here: while the science itself is more coherent than many critics have allowed, the novel's use of this scientific material is ambivalent, as the creature is created by invoking both contemporary science and an older tradition of necromancy and alchemy.[67] It should be asked to what purpose Shelley establishes this debate between science and magic. The magical and alchemical will not conform to the rule of scientific reason in that it has recourse to a supernatural world of spirits and essences. The novel negotiates the relations of dependence and disjunction between these concerns of science, alchemy and politics in its language and plot. The form of the novel offers itself as a useful intellectual tool, allowing these disparate forms of thought to jostle up against each other, not in resolution but in colloquy. The novel form, and in particular the gothic mode adopted by Shelley, allows for the contradictions, confusions and errors of the science to be overlooked and underplayed, incorporated into the creative act of reading.

Without doubt, Shelley had taken a keen interest in the representation of the science in the composition and revision of her novel. In the years when the novel was in its formative stages (1815–18), journals devoted to literary and cultural issues discussed a variety of scientific topics, such as electricity and magnetism, vivisection and evolution theory, as well as equally excited discussions of what would now be called pseudo-science, such as mesmerism and reanimation. Her diaries from 1816 record both her own reading of scientific work, and her enthusiastic commentary on the philosophical discussions at the Villa Diodati between herself and the poets Percy Bysshe Shelley (her husband-to-be), Lord Byron, and Dr John Polidori. In response to Byron's sociable suggestion '"We will all write a ghost story"', Shelley developed a ghost story out of the poets' 'conversations' on 'philosophical doctrines' on 'the nature of the principle of life'. Shelley recollects that they talked of Erasmus Darwin's 'experiments' in which a preserved 'piece of vermicelli' (a worm or vermicule) was restored to voluntary movement – referring to Darwin's speculations on the 'Spontaneous Vitality of Microscopic Animals' in *The Temple of Nature* (1803).[68] She mused that, 'Perhaps a corpse would be reanimated; galvanism had given token if such things: perhaps the component parts of a creature might be manufactured, brought together, and endued with vital warmth'.[69] Subsequently, the substantial revisions to this scientific material undertaken in the drafts of the novel, the first edition of 1818, and the heavily revised third edition of 1831, all point to her continued interest in fitting the science to her novel's purpose.

— ALCHEMY AND MODERN SCIENCE —

In the first chapter of his own narration, Victor Frankenstein regards his engagement with science as the 'genius that has regulated his fate'. Tellingly, he does not describe it as 'science', but 'Natural philosophy', the term used in the eighteenth century to describe both the physical sciences such as chemistry and physics, and the life sciences, biology and zoology. This distinction is not a slight one, for in the details of Victor Frankenstein's education as a 'man of science', and in his most famous experiment, the novel proposes a kind of argument about the nature of science. As a boy, untutored but enthusiastic, Victor is an alchemist, but as he is educated, he seems to abandon alchemy as a childish delusion, and to take up enlightenment science – chemistry and anatomy especially. In this transition, as Victor comprehends and rejects alchemical metaphysics as a species of superstition, the history of the scientific revolution, and the enlightenment, is played out in miniature.

Frankenstein's first engagement with natural philosophy is by chance: on a rainy day in a hotel near the mineral baths at Thonon, on the shores of Lake Geneva, in France, he idly picks up a book – a 'volume of the works of Cornelius Agrippa', a German alchemist of the sixteenth century (Heinrich Cornelius Agrippa of Nettesheim (1486?–1535)). Although he opens this book with apathy, he reports that his feeling is soon changed into enthusiasm by Agrippa's theory, an engagement he describes as a kind of enlightenment: 'A new light seemed to dawn upon my mind'. The work in question is unclear, but Agrippa was long out of print, and it might be best to think of little Victor reading a dusty old tome, as obscure in print as it is in thought. When Victor relates his exciting discovery to his instructor, his father, he replies, '"Ah! Cornelius Agrippa! My dear Victor, do not waste your time upon this; it is sad trash."' With hindsight, Victor the narrator (older and wiser) is able to contextualise this painful rebuff: remarking that Agrippa's views had been 'exploded' as chimerical, which is to say, fanciful and inaccurate. Instead they had been replaced by the 'real and practical' knowledge of 'a modern system of science'. Nonetheless, Victor remarks that Agrippa warmed his imagination (excited his passion and intellect), and as such, perhaps, 'the train of my ideas . . . received the fatal impulse that led to my ruin'. Disobeying his father, Victor continues to read avidly in the works of alchemists when he returns home to Geneva, consuming the works of Paracelsus and Albertus Magnus as well as those of Agrippa. Victor's tuition in alchemical thought is autodidactic. 'I read and studied the wild fancies of these writers with delight; they appeared to me treasures known to few beside myself.' Indeed, despite recognising the power of 'these secret stores of knowledge', young Victor keeps his reading secret from his father, whose censure he fears, even as he 'disclosed his discoveries' to his cousin Elizabeth, 'under a promise of strict secrecy'.[70] The knowledge that Victor learns from the alchemists is secret, and must itself be kept secret. In this way, it is unlike the enlightenment knowledge of the modern system of science, which is publicly manifested in experiment and must be made public to become knowledge.

Victor's study converts him into a 'disciple' of Albertus Magnus (1026?–1280), a Dominican friar and master of alchemy. The antiquarian Francis Barrett said of Albertus that 'he was in search of the *Philosopher's Stone*; that he was a famous *Magician*, and that he had formed a machine in the shape of a man, which served him as an oracle, and explained all the difficulties he proposed to it'.[71] Like Albertus, Victor:

> entered with the greatest diligence into the search of the philosopher's stone and the elixir of life. But the latter obtained my most undivided attention: wealth was an inferior object; but what glory would attend the discovery, if I could banish disease from the human frame, and render man invulnerable to any but a violent death![72]

In the period the novel was written, alchemy did not enjoy a high status amongst professional men of science, and neither did it enjoy a solid reputation amongst informed amateurs, although there were apologists for alchemy amongst antiquarians and connoisseurs. Barrett's compilation of Agrippa's thought, *The Magus, or Celestial Intelligencer* (1801), credulously detailed 'a complete system of Occult Philosophy' by supplementing Agrippa's material with cabalistic speculation, numerology, and hermetic philosophy, as well as more recent speculations on magnetism, and with biographies of the eminent alchemists (including Albertus Magnus, Paracelsus and Agrippa) (see Figure 8).[73] Nonetheless, alchemy was more generally a fugitive discipline in the opening decades of the nineteenth century. The fourth edition of the *Encyclopaedia Britannica* (1810) defined alchemy as 'that branch of chemistry which had for its principal objects the transmutation of metals into gold; the panacea, or universal remedy; an alkahest or universal menstruum; an universal ferment; and many other things equally ridiculous.'[74] The alchemist was by 1810 only a short step from the showman conjurer, spinning wonders at the fair, perpetrating artifice and imposture on a gullible public – a point of view that Victor's father appears to share.

Alchemy was, nonetheless, one of the places where science, or natural philosophy, was carried out before the emergence of the new science in

Figure 8. F. Barrett, engraved R. Griffith, 'Heads of Evil Daemons No. 2: Vessels of Wrath: Theutus, Asmodeus; The Incubus', in Francis Barrett, The Magus, or Celestial Intelligencer; Being a Complete System of Occult Philosophy *(London: Lackington, Allen and Co., 1801), II, opp. p. 44. British Library, London.*

the seventeenth century. Agrippa himself defended his 'natural magic' as a variety of natural philosophy:

> Natural Magick is taken to be nothing else, but the chief power of all the natural Sciences; which therefore they call the top and perfection of Natural Philosophy, and which is indeed the active part of the same; which by the assistance of natural force and faculties, through their mutual and opportune application, performs those things that are above Human Reason.

As Agrippa says, 'Alchymy, or Chymistry, is an Art.'[75] In Agrippa's work, there is material that appears to us obviously as magic: astrology, alchemy, mystical number symbolism, geomancy, incantations and rituals using pentangles. But there is also much of what the eighteenth century knew as natural philosophy: on the physical properties of the elements (chemistry), on treatments for diseases (medicine), and on the disposition of the stars (astronomy). This mixture, which appears to be contradictory and therefore unstable, is presented as a unified theory of the world: indeed, defenders argued that it is its inclusiveness and comprehensiveness that conferred it power. But such theory was attacked in the works of materialist and mechanistic empiricists like Newton and Copernicus, and gradually the magical elements of this philosophy were dissolved. The orthodoxy which replaced the natural magic was what later became known as the enlightenment: a materialist and pantheist philosophy of nature. This work was clearly a refutation of the occult philosophy of the magicians, but it was also only possible because of their work. Francis Bacon (1561–1626) was well versed in the Hermetic tradition of the magicians, and yet he did important work in mathematics and mechanical philosophy. Furthermore, as Margaret Jacob has argued, there was a residual interest in magic throughout the enlightenment, a 'blending of science and mysticism' sustained by the very same people who did so much to spread the innovations of the scientific revolution.[76]

However, Victor relates that his own experience in 'the raising of ghosts or devils' was unsuccessful, despite the promise of his favourite authors. Indeed, it is this failure, and the alchemists' ignorance of certain physical processes (distillation and 'the wonderful effects of steam') that leads him to become disillusioned with alchemy and to turn to the new science – or the 'science of natural philosophy' as he himself calls it. His fascination is first drawn by the spectacular demonstration of the vacuum afforded by use of an air pump, an experiment which proved that air was matter, famously dramatised as a gothic scenario in Joseph Wright of Derby's painting, *Experiment with an Air Pump* (1768). Secondly, he is offered a vivid lesson by the effects of lightening on a tree outside the family house in Belrive. Victor's discovery of electricity – as explained to him by his father – is the 'last stroke which completed the overthrow of Cornelius Agrippa, Albertus Magnus, and Paracelsus'. However, when Victor, at his father's urging, attends a series of lectures on natural philosophy, he finds them dull and incomprehensible: the professor's account of 'potassium and boron, of sulphates and oxyds' is too abstract, and Victor loses interest.[77] Modern scientific chemistry, then, having become a specialised discipline, offers no scope for the imagination, and young Victor forgoes its pleasures.

This indifference to the new science changes upon his entry to the University of Ingolstadt. The death of his mother turn Victor's thoughts once more to the nature of life, or rather, to 'that most irreparable evil, the void that presents itself to the soul' occasioned by death.[78] While science in England and France predominantly occurred outside the universities in public lecture halls and private laboratories, in Germany and Italy, the universities were at the forefront of scientific endeavour. The University of Ingolstadt, founded in 1472, was purportedly the *alma mater* of Faustus, a wanderer and vagabond who practised necromancy and alchemy in the early sixteenth century in association with Agrippa, and formed the basis, in works by Marlowe and Goethe, for the legendary magician who sold his soul to the devil in exchange for knowledge and power. The University of Ingolstadt was, by 1816 when the novel was written, an imaginary and even mythic place itself: it had relocated to Landshut in 1800, and to Munich in 1826. The myth with which it was often associated in these years was with the secret enlightenment conspiracy of the *Illuminati*, which had been founded there in 1776 by Adam Weishaupt. Mary Shelley records Percy reading to her 'the "History of the Illuminati", out of Barruel' in October 1814 in London.[79]

Victor's 'contempt' for 'the uses of modern natural philosophy' survives his tuition at Ingolstadt. While he learns much about recent innovations, such as the voltaic pile and galvanism, he is scornful of the lack of ambition in modern scientists. His education in enlightenment science is undertaken by two quite different teachers. He has little respect for the first, Monsieur Krempe, who is disparagingly described as 'a little squat man, with a gruff voice, and repulsive countenance'. At Victor's first interview with university science, Krempe pours scorn on his alchemical research, which he declares is 'nonsense'. 'Every instant that you have wasted on those books is utterly and entirely lost. You have burdened your memory with exploded systems, and useless names. [. . .] I little expected in this enlightened and scientific age to find a disciple of Albertus Magnus and Paracelsus.'[80] It is interesting here that when called upon to declare his learning at home, Victor turns to alchemy, even though his father's demonstration of electricity had supposedly caused him to reject it.

The bathetic and ridiculous portrait of the man of science offered by Krempe – ugly, dull and dismissive – is juxtaposed with the alchemists, whom Victor calls 'the masters of science', and whom he commends for their visions of 'immortality and power', given to views that 'although futile, were grand'. (Here the reader should not forget that the narrative, recounted in hindsight by Victor, is filtered through the beliefs he holds after his successful creation of the creature, when he sees the dangers, as well as the glory, of his endeavour). But while Victor refuses to go to the lectures of 'that little conceited figure', M. Krempe, he is drawn by curiosity and idleness to the lecturing room of Monsieur Waldman, an altogether more attractive figure:

> He appeared about fifty years of age, but with an aspect expressive of the greatest benevolence; a few grey hairs covered his temples, but those at the back of his head were nearly black. His person was short, but remarkably erect; and his voice the sweetest I had ever heard.[81]

Waldman's insight and kindness mark him as a man of vision, a 'scientist-as-hero', to use the phrase of Tess Cosslett, who appealed to those notions of genius favoured by the Romantic poets.[82] Waldman's attitude to Victor's alchemical heritage is more forgiving, as Waldman sees their work as a seamless continuum with modern practitioners of the discipline of chemistry.

> 'The ancient teachers of this science,' said he, 'promised impossibilities, and performed nothing. The modern masters promise very little; they know that metals cannot be transmuted, and that the elixir of life is a chimera. But these philosophers, whose hands seem only made to dabble in dirt, and their eyes to pore over the microscope or crucible, have indeed performed miracles. They penetrate into the recesses of nature, and show how she works in her hiding places. They ascend into the heavens: they have discovered how the blood circulates, and the nature of the air we breathe. They have acquired new and almost unlimited powers; they can command the thunders of heaven, mimic the earthquake, and even mock the invisible world with its own shadows.'

Victor Frankenstein finds here an enquiry compatible with his own quest. Waldman's dignified treatment of the alchemists, delivered 'without presumption or affectation' excites Victor's admiration. Agrippa and Paracelsus, he says, 'were men to whose indefatigable zeal modern philosophers were indebted for most of the foundation of their knowledge'. But when Victor becomes a disciple of Waldman's chemistry, an apprentice of his laboratory, he is also encouraged by Waldman to pursue 'every branch of natural philosophy'.[83]

Waldman is thus an important figure in Victor's science, yet he is an unusual 'man of science', a generalist in a period of increasing specialisation, an historian of science in a period consumed by a desire for the new and the innovative. Indeed, in the 1831 edition, Waldman's influence over Victor is almost preternatural, as if Waldman possessed the powers of the *magus* himself: his words appeared to Victor as 'the words of fate, enounced to destroy me', at whose sound, Victor says, 'I felt as if my soul were grappling with a palpable enemy; one by one the various keys were touched which formed the mechanism of my being: chord after chord was sounded, and soon my mind was filled with one thought, one conception, one purpose'.[84] Under Waldman's influence, Victor becomes a model student, applying himself with avidity to his studies, improving rapidly. 'My ardour was indeed the astonishment of the students; and my proficiency, that of the masters.' Victor's studies are still marked by passion and imagination (not the purposeful, systematic dullness of rationality), and indeed he relates that Professor Krempe often asked him, 'with a sly smile' how his studies of 'Cornelius Agrippa went on?'[85]

It is clear, then, that Victor has not abandoned alchemy or magic, but has supplemented it. The 'elixir of life' is not forgotten, but is pursued by another route, that of modern scientific chemistry and physiology. Lured by his thirst for discovery, his studies take him beyond the limits of agreed knowledge. 'None but those who have experienced them can conceive of the enticements of science. In other studies you go as far as others have gone before you, and there is nothing more to know; but in a scientific pursuit there is continual food for discovery and wonder'. Indeed, it is at this stage, 'animated by an almost supernatural enthusiasm', that Victor's enquiry takes on a new dimension. His enquiry now expands to tackle the 'bold' question: 'Whence . . . did the principle of life proceed?', which he begins to approach through the 'science of anatomy'. 'To examine the causes of life, we must first have recourse to death. I became acquainted with the science of anatomy: but this was not sufficient; I must also observe the natural decay and corruption of the human body'.[86] Victor's study of life begins with what might seem a perverse step, an examination of death, corruption and putrefaction. Yet this was a rhetorical, and pedagogical, move made by many contemporary physiologists. The writings of John Hunter, John Abernethy and William Lawrence, for example, all begin their analysis of the nature of life by comparing the properties of live matter to that which is dead. The distinguished surgeon and anatomist John Hunter, in his lectures in 1787, argued that the 'simple idea of life' is 'the principle of self-preservation, preventing matter from falling into dissolution', and 'preserving it from putrefaction'.[87] William Lawrence argued in his lecture 'On Life', delivered the Royal College of Surgeons in London in 1816, that 'The matter that surrounds us is divided into two great classes, living and dead.'[88]

In pursuing the origins of life amongst the manifestations of death, Victor has recourse to graveyards and charnel houses (repositories of bones). The scene of his science shifts from Waldman's university laboratory to the churchyard, and from day to night. His father's education has taught him not to be afraid of these abodes of horror, and we may picture him as the grave-robbing anatomist, fearlessly fossicking amongst the putrefying corpses of the recently buried.[89] 'I saw how the fine form of man was degraded and wasted; I beheld the corruption of death succeed to the blooming cheek of life; I saw how the worm inherited the wonders of the eye and brain.' Victor seems to be turning away from the enlightenment science that valued open and public knowledge demonstrated and verified by the lecture and experiment. In his graveyard laboratory, experiment is undertaken at night, out of sight and in secret. But although Victor walks on the dark side of science, he continues to experience enlightenment.

> I paused, examining and analysing all the minutiae of causation, as exemplified in the change from life to death, and death to life, until from the midst of this darkness a sudden light broke in upon me – a light so brilliant and wondrous, yet so simple, that while I became dizzy with the immensity of the prospect which it illustrated, I was surprised that among so many men of genius who had directed their inquiries towards the same science, that I alone should be reserved to discover so astonishing a secret.

The language of enlightenment here associates Victor's breakthrough with the discourse of modern science, even though it was a work of labour and toil that did not open 'upon me at once . . . like a magic scene' (a reference to the sudden appearance of an image in a magic lantern or slide show, rather than the work of a magician).[90]

His discovery is, however, not scientific in its nature, as it remains a secret. Scientific knowledge, as had been the case from the seventeenth century, was knowledge that was verifiable in public. 'Free and open communication of research is regarded as . . . a major component of the ethos governing science.'[91] Knowledge that is not shared is not science. But Victor's discovery is secret, and is a secret. Indeed, in his later explanations, he celebrates how his discovery remains a secret even to himself. The experiments which he has undertaken are manifested only by their result, not in practical or technical demonstration, even though 'the stages of the discovery were distinct and probable'. The discovery is whole and indivisible. 'This discovery was so great and overwhelming that all the steps by which I had been progressively led to it were obliterated, and I beheld only the result'.[92] The balance of evidence here reveals that this discovery is alchemical.

The nature of Victor Frankenstein's discovery is such that those who understand it might be derided as mad, or ascribe it to 'some miracle'. Victor claims he had 'succeeded in discovering the cause of generation and life; nay, more, I became myself capable of bestowing animation upon lifeless matter'. The clarity of this description is not supported by the rest of Victor's narration, which clothes his breakthrough in the obscurity of esoteric secrecy. The only public demonstration of the research will be the creation of the creature. No other researchers may follow Victor, he says, because his experience has shown that the power he now possessed was too great for the mere human scientist to bear. Indeed, the only public knowledge demonstrated by his discoveries is not scientific but moral and political: 'Learn from me, if not by my precepts, at least by my example, how dangerous is the acquirement of knowledge'.[93]

The sole test of his experiment, according to the public standards of science, is to behold the results. The rest of the novel, then, functions as a record of that experiment, through to its final conclusions, as if *Frankenstein* is the *Philosophical Transactions*, a scientific paper gone to seed. Armed with the 'astonishing' power of 'bestowing animation', Victor sets about 'the creation of a human being', the accomplishment of which confirms his mastery. 'My imagination was too much exalted by my first success to permit me to doubt of my ability to give life to an animal as complex and wonderful as man.' So that the work might proceed more quickly, he settles upon one of 'gigantic stature, that is to say about eight feet in height, and proportionably large'. The work is arduous, but the reward is great.

> No one can conceive the variety of feelings which bore me onwards, like a hurricane, in the first enthusiasm of success. Life and death appeared to me ideal bounds, which I should first break through, and pour a torrent of light into our dark world. A new species would bless me as its creator and source; many happy and excellent natures would owe their being to me. No father could claim the gratitude of his child so completely as I should deserve theirs.

Victor remains in search of the secret, and his search remains itself secret. He says that he 'pursued nature to her hiding places', and 'disturbed . . . the tremendous secrets of the human frame'. In addition, he complains of the 'horrors of my secret toil', and explains how he kept his laboratory, his 'workshop of filthy creation' hidden 'in a solitary chamber, or rather cell, at the top of the house'.[94] In the pursuit of this knowledge, he neglects the passing of time and the seasons, and even forgets his precious family.

The creation scene itself, at the beginning of chapter four in the 1818 edition, was the first section Shelley composed. The pathetic fallacy of the opening lines – 'on a dreary night of November' – now seems banal and over-determined. But the scene summarises this ambivalent encoding of alchemy and science. 'With an anxiety that almost amounted to agony, I collected the instruments of life around me, that I might infuse a spark of being into the lifeless thing that lay at my feet'.[95] Marilyn Butler has astutely suggested that this implies the presence of scientific apparatus. Referring to the research on electricity in the animal nervous system conducted by Luigi Galvani (1737–98), her suggestion is that the 'spark of life' that is here infused is electrical in nature. 'Frankenstein may have calculated he needed a gigantic Voltaic battery'.[96] The term 'instrument' is indeed used in a similar fashion earlier in the novel, but Waldman earlier describes the alchemists as 'instruments' of research.[97] Victor's procedure also calls to mind the vitalist theories of contemporary physiologists such as the anatomist John Abernethy, who argued in 1814 that life was an effect of 'a subtile, active, vital principle, pervading all nature [. . .], and denominated the *Anima Mundi*.'[98] But as well as this medical science, the scene continues to recall the alchemical. The location suggests the gothic, both in its midnight hour, the inclement weather and his isolated garret. That he is alone and without witnesses testifies that this is not a scientific demonstration. Other aspects of the scene reflect an alchemical discourse too. Victor says that the 'spark of being' is infused into the 'lifeless' material. Infusion is a process known to modern chemistry, but it has an alchemical genealogy. While the term 'spark' hints at electrification, 'infuse' implies that he pours in a liquid, or steeps the material in a soluble solution, suggesting the presence of the *alkahest*, or universal solvent said to initiate alchemical transmutations.

— SECRECY AND SUBVERSION —

While scientific enlightenment was often associated with utopian radicalism in the early nineteenth century, the disruptive and subversive appeal of alchemy found a resonance in radical secret societies, including the Freemasons and the *Illuminati*. Georg Simmel suggests that reform and secrecy are structurally related, as both reformers and secret societies propose an alternative version of the truth or social conditions. 'Secrecy secures . . . the possibility of a second world alongside the obvious world, and the latter is most strenuously affected by the former.' As such, secret societies enter into combination with treason and subversion: 'the secret society, purely on the ground of its secrecy, appears dangerously related to conspiracy against existing powers'.[99] The *Illuminati* were the paradigmatic example of the fertilisation of radical politics by the alchemical culture of secrecy. They were, in short, political magicians, necromancers of revolution.

Alchemical research was secret, not merely in response to official persecution, but because it was a kind of knowledge which could only be revealed to the initiated (a version of this is maintained to this day in the Hippocratic oath pledged by medical doctors). Although this is much more pronounced in the third edition of 1831, where he talks of his desire to 'divine' the 'secrets of nature',[100] Victor announces in the first edition that to him, 'The world was . . . a secret, which I desired to discover'.[101] Victor's notorious secrecy, and the secret knowledge to which he aspires (the two are not the same), recapitulate the characteristic esotericism of pre-modern natural philosophy. This secrecy is moreover pervasive in the novel: as many readers note, ambiguity and obscurity are central to the novel's tone. Victor's secret, the secrets of nature, is kept secret throughout the book. We don't know how he does it. In this way, the novel itself functions as an alchemical structure: it replicates the secretive form and content of alchemical researches.

The novel does reveal its secret, of course, in the fact of the creature, the successful production of Victor's secret arts and the practical demonstration of the success of his experiment. The second volume of the novel, narrated by the creature itself, demonstrates the extent of Victor's success, and also the nature of his failure. In a sense, the creature's performance in these chapters assesses alchemy's secret knowledge by example. The creature's account of his education, his attempts at socialisation, and his unwitting rebuff by the De Laceys (blinded by social conditioning), make the creature an eloquent emblem for a generic, natural man. Without his own name, and variously called 'monster', 'wretch', 'demon', 'creature', 'devil', and 'fiend', the creature stands outside civilised society. Victor's rejection of the creature as it opens its eyes to life initiates his expulsion from society.

> His limbs were in proportion, and I had selected his features as beautiful.
> Beautiful! – Great God! His yellow skin scarcely covered the work of muscles
> and arteries beneath; his hair was of a lustrous black, and flowing; his teeth
> of a pearly whiteness; but these luxuriances only formed a more horrid contrast

with his watery eyes, that seemed almost of the same colour as the dun white sockets in which they were set, his shrivelled complexion, and straight black lips.[102]

Despite the beauty of the constituent parts, the monster is not beautiful. In coming together, the mix has become sordid and hideous, so that women and children instinctively recoil.[103] Although many contemporaries, such as Rousseau, argued that man possessed an innate innocence at birth, Victor perceives his progeny as vicious and a monster. 'I beheld the wretch – the miserable monster whom I had created'.[104] Victor's judgement about the monster is based on his appearance: and as such is constructed as an elemental revulsion. Yet it might be noted that this judgement is not simply one of disinterested aesthetics. Rather, the language in which Victor casts the creature is embedded within contemporary discourse on race and class difference. As a number of critics have observed, the novel's deployment of fear around the creature constructs him as both racially different and as a vision of the modern, alienated labouring poor – an allegiance most clearly expressed in the slave.[105]

Victor's rejection of his un-dead progeny, 'the demoniacal corpse to which I had so miserably given life', denies the creature family and domestic affection, and leads to his subsequent transformation into vengeance and malevolence.[106] The creature's reign of terror is not the result of the innate evil of the un-dead monster, however, but is traced to his unsocialised education. Despite Victor's abdication of responsibility, the orphaned creature manages to survive through his own instinctual abilities, somewhat like Robinson Crusoe on his desert island. Through his observations of the De Lacey family, the creature acquires language and literacy, and observes the effects of domestic affection. His voyeuristic education in book-knowledge begins with a difficult philosophical treatise by Constantin Volney, *The Ruins: or a Survey of Empires* (1795), through which the creature 'obtained a cursory knowledge of history, and a view of the several empires at present existing in the world; [and] an insight into the manners, governments, and religions of the different nations of the earth'.[107] In Volney, the creature learns not only about the world and history, but of the powerful desires that drive it, of '*self-love, aversion to pain, and desire of happiness*'.[108] In Volney, the manifestations of society and civilisation (food, shelter, clothing, love, family) arise naturally from the basic human wants and desires. What the creature learns in his voyeuristic 'reading' of Volney is that he is a savage, in that particular enlightenment sense of a being in the primitive condition of all mankind. From his innate yearnings, the creature discovers his humanity. His later encounters with Milton's *Paradise Lost* (1667), Plutarch's *Lives* (c. 100 AD) and Goethe's *Sorrows of Werter* (1774), offer the creature a moral inquiry into the conduct of the individual in society. From Goethe he reads of 'the gentle and domestic manners', and observes of his own 'feelings and condition' that he was 'myself similar, yet at the same time strangely unlike' other men.[109] The creature's unhappy realisation is that he has an innate capacity for reason and feeling, but that inalienable qualities of birth and origins deprive him of justice and society.

The creature's heartfelt yearnings for a wife (as both companion and mate) express the humanity Victor does not accept. That Victor is capable of repeating the experiment demonstrates that it succeeded because he understood the principle of the origin of life, rather than being the result of serendipity or the miraculous. The creature's infertility confirms his singularity, but also his unnatural hybridity: Erasmus Darwin had observed that, 'The reproduction or generation of living organized bodies, is the great criterion or characteristic which distinguishes animation from mechanism.'[110] Victor's justifies his subsequent decision to abort his second 'horrible and irksome' experiment in creation before the female companion is completed by reconsidering the future consequences of his action. Victor's hatred for the creature, manifested first in his aesthetic revulsion at his appearance, now addresses his kind or race. Victor's rationale is that with a female to bond and mate with, the monster will breed a race of monsters.

> Even if they were to leave Europe, and inhabit the deserts of the new world, yet one of the first results of those sympathies for which the daemon thirsted would be children, and a race of devils would be propagated upon the earth, who might make the very existence of the species of man a condition precarious and full of terror.[111]

Victor's fear, recapitulating conservative debate on slave emancipation, expresses a hatred akin to racism. In Victor's estimation, the creature's wretched monstrosity prefigures the future course of civilisation, concatenating fears of revolution, emancipation, modernity and monstrosity. This concern with the future has provoked many to read the novel's engagement with science as a prophylactic warning (and encouraged those who see it as an early venture in science fiction). The novel expresses doubts about the enlightenment doctrine of scientific perfectibility and of scientific progress, and voices an anxiety about the unforeseen consequences of scientific and technological change. Like Brown's *Wieland*, however, the debate on the nature of science and enlightenment hosted by *Frankenstein* articulates an enquiry into the state of society, gothicising both the spectre of radical reform and its political double, conservative reaction.

— NOTES —

1. Erasmus Darwin, *Zoonomia; or, the laws of Organic Life*, 3rd edn, 4 vols (London: J. Johnson, 1801), II, p. 63.
2. See Dorinda Outram, *The Enlightenment* (Cambridge: Cambridge University Press, 1995); Ernst Cassirer, *The Philosophy of the Enlightenment*, trans. Fritz Koelln and James Pettegrove (Princeton: Princeton University Press, 1951), Thomas L. Hankins, *Science in the Enlightenment* (Cambridge: Cambridge University Press, 1985); Geoffrey Sutton, *Science for a Polite Society: Gender, Culture and the Demonstration of Enlightenment* (Oxford: Westview, 1995).
3. Jan Golinski, *Science as Public Culture: Chemistry and Enlightenment in Britain, 1760–1820* (Cambridge: Cambridge University Press, 1992), pp. 188–235.
4. Theodor W. Adorno and Max Horkheimer, *Dialectic of Enlightenment*, trans. John Cumming (1944; London: Verso, 1979), p. 3.
5. William Dunlap, *Memoirs of Charles Brockden Brown, the American Novelist* (London: Henry Colburn and Co., 1822), p. 91.
6. Charles Brockden Brown, 'On the Cause of the Popularity of Novels', *Literary Magazine and American Register*, 7, 45 (June 1807), p. 412.
7. Charles Brockden Brown, *Wieland; or, The Transformation. An American Tale*, ed. Jay Fliegelman (1798; New York: Penguin Books, 1991), p. 3.
8. Brown, *Wieland*, p. 5.
9. Brown, *Wieland*, p. 3.
10. Brown, *Wieland*, p. 21n.
11. Dunlap, *Memoirs*, pp. 94–5.
12. Dunlap, *Memoirs*, p. 91.
13. *Literary Magazine and British Review*, IV (May 1790), pp. 336–41; *American Museum, or, Universal Magazine*, 11 (April 1792), pp. 146–9.
14. Warren S. Walker, 'Lost Liquor Lore: the Blue Flame of Intemperance', *Journal of Popular Culture*, 16, 2 (1982), pp. 17–25.
15. Brown, *Wieland*, pp. 12, 13.
16. Brown, *Wieland*, p. 26.
17. Brown, *Wieland*, p. 66.
18. Brown, *Wieland*, pp. 57, 59, 60.
19. Brown, *Wieland*, pp. 77–8.
20. Brown, *Wieland*, p. 149.
21. Brown, *Wieland*, p. 206.
22. Brown, *Wieland*, pp. 203–4.
23. *New York Weekly Magazine*, II, 55 (20 July 1796), p. 20; II, 56 (27 July 1796), p. 28.

24. Karen Halttunen, *Murder Most Foul: the Killer in the American Gothic Imagination* (Cambridge, MA: Harvard University Press, 1998), pp. 136–41.
25. Brown, *Wieland*, p. 226.
26. Brown, *Wieland*, p. 230.
27. Brown, *Wieland*, p. 226n.
28. Joannes Baptista De La Chapelle, *Le Ventriloque, ou l'engastrimythe* (Londres: De L'Etanville, 1772).
29. *Monthly Magazine and American Review*, I, 2 (May 1799), p. 135.
30. 'Ventriloquism', *Encyclopaedia Britannica; or, a Dictionary of Arts, Sciences, and Miscellaneous Literature*, 3rd edn (Edinburgh: A. Bell and C. Macfarquhar, 1797), XVIII, pp. 637–9, p. 637.
31. Leigh Eric Schmidt, 'From Demon Possession to Magic Show: Ventriloquism, Religion, and the Enlightenment', *Church History*, 67, 2 (1998), pp. 274–304.
32. Thomas Blount, *Glossographia, or a dictionary interpreting all such hard words . . . as are now used* (London: Tho. Newcomb, 1656).
33. Thomas Hobbes, *Leviathan*, ed. Richard Tuck (Cambridge: Cambridge University Press, 1991), p. 304.
34. Francis Hutchinson, *An Historical Essay Concerning Witchcraft* (London: Knaplock, 1718), pp. 8–9.
35. Schmidt, 'Demon possession', pp. 282, 284.
36. 'Ventriloquism', *Encyclopaedia Britannica*, 3rd edn (1797), XVIII, pp. 637, 640–1.
37. Brown, *Wieland*, p. 3.
38. Brown, *Wieland*, pp. 248, 28, 187, 189, 190.
39. Pamela Clemit, *The Godwinian Novel: the Rational Fictions of Godwin, Brockden Brown, Mary Shelley* (Oxford: Clarendon Press, 1993), p. 130.
40. Edmund Burke, *Reflections on the Revolution in France*, ed. Conor Cruise O'Brien (Harmondsworth: Penguin, 1976), pp. 262–3.
41. Charles Brockden Brown, *An Address to the Government of the United States on the Cession of Louisiana to the French*, 2nd edn (Philadelphia: John Conrad, 1803), pp. 48–9.
42. James Roger Sharp, *American Politics in the Early Republic: The New Nation in Crisis* (New Haven: Yale University Press, 1993), pp. 8–10, 92–184; Henry F. May, *The Enlightenment in America* (New York: Oxford University Press, 1976), pp. 252–69.
43. Brown, *Wieland*, p. 34.
44. Burke, *Reflections on the Revolution in France*, p. 265.
45. Gordon S. Wood, 'Conspiracy and the Paranoid Style: Causality and Deceit in the Eighteenth Century', *William & Mary Quarterly*, 3rd ser., 39 (1982), pp. 407–8.
46. John Robison, *Proofs of a Conspiracy Against all the Religions and Governments of Europe, Carried on in the Secret Meetings of Free Masons, Illuminati, and*

Reading Societies, 4th edn (London: T. Cadell and W. Davies; Edinburgh: W. Creech, 1798), pp. 10–12.

47. Augustin Barruel, *Memoirs, Illustrating the History of Jacobinism*, trans. Robert Clifford, 4 vols (London: T. Burton, 1798) I, pp. ix, xiv.

48. Robison, *Proofs of a Conspiracy*, pp. 501, 535, 14.

49. Vernon Stauffer, *New England and the Bavarian Illuminati* (New York: Columbia University, 1918); Richard Buel, *Securing the Revolution: Ideology in American Politics, 1789–1815* (Ithaca and London: Cornell University Press, 1972).

50. Jedidiah Morse, *A Sermon, Delivered . . . May 9, 1798* (Boston, 1798), quoted in May, *Enlightenment*, p. 262.

51. Timothy Dwight, *The Duty of Americans in the Present Crisis* (New Haven: Thomas and Samuel Green, 1798), p. 11.

52. *The Diary of Elihu Hubbard Smith (1771–1798)*, ed. James E. Cronin (Philadelphia: American Philosophical Society, 1973), pp. 454–62; *Diary of William Dunlap (1766–1839): The Memoirs of a Dramatist, Theatrical Manager, Painter, Critic, Novelist, and Historian*, 3 vols (New York: New York Historical Society, 1930), I, pp. 305, 316–17, 322–4.

53. Harry R. Warfel, 'Charles Brockden Brown's German Sources', *Modern Language Quarterly*, 1 (1940), pp. 357–65.

54. *New York Weekly Magazine*, I, 20 (18 November 1795), p. 157.

55. Robison, *Proofs of a Conspiracy*, pp. 119, 121.

56. Brown, *Carwin*, pp. 315–16.

57. Brown, *Carwin*, p. 316.

58. Robert Southey, *New Letters*, ed. Kenneth Curry, 2 vols (New York and London: Columbia University Press, 1965), I, p. 75.

59. Brown, *Carwin*, p. 317.

60. Brown, *Carwin*, p. 321.

61. Dunlap, *Diary*, I, pp. 338–9.

62. Brown, *Carwin*, p. 345.

63. Mary Shelley, *Frankenstein: or the Modern Prometheus. The 1818 Text*, ed. Marilyn Butler (Oxford: Oxford University Press, 1994). Further references to this edition unless otherwise specified.

64. Maurice Hindle, 'Vital matters: Mary Shelley's *Frankenstein* and Romantic science', *Critical Survey*, 2, 1 (1990), pp. 29–35, p. 29.

65. Anne K. Mellor, *Mary Shelley: her Life, her Fiction, her Monsters* (London: Routledge, 1988), pp. 89–114; Marilyn Butler, 'Introduction', in Shelley, *Frankenstein*, pp. [ix]–li; and Samuel H. Vasbinder, *Scientific Attitudes in Mary Shelley's Frankenstein* (Ann Arbor, MI: UMI Research Press, 1976).

66. Mary Shelley, *Frankenstein, or the Modern Prometheus (The 1818 Text)*, ed. James Reiger (Indianapolis and New York: The Bobbs-Merrill Company, 1974), p. xxvii.

67. Crosbie Smith, 'Frankenstein and natural magic' in *Frankenstein, Creation and Monstrosity*, ed. Stephen Bann (London: Reaktion Books, 1994), pp. 39–59.

68. Erasmus Darwin, 'Additional Notes', *The Temple of Nature; or, the Origin of Society: a poem* (London: J. Johnson, 1803), pp. 1–11.
69. 'Introduction to Standard Novels Edition (1831)', Shelley, *Frankenstein*, p. 194.
70. Shelley, *Frankenstein*, I, i, pp. 22, 23.
71. Francis Barrett, *The Magus, or Celestial Intelligencer; being a complete system of Occult Philosophy* (London: Lackington, Allen and Co., 1801), p. 180.
72. Shelley, *Frankenstein*, I, i, p. 23.
73. Barrett, *Magus*, p. iii.
74. *Encyclopaedia Britannica*, 4th edn (London: Vernor, Hood and Sharpe, 1810), I, p. 570.
75. Henry Cornelius Agrippa, *The Vanity of the Arts and Sciences* (London: R. Everingham for R. Bentley, and D. Brown, 1694), pp. 110, 312.
76. Margaret Jacob, *The Radical Enlightenment: Pantheists, Freemasons and Republicans* (London: George Allen & Unwin, 1981), p. 35.
77. Shelley, *Frankenstein*, I, i, pp. 24, 25.
78. Shelley, *Frankenstein*, I, ii, p. 27.
79. 23, 25 August; 9, 11 October, *Mary Shelley's Journal*, ed. Frederick L. Jones (Norman: University of Oklahoma Press, 1947), pp. 11, 19.
80. Shelley, *Frankenstein*, I, ii, p. 29.
81. Shelley, *Frankenstein*, I, ii, pp. 29, 30.
82. Tess Cosslett, *The 'Scientific Movement' and Victorian Literature* (Brighton: Harvester, 1982), pp. 6–7.
83. Shelley, *Frankenstein*, I, ii, pp. 30–1.
84. Mary Shelley, *Frankenstein, or the Modern Prometheus*, ed. M. K. Joseph (1831; Oxford: Oxford University Press, 1969), iii, p. 48.
85. Shelley, *Frankenstein*, I, iii, p. 32.
86. Shelley, *Frankenstein*, I, iii, p. 33.
87. John Hunter, *Lectures on the Principles of Surgery*, in *The Works of John Hunter, F.R.S.*, ed. James F. Palmer, 4 vols (London: Longman, Rees, Orme, Brown, Green, and Longman, 1835), I, pp. 223, 225.
88. William Lawrence, *An Introduction to Comparative Anatomy and Physiology* (London: J. Callow, 1816), p. 121.
89. Tim Marshall, *Murdering to Dissect: Grave-robbing, Frankenstein and the Anatomy Literature* (Manchester: Manchester University Press, 1995).
90. Shelley, *Frankenstein*, I, iii, pp. 33–4.
91. William Eamon, 'From the secrets of nature to public knowledge', in David C. Lindberg and Robert S. Westman, eds, *Reappraisals of the Scientific Revolution* (Cambridge: Cambridge University Press, 1990), p. 333.
92. Shelley, *Frankenstein*, I, iii, p. 34.
93. Shelley, *Frankenstein*, I, iii, pp. 34, 35.
94. Shelley, *Frankenstein*, I, iii, pp. 35–6.
95. Shelley, *Frankenstein*, I, iv, p. 38.
96. Shelley, *Frankenstein*, p. 255n.

97. Shelley, *Frankenstein*, I, iii, p. 33, ii, p. 31.
98. John Abernethy, *An Enquiry into the Probability and Rationality of Mr. Hunter's Theory of Life* (London: Longman, Hurst, Rees, Orme and Brown, 1814), p. 52.
99. Georg Simmel, 'The Sociology of Secrecy and of Secret Societies', trans. Albion Small, *The American Journal of Sociology*, XI, 4 (1906), pp. 441–98, pp. 462, 498.
100. Shelley, *Frankenstein*, ed. Joseph (1831), ii, p. 37.
101. Shelley, *Frankenstein*, I, i, p. 21.
102. Shelley, *Frankenstein*, I, iv, p. 39.
103. Elizabeth Bohls, 'Standards of Taste, Discourses of "Race," and the Aesthetic Education of a Monster: Critique of Empire in *Frankenstein*', *Eighteenth-Century Life*, 18, 3 (1994), p. 31.
104. Shelley, *Frankenstein*, I, iv, p. 39.
105. Franco Moretti, *Signs Taken for Wonders: Essays in the Sociology of Literary Forms*, trans. Susan Fischer, David Forgacs and David Miller (London: Verso Editions and NLB, 1983), pp. 83–108; and Chris Baldick, *In Frankenstein's Shadow: Myth, Monstrosity and Nineteenth-century Writing* (Oxford: Clarendon, 1987), pp. 86–91.
106. Shelley, *Frankenstein*, I, iv, p. 40.
107. Shelley, *Frankenstein*, II, v, p. 95.
108. Constantin François Chasseboeuf, Comte de Volney, *The Ruins: or, A Survey of the Revolutions of Empires* (London: A. Seale, 1795), p. 39.
109. Shelley, *Frankenstein*, II, vii, p. 103.
110. Darwin, *Temple of Nature*, ad. notes, p. 33.
111. Shelley, *Frankenstein*, III, iii, p. 138.

CHAPTER FIVE

Vampires, credulity and reason

Vampire controversy in the 1730s; vampire verse by Coleridge, Southey, Stagg and Byron; John William Polidori, The Vampyre (1819); Bram Stoker, Dracula (1897)

The vampire is the most notorious of the 'grim and grisly ranks of the Un-Dead', that genus of gothic monster, neither dead nor alive, first identified by Bram Stoker in *Dracula* in 1897.[1] According to many accounts, the vampire has a history as extended as the perversely prolonged existence of the undead, but in many respects, this history is a distorted and deforming myth. In the 1920s, the Rev. Montague Summers, one of the founding fathers of the new criticism of the Gothic novel, produced two influential works of vampire scholarship: *The Vampire: His Kith and Kin* (1928), and *The Vampire in Europe* (1929). With pedantic yet obfuscatory zeal, these two works explored a dizzying range of vampire stories and references across an impressive range of periods and cultures. His research was, however, based firmly in the work of nearly two centuries of critical analysis and antiquarian research. In strategy and execution, Summers's work sought to demonstrate the ubiquity of the vampire across global culture, from the primitive to the civilised, and to trace textual evidence for the vampire back into deep history: a myth whose 'tradition is world wide and of dateless antiquity.'[2] But rather than being 'ancient and everywhere' in Ken Gelder's phrase,[3] the vampire's origins can be located quite precisely in the mid-eighteenth century, a particularity that behoves careful historical attention. The vampire has a perverse modernity: a terror of recent invention manifested as a monster from time out of mind, from deep history.

Reports of vampire attacks, ever since the first from Central Europe in the 1730s, have debated questions of credulity, superstition and reason. Exploiting the gothic tone's creative uncertainty, enveloped in gloom and obscurity, vampire texts stage battles between reason and superstition. To eighteenth-century rationalists as much as nineteenth-century folklorists, the vampire superstition required authentication or disavowal. In the non-verifiability of the vampire (caught between reason and superstition, truth and fiction), the gothic novel finds an analogy for structures of moral inconsistency, confusing vice and virtue, and sexual perversity. Gothic vampire narratives, in prose and verse, deployed a scepticism about the vampire's truth in order to articulate a debate on codes of social behaviour (commercial, libertine and sentimental). The vampire texts do not offer a synthesis of their various constituent discourses, but do ask the reader to bring them into conjunction, to allow one discourse to elucidate, criticise or substantiate the others in a ramifying series of fears, histories, events.

— I. THE 1730s VAMPIRE CONTROVERSY —

The term 'vampire' was first used in English in a newspaper report, published in the *London Journal* in March 1732. The report, received by private letter from Vienna, announced the sensational discovery in Hungary 'of Dead Bodies sucking, as it were, the blood of the Living; for the latter visibly dry up, while the former are filled with Blood'. The report signals its strained credulity by describing this a 'sort of Prodigy'; that is, an amazing or marvellous monster, out of the normal course of nature, from which omens could be drawn: 'The fact at first Sight seems impossible and even ridiculous; but the following is a true Copy of a Relation attested by unexceptionable Witnesses, and sent to the Imperial Council of War'. The report stated:

Medreyga in *Hungary, Jan.* 7. 1732
Upon a current Report, that in the Village of *Medreyga* certain Dead Bodies (called here *Vampyres*) had killed several persons by sucking out all their Blood, the present Enquiry was made by the Honourable Commander in Chief; and Capt. Goschutz of the company of Stallater, the *Hadnagi* Bariacrar, and the Senior Heyduke of the Village, were severally examined: Who unanimously declared, that about 5 Years ago a certain Heyduke named Arnold Paul was killed by the Over turning of a Cart Load of Hay, who in his Life-time was often heard to say, that he had been tormented near Caschaw, and upon the borders of Turkish Servia, by a *Vampyre*; and that to extricate himself, he had eaten some of the Earth of the *Vampyres* Graves, and rubbed himself with their Blood.
That 20 or 30 Days after the Decease of the said Arnold Paul, several Persons complained that they were tormented; and that, in short, he had taken away the Lives of four Persons. In order, therefore, to put a Stop to such a Calamity, the Inhabitants of the Place, after having consulted their *Hardnagi* [sic], caused the Body of the said Arnold Paul to be taken up, 40 Days after he had been dead, and found the same to be fresh, and free from all manner of Corruption; that he bled at the Nose, Mouth, and Ears, as pure and florid Blood as ever

was seen; and that his Shroud and Winding Sheet were all over bloody; and lastly, his Finger and Toe Nails were fallen off, and new ones grown in their room.

As they observed from all these Circumstances, that he was a *Vampyre*, they according to Custom drove a Stake through his Heart, at which he gave a horrid Groan, and lost a great deal of Blood. Afterwards they burnt his Body to Ashes the same day, and threw them into his Grave. These good Men say farther, that all such have been tormented or killed by the *Vampyres*, became *Vampyres* when they are dead; and therefore they served several other dead Bodies as they had done Arnold Paul's, for tormenting the Living.

> Signed,
> Batruer, *First Lieutenant of the Regiment of* Alexander.
> Flickhenger, *Surgeon Major of the Regiment* of Furstemburch.
> – three other Surgeons.
> Gurschitz, *Captain* a Stallath.[4]

The controversy this account created in England was exacerbated by the status of the *London Journal*, which as the mouthpiece of propaganda for the ministry of Sir Robert Walpole claimed a reputation for reliability.

The story of Arnold Paul became the subject of much discussion amongst polite London society. *The London Journal*'s account engendered a series of replies in other journals, and the whole exchange was recorded in excerpts in *The Gentleman's Magazine*, the biggest selling journal of the period.[5] The pseudonymous essayist Philip Sidney, Esq., in *Applebee's Original Weekly-Journal*, 27 May 1732, noted, 'The late strange *Hungarian* story of the *Vampyres* ... hath occasioned many controversies in Conversation, whether in Reason we ought to yield any belief to it, or no'. Although Sidney found the truth of this account from Hungary difficult to establish, the sensational topic was appropriate to the crime reports and translations of foreign fiction for which *Applebee's Journal* was renowned. Lamenting that the 'Proposition' was 'incongruous to our senses', he replied that some natural phenomena – such as the magnetic properties of lodestone or the artificial incubation of chicken eggs – had similarly stretched comprehension when first discovered. Nonetheless, the essay concludes that in the case of 'the Vampyres ... our Reason will of itself determine it to be false', and that the testimony of the witnesses is a form of delusion:

> We may so far credit the Witnesses who assert it, as to believe they did not intend to impose upon us, but either thro' want of Capacity of judging, or want of Capacity of enquiring, have been imposed on themselves, and have only represented things to us, in the same Light they stood to them.

> This will effectually solve the Credibility of the Story, which gave Birth to this Dissertation, we may admit that those who attest it tell Truth as far as they are Judges of Truth, but we are not therefore to sink our Judgements to the same level with theirs, and receive as an object of belief a matter utterly Repugnant to Reason and our Senses.

Sidney reasserts that 'rationally and experimentally we know, that Death totally deprives [human Bodies] of all faculties', so that they 'are absolutely unfit afterwards, to act in such a manner as would be consistent with such Stories'.[6] In this way, *Applebee's Journal* finds in the vampire story an instance of the central epistemological problem for the mid-eighteenth century: how to establish the truth-value of reports transmitted in writing (where the report itself must be its own authority). Such questions of truth were central to the novel genre too: what was 'new' about the novel, Michael McKeon has argued, was the analogy it constructed between epistemological problems (questions of truth) and social problems (questions of virtue).[7]

The *London Journal* report signals the difficulty of establishing its own credibility. It legitimates itself by deploying well-known techniques for establishing the fact of events, but also reveals concerns about ambiguity and deception. These authenticating techniques were as well known from the novels of Daniel Defoe as the early journalism of the seventeenth-century newspapers. The *London Journal* report vouches for the credibility of the author and narrator by establishing their status of eyewitnesses. Nonetheless, there are some odd moments, as the narrative voice shifts between the undersigned surgeons and officers, putatively still narrating their own story, and the *London Journal* narrator, who in the final paragraph comments on 'These good Men'. Such authenticating techniques reinforce the probity of the investigation by showing how the officers of the enquiry were invested with the proper authority and education, how they deployed an empirical methodology, and interrogated persons of local repute and importance (the *Hadnagi* is the village elder, and the representative of authority in the locality). The *London Journal* report, although apparently only an enclosure in a private letter, also faithfully replicates the narrative structure and legalistic tone of the official report, elaborating the circumstantial detail of events, such as listing the organs from which Paul bled, and adopting a medical language to describe the condition of his blood ('pure and florid'). However, the scrupulous accuracy of observational detail is mitigated by the imprecise approximation of important facts concerning Paul's death (about '20 or 30 Days after' his decease, 'about 5 years ago'). As the essayist in *Applebee's Original Weekly-Journal* observes, the undersigned officers are not eyewitnesses to Arnold

Paul's vampiric attacks, but are only eyewitnesses to the villagers' stories. The whole is a retrospective relation of a series of events that happened 'about 5 years ago': despite the rhetoric of eyewitness observation, despite the legal language, despite the legitimating narrative structures of the official report, the entirety of the events are secondhand. The topic of the account is not the vampire, in fact, but the folk beliefs of a village in rural Hungary.

WALPOLE, THE NEW COMMERCIAL SOCIETY AND THE EXCISE VAMPIRE

As the *London Journal* was the foremost outlet for ministerial political propaganda, the vampire story was soon embroiled in political controversy. The leading opposition journal, *The Craftsman*, at that time enjoying its most celebrated and popular period, replied with a biting satire that deployed the vampire story against the government. The anonymous essayist in *The Craftsman* observed the story's celebrity: 'One evening last Week I call'd to see a Friend and met a Company of Gentlemen and Ladies, engaged in a Dispute about *Prodigies*, occasioned by a very remarkable Event which lately happen'd in *Hungary*.' The fictional narrator, Caleb D'Anvers, a lawyer and habitué of coffeehouses and salons, reports a 'Conversation' about this 'extraordinary narrative' between himself, a grave Doctor of Physick, who speaks for reason and philosophy, and a beautiful young lady – 'a great Admirer of strange and wonderful Occurrences'. The essay's gendering of credulity as feminine and reason as masculine is not accidental. The Doctor 'endeavour'd to ridicule' the vampire report as a 'romantick Story' (one that identifies with the genre of the romance), of the kind news-writers had recourse to during the 'dead Season' when real news was scarce. The 'young Lady', on the other hand, was impressed not only with the authorities who legitimated the story, but also with its air of verisimilitude: noting that 'the Time, the Place, and the Names . . . were particularly mentioned', in the manner of an 'authentick Account' rather than a fictional romance.[8]

Caleb D'Anvers, when called upon to adjudicate the dispute, reviews the account through his *'political Spectacles'*, by which means 'I soon discover'd a secret Meaning in it' in the *'allegorical Style'*, a mode adopted in 'the States of Hungary' because they are governed 'with a pretty hard Rein'. 'This relation of the *Vampyres* is a Piece of that Kind [allegory], and contains a secret Satire upon the Administration of *those Countries*.'

You see that the Method, by which these *Vampyres* are said to torment and kill the *Living*, is by *sucking out all their Blood*; and what, I pray, is a more common phrase for a *ravenous Minister*, even in this Part of the World, than a *Leech*, or a *Blood-sucker*, who preys upon human Gore, and fattens Himself upon the Vitals of his Country? [. . .] I look upon all *Sharpers*, *Usurers*, and *Stockjobbers* in this Light, as well as *fraudulent Guardians*, *unjust Stewards*, and the *dry Nurses of great Estates*. [. . .] It will not be deny'd that many of the *late South-Sea Directors* were Tormentors of this Sort; and I heartily wish that the *present managers of that Company* may not furnish us with some Instances of the same Nature.[9]

Drawing out the 'parable', D'Anvers cleverly finds extensive parallels: like a vampire coming from the grave, the corrupt minister's scheme of taxation plagues society long after his fall from office; like the manner in which Arnold Paul's corpse was found in the grave 'free from corruption', the remains of political corruption endure in the real world; and like the stake needed to kill the vampire, the corrupt minister can only be deposed by 'means of a certain Parliamentary emetick' – an election or impeachment.

The Craftsman's attack inserts the vampire account into a debate on political corruption, which it explicitly links with the commercial ideology of the incumbent ministry of Walpole. In the period since the revolution of 1688, England's conspicuous economic transformation had been led by the foundation of new financial institutions, such as the Bank of England (1694), and the South Sea Company (1711); in which stockjobbers and joint-stock companies enjoyed a new prominence. The new culture of commerce created a glittering and refined society of wealthy consumers, especially in London, conspicuously displaying their taste in ever-varied consumption of luxuries. Debacles such as the collapse of the stock market in 1720–1 (the South Sea Bubble) suggested a spirit of merciless and alienating competition engendering corruption, indebtedness and misery. Support for the new economic order – and Walpole's ministry – was strong among the Court (the King's followers), the great Whig landowners and the 'moneyed interest' (large financial interests in the City of London). *The Craftsman*, edited by Nicolas Amhurst, was at the centre of opposition to the Court Whigs, established to service the interest of the opposition leaders William Pulteney (a disaffected Whig) and Henry St John, Viscount Bolingbroke (a Jacobite and Tory).[10] *The Craftsman*'s attack on the ministry found a telling parallel between the new economic order's promotion of debt and financial innovation, and Walpole's systematic corruption by which the allegiance of 'place-men' was bought by the distribution of sinecures and lucrative contracts. Walpole was the subject of much personal political satire: frequently depicted as a kind of monster or leviathan, swollen with power and wickedness, or as a vast caterpillar consuming the life-blood of the country.[11]

The public notice occasioned by this sensational story in a ministerial paper no doubt appeared as a provocation to the opposition papers, especially as the story adumbrated a long-standing satirical figure, that of the blood-sucker, with which satirists had attacked tax-gatherers, stock-jobbers and corrupt politicians. The term 'blood-sucker' (an animal which sucks blood, especially the leech) appeals to the sanguinary principle that wealth and money are a kind of vitality that circulates in the economy like blood in the body, exploiting the 'hypothetical Allegory (betwixt the natural Body and Body politick)' remarked upon by one of Bolingbroke's pamphleteers.[12] Roger L'Estrange in 1668 had satirically equated 'a certain *Tax-gatherer*' with a 'sort of Blood-Sucker' found in hell, 'an Informing, projecting Generation of men, and the very bane of a Kingdom'.[13] John Trenchard, attacking the fraudulent practices of the stockbrokers of the South Sea Company in 1720, complained they were 'Blood-suckers of the People' who should 'make the people some Amends, by restoring the Blood that they have sucked'.[14] In such usages, the force that makes men prey on the vital force of others is commercial competition: blood-sucking is a metaphor for seeking personal advantage and by extension, for selfish greed and upward social mobility. In 1733, Charles Forman, a pamphleteer and political commentator, attacked merchants who export coin for personal advantage to the detriment of trade. Of these merchants (the forerunners of foreign-exchange dealers), Forman says:

> Our Merchants, indeed, bring Money into their Country, but, it is said, there is another Set of Men amongst us who have as great an Address in sending it out again to foreign Countries without any Returns for it, which defeats the Industry of the Merchant. These are the *Vampires* of the Publick, and Riflers of the Kingdom.[15]

The Craftsman, in the weeks and months prior to the appearance of the vampire essay (No. 307, 20 May 1732), is filled with monsters and blood-sucking parasites. Essay No. 306 (13 May 1732) attacks the tyrannical abuses of corrupt ministers, as being '*Monsters*' pestering the nation; that of 18 April 1732 calls for a bleeding of the rich veins of the Directors and proprietors of the South Sea Company. The figure of the vampire in *The Craftsman* No. 307 satirises the agents of the new commercial society: its politicians, the new financial innovators, stockbrokers, libertines and projectors, exposing their wealth, refinement and modernity as a kind of preternatural corruption. The vampire figures modernity in its commercially corrupting form, articulated both in economic and moral dimensions: venal business practices, autocratic government, tyrannical taxation, moral laxity, and sexual perversion.

The figure of the tyrant vampire was used in political propaganda later in the eighteenth century too. In Oliver Goldsmith's satire on modern society, *The Citizen of the World* (1760), a corrupt magistrate is described as a vampire, preying on the blood of his convicted criminals – reflecting Goldsmith's distaste for the judicial system which paid magistrates according to how many convictions they made. The mercenary magistrate, complains the narrator, behaves like a Hyena at first:

> naturally it is no way ravnous, but once it has tasted human flesh, it becomes the most voracious animal of the forest, and continues to persecute mankind ever after; a corrupt magistrate may be considered as a human hyena, he begins perhaps by a private snap, he goes on to a morsel among friends, he proceeds to a meal in public, from a meal he advances to a surfeitt, and at last sucks blood like a vampire.[16]

The vampire, to Goldsmith, embodies both luxurious and immoral corruption, appealing both to the haemovorous nature of the vampire, and the sense of civic corruption. During the French Revolution, the term 'blood-sucking vampires' was political shorthand for the commercial aristocracy, such as the Farmers General, who levied the taxes on food around Paris.[17] In 1792, Lord Malmesbury suggested that the Duke of Portland was so much under the influence of Charles James Fox that Fox was his 'vampire – he fascinates him, benumbs the operation of his reason & judgment & even of his conscience'.[18] The vampire here is measured by its effects on the nervous system, not its bite or preferred type of nourishment. In a range of texts, Chris Baldick has identified the significance of the vampire as a metaphor in the political economy of Karl Marx, as a compelling and grisly allegory for the modern economic condition.[19] Commenting on the passage of legislation limiting working hours, in 1864 Marx characterised the endless demand for labour in 'British industry, which vampire-like, could but live by sucking blood, and children's blood, too.'[20]

— ANTIQUARIAN VAMPIRES AND THE BIRTH OF FOLKLORE —

The political controversy in London in 1732 aroused by the story of 'the Hungarian *Vampyres*' established the demand for such truth-stretching prodigies. A Europe-wide craze for vampire scholarship emerged amongst learned gentlemen of varied disciplines, physicians and antiquarians especially. In Germany, the publishers of Leipzig – the centre of the German book-trade – churned out tracts and dissertations collating material on the vampire (see Figure 9). This flood of literature retold, and elaborated, the narrative of Arnold Paul. Biblical scholars and antiquarians searched for precedents, while medical writers issued dissertations assessing the

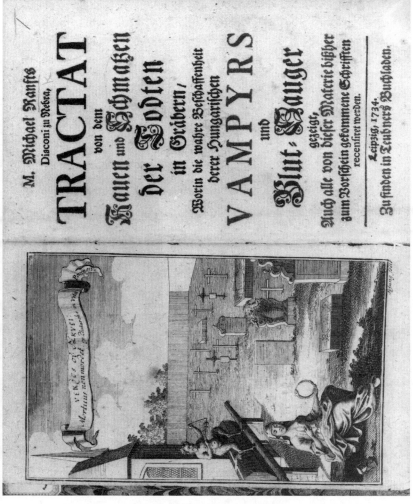

Figure 9. The Vampire Controversy: frontispiece and title page of M. Michael Ranfts, Tractat von dem Kauen und Schmatzen der Todten in Gräbern, worin die Wahre Beschaffenheit berer Hungarischen Vampyrs und Blut-Sauger gezeigt, auch alle von dieser Materie bissher zum Vorschein gekommene Scrigten recensiret werden (Leipzig: Teuber's Buchladen, 1734); British Library, London.

physiology of the blood-sucking revenants. Many reports replicated the concern for credulity and reason. One such was offered in the travel-journal by an anonymous 'person of curiosity' and member of the Royal Society (London), entitled 'The Travels of three English Gentlemen, from Venice to Hamburgh, being the grand Tour of Germany, in the Year 1734', published in 1744 in the *Harleian Miscellany*. This account offers a scholarly digest of geographical and cultural observation about the Hapsburg duchy of Carniola (now Slovenia), taking notice of local antiquarian research into the manners and customs of the 'Sclavonic' 'natives'. In particular, they notice that the locals 'pay some regard' to tales of 'Vampyres, said to infest some parts of the Country'. 'These Vampyres, are supposed the bodies of deceased persons, animated by evil spirits, which come out of the graves, in the night-time, suck the blood of many of the living, and thereby destroy them.' To the sceptical English eye of the narrator, such accounts are ridiculous. Tales of vampires, he says,

> will, probably, be looked on as fabulous and exploded, by many people in England; however it is not only countenanced by Baron Valvasor, and many Carnioleze noblemen, gentlemen, &c. as we were informed; but likewise actually embraced by some writers of good authority.

Taking notice of further scholarly research, the narrator accumulates an impressive-looking pile of references, delineated in the obsfuscatory and Latinate abbreviations of the scholar and pedant. Latinising the name of the physician Joannes Heinrich Zopff to 'M. Jo. Henr. Zopfius.', they describe his dissertation on vampires as 'extremely learned and curious', a joke suggestive of bathetic pedantry.[21]

A satirical reflection on such work was offered in 1738 by the French philosopher, John Baptist Boyer, Marquis D'Argens, in his 'oriental tale' entitled *Lettres Juives* (translated into English as *The Jewish Spy* in 1739), being, as the subtitle has it, 'a Philosophical, Historical and Critical Correspondence' between an educated Jewish visitor to Paris, Aaron Monceca, and a learned Rabbi in Constantinople. This epistolary satire, in the manner of the Persian tale genre, uses Monceca's detached and sceptical description of French culture to defamiliarise, and expose the follies of, polite society, the abuses of scientific and scholarly learning, and the superstition of the church. Monceca's orientalist yet enlightened values of rationality and materialism ironically contrast with the debased state of learning in the civilised world: 'Ignorance has in this Kingdom a firm Support from the Monks'.[22] In a letter reviewing the vampire controversy, Monceca notes that he has read 'the Relation of a Prodigy inserted in an 'historical Journal', referring the reader to the *Mercure Historique et Politique* for October 1736. As Monceca adds, the vampire 'prodigy' is primarily a question of knowledge: 'the facts contained therein are absolutely irreconcilable to Philosophic Speculations, and all the Efforts of the reasoning Faculty'. The report starts with a testimonial to its authenticity:

> We have had in this Country a new Scene of Vampirism, which is duly attested by two Officers of the Tribunal of *Belgrade*, who took Cognizance of the Affair on the Spot, and by an Officer in his Imperial Majesty's Troops at *Gradisch* (in *Sclavonia*) who was an Eye witness of the Proceedings.

The anecdote, located in the village of Kisilova, three leagues from Gradisch in Sclavonia, concerns the death of an elderly man, who returns from beyond the grave to bother his son for food. The son dutifully provides him with nourishment over several nights, until one morning the son is found dead. The village Magistrate reports the death to the Tribunal at Belgrade, who dispatches two Commissioners, 'with Instructions to examine closely into the affair'. Observing the fresh colour and 'quick and strong' respiration of the old man in his grave, their inquiry concludes that he was 'a notorious *Vampire*', and so has the Executioner strike a 'Stake thro' his heart'. These perplexing events defy reason:

> Thanks be to God, we are as far as any People can be from giving in to Credulity, we acknowledge that all the Lights of Physick do not enable us to give any Account of this Fact, nor do we pretend to enter into its Causes. However, we cannot avoid giving Credit to a Matter of Fact juridically attested by competent and unsuspected Witnesses, especially since it is far from being the only one of the kind.[23]

The letter continues with further references (to French periodicals) that outline the Arnold Paul story.

In the subsequent discussion, Aaron Monceca suggests that 'the strange Stories that have been related of Vampires' might allow his correspondent to 'judge of the Matter' by comparing 'the Circumstances of one Story' with the other.

> There are two different Methods whereby the Falsity of this Opinion, that dead Persons can return and suck the Living may be demonstrated; that is to say, the Fact may be shown to be impossible. First, by explaining the means of physical Causes all that is attributed to Vampirism, and secondly, by denying totally the Truth of these stories.

Monceca admits that 'the Names of the Person who have signed this Relation give such an Authority thereto, as serves to render it credible', but argues that in 'Philosophical Matters' (science), the opinion of such men (soldiers) is not to be trusted. Furthermore, 'People' might 'fancy that they have been sucked by Vampires' and firmly believe this to be a legitimate explanation of events, even though they have another material cause. As Monceca observes, the notion of vampirism is a true belief amongst the people, a kind of popular delusion, in which he discovers 'all the Marks of an epidemic Fanaticism'. He concludes: 'The Impressions of their own Fears was the true Cause of their Destruction ... This pretended Vampirism is the pure Effects of a heated Imagination.'[24]

The most celebrated example of vampire scholarship in the eighteenth century was that of a French Benedictine monk and biblical scholar, Dom Augustin Calmet, whose work received the 'Approbation' (formal approval) of the Sorbonne and the Benedictine order. His *Dissertations upon the Apparitions of Angels, Daemons, and Ghosts, And concerning the Vampires of Hungary, Bohemia, Moravia, and Silesia*, published in French in 1746 and translated into English in 1759, collated and assessed accounts of vampires, blood-sucking revenants, and incorruptible corpses, establishing analogies for them in biblical and classical sources, and in further travel accounts.[25] Like many deistic philosophers, Calmet thought that the prevalent reports of vampires demonstrated, the presence of God in the world. A world without such practical manifestations of the supernatural as apparitions, witches and vampires was akin to a world without God. His book confused the reviewers when translated into English in 1759: *The Monthly Review* opined that he believed in the miraculous stories even as he discredited them, 'so that, on the whole, we are at a loss to say, whether his book is most likely to do good or harm among the ignorant and superstitious; for whose instruction, however, he plainly intended it'.[26] Although not especially popular when first issued, Calmet's book gained a certain notoriety (and even an antiquarian 'authenticity' of its own) when translated again in the nineteenth century, as *The Phantom World* (1850), by the Anglican clergyman Henry Christmas.[27]

Calmet's method is scholarly (based on printed sources), not empirical: he repeats the narratives of Arnold Paul and D'Argens's old man from Kisilova.

> I shall therefore examine this question as an historian, as a philosopher, and as a divine. As an historian, I shall endeavour to discover the truth of the facts; as a philosopher, I shall consider their causes and circumstances; and lastly, the light which theology affords will enable me to draw from it some consequences, with a view to religion.

To enlightened English minds, Calmet's pedantic credulity gave evidence of the superstitious gallimaufry of the Catholic church. Although Calmet was careful not to state that he actively believed in the existence of vampires, his dissertation consistently refuses to make explicit truth-judgements, even when the documents themselves signal their fictionality or mediation.

> I write not in hopes of convincing freethinkers, and scepticks, of the existence of vampires, nor even of the apparitions of angels, devils and ghosts; nor to frighten weak and credulous minds with stories of surprising apparitions. On the other side, I do not expect to cure the errors of the superstitious, or the prejudices of the people, nor even to correct the abuses which spring from their unenlightened belief. [. . .] I must further desire my reader to make a distinction between the facts themselves which are related and the manner of their being brought about.[28]

Calmet's research is less interested in the factuality of the vampire than the prevalence and meaning of stories about vampires in popular culture. He quotes from 'poets and authors of little credit', because 'these authors' can be 'witnesses of the opinions which generally prevailed at the time'.

The study of the popular beliefs of the common people was also an investigation into 'superstition', a central target for the rationalising Protestant enlightenment. John Trenchard, in *The Natural History of Superstition* (1709), speculated that superstition, from 'Heathen Gods and Goddesses, Oracles and prophets, Nimphs and Satyrs' to 'Furies and Demons, most of the stories of the Conjurers and Witches, Spirits and Apparitions, fairies and Hobgoblins' proceeded from 'ignorance of Causes' and the deceptions of others. 'Tis this Ignorance of Causes, &c. subjects us to mistake the Phantasms and Images of our own brains (which have no existence any where else) for real beings.'[29] In 1762, an anonymous essayist argued that, 'The tyranny of *Superstition* over the minds of mankind has certainly been more extensive, more lasting, and despotick, than any other empire in the world ever was.' Coding superstition as the exploded notions of ancient times, he depicted the resistance of modern reason as a justified rebellion against a tyrant. Here, superstition was a species of Jacobite subversion, reliant on that belief in witchcraft and demons in 'Catholick countries; where ignorance and superstition, mixt with priestly cunning, have totally captivated and enslaved the minds of the common people'.[30]

Both enlightenment philosophers and Protestant deists argued that superstitious popular beliefs, such as the vampire, were being expunged by rational science. Even Calmet argued that by the 1740s, the vogue for vampire stories had already passed: They were already a popular delusion to be 'treated with contempt and ridicule.'[31] The French *philosophes* of the *Encyclopédie* (1751–76) dismissed the 'pretended demons' of the vampires as part of the 'history of superstition', kept alive only by Calmet's 'absurd work'.[32] In 1786, Horace Walpole expressed surprise and disdain that in an age when 'credulity and superstition are so far exploded', George II, 'though not apt to believe more than his neighbours, had no doubt of the existence of vampires and their banquets on the dead'.[33] Voltaire, in his *Philosophical Dictionary*, declared Calmet's work an historical scandal, a grotesque survival of superstitious unreason:

> What! is it in our eighteenth century that vampires exist? Is it after the reigns of Locke, Shaftesbury, Trenchard, and Collins? Is it under those of D'Alembert, Diderot, St Lambert, and Duclos, that we believe in vampires, and that the reverend father Dom Calmet ... has printed and reprinted the history of the vampires?[34]

As the eighteenth century came to an end, it seemed to men of education that the superstitious popular belief about vampires had been laid to rest, killed off by reason. However, at the end of the eighteenth century, study of popular superstition was influenced by a more credulous (albeit no less enlightened) investigation into popular tales by antiquarians. William Beckford argued that 'primitive fables' enliven the imagination:

> Tales handed down from generation to generation carry with them strong intrinsic recommendation. The wayward fancy of man is always apt to make an excursion beyond the bounds of this working-day world, and take its sport in the millennium of possibilities. But this playful disposition is most indulged in the careless infancy of the race.[35]

Beckford suggests that the 'bewitching power' of vulgar tales allowed scholars access to an otherwise inaccessible pre-history. Study of primitive fables gave evidence of foundational values of subsequent civilisation: either demonstrating the progress of refinement and politeness, or the original virtues now eclipsed by corruption and folly. Popular tales – such as those of the vampire – were an important resource for the period's increasing curiosity about the beliefs of the people. Such investigations, undertaken in the spirit of the enlightenment, reconstructed national 'culture' as belonging to the people. Popular culture is both countermanded and created in this research, as scholars make clear distinctions (and erect barriers of status) between the world of the vulgar and the polite, the superstitious and the enlightened. The vampire tales constitute an early and paradigmatic example of how popular superstition was collected and recorded by antiquarian research, a process that not only transformed oral tradition into written account, but also retheorised the value and significance of vulgar or plebeian culture. By attending to the oral stories of ordinary people, and scrupulously recording their orality (that they are spoken), the antiquarian established a text that, it could be argued, offered a transparent transition from the village elder's rambling anecdote to the comfortable study of the enlightened researcher. In the antiquarian collection, belief which was fugitive and unofficial was granted (or assumed) an official imprimatur.

II. ROMANCE VAMPIRES AND THE ROMANTIC POETS

The vampire's antiquarian historicism attracted the attention of a group of English poets, led by Samuel Taylor Coleridge and Robert Southey, in the last years of the eighteenth century. Turning to materials drawn from gothic romance and vulgar tales, and reading voraciously in travel accounts and antiquarian research, they sought to furnish their poetry with fresh and exciting images and language. Out of such popular tales and superstitions, they aimed to create powerful yet refined poetry of a new and radical form, simple, moving, and significant. Coleridge's first engagement with the supernatural vampires was through the low German terror novels of the 1790s. Johann Wolfgang von Goethe had, in 'The Bride of Corinth', demonstrated how low gothic material might be elevated into poetry. First published in Schiller's periodical *Die Horen* in 1797, Goethe's ballad depicted a seductive young woman who is revealed as a life-sapping spectre escaped from her coffin.[36] Coleridge's 'Christabel', written in the period 1797–1800, was not published until 1816, and was still unfinished even then. Similarly cast in the 'popular' poetic form of the ballad, gothic material is suffused through the poem in uncanny and enigmatic imagery. Despite a few half-ordered premonitions, Christabel never comprehends the threat posed by her vampiric assailant, a beautiful young woman called the Lady Geraldine; and indeed, in the poem's half-finished state, the reader cannot fully comprehend her threat either. Instead the gothic tone envelope the reader in a dark foreboding, catching at half-glimpsed terrors:

Then drawing in her breath aloud,
Like one that shuddered, she unbound
The cincture from beneath her breast:
Her silken robe, and inner vest,

Dropt to her feet, and full in view,
Behold! her bosom and half her side –
A sight to dream of, not to tell! (ll. 247–253)

Geraldine's deformed breast – in an earlier manuscript version described more dramatically as 'Hideous, deformed and pale of hue'[37] – recapitulates a popular superstition about witches uncovered in Coleridge's reading among the antiquarians. Forced by circumstance to share a bed, Geraldine bewitches Christabel: 'In the touch of this bosom there worketh a spell'. When Christabel wakes, her innocent happiness is bewilderingly discomposed, and she recognises in herself an unnamed and elusive sense of sin, while Geraldine is so refreshed with lively vigour that 'her girded vests/ Grow tight beneath her heaving breasts'. In 'Christabel', Coleridge turns his uneasy insinuation of sexual attraction between women into a gothic effect. As Arthur Nethercot concludes, 'What else could such a creature be but a vampire?'[38] Both Coleridge and Goethe construct the seductions of these female demons as supernatural, inviting speculation that they are vampires.

In Robert Southey's long orientalist metrical romance *Thalaba the Destroyer* (1801), antiquarian research and travel journals authenticate the poem's exoticism. Designed as 'a continuation of the Arabian Tales', the twelve-book poem had, he hoped, 'all the pomp of Mohammedan fable, relieved by scenes of Arabian life & then contrasted again by the voluptuous of Persian scenery & manners'.[39] Amongst the numerous exotic touches is a vampire: one of the walking dead reanimated by a demon, and destroyed according to the expert method of transfixion. Though dead, the corpse of the 'Arabian maid' Oneiza wanders the passages of her tomb by night, possessed by a demon. The hero Thalaba and his father-in-law Moath find her there, her lineaments changed by death to 'livid cheeks, and lips of blue'. Moath, urged by Thalaba, takes action:

thro' the vampire corpse
He thrust his lance; it fell,
And howling with the wound
Its demon tenant fled.[40]

To this brief interlude, Southey appends an extensive footnote that makes reference to the mid-eighteenth century vampire scholarship, noting in particular the narrative of Arnold Paul from D'Argens's *Jewish Spy* (1738) and a traveller's account of a related superstition of the 'Vroucolacas' in Greece by Joseph Pitton de Tournefort (1718), both extensively discussed in Calmet.[41] Although not entirely congruent with *Thalaba's* Persian location, the ease with which Southey's orientalism absorbed the Hungarian and Greek (Christian) sources of the vampire anecdotes was revealing: all exotic culture might be levelled into one primitive and superstitious discourse.

Inquiry concerning vampires continued to arouse the discriminating eye of the antiquarian too. John Herman Merivale (1779–1844), a 28-year-old lawyer with interests in antiquarian scholarship and poetry, published a series of articles on the vampire and other popular superstitions in John Aikin's popular miscellany *The Athenaeum*. Merivale, in the guise of 'Arminius', published a curiously antiquated poem, 'The Dead Men of Pest', related by a pedantic scholar (a 'learned pedagogue') in the vulgar manner of the seventeenth-century travel satire by Thomas Coryate, *Coryats Crudities* (1611). Described as 'a romance', Merivale's parody of medieval English poetry 'is built upon one of the most extraordinary events recorded in the annals of the human mind'.[42] The poem relates a visit to the strangely deserted 'towne of Pest' (now part of Budapest, Hungary), where a skeletal old man relates how the town has been depopulated by a 'demonne guest' named the 'vampire' who burst from his grave and 'suck'd our bloud'.[43] Suggesting in his explicatory note that his source for this information was *The Gentleman's Magazine*, and pressed by a corespondent for more details of these 'curious particulars', Merivale replied with two extensive summaries of popular superstitions regarding 'Vampyres or Blood-Suckers': the first, derived from the 1732 magazine articles, narrated the history of Arnold Paul;[44] and the second, a survey of Calmet's research.[45]

Such 'curious' and 'romantic' resources were not ignored by poets. John Stagg (1770–1823), the blind bard of Cumberland, versified the material in his 152-line ballad 'The Vampyre', published in his antiquarian collection *The Minstrel of the North: or, Cumbrian Legends. Being a Poetical Miscellany of Legendary, Gothic, and Romantic, Tales* (1810). To Stagg, the vampire history can be collated with 'Gothic stories prevalent in the North' of England, suggesting that as a gothic romance, the vampire transcends (or ignores) national boundaries. Stagg relates that 'the story of the *Vampyre* is founded on an opinion or report which prevailed in Hungary' asserting that 'in several places dead persons had been known to leave their graves, and by night, to revisit the habitations of their friends, whom, by suckosity, they drained of their blood as they slept'.[46] The vampiric attack on Herman by his recently departed friend Sigismund begins when he is disturbed by bad dreams at midnight. Rendered wan and distracted by a 'vulture-like' distress, Herman's decline worries his wife Gertrude. Herman explains that he is visited by Sigismund's restless ghost at midnight.

Close to my side the goblin lies,
And drinks away my vital blood!

Sucks from my veins the streaming life,
And drains the fountain of my heart. (ll. 71–4)

After 'banqueting by suckled gore' Sigismund retires to his sepulchre, and Herman is left exhausted, spent and in agony. Herman advises Gertrude to stake his corpse with a 'jav'lin' (l. 95) through the heart to prevent him suffering 'this horrid fate' (l. 93). Herman instructs Gertrude to wait beside his bed to scare away the demon just as Herman dies. She surprises 'The shade of Sigismund' (l. 120) at his work:

His jaws cadaverous were besmear'd
With clotted carnage o'er and o'er,
And all his horrid whole appear'd
Distent, and fill'd with human gore! (ll. 125–28)

With Herman dead, the town council open Sigismund's grave and find him 'warm as life, and undecay'd' (l. 140). Interring Herman beside him, they drive sharpened stakes through their carcasses to ensure that 'no longer they can roam'. In Stagg's capable hands, the gothic properties of the antiquarian vampire histories are translated, without losing enlightening and entertaining details, into verse. But the desuetude with which Stagg's 'The Vampyre' has fallen – despite being the first work so titled in English – suggests that his versification failed to ignite the imagination of his readers, and the critics. Such a fate did not befall the vampire tales of more self-publicising writers.

BYRON'S *THE GIAOUR* (1813): THE VAMPIRE AS MODERN TYRANT

In his long orientalist poem *The Giaour* (1813), Byron found in the vampire figure a vivid if obscure image of depravity and corruption. Concerned with the beliefs and customs of Islam, *The Giaour*, like *Thalaba*, took the form of an extended and fragmentary ballad recounting a violent love story. *The Giaour* is set against an indistinct context of warfare and violence, scenes of which are identifiable with the brutal suppression of the Albanian banditti in the Morea peninsula (the Peloponnesus) by the Turkish forces of Hassan Ghazi in 1779. Byron claimed he heard the love story recited 'by one of the coffee-house storytellers who abound in the Levant, and sing or recite their narratives' – although other evidence in his correspondence suggests the narrative was based on Byron's own rakish experiences in Piraeus.[47] In the poem, Leila, a pale and beautiful Circassian slave in the Harem of a Moslem warlord, Hassan, falls in love with a mysterious Christian, known only as the Giaour, a word meaning the infidel or stranger. When Hassan discovers his concubine's adultery (that Leila 'has wrong'd him with the faithless Giaour', l. 458), she is punished, according to a Turkish custom outlined in the poem's 'Advertisement', by being sewn into a sack and thrown into the sea. In revenge, the Giaour joins a band of Albanian banditti (the Arnauts), who kill Hassan in an ambush in the mountains. The Giaour, in exile at a monastery, is driven near to madness by his sense of loss, and is visited by Leila's spirit, unconstrained by her watery grave. The 'excessively melodramatic'[48] plot, reminiscent of a 'Grade C movie'[49] shows Byron's continued interest in the subversive appeal of Gothic vulgarity. By contrast, the lurid events are juxtaposed with explanatory footnotes whose mix of sober scholarship and dismissive irony was characterised by Marilyn Butler as an 'urbane Voltairean detachment.'[50] As Nigel Leask observes, The Giaour's hybridisation of the 'traditional ballad' and 'self-conscious antiquarianism', has, curiously, its own 'problematic modernity'.[51]

The poem's fragmentary structure, reflecting a complex composition over serial editions in 1813,[52] underscores its multiple narrators. The first section, detailing Greek history, is narrated by an educated Englishman bewailing the degraded state of the modern Greeks under Turkish rule. The poem then switches to Leila's tale of double murder and revenge (from l. 168), supposedly related by a Moslem fisherman, before a transition in the final section (from l. 787) to a friar, from the monastery where the Giaour resides, reporting his anguished, but unrepentant, confession.[53] The central tale of love and murder is written from the fisherman's Islamic point of view, to whom the Giaour is the alien intruder, and Hassan an honourable warrior. The poem works hard to establish a sympathetic portrait of the Moslem warrior, whose sensitive manners, civilised customs and manly courage the reader is asked to admire.

The vampire state underscores this differential equation between Hassan's Islamic felicity and the Giaour's afflicted state. The fisherman contrasts the Giaour's future state with the peaceful afterlife of the glorious Hassan (piously slain in battle), who is destined for the Houris of Paradise. The fisherman curses the Giaour with an unquiet grave, where, interrogated by the inquisitors of the dead, Monkir and Nekir, he is fated to wander forever in the 'inward hell' of Eblis, 'the Oriental Prince of Darkness'. Even in the grave, he says, the Giaour will not find peace, but will be transformed into a vampire, to feed upon his own family.

> But first, on earth as Vampire sent,
> Thy corse shall from its tomb be rent;
> Then ghastly haunt thy native place,
> And suck the blood of all thy race,
> There from thy daughter, sister, wife,
> At midnight drain the stream of life;
> Yet loathe the banquet which perforce
> Must feed upon thy livid living corse. (ll. 755–62)

The fisherman suggests that the Giaour is a kind of parasite, whose desires are perverted into illegitimate channels (adultery) and whose outward vampirism signals his moral corruption. The Giaour's love for Leila (explored more fully during his later confession) is transfigured into a self-destructive lust, overwhelming his family and his heirs.

The footnote appended to 'the Vampire' declares its reliance on the Southey's 'notes on Thalaba', relating that 'The Vampire superstition is still general in the Levant'. The fisherman imagines the loathsome state of the Giaour's vampirised corpse, undead in the grave:

> Wet with thine own best blood shall drip,
> Thy gnashing tooth and haggard lip;
> Then stalking to thy sullen grave –
> Go – and with Gouls and Afrits rave;
> Till these in horror shrink away
> From Spectre more accursed than they! (ll. 781–86)

Here again, Byron's footnote reveals his reliance on Southey's research in Calmet:

> The freshness of face, and the wetness of the lip with blood, are the never-failing signs of a Vampire. The stories told in Hungary and Greece of these foul feeders are singular, and some of them most *incredibly* attested.

These stories Byron finds '*incredibly* attested', although it is unclear whether he finds the testimony of such supposedly learned men incredible, or that it is incredible that anyone could doubt their attestations. There are further difficulties here. The fisherman's curse constructs the 'foul-feeding' Vampire as Islamic folklore, although the footnotes make it clear that Byron understands the belief is present amongst the Christian population of Greece and Hungary. The ironic distance the footnoter adopts towards the folkloric material, constructs the vampire as both exotic and archaic, a figure out of history. The bloody excesses of the vampire's quasi-incestuous violence mark the Giaour as a tyrant. As well as elusive connections to contemporary controversies about the Greek struggle for independence,[54] Byron courts an identification between his self as demon-hero and the Giaour. As Marilyn Butler suggests, the 'vampirish Giaour' is a 'Gothic self-projection', cemented by later writers, Polidori and Coleridge included.[55] In *The Giaour*, then, the vampire signals the corruption of heroic action in the modern world. In the modern Christian hero we see nothing but an ancient foul-feeder, a base and unlovely vampire recast as a stateless, nationless 'stray renegade'.

Southey, Merivale, Stagg and Byron all make an effort to signal their research amongst the mid-eighteenth-century vampire antiquarians, variously referencing the magazine reports, Calmet, Tournefort, and D'Argens. Their poetic invocations of the vampire establish and display their research in a scholarly machinery of notes, prefaces and appendices. Their theatrical erudition works an authenticating magic (legitimation): it locates the vampire in the past (as a figure from history, and hence, as a figure of history); and demonstrates the influence of the romance genre.

— JOHN WILLIAM POLIDORI, *THE VAMPYRE* AND BYRON —

The vampire of the romantic poets was celebrated most famously in John William Polidori's novella *The Vampyre* (1819), the first prose fiction in English with such a title. Polidori's narrative was, by a drawn-out process, the product of the same ghost-story competition, proposed by Byron at the Villa Diodati near Geneva in the summer of 1816, that led to Mary Shelley's *Frankenstein* (1818). Byron too began a story, abandoned after 2,000 words: an enigmatic gothic tale concerning a seductive and wealthy man, Augustus Darvell, on a tour of Europe and the Orient, whose mysterious death suggests that he is some sort of supernatural being, an immortal or revenant.[56] Polidori, attached to Byron as his personal physician, nonetheless nurtured hopes of a career in writing. His journal repeatedly reports that he was beginning his ghost story (18 June and 19 June).[57] Mary Shelley, writing in 1831, remembered that, 'Poor Polidori had some terrible idea about a skull-headed lady who was so punished for peeping through a keyhole – what to see I forget – something very shocking, and wrong, of course.'[58] Although no trace of this story remains, Polidori later completed a gothic novel, *Ernestus Berchtold: or the Modern Oedipus* (1819). A complicated tale of hidden incest, the narrator, Ernestus Berchtold, is a foundling who falls in love with and marries his sister, while Ernestus's twin sister Julia is seduced and abandoned by her brother. These terrible 'domestic afflictions', it is later revealed, are the result of his father's dealings with a demon. In return for wealth, the demon exacts a domestic punishment on the family, caused and revealed by the family's incestuous relations.[59]

In addition, on the '*ground-work*' of Byron's unfinished tale of the gothic immortal, Augustus Darvell, Polidori constructed a novella, *The Vampyre*.[60] The manuscript was sent by an unknown person to Henry Colburn, the editor of the reactionary journal *The New Monthly Magazine*. Recognising the manuscript's value as controversy (social and political, given Byron's notorious rakery and support for liberation struggles in the Levant), and without Polidori's consent or knowledge, Colburn published the story in his magazine and, almost simultaneously, as a separate volume. Both editions carried the fraudulent subtitle 'A Tale by Lord Byron'. The scandal was immediate.[61] Both Byron and Polidori were aggrieved: Byron exclaimed 'Damn "the *vampyre*" . . . It must be some bookselling imposture' and wrote a disclaimer to a Parisian English-language journal, *Galignani's Messenger*, that had repeated the attribution. He proclaimed, 'I am not the author and never heard of the work in question until now. [. . .] I have besides a personal dislike to "Vampires" and the little acquaintance I have with them would by no means induce me to divulge their secrets.' Byron's publication of his own fragmentary tale with *Mazeppa* was intended to prove his innocence of 'the thing in the Magazine'.[62] Polidori, who had written to Colburn the day after it appeared, stating 'The Vampyre is *not* Lord Byrons but was written *entirely* by me', publicly acknowledged his authorship in the May issue of *The New Monthly Magazine*.[63]

When the story was published in April 1819, the editor of *The New Monthly Magazine* had attached to it a series of prefatory introductions.[64] The first was a brief editorial statement composed by the sub-editor of *The New Monthly Magazine*, Alaric Watts, and altered by Colburn so as to fraudulently suggest Byron as author: a subterfuge that precipitated Watts's immediate resignation.[65] The second item was called the 'Extract of a Letter from Geneva', often assumed to be by Polidori, but which is more convincingly ascribed to another hand, perhaps working from Polidori's journal. The editor of that journal, William Michael Rosetti, argued it was Madame Gatelier,[66] and Polidori's most recent biographer, David Macdonald, has proposed an obscure hack called John Mitford, who later fabricated a scandalous memoir of Byron's sexual intrigues.[67] The third introductory section, signed ' – ED.' in the magazine and probably by Alaric Watts or perhaps Mitford, set about explaining 'The superstition upon which this tale is founded'.

The preliminaries to *The Vampyre* summarise extant vampire knowledge. Rather than suggesting that the editor could not assume readers' prior knowledge of this 'singularly horrible superstition', it has a tonal effect, locating the novella within discourse of antiquarianism and establishing for it a romantic-poet pedigree. The introduction repeats the 'curious, and of course, *credible*' narrative of Arnold Paul, laudably sourcing it to 'the London Journal of March, 1732', but subsequently censuring it as a 'monstrous rhodomontade'.[68] The introduction credits the research of Southey in *Thalaba* and its use by Byron in *The Giaour*; and recognises their reliance on Calmet and Tournefort. An ironic suspicion about the truth of vampire investigations helps secure the antiquarian foundations of the introduction, and at the same time, indulges the supernatural elements of popular tales. Watt's contribution to the debate reinforces the sexual element of the vampire stories. Vampires, he says, feed 'upon the blood of the young and beautiful' (an odd description of Arnold Paul, surely), and make their 'visitations on those beings [they] loved most while upon earth'.[69] *The New Monthly Magazine*'s research underlines, but also mystifies, how much Polidori has altered the vampire tale material. The vampire remains exotic, oriental, vulgar, folkloric, perverse, supernatural, superstitious, and to the sceptic, faintly ridiculous: but in Polidori's hands, he is now also a seductive rake, resident in an aristocratic culture and at home in the metropolis.

The nobleman eventually proclaimed as 'a VAMPYRE!' in the last line dissimulates his blood-sucking practices under the guise of rakery. Lord Ruthven is a sexual predator whose testified vampirism takes the form of sexual seduction. His haemovorous tendencies are a sexo-culinary perversion that merely underline his immoral pursuit of women. His interest in these women is not, however, simply in sex: he spurns the advances of the 'common adultress' Lady Mercer who 'threw herself in his way' and offered herself to him. Instead, Ruthven uses his 'winning tongue' (his seduction is verbal) to target especially the 'virtuous wife and innocent daughter', whom he approaches by the devious means of professing an 'apparent hatred of vice'. Cloaking himself in virtue, he is able to seduce and dishonour precisely those women who were most virtuous: 'those females who form the boast of their sex from their domestic virtues'.[70] His seductions do not have sex as their target, but a more moral quarry, virtue itself. Ruthven's strategy has a long heritage in eighteenth-century fiction, exemplified by Richardson's rake Lovelace in *Clarissa* (1748–9) and Laclos's Valmont in *Les Liaisons Dangereuses* (1789). Polidori suggests that the life of the morally virtuous is really a kind of hypocrisy, that moral certainty masks a more fluid construction of not virtue but vice. The rake and the vampire are both devices for exposing the epistemological complexity of moral judgement. The medium of the novel (even a short one) allows the particularities of case histories to be explored and dissected. James Twitchell has argued that the 'myth' of the vampire 'is loaded with sexual excitement; yet there is no mention of sexuality. It is sex without genitalia, sex without love – better yet, sex without mention.'[71] That there is no mention of sex in Polidori's tale is just not true, although it is true that there is no 'genitalia' (a term not coined until 1876). Reading this story as failing to express a more explicit sexuality is to fail to read it in an historically sensitive manner. To contemporaries, Polidori's sexual language was, if anything, too explicit, and certainly seemed as explicit as it might possibly be in a public journal addressed to women and men of moral character. As Polidori discovered, the language of libertinism deliciously adulterated mere sexuality with radical politics and social gossip. Like Ruthven, Byron's aristocratic status was permeated with a carnival of transgressive qualities: rebellion and liberty, banditti and revolution, atheism and idolatry, Jacobinism and subversion. Such libertinism, even when ironic, portrayed the aristocratic rake as a radical articulation of that particular kind of masculine sexuality explored in earlier gothic novels by Lewis and Dacre. Similarly, the model of female sexuality deployed in The Vampyre shares many features with an historically-enduring misogynist model of femininity: that every woman self-fashioned after the model of virtue conceals a hidden yearning for sexual expression.

The conventionality of The Vampyre's construction of both rakish masculinity and feminine passivity coalesces in Aubrey, the sensitive young gentleman he befriends in London. To Aubrey's aestheticised sentimentalism, the world is read as if 'romance', and like the heroine of Austen's Radcliffean parody, he thinks that 'the dreams of poets were the realities of life'. As Aubrey watches Ruthven, his sense of judgement wanes:

> the very impossibility of forming an idea of the character of a man entirely absorbed in himself, who gave few other signs of his observation of external objects, than the tacit assent to their existence, implied by the avoidance of their contact: allowing his imagination to picture everything that flattered its propensity to extravagant ideas, he soon formed this object into the hero of a romance, and determined to observe the offspring of his fancy, rather than the person before him.

Ruthven's self-supporting autonomy bewilders Aubrey's aestheticised perceptions so much so that Aubrey can only see his own desires. Ruthven induces in Aubrey a solipsistic retirement from the real world into a land of reverie and dream, where the mind's expansive powers might go unchecked. This retirement, like a narcotic, promises release, but threatens corruption: Aubrey is flattered when Ruthven agrees to undertake an educational tour of the Continent, hoping it will allow him 'to take some rapid steps in the career of vice'. Ruthven, generous towards those overwhelmed by vice, but parsimonious to the virtuously indigent, has a counter-sentimental note, reversing conventional morality, while broadly accepting its language and terms of value. In Rome, however, Aubrey is informed by his guardians of Ruthven's inhuman perversity, and is persuaded to break off his travelling arrangement. His guardians 'urged, that his [Ruthven's] character was dreadfully vicious, for that the possession of irresistible powers of seduction, rendered his licentious habits more dangerous to society'. They inform him that the hitherto virtuous women he had seduced, were now abandoned 'to infamy and degradation' and did not 'scruple to expose the whole deformity of their vices to the public gaze.'[72] Ruthven's seduction marks his victims (in a manner like that of disease) and permanently alters them.

By contrast, Aubrey's resort to antiquarian pursuits amongst the ruins of Greece offers normative pleasures, virile and sentimental, in the shape of the beautiful Greek woman Ianthe. While he makes drawings of ruined buildings, he also takes an interest in her tales of local folklore, especially as she believes these stories so earnestly. 'She told him the tale of the living vampyre ... forced every year, by feeding upon the life of a lovely female to prolong his existence for the ensuing months.' Although Aubrey tried to 'laugh her out of such idle and horrible fantasies', she proffers authoritative witnesses to prove her testimony. Her parents 'affirmed [the vampyre's] existence, pale with horror at the very name'.[73] Polidori's tale recapitulates the epistemological structure encountered in the folkloric accounts: folklore beliefs constitute a primitive belief system inimicable to enlightened reason. Despite the gulf of language, class and nation between them, Aubrey's love for Ianthe brings him to consider marrying her (which is to say, a normative expression of the kinds of desire perversely articulated by Ruthven). Aubrey's enlightened scepticism about vampires, ironically, merely underscores the distance between their worlds.

The scene of Ianthe's death – in a wood supposed the 'resort of the vampyres in their nocturnal orgies' – rudely obtrudes the vampire's libertine sexual world into Greek sentimental primitivism. Ianthe's 'lifeless corse' shows signs of vampirism:

> There was no colour upon her cheek, not even upon her lip; yet there was a stillness about her face that seemed almost as attaching as the life that once dwelt there: – upon her neck and breast was blood, and upon her throat were the marks of teeth having opened the vein: – to this the men pointed, crying, simultaneously struck with horror, "a Vampyre, a Vampyre!".

Polidori stages the epistemological problem of the vampire's verifiability as a drama of disappearance and reappearance. Though he has witnessed Ruthven's death, accompanied by mysterious auguries, Aubrey is horrified to find a man exactly resembling him on his return to England. Aubrey's bewildered claims that 'the dead rise again' do not convince society in the same way that such assertions, made without the narrator's confidence, fail to convince the reader. The recursive loop of the narrative's conclusion, as Aubrey's sister is dishonoured and married to 'the monster' Ruthven, completes the return of the vampire theme, as the last line proclaims 'Aubrey's sister had glutted the thirst of a VAMPYRE!'[74] The narrator refuses to clarify the nature of Ruthven's reappearance: at times it seems no more than a confusing likeness between doubles, whilst at others, it is a work of supernatural agency. At times, the narrator suggests Aubrey's insanity has bewildered his judgement, whilst at others it is only Aubrey who can see through Ruthven's dissimulations. The unverifiability of Ruthven's vampirism encodes the destabilising structure of his moral inconsistency, already seen in his peculiar confusion of vicious and virtuous, polite refinement and base urges, wealth and debt.

The scandal around the publication of *The Vampyre* did nothing for its reputation or that of Polidori. He was now associated with the grub-street hacks who promoted themselves through scandalous parodies of Byron and his verse. Whatever the skill of his narration, the story confirmed the vampire tale as vulgar matter, originating in a superstition of the lowest strata of society and the oriental periphery of Europe. In Polidori's hands, this gothic material was not even dignified by poetry, and was associated with the lowest kind of sexual scandal. Such effects are of course paraded as virtues by the text itself: this is a text which beseeches its own perverse rejection (noticeable in the careful way it distinguishes between the realm of the virtuous and that of scandal). Noticing distinctions between class and sexual identification, *The Vampyre* provides its own theory of how to read transgressive acts, mapping the epistemological problem of credulity and reason onto the social dynamic of the inconsistent verifiability of virtue.

— VAMPIRES AND THE SCIENCE OF FOLKLORE —

The Vampyre serves as a prototype for the nineteenth-century codification of popular culture as folklore. Alongside the editor's scholarship, the tale itself locates the vampire in the vulgar tales of primitive Greek society, here understood as a repository of ancient cultural knowledge. The term 'folk-lore' was first coined in English by a literary antiquarian, William John Thoms (1803–85), in 1846: that which 'we in England designate as Popular Antiquities, or Popular Literature, would be most aptly described by a good Saxon compound, Folk-Lore, – The Lore of the People'.[75] Thoms proposes that the term 'folk-lore' has an origin in deep Saxon history (giving a gothic tincture to the debate), although a more immediate precedent would have been the German *Volkskunde*. The term gained popularity amongst those scholars and scientists engaged in the collection and classification of primitive belief and thought of the people. In the mid-nineteenth century, the increasing intellectual prestige of this 'serious cultural inquiry'[76] manifested an increased method-ological introspection, and the foundation of institutions for folklore study (the Folk-Lore Society in 1878; and a specialised journal, *The Folk-Lore Record*, in 1878). Disciplinary self-consciousness brought new rigour and confidence to the handling of epistemological uncertainty in folk-lore study. The Russian folklorist William Ralston (1828–89) displayed little sign of nervousness about credulity when he instructed:

> It is impossible to impress too strongly on collectors the absolute necessity of accurately recording the stories they hear, and of accompanying them by ample references for the sake of verification. The temptation to alter, to piece together, and to improve, is one which many minds find extremely seductive; but yielding to it deprives the result of any value, except for the purposes of mere amusement.[77]

The new folklore discipline was to adhere to principles and practices constructed as 'scientific'. From such self-conscious methodology, folklore could be constructed as a 'discipline' alongside anthropology, with which it shared many interests. But while folklore considered itself the study of one's own culture (down the scale of class to the vulgar and peasants), in anthropology the object was the comparative study of multiple cultures (across cultural difference).[78] The ideological and political importance of the new folklorist's object of study was founded in increasing percep-tion that the common people had preserved in their folklore the unique virtues and founding principles of the nation. Just as primitive English liberty was identified in the martial vigour of Arthurian romance, so too the ancient superstitions of central Europe confirmed the pervasive Catholic tyranny.

Mid-nineteenth-century folklore research on vampires continued to rely heavily on eighteenth-century antiquarian speculations, such as those by D'Argens and Calmet. Elihu Rich's article on 'Vampires' for Edward Smedley's *The Occult Sciences* summarised Calmet's *Dissertation* (1746), itself retranslated in 1850 by Henry Christmas.[79] The English anatomist Herbert Mayo (1796–1852), in a book entitled *The Truths Contained in*

Popular Superstitions (1848), offered scientific explanations for a range of supernatural or superstitious phenomena. Dependent on Calmet, Mayo explained vampirism as a medical state (the near-death experience, in unconsciousness), which he calls the 'death-trance' or 'suspended animation' (from the German '*scheintod*').[80] The leading British anthropologist of the nineteenth century, Edward Tylor, argued in *Primitive Culture* (1871) that such 'nocturnal demon[s]' as vampires were not 'mere creations of groundless fancy', but had 'causes conceived in spiritual form to account for specific facts of wasting disease' and nightmare. Because, says Tylor, 'certain patients are seen becoming day by day, without apparent cause, thin, weak, and bloodless', primitive man responds by 'producing' a 'satisfactory explanation' in the world of spirits. The primitive invents the 'doctrine' that 'there exist certain demons which eat out the souls or hearts or suck the blood of their victims'.[81] Tylor's research, reliant on Calmet, follows other Victorian materialists such as Mayo, in ascribing a core physiological condition (trance or consumption) to which the folklore is a 'savage' explanation. Recourse to superstition such as the vampire, Tylor suggests, is a kind of atavism, a return to barbarous ancestral beliefs, a falling back from modernity into deep gothic history.[82]

The research of Victorian materialist folklorists described a cycle of credulity: the scientific method of folklore study authenticated the collection and analysis of popular superstitions; the properly sceptical scientist offered material explanation for primitive beliefs of folklore; the folklorist, disseminating primitive folklore belief beyond their core culture, established key figures, such as the vampire, as ubiquitous. In these conditions, the speculative and congenitally credulous posture of the fiction-writer located fertile creative potential in vampire folklore. There was a considerable body of vampire fictions in the nineteenth century, although space necessitates that this chapter engages in depth with but one example, Stoker's *Dracula*. Charlotte Brontë's *Jane Eyre* (1847), George Eliot's *Middlemarch* (1847), and Charles Dickens's *Bleak House* (1853), found the vampire motif a powerful metaphor. In *Jane Eyre*, for example, Mr Rochester's insane wife, Bertha Mason-Rochester, locked away in the attic of Thornfield House, is described by Jane as having a 'discoloured face – it was a savage face', with 'red eyes, and the fearful blackened inflation of the lineaments; . . . the lips were swelled and dark; the brow furrowed: the black eyebrows widely raised over the bloodshot eyes.' The disfigured face of the madwoman, Jane concludes, reminded her 'Of the foul German spectre – the vampire.'[83] Jane's imagination makes the analogy to the literary property of the vampire in order to highlight how the scene's paralysing terror was produced by her own credulous misgivings. Sheridan Le Fanu's novella 'Carmilla' (1872) produces and ironises the credulous construction of the vampire in Laura's seduction by the beautiful female vampire, Carmilla. Located in Styria, an Austrian province near Hungary, the story establishes the vampire or *oupir* as an 'appalling' local superstition. In the winding-up of the story, Carmilla is revealed as the demon vampire of the Countess Mircalla Karnstein, a fact 'proven' by statement and demonstration: even the sceptical state that 'it is difficult to deny, or even to doubt, the existence of such a phenomenon as the Vampire'. Le Fanu offers the reader only Vordenburg's 'voluminous digest' of the 'curious lore', derived from Calmet, ironically portrayed as a 'minute and laborious investigation of the marvellously authenticated tradition of Vampirism'.[84] In 'Carmilla', the epistemological problem of the vampire is a contest between the persuasive pathos of fiction, in which Carmilla's seduction of Laura is represented as a verifiable vampirism, and the arcane but bathetic research of the antiquarians.

— III. HISTORY, THE VAMPIRE AND *DRACULA* —

The ironic prefatory note appended to the beginning of Bram Stoker's *Dracula* (1897), explaining the fictional editor's work of arrangement and transcription, implies that the volume's purpose is broadly within the bounds of folkloric antiquarianism: a collection and summary of an investigation of the phenomenon of the vampire, in which this folkloric 'monster' is shown to be pursued, overtaken and defeated by the actions of modern science. The 'history' of the vampire it relates, 'almost at variance with the possibilities of latter-day belief', is defended from error by an array of modern strategies of recording, reliant on the interpretation of observed phenomena, pursued in discourses from medicine, to legal and commercial records, and travel journals. The novel's self-conscious modernity relies on the polyphonic variety instanced in its collection of papers, to which the author has acted only as editor, placing them in sequence and eliding extraneous matter.[85] The novel is composed of fragments supposedly inscribed, typed and recorded by a number of different people in a range of different modes: diary, shorthand journal, familiar letter, bills of exchange, newspaper cuttings and official reports. New media technologies are enthusiastically adopted into the fabric of the novel, underlining the discursive modernity of the novel: shorthand, 'phonograph' (a device which records the voice on wax cylinders, invented in 1877), the telegram and the typewriter.[86] Modern science in the novel is especially associated with Dr John Seward's variety of experimental and institutional medical psychiatry, played out in his mode of observation and narration as much as his treatment of the 'zoophagous' lunatic Renfield or the vampirised Lucy. Professor Van Helsing, by contrast, is a curious hybrid, a linguistically challenged polymath whose research incorporates recent medical innovations (such as blood transfusion) alongside para-scientific practices such as mesmerism and hypnotism; as well as an interest in the antiquarian and metaphysical.[87]

Dracula begins with a twofold journey: a train journey east into Hungary, and back into the uncivilised, primitive world of folklore. Harker, adopting the techniques of travel writing, records his curiosity about exotic places, but also makes careful record of modes of transport and places of rest (railways and coaches, hotels and inns). Stoker's notes of his research record his reliance on Victorian travel guides (like Baedecker) and travel accounts.[88] The journey is nonetheless enveloped by an obscuring gothic tone. Despite his preparatory reading, he is not well-informed and repeatedly asks the 'Count' for explanations. As Harker nears his destination, his journey traverses time as well as space: the well-ordered train timetables and light-filled stations give way to a more disordered and chaotic experience that is, though unstated, barbarous. Finally, as civilisation is left behind, railways give way to carriages, and German cities give way to increasingly orientalised locations populated by superstitious peasants. The gathering gloom surrounding Harker culminates in a long nightmarish journey by night in a *calèche* besieged by wolves. In his journey to Transylvania, Harker travels back to a pre-modern feudal world populated by uneducated and fearful peasants: the land of folklore and superstition.

The novel's author, Bram Stoker, performed this journey in the library of the British Museum in London. For Stoker, the search for Dracula was a kind of scholarship. The novel produces its own drama of scholarship when Harker notes, before departure, that,

> Having some time at my disposal when in London, I had visited the British Museum and made search amongst the books and maps of the library regarding Transylvania; it had struck me that some foreknowledge of the country could hardly fail to have some importance in dealing with a noble of that country.[89]

Harker's construction of scholarship as the preserve of leisure (not labour) contrasts both with his lowly status as a recently qualified lawyer and the novel's tawdry self-representation as a sensation shocker, bound in yellow boards. Theatricalising the scene of research on the first page of the novel prepares the unwary reader for the later appearance of recondite knowledge of specialist disciplines, from undigested medical reportage to arcane orientalist folklore to concentrated and weighty history.

Stoker transforms the vampire historiography by grafting onto it an unrelated, but symbolically resonant, Eastern European history. He identifies Count Dracula with a specific historical figure, albeit of somewhat controversial bearing and lineage. This particularity renders the novel's engagement with history more richly textured, but also less metaphorically unstable (fixity inducing simplicity). Dracula relates to Harker his allegiance to the dynasty or house of Dracula, through which he lays claim to a long aristocratic tradition of heroism and chivalry. In speaking of the history of Transylvania, Harker notes the odd effect wrought by his aristocratic pride in his 'house': 'he spoke as if he had been present' at all the significant battles in the history of Transylvania. '"We Szekelys have a right to be proud, for in our veins flows the blood of many brave races who fought as the lion fights, for lordship.' Adopting an aristocratic discourse, Dracula takes pride in his family's lineage, or blood-lines. To the Dracula family, he states, 'for centuries was trusted the guarding of the frontier of Turkeyland', referring to the keenly contested border between Christian Europe and the Muslim Ottoman empire.[90] The blood-line of the Draculas is gauged in the blood spilt in their defence of the cross and the King.

The dynastic history related by Dracula to Harker is, however, deliberately obscure, fusing a variety of different historical figures in their common cause of liberty. The house of Dracula, the novel proposes, organised both Wallachian resistance to the Turk, and also to Hungarian overlords:

> for our spirit would not brook that we were not free. Ah, young sir, the Szekelys
> – and the Dracula as their heart's blood, their brains, and their swords – can
> boast a record that mushroom growths like the Hapsburgs and the Romanoffs
> can never reach.[91]

Dracula recodes ancient liberty as a blood-line: representing the spirit of Wallachian liberty in the Dracula clan, whose endurance he ruefully compares with the comparatively recent appearance of the ruling imperial families of Austro-Hungary and Russia (Hapsburg and Romanoff, respectively). Count Dracula claims – or assumes – a blood relation with a notorious Wallachian warlord (or Voïvode), now popularly known as Vlad the Impaler. The events Dracula describes occurred in 1460, when the Voïvode Dracula instigated a rebellion against the Turkish rule by launching a daring raid across the Danube, deep into Turkish territory. In the face of vastly superior forces, he had to fall slowly back in retreat, laying waste to his own territory whilst launching damaging raids on the enemy. His incursions were characterised by the deliberate and widespread use of terror as a weapon: Vlad's favourite method of execution was live impalement, and there were many large-scale massacres of peasant non-combatants (in the town of Amlas on 24 August 1460, St Bartholomew's Day, there were 20,000 killed).[92] His notoriety spread widely, even after his defeat and capture: in the fifteenth century there were histories of his exploits with titles like:

> The shocking story of a Monster and Beserker called Dracula, who committed such unchristian deeds as killing men by placing them on stakes, hacking them to pieces like cabbage, boiling mothers and children alive and compelling men to acts of cannibalism.[93]

Accounts of the Voïvode Dracula's atrocities, circulated by myriad enemies who sought to discredit him, 'soon portrayed him as one of the great demented psychopaths of history'; while others cast him as an heroic Christian crusader or, as in post-war revisionist Rumanian history, liberator of the Wallachians.[94] Dracula's own account of his history is something of a whitewash.

Count Dracula's autobiography, recorded through the mediation of Harker's prodigious memory, relies on the same body of work that Stoker had found in the British Museum Library concerning the folklore of the vampire. Versions of Dracula's story are found in the eccentric travel journal of Major E. C. Johnson, called *On the track of the crescent: Erratic notes from the Piraeus to Pesth* (1885), and earlier, in a history of the region penned by the British ambassador, William Wilkinson, called *Account of Wallachia and Moldavia: with various political observations relating to them* (1820) – that Stoker had first come across in the Whitby Public Library in the summer of 1890.[95] In these accounts, the Voïvode Dracula (father and son) are less heroic figures than Dracula suggests, and their contribution to the contest between Christianity and Islam in Wallachia and Transylvania was less than honourable. Of all Stoker's sources, only Wilkinson refers to 'Dracula' by name, referring to three different Voïvodes, and even this is not clear (father, son, and another – the voïvodate was not normally hereditary). As Clive Leatherdale notes, the answer to the question of who Dracula was remains a 'guess'.[96] None of Stoker's sources, including Wilkinson, refer to Vlad Tepes, the Impaler. Indeed, as an immortal, Count Dracula could be all these different historical figures. The novel, in short, does not represent events of the past as they are recorded in the historical chronicle, but creatively remakes and deploys them in the drama of plot and character.

Wilkinson suggests that the Voïvode Dracula expressed the liberty of his people, but his defeat and treachery 'laid the foundations of that slavery, from which no efforts have yet had the power of extricating them with any lasting efficiency'. Dracula's fearless bravery was also distinctly unreliable. Wilkinson supplied a curious footnote: 'Dracula in the Wallachian language means Devil. The Wallachians were, at that time, as they are at present, used to give this as a surname to any person who rendered himself conspicuous either by courage, cruel actions, or cunning'.[97] The Voïvode certainly commanded fanatical loyalty: Leopold Von Ranke remarks in his *History of Servia* (1847) that,

> The more powerful chiefs in war, who styled themselves Woiwodes, were not only commanders of districts, but they had a force of their own – the Momkes – the only cavalry troops in the country. The Momkes were people settled on the land, and descended from good families; they ate with their leader, and were provided by him with horses and handsome apparel. Though not paid, they received valuable presents, and shared his booty. For this they were bound to their chief in life and in death; and they always formed his suite. They served him as readily against other enemies as against the Turks.'[98]

Like banditti in gothic novels, the Voïvode's rule was characterised by heroic defence of liberty, but also treachery and bloody atrocity. Dracula's aloof aristocratic superiority – symbolised by his blood – finds an expression for the liberty of his people, even though they do not share his blood.

The novel's conception of this contested historical figure is self-consciously scholarly. In the middle of the novel, Professor Abraham Van Helsing forms a 'board or committee' for the study of available knowledge about 'the kind of enemy with which we have to deal', offering both 'the history of this man' and an investigation of 'the teachings and records of the past', which is to say 'tradition and superstition'. Van Helsing lectures his assembled committee (Lord Godalming, Dr Seward, Mr Quincey Morris, Mina and Jonathan Harker), instructing them not only in vampire 'lore' but also in how to read it. Van Helsing's academic structures and his interdisciplinary approach to vampire research, dramatise the epistemological confusion of enlightenment supernaturalism (simultaneously emasculating the similar debate in the reader's mind). At first 'a sceptic', having trained himself 'to keep an open mind', Van Helsing suddenly perceives the truth in a flash of enlightenment '"See! See! I prove; I prove."' He concludes, 'Tradition and superstition are everything': adding, 'A year ago which of us would have received such a possibility' as the vampire 'in the midst of our scientific, sceptical, matter-of-fact nineteenth century'.[99]

The subsequent summary of the vampire folklore is erudite and well-researched, although the only reference is to a man who did not pursue vampire research, Arminius Vambéry, a celebrated Hungarian traveller and scholar of oriental languages who Stoker had met briefly in London in 1890.[100] Vambéry, who by his own testimony wrote twelve languages and read twenty, was one of the foremost experts on Eastern European and Central Asian linguistics and history, and a 'zealous defender of British interests in Asia'.[101] His history of Hungary mentions neither vampires nor Vlad the Impaler.[102] In the novel, Van Helsing appeals to his expertise in such matters: 'I have asked my friend Arminius, of Buda-Pesth University, to make his record; and from all the means that are, he tell me of what he has been.' The memorandum of Hungarian history prepared for Professor Van Helsing's inter-disciplinary committee on vampires concludes that Count Dracula is both a vampire and the Voïvode Dracula:

> He must, indeed, have been that Voivode Dracula who won his name against the Turk, over the great river on the very frontier of Turkey-land. If it be so, then he was no common man, for in that time, and for centuries after, he was spoken of as the cleverest and the most cunning, as well as the bravest of the sons of the "land beyond the forest" [lit. Transylvania]. That mighty brain and that iron resolution went with him to his grave, and are even now arrayed against us.[103]

The same qualities that identify the Voïvode Dracula as historical (uncommon bravery and clever cunning), Van Helsing discovers, also mark his modern threat as powerful and innovative.

The historical figure, the Voïvode Dracula, was not a vampire; despite his reign of terror, he was not a revenant and blood-sucker. Christopher Frayling confirms that Bram Stoker was the first to confuse the 'mass-murderer' with the folk-tale vampire.[104] Stoker's marriage of the folkloric vampire (revenant blood-sucker) to the Transylvanian warlord reanimated the longstanding connection between the vampire and the tyrant. As David Punter argues, Dracula offers a lively metaphor for the hereditary principal of the aristocracy.[105] He embodies the historical involution of aristocratic claims to noble blood, a quality of breeding that can only be located in lineage and history, and not in innovation or creation. However, the same principle articulates a perverse version of ancient constitution discourse too. Dracula insists that his people's spirit of liberty is encapsulated in the Dracula blood-line as a property of his blood: his demonic and uninterrupted corporeal existence preserves that liberty from the deep past to the present. Dracula appears to be a strange anachronism: a figure out of history as well as a figure draped in history.

— MODERNITY AND ATAVISM IN THE VAMPIRE —

Against the ancient supernaturalism of the vampire patriarch (warlord, tyrant, extortionist), the novel opposes a multivocal modernity: technologies of reason (communication, transport, medicine, psychiatry, police) and civilisation (domestic femininity, the family, sentimental love, moral standards). Even here, however, Stoker queers the pitch. The narratives of Mina and Lucy begin as conventional plots of love-driven 'romance', cast in deliberate counterpoint to Harker's and Seward's stories of exotic travel, perverse sexuality and lunatics. The excitement displayed by the young women in describing their suitors and courtship rituals, constructs them as modern women, both choosing between men and confident in their judgement. The pleasures and satisfactions offered to the women by sentimental love, and the domesticity of marriage reassert a more conservative construction of femininity, especially as the novel offers such homely virtues as the most powerful force against the vampire, even as a motivation for the scientific men. The novel's English speakers value 'middle class' virtues of family and love against Dracula's aristocratic claims to lineage and blood. The contest between political ideologies is here manifested in the sexual arena too: the English confine legitimate sexuality to the marital bed and the ideology of love, while Dracula's alien sanguinary desires suggest wilder passion and perverse sexual practices (oral sex, tribadism, homosexuality).

The correspondence between Lucy and Mina suggests, in its frank exchange of views on men, that marriage is desirable only to achieve independence and to enjoy a sexuality whose force they feel already. Lucy is entertained, not threatened, by her trio of suitors, and enjoys reading the spectacle she makes of herself choosing between them (a structure both voyeuristic and masturbatory). Mina ironically compares such 'appetites' with a modern reconstruction of femininity, the 'New Woman'.[106] The discourse of the 'New Woman' offered a revision of the model of the passive domestic woman, during the last decades of the nineteenth century. Self-consciously feminist and revisionist, the account of middle-class feminine behaviour in New Woman discourse was based on a new model of sexual independence. It assumed that a desiring, actively sexual woman was not only permissible but healthy, and offered a broad attack on the accepted standards of women's behaviour as repressive, illiberal and unjustified. As well as promoting smoking, cycling and leaving off wearing corsets, proponents mounted a critique of marriage, and support for educational equality, female emancipation and employment in the professions. In the view of the press, however, the New Women were perceived as an attack on received moral standards: they were accused of being promiscuous, unruly and self-interested; of being masculine, socialist and revolutionary; of being flat-chested, androgynous and humourless.[107] Mina's professionalism, seen throughout the novel in her intelligent analyses and technological proficiency, can be construed as New Woman discourse, but so too can Lucy's vampirised sexuality. Such satirical ambivalence suggests the depth of Stoker's critical curiosity about the realignments of gender in Victorian culture.

As many recent critics of *Dracula* have noted, the novel expresses a polyvalent curiosity about sexuality and gender, noting especially how the vampire theme allows topics that normally remain unspoken to be raised and addressed. This transgressive quality of the text is liberated, in the novel's view, by the vampire's transgressive qualities. The count's vampirisation of Harker in Castle Dracula, and then of Lucy Westenra, recasts the seductive quality of the vampire's blood-sucking haemophagy into a perverse eroticism. In a soporific reverie induced by Dracula's ministrations, Harker dreamily describes the approach of 'three young women, ladies by their dress and manner' (a codicil that implies that their lady-like appearance contrasts with their lascivious, whore-like actions). While the tone of Harker's journal had begun with the crisp empiricism of the travel journal, he has already experimented with more feminised discourses (gothic terror and romance). The language of his description of the women reverts to libertinism.

> Two were dark, and had high aquiline noses, like the Count's, and great dark, piercing eyes, that seemed to be almost red when contrasted with the pale yellow moon. The other was fair, as fair as can be, with great wavy masses of golden hair and eyes like pale sapphires. I seemed to know her face, and to know it in connection with some dreamy fear, but I could not recollect at the moment how or where. All three had brilliant white teeth, that shone like pearls against the ruby of their voluptuous lips. There was something about them that made me uneasy, some longing and at the same time some deadly fear. I felt in my heart a wicked, burning desire that they would kiss me with those red lips.[108]

The seductive women display their sexually adventurous qualities on their bodies, especially their 'voluptuous lips', which signal to Harker their erotic intentions. Although many critics have tried to establish the identity of these women, the dreamy tone of the passage obscures certainty.[109] Their coquettish actions, their explicit discussion of 'kisses', and their sweet-but-bitter breath, redolent of blood, inaugurates a series of cryptic encounters which suggestively pun sex with the vampire's bite:

The fair girl went on her knees and bent over me, fairly gloating. There was a deliberate voluptuousness which was both thrilling and repulsive, and as she arched her neck she actually licked her lips like an animal, till I could see in the moonlight the moisture shining on the scarlet lips and on the red tongue as it lapped the white sharp teeth. Lower and lower went her head . . . I closed my eyes in a languorous ecstasy and waited – waited with beating heart.[110]

It is clear, in one sense, that 'the fair girl' is preparing to bite his neck – Harker notes that he can feel the sharp points of her teeth at the 'supersensitive skin of my throat'. Yet the same encounter also feels like a sexual skirmish, in which Harker fantasises that the she-vampire will give him oral satisfaction by fellatio.[111] The term 'fellatio' was coined by the classical scholar Leonard Smithers in 1887 ('The patient (fellator or sucker) provokes the orgasm by the manipulation of his (or her) lips and tongue on the agent's member'),[112] and, adopted by the late-Victorian sexologist Havelock Ellis, was rapidly incorporated into the nascent discourse of psychology.[113] Stoker's punning suggestion of the sexuality of vampiric encounter elaborates the novel's polymorphic exploration of suckers (sanguine and sexual, political and financial).

After this, in the extended section of the novel where Dracula seems to have the upper hand, the encounters between vampires and mortals are tinctured with this perverse eroticism – Lucy sleepwalking in Whitby, Dracula's nightly visits in London and Hillingham, even the transfusions to keep her alive. Against such libertine discourse, the novel places the estranged chastity of Van Helsing's medical science, and, intriguingly, Mina's competent performance of the modern woman, both mother and warrior. Mina's professionalism as committee secretary, her career as a teacher, her adept concern for decorum, all suggest that she manages more successfully than others to fashion herself into a modern woman (even, it has been argued, a New Woman).[114] These qualities – passive, obedient yet resilient – serve her well in her confrontation with Dracula. But Mina's encounter with Dracula exposes her to an hyperbolic emotional world, redolent of a terror and sexuality that she plainly cannot name. The Count forces Mina to drink his blood, 'like a child forcing a kitten's nose into a saucer of milk', as Dr Seward remarks. In her own words, she comments:

"He pulled open his shirt, and with his long sharp nails opened a vein in his breast. When the blood began to spurt out, he . . . seized my neck and pressed my mouth to the wound, so that I must either suffocate or swallow some of the – Oh, my God, my God! what have I done?"[115]

Rubbing the 'pollution' from her lips, as Seward says, Mina is unable to name what has happened. She has been vampirised, and understands this as a kind of dishonouring that renders her 'unclean' (unchaste). Mina of course recovers, and in the winding-up of the story she 'achieves' the rewards of marriage and motherhood, suggesting that the 'Good' woman she embodies is approved by Stoker. But her vaunted power (wielding a giant revolver in the final battle) is equally a kind of prison: unable to articulate her own experiences, victim of her perfected passivity, Mina's status as woman dispossesses her of agency and independence.

Although the battle depicted in the novel, between reason and the supernatural, science and folklore, leads eventually to the defeat of the vampire, the committee of modernists achieve their victory not by dint of their science, but their credulous retreat into folklore remedies. By the end of the novel, the scientists have given up on both a material and a 'mental', or psychiatric, cause for the vampiric phenomena. Instead they recognise, as Mina did intuitively, that the vampire is an atavism, a regression to the primitive past of folklore and superstition. Their pursuit of Dracula is a work of rational and logical detection (clues are uncovered, leads are traced), and the chase back to his Transylvanian lair is accomplished with clearly modern forces (railways, the latest Winchester repeating rifles). However, when their enemy is cornered and vanquished, they resort to exotic and primitive knives (Jonathan's Kukri and Morris's bowie), and then finish him off with the same kind of sharpened stake, recommended by custom, used in 1732 to despatch Arnold Paul. Dracula has caused them to abandon their faith in material science and modernity in an analogous way to his catalysation of their latent sexuality: both are structured as transgressions. Despite the novel's self-conscious celebration of its up-to-the-minute modernity, the supernatural discourses of folklore win out. The reassertion of superstition, the novel argues, adheres in the relation between the vampire property and the form of the novel. As long as the novel wants to invest the vampire with a sense of possibility, the reassertion of reason and science, by which terrors are exposed as frauds, will be figured as bathos. If Stoker's 'horrid details' are to last to the end, there can be no exposure of their irrationality, and the novel perforce ends credulously.

— NOTES —

1. Bram Stoker, *Dracula*, ed. Maud Ellman (Oxford: Oxford University Press, 1996), p. 370.
2. Montagu Summers, *The Vampire: His Kith and Kin* (London: Kegan Paul, Trench, Trubner & Co., 1928), p. 22.

3. Ken Gelder, *Reading the Vampire* (London: Routledge, 1994), p. 25.
4. *The London Journal*, No. 663 (Saturday, 11 March 1731–2).
5. *The Gentleman's Magazine*, II, 15 (March 1732), p. 682.
6. *Applebee's Original Weekly-Journal* (27 May 1732), p. [1].
7. Michael McKeon, *The Origins of the English Novel, 1600–1740* (Baltimore: The Johns Hopkins University Press, 1987), pp. 65–89.
8. *The Country Journal: or The Craftsman*, No. 307 (Saturday, 20 May 1732), [unpaginated].
9. *Craftsman*, No. 307.
10. Simon Varey, 'Introduction', in Henry St John, Viscount Bolingbroke, *Lord Bolingbroke: Contributions to the Craftsman*, ed. Simon Varey (Oxford: Clarendon Press, 1982), pp. xvi–xxv.
11. See Isaac Kramnick, *Bolingbroke and his Circle: the Politics of Nostalgia in the Age of Walpole* (London: Oxford University Press, 1968), pp. 39–55; and Shelley Burtt, *Virtue Transformed: Political Argument in England, 1688–1740* (Cambridge: Cambridge University Press, 1992), pp. 88–109.
12. *Reflections Upon a Pamphlet. Entitled Observations Upon the Laws of Excise* (London: J. Roberts, 1733), p. 8.
13. Roger L'Estrange, *The Visions of Dom Francisco de Quevedo Villegas, Knight of the Order of St James* (1668; 4th edn, London: H. Herringman, 1671), p. 15.
14. John Trenchard, *Cato's Letters; or, Essays on Liberty, Civil and Religious, and other Important Subjects*, 4 vols, 3rd edn (London: W. Wilkins, T. Woodward, J. Walthoe and J. Peele, 1733), I, p. 144.
15. Charles Forman, *Some Queries and Observations Upon the Revolution in 1688, and its Consequences* (London: Olive Payne, 1741), p. 11n.
16. Oliver Goldsmith, *Collected Works*, ed. Arthur Friedman, 6 vols (Oxford: Clarendon Press, 1966), II, p. 329.
17. Simon Schama, *Citizens* (London: Viking, 1989), pp. 73, 754.
18. Lord Malmesbury to the Duke of Leeds, 29 December 1792; quoted in L. G. Mitchell, *Charles James Fox* (Oxford: Oxford University Press, 1991), p. 132.
19. Chris Baldick, *In Frankenstein's Shadow: Myth, Monstrosity and Nineteenth-century Writing* (Oxford: Clarendon, 1987), p. 128.
20. Karl Marx, *The First International and After*, ed. David Fernbach (Harmondsworth: Penguin, 1974), III, p. 79.
21. 'The Travels of three English Gentlemen, from Venice to Hamburgh, being the Grand Tour of Germany, in the Year 1734. (MS)', *The Harleian Miscellany*, ed. Samuel Johnson, 8 vols (London: T. Osborne, 1744–6), IV, pp. 365, 375–6.
22. John Baptist Boyer, Marquis D'Argens, *The Jewish Spy: being a Philosophical, Historical and Critical Correspondence, By Letters* (London: D. Browne and R. Hett, 1739), I, p. ix.
23. D'Argens, *Jewish Spy*, IV, pp. 122–4.

24. D'Argens, *Jewish Spy*, IV, pp. 127, 128.
25. Augustin Calmet, *Dissertations upon the Apparitions of Angels, Daemons, and Ghosts, And concerning the Vampires of Hungary, Bohemia, Moravia, and Silesia* (London: M. Cooper, 1759).
26. *The Monthly Review or Literary Journal*, XX (1760), p. 564.
27. Augustin Calmet, *The Phantom World: or, the Philosophy of Spirits, Apparitions, &c.*, trans. Henry Christmas, 2 vols (London: Richard Bentley, 1850).
28. Calmet, *Dissertations upon the Apparitions*, pp. vii–viii.
29. John Trenchard, *The Natural History of Superstition* (London: A. Baldwin, 1709), pp. 9, 11.
30. *Anti-Canidia: or, Superstition Detected and Exposed. In a Confutation of the Vulgar Opinion concerning Witches, Spirits, Demons, Magick . . . &c* (London: R. and J. Dodsley, [1762?]), pp. 3, 34
31. Calmet, *Dissertations upon the Apparitions*, p. 179.
32. *Encyclopédie, or Dictionnaire Raisonné des Sciences, des Arts et des Metiers* (Neufchatel: Samuel Faulche, 1765), XVI, p. 828.
33. Horace Walpole, *Letters*, ed. Paget Toynbee, 16 vols (Oxford: Clarendon Press, 1905), XIII, pp. 357–8.
34. Marie-François Arouret de Voltaire, 'Vampires', *A Philosophical Dictionary*, 6 vols (London: John and Henry L. Hunt, 1824), VI, pp. 304–8.
35. William Beckford (trans.), *Popular Tales of The Germans*, 2 vols (London: J. Murray, 1791), I, p. vi.
36. J. W. von Goethe, 'The Bride of Corinth', *Goethe, with plain prose translations of each poem*, trans. David Luke (Harmondsworth: Penguin, 1964), pp. 159–68.
37. William Hazlitt, *Examiner* (June 1816), quoted in S.T. Coleridge, *The Complete Poems*, ed. William Keach (Harmondsworth: Penguin, 1997), p. 509n.
38. Arthur H. Nethercot, *The Road to Tryermaine: a Study of the History, Background and Purposes of Coleridge's 'Christabel'* (Chicago: The University of Chicago Press, 1939), p. 56.
39. Robert Southey, *Thalaba the Destroyer: a metrical romance*, 2 vols (London: T. N. Longman and O. Rees, 1801), p. vii; Robert Southey to William Taylor, 5 October 1798, quoted in Mark Storey, *Robert Southey: a Life* (Oxford: Oxford University Press, 1997), p. 120.
40. Southey, *Thalaba*, VIII, pp. 102–4.
41. Joseph Pitton de Tournefort, *A Voyage into the Levant*, 2 vols (London: D. Browne et al., 1718).
42. John Herman Merivale, 'The Dead Men of Pest, A Hungarian Legend', *The Athenaeum*, I, 4 (April 1807), pp. 362–6, p. 362.
43. John Herman Merivale, 'The Dead Men of Pest', *Poems Original and Translated. Now first collected* (London: William Pickering, 1838), p. 71.

44. 'On Some Popular Superstitions, More Particularly on that relating to Vampyres or Blood-Suckers', *Athenaeum*, II, 7 (July 1807), pp. 19–25.

45. 'On Vampires', *Athenaeum*, III, 18 (June 1808), pp. 520–5.

46. John Stagg, 'The Vampyre', *The Minstrel of the North: or, Cumbrian legends. Being a Poetical Miscellany of Legendary, Gothic, and Romantic, Tales* (London: for the author by J. Blacklock, 1810), pp. 261–8, p. 261.

47. 'The Giaour' (1813) in *Lord Byron, The Complete Poetical Works*, ed. Jerome J. McGann, 7 vols (Oxford: Clarendon Press, 1981), III, p. 414n.

48. Daniel P. Watkins, 'Social Relations in Byron's *The Giaour*', *ELH*, 52 (1985), pp. 873–92, p. 874.

49. Leslie A. Marchand, *Byron's Poetry: a Critical Introduction* (London: John Murray, 1965), p. 63.

50. Marilyn Butler, 'The Orientalism of Byron's *Giaour*', in Bernard Beatty and Vincent Newey, *Byron and the Limits of Fiction* (Liverpool: Liverpool University Press, 1988), p. 87.

51. Nigel Leask, *British Romantic Writers and the East: Anxieties of Empire* (Cambridge: Cambridge University Press, 1992), p. 29.

52. Michael G. Sundell, 'The Development of *The Giaour*', *Studies in English Literature, 1500–1900*, IX (1969), pp. 587–99.

53. See also Karl Kroeber, *Romantic Narrative Art* (Madison, WI: University of Wisconsin Press, 1960), pp. 139–40 or Jerome McGann, *Fiery Dust: Byron's Poetic Development* (Chicago and London: The University of Chicago Press, 1968), pp. 143–44.

54. Watkins, 'Social Relations', pp. 873–92.

55. Butler, 'Byron's *Giaour*', p. 94.

56. Lord Byron, 'Augustus Darvell', in John Polidori, *The Vampyre and other Tales of the Macabre*, ed. Robert Morrison and Chris Baldick (Oxford: Oxford University Press, 1997), pp. 246–51. Subsequent references to this edition unless otherwise stated.

57. William Michael Rossetti (ed.), *The Diary of Dr. John William Polidori, 1816, Relating to Byron, Shelley, etc.* (London: Elkin Mathews, 1911), pp. 126–32.

58. Mary Shelley, 'Introduction [1831]', *Frankenstein*, ed. M. K. Joseph (Oxford: Oxford University Press, 1987), p. 7.

59. John William Polidori, *Ernestus Berchtold, or the Modern Oedipus*, ed. D. L. Macdonald and Kathleen Scherf (Toronto: University of Toronto Press, 1994).

60. 'John W. Polidori to Mr. Editor', *The New Monthly Magazine* (old series) 11, 64 (May 1819), p. 332.

61. The fullest account is offered in David Macdonald, *Poor Polidori: a Critical Biography of the Author of The Vampyre* (Toronto: University of Toronto Press, 1991), pp. 177–203.

62. *Byron's Letters and Journals*, ed. Leslie A. Marchand, 12 vols (London: John Murray, 1973–82), VI, pp. 114, 118–19, 140.

63. 'Polidori to Mr. Editor', *The New Monthly Magazine*, p. 332.
64. 'The Vampyre', *The New Monthly Magazine* (old series) 11, 63 (April 1819), pp. 193–206, reprinted as 'Appendix A', in Polidori, *The Vampyre*, ed. Morrison and Baldick, pp. 235–43.
65. Henry R. Viets, 'The London Editions of Polidori's *The Vampyre*', *Papers of the Bibliographical Society of America*, 63 (1969), pp. 83–103, pp. 90–1.
66. Rosetti (ed.), *Diary of Polidori*, p. 13.
67. John Mitford, *The Private Life of Lord Byron; comprising his voluptuous Amours, secret intrigues, and close connection with various Ladies of Rank and Fame* (London: H. Smith, [1828]).
68. Polidori, *Vampyre*, p. 241.
69. Polidori, *Vampyre*, pp. 240, 242.
70. Polidori, *Vampyre*, pp. 3–4.
71. James Twitchell, 'The Vampire Myth', *American Imago*, 37 (1980), pp. 83–92, p. 88.
72. Polidori, *Vampyre*, pp. 4, 5, 7.
73. Polidori, *Vampyre*, pp. 9, 10.
74. Polidori, *Vampyre*, pp. 12, 18, 23.
75. Ambrose Merton [William John Thoms], 'Folk-Lore', *Athenaeum*, 22 August 1846 (No. 982), pp. 862–3.
76. Richard M. Dorson, *The British Folklorists: a History* (London: Routledge Kegan Paul, 1968), p. 1.
77. William Ralston, 'Notes on Folk-Tales', *The Folk-Lore Record*, I (1878), pp. 71–98, p. 72.
78. Uli Linke, 'Folklore, Anthropology, and the Government of Social Life', *Comparative Studies in Society and History*, 32:1 (1990), pp. 117–48, p. 123; Tahal Asad (ed.) *Anthropology and the Colonial Encounter* (London: Ithaca, 1973).
79. Edward Smedley, W. Cooke Taylor, Henry Thompson and Elihu Rich, *The Occult Sciences: sketches of the traditions and superstitions of past times, and the marvels of the present day* (London and Glasgow: Richard Griffin and Co., 1855), pp. 66–71.
80. Herbert Mayo, *On the Truths Contained in Popular Superstition*, 2nd edn (1848; Edinburgh and London: William Blackwood, 1851), pp. 20–41.
81. Edward B. Tylor, *Primitive Culture: Researches into the Development of Mythology, Philosophy, Religion, Language, Art and Custom*, 2 vols (London: John Murray, 1871), II, pp. 175–6.
82. Patrick Brantlinger, 'Imperial Gothic: Atavism and the Occult in the British Adventure Novel, 1880–1914', *English Literature in Transition*, 28 (1985), pp. 243–52.
83. Charlotte Brontë, *Jane Eyre*, ed. Q. D. Leavis (Harmondsworth: Penguin Books, 1966), pp. 310–12.
84. Sheridan Le Fanu, 'Carmilla', *In a Glass Darkly*, ed. Robert Tracy (Oxford: Oxford University Press, 1993), pp. 315–16.

85. Stoker, *Dracula*, p. xxxviii.
86. Jennifer Wacke, 'Vampiric Typewriting: *Dracula* and its Media', *ELH*, 59 (1992), pp. 467–93.
87. John Greenway, '*Dracula* as a Critique of "Normal Science"', *Stanford Literature Review*, 3, 2 (1986), pp. 213–30.
88. Clive Leatherdale (ed.), 'Complete List of Bram Stoker's Sources for *Dracula*', *Bram Stoker's Dracula Unearthed* (Westcliff-on-Sea, Essex: Desert Island Books, 1998), pp. 18–19.
89. Stoker, *Dracula*, p. 1.
90. Stoker, *Dracula*, pp. 28–9.
91. Stoker, *Dracula*, p. 29.
92. See Clive Leatherdale, *Dracula: the Novel and the Legend: a Study of Bram Stoker's Gothic Masterpiece* (Wellingborough, Northamptonshire: The Aquarian Press, 1985), pp. 89–100.
93. See Raymond T. McNally and Radu Florescu, *In Search of Dracula: the History of Dracula and Vampires* (London: Robson Books, 1994), p. 84.
94. Leatherdale, *Dracula: Novel and Legend*, p. 94.
95. Christopher Frayling, *The Vampyres: Lord Byron to Count Dracula* (London: Faber & Faber, 1991), pp. 317–18.
96. Leatherdale (ed.), *Dracula Unearthed*, p. 68n.
97. William Wilkinson, *Account of Wallachia and Moldavia: with various political observations relating to them* (London: Longman, Hurst, Rees, Orme, and Brown, 1820), p. 19, 19n.
98. Leopold Von Ranke, *A History of Servia, and of the Servian Revolution*, trans. Louisa May Kerr (London: John Murray, 1847), pp. 185–6.
99. Stoker, *Dracula*, pp. 236, 238.
100. Barbara Belford, *Bram Stoker: a Biography of the Author of Dracula* (London: Weidenfeld and Nicolson, 1996), p. 260.
101. Arminius Vambéry, *The Story of My Struggles: the memoirs of Aminius Vambéry* (London: T. Fisher Unwin, 1904), p. 358.
102. Arminius Vambéry, *Hungary in Ancient, Mediaeval, and Modern Times*, 2nd edn (London: T. Fisher Unwin, 1887).
103. Stoker, *Dracula*, p. 240.
104. Christopher Frayling, 'Vampyres', *London Magazine*, n.s. 14:2 (June/July 1974), pp. 94–104, p. 101.
105. David Punter, *The Literature of Terror: A History of Gothic Fictions from 1765 to the Present Day* (New York: Longman, 1980), p. 257.
106. Stoker, *Dracula*, p. 88.
107. Elaine Showalter, *Sexual Anarchy: Gender and Culture at the Fin de Siècle* (London: Virago Press, 1992), pp. 38–58; and Sally Ledger, 'The New Woman and the Crisis of Victorianism', in Sally Ledger and Scott McCracken (eds), *Cultural Politics at the Fin de Siècle* (Cambridge: Cambridge University Press, 1995).
108. Stoker, *Dracula*, p. 37.

109. Showalter, *Sexual Anarchy*, p. 180; Leatherdale, *Dracula: Novel and Legend*, pp. 148–9; Gelder, *Reading the Vampire*, p. 73.
110. Stoker, *Dracula*, p. 38.
111. See also Christopher Craft, '"Kiss me with those red lips": Gender and Inversion in Bram Stoker's *Dracula*', in Elaine Showalter (ed.) *Speaking of Gender* (London: Routledge, 1990) p. 218.
112. *Priapeia, or the Sportive Epigrams of Divers Poets of Priapus*, trans. Leonard C. Smithers (Athens [actually London]: Erotika Biblion Society, 1888), p. 142. The term 'fellatio' was adopted, in an explicitly homosexual context, by the sexologist Havelock Ellis in *Sexual Inversion* (published and suppressed in 1897, and included as volume II of *Studies in the Psychology of Sex* (1901)).
113. The equation of semen with vampirised blood is made explicitly in Ernest Jones, *On the Nightmare* (London: The Hogarth Press, 1931), p. 98.
114. Carol A. Senf, *Dracula: Between Tradition and Modernism* (New York: Twayne Publishers, 1998), pp. 56–8.
115. Stoker, *Dracula*, p. 288.

CHAPTER SIX

Zombies and the occultation of slavery

*Lafcadio Hearn, Two Years in the French West Indies
(1890); William Seabrook, The Magic Island (1929);
white zombie tales by Weston, Wellman, Meik and
Bromley; Victor Halperin, White Zombie (1931);
Val Lewton, I Walked with a Zombie (1943)*

In the last decades of the twentieth century, the zombie, or the living
dead, has become a staple figure of the B-grade horror film. One cinema
database lists over eighty films featuring the zombie, with over thirty
made in the 1980s alone.[1] With the exception of George Romero's 'cult'
classic, the trilogy of *Night of the Living Dead* (1968), *Dawn of the Dead*
(1979) and *Day of the Dead* (1985), these zombie films are, by and large,
forgotten by cinema audiences, and difficult to locate. Even the titles
of zombie films, promiscuously mixing themes and genres, suggest their
popular culture status: *Teenage Zombies* (1959); *The Incredibly Strange
Creatures Who Stopped Living and Became Mixed-Up Zombies* (1963); *Space
Zombies* (1969); *Zombi Holocaust* (1979); *Hard Rock Zombies* (1984);
Redneck Zombies (1987); *Zombie Ninja Gangbangers* (1997); and *Interview
with a Zombie* (1997). There are zombie films cast in the mode of science
fiction, westerns, comedies, and pornography. Zombies in the cinema
appear as, or alongside, vampires, werewolves, Nazis, bikers, prostitutes,
and metalheads. The numerous pulp fictions of the zombie also indulge
their low cultural status.[2] Such self-consciously popular-culture films and
fictions aspire to dismissive critical notice, gesture towards their own
disposability, and advertise their 'pulp' provenance: defining, in the
process, a postmodern paradigm for the zombie. In endlessly proliferating
variations, the zombie fails to stop signifying, and predicates a kind of
ontological exhaustion. Indeed, in recent decades, the term zombie has
been emptied of all but its popular culture glamour: an American glam-
rock/thrash-metal band, *White Zombie*; an alcoholic cocktail using
over-proof rum; a virtual-reality computer game; a genre of ironic postmodern cartoons about suburban life; a termination process in the C
computer language; and even a philosophical model of the subconscious.

Drained of almost all its original significance, the postmodern era threatens to occlude the zombie's enduring and distinctive history.

ANSWERING THE QUESTION
'WHAT IS A ZOMBIE?'

In a gothic typology, the zombie can be categorised alongside the vampire as one of the 'un-dead', a medieval designation picked up by Bram Stoker in *Dracula* (1897) to describe the victims of the vampire who were clinically dead but not yet at rest. This enigmatic state, 'dead-and-alive' as the *Oxford English Dictionary* has it, perversely mixes the different schemes of knowledge of medicine and theology. The zombie has its own particular history, however, in the walking dead associated with the voodoo religion of the Caribbean state of Haiti. Descriptions, definitions and accounts of the zombie have been offered by anthropologists, sociologists and medical writers. The anthropologists and folklorists have not been concerned to prove or disprove the actual existence of the zombie: rather, they analyse the meaning of the zombie 'myth' within its primary culture in Haiti. In a French study of voodoo published in 1957, the French anthropologist Alfred Metraux defined the '*Zombi*' as a 'person from whom a sorcerer has extracted the soul and whom he has thus reduced to slavery. A *zombi* is to a certain extent a living corpse.' Metraux points out that in the syncretic religion of Voodoo (which amalgamates the rites and theological beliefs of diverse African religions with Catholicism), the widespread belief in black magic and sorcery explains how occult forces immanent in things and human beings are manipulated by the *hungan* or voodoo priest for personal ends. The *zombi* is the product of one such ritual: a person is raised from the dead by the supernatural power of the *hungan* through a process that is ritualised, obscure and secret (known only to adepts). Although zombies are restored to life, they do not reoccupy their previous place in society. 'He moves, eats, hears what is said to him, even speaks, but he has no memory and no knowledge of his condition.' In this condition, the zombie can be directed to work like a 'beast of burden' at whatever work his master identifies.[3] Other anthropologists have elaborated important differences between kinds of *zombi*. Hans-W. Ackermann and Jeanine Gauthier, in 'The Ways and Nature of the Zombi' (1991), discern distinctions between the *zombi* of the body (the living dead) and the *zombi* of the soul (akin to the *duppy* of Jamaican folklore).[4] Maximilien Laroche's study 'The Myth of the Zombi' (1976) delineated the extensive connections between the African myths of the living dead and the Haitian *zombi*; an 'evolution',

Laroche argues, imbricated in the history of slavery and the experience of colonial oppression.[5]

A different approach is taken by those researchers who investigate and assess the factual validity of reports of zombies in folklore, newspaper reports, and the accounts of eyewitness observers. The most famous of these researchers is Wade Davis, a participant in a cross-disciplinary investigation called 'The Zombie Project' in Haiti between 1982 and 1985 led by the Centre de Psychiatrie et Neurologie Mars-Kline in Port-au-Prince, that undertook a systematic investigation of popular reports of zombies. The project found a man, Clairvius Narcisse, who had been pronounced dead in 1962 at the Albert Schweitzer Memorial Hospital and buried in the presence of reputable witnesses: in 1980, a man claiming to be Narcisse returned to his village, stating that his brother had made him a zombie eighteen years before because of a land dispute.

The focus of Wade Davis's research was a material cause for zombification, in particular using ethnological, botanical and pharmacological methods to analyse a hypothesised 'zombie powder' that drugged humans and turned them into zombies. Davis presented his research in two texts: the first, *The Serpent and the Rainbow* (1985), was narrated as a travel adventure, and later made into a far-fetched horror film of the same name by Wes Craven; the second, *Passage of Darkness* (1988), is a sober academic account of his search for the folk toxin.[6] Davis argues that zombification is an essentially criminal practice effected by powerful psychoactive chemicals, called tetrodotoxins, derived from tropical flora and fauna, including puffer fish. These drugs, he proposes, incapacitate the body so as to suppress pulse and all vital signs. In this state, the body might be buried, even though the victim retains subdued consciousness throughout. He concludes that the devastating psychological effect of these drugs, of being buried alive, and dug up, combined with the effect of other powerful hallucinatory drugs from the datura and solanum families, might possibly bring about the effect of the *zombi*, especially on victims firmly believing in a voodoo world view where such events are possible. Davis's hypothesis of a pharmacological explanation for zombification was attacked by Mark Kemp, who questioned the scientific validity of Davis's work on tetrodotoxins,[7] while Ackermann and Gauthier suggest that the various zombie powders are simply sympathetic medicines with no proven pharmacological effectiveness: a 'perverse homeopathy'. Instead, they propose that many *zombi* stories can be explained as observations of exploited or vagrant mentally ill persons.[8] However, the most recent investigation by the anthropologist Richard Littlewood and the medical doctor Chavannes Douyon has revealed that in three cases of reported zombification in Haiti, two were shown by DNA testing to be cases of mistaken identity, whilst one was consistent with Davis's theory of poisoning by tetrodotoxins.[9]

— I. SLAVERY AND THE ZOMBIE —

This section replaces the question 'what is a zombie' (or 'does the zombie exist') with a proposition of a different order: 'how is the zombie represented in Western culture', looking at examples drawn from history writing, political commentary, fiction, and cinema. The zombie, like the vampire, foregrounds the place of folklore belief in modernity's age of reason. The zombie allows for the remembering and occultation of the history of African slavery in the American colonies, invoking the memory of slave resistance and rebellion, not as a trope of abolition and emancipation, but as fear about what that resistance implies about the communities and nation-states which are its legacy.[10]

The first accounts of the zombie are found in eighteenth-century histories of the West Indian sugar colonies. Describing the secret religious rituals of the African slave labourers, historians regularly figure slave religions in a gothic mode to signal the slaves' morally degraded condition. These accounts are often produced at, or inscribe, moments of cultural and political tension between racially-identified interest groups in the slave colonies, such as rebellion, abolition, emancipation and independence. The zombie, like the cannibal, is an ideologically motivated rhetorical device deployed to demonstrate and establish the moral superiority of civilised colonial authority over the barbarous slaves. This moral superiority – formalised into scientific theories of racial superiority – justified the continued use of military violence and legal process to maintain colonial authority. Authority in the slave plantation was absolute and tyrannical. Slave societies and the slave plantation system appeared to contemporaries as gothic institutions, vast prisons clanking with chains. As an apologist for slavery, the Jamaican slave-owner Bryan Edwards commented, 'In countries where slavery is established, the leading principle on which government is supported is fear.'[11]

In European constructions of the moral status of slavery, death and honour played an important part. Apologists for colonial slavery argued in the manner of John Locke that 'The perfect condition of *Slavery* is nothing else, but *the state of War continued, between a lawful Conqueror, and a Captive*'.[12] Bryan Edwards argued in 1793, that the slaves were legally purchased captives fairly taken in a just war, who, upon capture, had agreed to perpetual labour (slavery) in exchange for life (deferring execution). The state of slavery, in this account, is nothing but the state of death postponed: a desocialised and depersonalised condition described by Orlando Patterson as 'social death'.[13] Furthermore, Edwards argued, 'Negroes in a state of slavery' represented 'human nature in its most debased and abject state'. Slavery on the sugar plantations, Edwards notes, 'degrades and corrupts the human mind in a deplorable manner', the signal instance of which was the frequent slave rebellions throughout the eighteenth century.

Descriptions of rebellions typically retailed examples of slave depravity, indicating how slaves acted without restraint. It is true that slave rebellions were characterised by exceptionally brutal violence, both on the side of the rebel Africans (fighting for their freedom and with nothing to lose) and the forces of colonial order (outnumbered, seemingly without legal restraint, and determined to re-establish profitable law and order). During Tacky's revolt, in Jamaica in 1760, Edwards records how the rebels 'butchered' many white overseers 'in the most savage manner, and literally drank their blood mixed with rum'. When order was restored, three of the rebels were executed in a manner designed to be both exemplary and horrific:

> one was condemned to be burned, and the other two hung up alive in irons, and left to perish in that dreadful situation. The wretch that was burned was made to sit on the ground, and his body being chained to an iron stake, the fire was applied to his feet. He uttered not a groan, and saw his legs reduced to ashes with the utmost firmness and composure.[14]

Lurid accounts of slave atrocities, and vengeful exemplary executions, functioned in contemporary journalism as a species of gothic horror, depicting moments of savagery perpetrated both by rebel slaves and the slave-owning authorities outside the bounds of civilised behaviour. Such scenes of colonial rebellion and punishment offered British society its most compelling examples of pure terror.

Observers had long been aware that the slaves, kidnapped from Africa, harboured in their society secret religious and political organisations. Edwards's attention was drawn to 'the malicious contrivances and diabolical arts of some practitioners in Obeah, a term of African origin, signifying sorcery and witchcraft'. Such religious practices amongst slave communities had long been noted in the British West Indies, and were widely understood to be of African and creole origin. Obeah, Edwards admits, had 'so powerful an effect on the Negroes, as to bias, in a considerable degree, their general conduct, dispositions, and manners'. Edwards explains that obeah has now become in Jamaica the general term to denote those Africans who in that island practise witchcraft or sorcery, comprehending also the class of what are called Myal-men, or those who, by means of a narcotic potion, made with the juice of an herb (said to be the branched *Calalue* or species of *Solanum*) which occasions a trance or profound sleep of a certain duration, endeavour to convince the deluded spectators of their power to re-animate dead bodies.[15]

Edwards's account describes but does not name the zombie.

Writing in his *History of Jamaica* (1774), Edward Long described the widespread belief amongst the slaves 'in the apparition of spectres'. The 'supernatural powers of the African obeah-men' he describes as 'pretended conjurers', who ascribe to magic what is the 'natural operation' of some 'poisonous juice, or preparation, dextrously administered by these villains'. In the secret society of the *myal dance*, the obeah-man uses his medical charlatanism to promise a restoration of 'the body to life' after death.

> The method, by which this trick was carried on, was by a cold infusion of the herb *branched colalue* [*Solanum Nigram*]; which, after the agitation of dancing, threw the party into a profound sleep. In this state he continued, to all appearance lifeless, no pulse, nor motion of the heart, being perceptible; till, on being rubbed with another infusion (as yet unknown to the Whites), the effects of a the colalue gradually went off, the body resumed its motions, and the party, on whom the experiment had been tried, awoke as from a trance, entirely ignorant of anything that had passed since he left off dancing.[16]

Under the plantocrat's superior surveillance, the colonial science of botany exposes the machinations of the myal secret society as theatrical imposture.[17] Rather than truly raising the slain warrior from the dead, the obeah man simply presents a cunning but essentially theatrical demonstration of the suspension of animation (that which might now be called an unconscious state).

Both Long and Edwards recognised the important role played by obeah in slave rebellions. Obeah-men were often leaders of rebellions: the preparations of their sympathetic medicine and natural magic were used to instil courage in rebel soldiers. Amongst the maroons (communities of rebel slaves), obeah was central to social organisation and self-definition. Obeah became, in this manner, a byword for subversion as the most celebrated focus of African resistance to slavery. In his *Account of the Maroon Negroes in the Island of Jamaica* (1801), Edwards confirmed 'the prevalence of *Obi* and the supernatural power of their *Obeah* men', complaining that they were 'attached to the gloomy superstitions of Africa (derived from their ancestors) with such enthusiastick zeal and reverential ardour, as I think can only be eradicated with their lives'.[18] According to Philip

Thicknesse, a lieutenant in the colonial army raised to suppress the maroons in 1739–40, the ordinary British soldiers were also greatly in fear of the obeah witch-doctors. Thicknesse describes the fearsome appearance of the 'obea-woman' of the maroon leader, Captain Quoha, who wore 'the upper teeth of our men, slain in [battle] . . ., drilled thro' and worn as ankle, and wrist bracelets'. The ferocity of the obeah-women gave the soldiers a great fear of being taken alive as a prisoner, 'for that *only* was our fear, we would have compounded for immediate death; but we dreaded the sentence of death, and the execution of it, from the hands of that horrid wretch, their *Obea woman.*'[19]

Representations of obeah, on the other hand, were often used in European texts to exemplify the barbarity and savagery of slave society, and as such, to justify the habitual violence of slavery as an institution. The practices of obeah and the figure of the obeah-man or witchdoctor, function as a gothic force in these texts: a source and index of terror. Plantocratic historiography argued that obeah's origins lie in the deep past. Edwards proposed that the etymology of 'the term *Obeah, Obiah,* or *Obia*' was probably an ancient Egyptian worship of the snake-demon *Ob.* Derived from Jacob Bryant's antiquarian study of ancient mythology (1774), Edwards suggested that the ancient heresy arrived in the slave colonies by way of the 'ancient oracular Deity of Africa' known as 'the Basilisk or Royal Serpent'.[20] The physician Benjamin Moseley, surgeon-general to Jamaica from 1768–84, argued that Obi, as he called it, represented lost or forgotten knowledge akin to alchemical magic. Moseley declared that 'the science of Obi is very extensive' and 'has its origin, like many customs among the Africans, from the ancient Egyptians'. Obi's antiquity allies it with a kind of gothic culture: a knowledge preserved 'from the antients' which is here transmitted to modern medical science by the slaves. He comments that they were 'deeply skilled in magic, and what we call the *black art,* which they brought with them from Africa'. As a doctor, Moseley was interested in the obi-men as native practitioners of sympathetic medicine. The obeah-men's knowledge of the medicinal powers of tropical plants, and their ability to 'administer a baleful dose from poisonous herbs, and calculate its mortal effects' suggests to him a likeness with the medieval alchemists Roger Bacon and Thomas Aquinas, who also practised sympathetic medicine. Associated with gothic superstition, secret societies, and occult mystery, Moseley insinuates obeah into contemporary conspiracy theory. Gullible slaves, he argued, were susceptible to the influence of the obeah-men, who taught them 'the mysteries of sigils [occult signs or devices supposed to have mysterious powers], spells, and sorcery; and *illuminated* [them] in all the occult science of OBI'.[21] Here, Moseley reasons that the secret societies of the obeah cult are equivalent to the *Illuminati*, the secret societies devoted both to enlightenment science and alchemical mystery: in short, they are subversive and revolutionary associations given to esoteric supernaturalism. By contrast, the journals of Maria Nugent and Matthew Lewis emasculate the dangerous threat of resistant slave culture by recasting their observations of Jamaican obeah in a quaintly picturesque mode.[22]

— REBEL SLAVES AND THE DEVIL-KING ZOMBI —

The first time the term 'zombie' was used in English was 1819, in an account of the maroon republic of Palmares in Robert Southey's *History of Brazil*. He described how this enduring rebel black republic in the Brazilian state of Pernambuco was 'the resort of the negroes who from time to time were able to escape from slavery'. The well-organised population of 30,000 professed Christianity, but this was 'a religion which they had received in so corrupt a form, that it was scarcely possible for them, ignorant as they were, to make it more unlike its divine original'.[23] By the 1690s, the maroon republic had 'acquired strength and audacity' as a well-organised military force under the rule of an 'elected chief' known as the Zombi, chosen for his justice and valour.

> Perhaps a feeling of religion contributed to this obedience; for Zombi, the title whereby he was called, is the name for the Deity, in the Angolan tongue. They retained the use of the cross, some half-remembered prayers, and a few ceremonies which they had mingled with superstitions of their own, either what they preserved of their African idolatry, or had invented in their present state of freedom.[24]

As Southey makes clear, the Zombi is integral to the maroon society's freedom (he is the expression of their republican liberty) and has a significant role in transculturated creole religion.[25] In a footnote, Southey explores the derivation of the term Zombi: he explains that Rocha Pitta, his Portuguese source,

> says the word means Devil in their language. This appeared to me so unlikely that I examined a book of religious instructions in the Portugueze and Angolan languages, to ascertain the fact; and there I found that *NZambi* is the word for Deity; . . . *Cariapemba* is the Devil. It is not used in the sense of *Lord*, which might explain its application here without any religious import, . . . but of *Deity*.[26]

Southey's reluctance to countenance Rocha Pitta's equation of 'Zombi' with 'Devil' signals his refusal to accept such a semiotically confusing political entity: a black republic led by a devil-king.

The zombie is also noted in late eighteenth-century French reports of slave culture in St Domingue (later known as Haiti), where it is reported as a creole word meaning ghost or revenant. Throughout the 1790s, St Domingue had been wracked by both an orthodox slave rebellion and a republican revolution inspired by events in metropolitan France. Méderic Louis Élie Moreau de Saint-Méry, a French émigré from St Domingue who settled in Philadelphia, published his *Description Topographique, Physique, Civile, Politique et Historique de la Partie Française de L'Isle Saint-Domingue* in 1797 to supply the demand for information about the revolution. Although Moreau de Saint-Méry's account confines itself to the colony's *ancien régime* (before 1789), the reading public in America and Britain were curious about how the much-denigrated rebel slave army had repelled well-armed and disciplined European troops. Moreau de Saint-Méry's account of the slaves describes their appearance, their fertility, their practices of child-rearing, their health, the manners of their women, their dances and music (*Calenda, Bomboula*), and their *Vaudoux* cult. Voodoo is primarily understood by Moreau de Saint-Méry as a dance, around which a ritual worship of the snake and a cult of secrecy have developed. After describing the appearance of the voodoo king and queen, he comments that their dance is 'accompanied by the most horrible things that delirium is capable of imagining'. He observes that the oracle speaks through the mouth of the priestess ('La Reine *Vaudoux*') while she is in a convulsive state induced by the ceremonial dance. The ritual finishes 'in a nearby room, where disgusting prostitution exercises in the dark its most hideous empire'. Moreau de Saint-Méry complains of the difficulty the whites have in penetrating the secrets of the mysterious voodoo cult, and indistinctly suggests that it has played an important role in slave rebellions. Almost in an aside, he mentions that amongst the slaves there is a pronounced dread of night, generated by their fear of revenants, ghosts and werewolves. Amongst these ghosts he notes 'the story of the Zombi', which, as he explains in a footnote, is 'A creole word meaning spirit, revenant'.[27]

The nineteenth century saw a burgeoning interest in the culture and religion of black society in the sugar colonies of the Caribbean, not only in Haitian voodoo, but also the varieties of obeah observed in the rest of the West Indies. Nineteenth-century accounts of the Haitian republic repeatedly instanced the voodoo cult as a sign of the nation's political exceptionalism, social corruption and inherent instability. The free and independent Republic of Haiti was an anomaly in the region, and as such had few friends or allies. The once-rich sugar plantation economy almost completely collapsed as the freed slaves abandoned the plantation system in favour of subsistence farming. Declining into a state of economic ruin, Haitian society became highly stratified: an elite composed mostly of mulattos modelled their life and culture on France, speaking French and adhering to the Catholic religion; while the masses, mostly black peasants, whose culture was a unique acculturation of European and African influences, spoke their own Haitian creole language and prac- tised the folk religion of voodoo. Voodoo was the distinctive principle of Haitian mass culture: it had played a crucial part in the early stages of the revolution and remained a central pillar of black resistance and independence.[28]

The notoriety of voodoo in Anglophone writing on Haiti was cemented by a British diplomat, Sir Spencer Buckingham St John, in *Hayti: or, The Black Republic* (1884). Demonstrating that the 'Black Republic' was, in spite of its democratic and civilised pretensions, nothing but a tyran- nical military despotism, St John presented sensationalised accounts of 'vaudoux' criminal practices, including child sacrifice and cannibalism.[29] The British historian of empire James Anthony Froude, Professor of History at Oxford, followed a similarly controversial path in his assess- ment of the political maturity of the West Indies colonies, *The English in the West Indies; or, The Bow of Ulysses* (1888). Defending the 'benef- icent despotism of the English Government', Froude drew a contrast with Haiti, where he found a gothicised dystopia, 'where they eat the babies, and no white man can own a yard of land'. Following St John, Froude offers voodoo as the signal of Haitian political corruption: 'Behind the immorality, behind the religiosity, there lies active and alive the horrible revival of West African superstitions: the serpent worship, the child sacri- fice, and the cannibalism. There is no room to doubt it.'[30] Recast in a flagrantly sensationalised version, the representation of voodoo served the negrophobic paternalism central to colonial ideology. As the black Trinidadian intellectual J. J. Thomas argued, in his reply *Froudacity* (1889), the example of Haiti was a rhetorical ploy in English argument, designed to scapegoat black political aspirations as a variety of extremist radicalism.[31]

LAFCADIO HEARN'S ZOMBIE STORIES: HISTORY AS SPECTRE

Harper's Magazine commissioned in 1887 a series of articles on folklore and popular culture from the travel-writer and literary critic Lafcadio Hearn (1850–1904), perhaps reflecting the increasing curiosity in America in the geo-politics of the West Indies. For at least a decade, whilst resident in New Orleans, Hearn had been collecting 'Creole legends, traditions and songs'.[32] A cruise to Guiana was followed by a more extended sojourn of two years in the French colony of Martinique. Hearn's magazine articles, and other material, were developed into a well-received travel journal called *Two Years in the French West Indies* (1890) and a novel, *Youma*, that gave an account of the Martinique slave rebellion of 1848.[33] As a folklorist, Hearn found in the West Indies an archive of gothic customs and beliefs concerning ghosts, zombies and revenants. But to Hearn, these Creole superstitions and stories were not only exotic or picturesque folkways: they also hosted an argument about race. In 'La Verette and the Carnival in St Pierre, Martinique', Hearn's well-shaped narrative detailed the fate of some of his neighbours in a retiring back street of Martinique during the carnival in 1887.[34] Amongst the narrator's neighbours were a benevolent black female witchdoctor, Maum-Robert, and the family of the widow Yzore, a beautiful pale-skinned mulatto *calendeuse*, impoverished after the death of her upper-class husband. Hearn's description of the commencement of the carnival is overlaid with the onset of 'La Verette', a plague of smallpox. The carnival, with its picturesque masquerade costume, is equated with the disfiguring contagious disease. For Hearn, carnival costume and dancing recalled the African heritage of the populace, but also their history of slavery and emancipation. In the music and popular song, for example, he finds signs of the 'old African method of chanting at labor'. Many revellers wear the *Congo*, a dress mimicking that worn by workers on the plantations under slavery. There are also more threatening figures: *Ti Nègue gouos-sirop* (the little molasses negro) is smeared in molasses and soot, so as to recall the original African ancestor, while the *guiablesse* (Devil-woman) is a tall young woman robed in black, recalling a Martinique superstition about plantation seductresses. Nonetheless, the mass of masks has an uncanny effect, for as Hearn remarks: 'it is not in the least comical; . . . it is void of all character – expressionless, void, dead'. The carnival is dominated by the *Bon-Dié* (good-God), who scatters the devils and diablesses, but also by the Devil and his *Zombis* – a crowd of nearly 300 chanting boys. As the carnival season winds down, the plague picks up speed, and Ysore is but one more victim. Her orphaned children, whose brilliant white skin had originally attracted the narrator's interest, have only the old witch-doctor to look after them. Fearful of their precarious future, Maum-Robert utters 'the dark thought' that these 'three little penniless white ones' would be better off dead, saying, '"let me go call your father from the cemetery to come and take you also away!"'[35]

The essay's horror at the future faced by these 'white' children in the hands of the black witch-doctor articulates Hearn's race-politics. Hearn's travel journal 'A Midsummer Trip to the Tropics' had found the naked bodies of the men, boys and women he encountered in Martinique both beautiful and erotic; but nonetheless, his work is bisected by a powerful racism. Like Froude, he articulates the economic decline of the West Indies after emancipation as an argument about civilisation in which race is central. He sees island culture and society, increasingly dominated by its black majority, as a 'contest' for 'racial supremacy' in which the 'heroism' and 'civilisation' of the white 'races of the North' are devoured and effaced by the decadent blacks.[36] Hearn's notions on race, not unusual for this period, are pursued more explicitly in a short essay, first published in *The Cosmopolitan* in June 1890, called 'A Study of Half-Breed Races in the West Indies'. In contrast to the United States, Hearn implies, West Indian colonies are characterised by a considerable number of people of mixed race – unions between 'a savage and a civilised race': 'The greatest error of slavery was that which resulted in the creation of mixed races – the illegitimate union between the white master and the African woman, whose offspring remained slaves by law.'[37] The profound racism of Hearn's horror relies on race ideology for its strongest claims. The 'half-breed' blurred the distinction implicit and fundamental to new world slavery, of the biological and political difference between master and slave (white and black). As the post-colonial theorist Robert Young has recently argued, the identification between whiteness and mastery on the one hand, and blackness and slavery on the other, underpinned much mid-nineteenth-century thinking on race. Miscegenation threatened this equivalence and, by extension, those distinctions of culture and civilisation that were the defining criteria of Western modernity.[38] Hearn argued that the figure of the half-breed illuminated in 'the simple minds of the blacks ... the injustice of their condition', and as such, destroyed the sentiments of filial affection and duty that had hitherto governed the master-slave relationship. The '*infâme mulatre*' combined 'the proud white life in its veins' with the 'mutinous obstinacy and ... displays of aggressiveness' of the black slaves. Hearn concluded that the emergence of mulatto populations in the West Indies, given to 'Treachery and resolve, duplicity and courage', undid slavery from the inside. In Hearn's view, the 'ruin of the colony' of St Domingue (Haiti) can be traced to miscegenation. But Hearn's fear of the half-breed is also a kind of self-hatred: the 'very existence' of mulatto people, he states, 'tended above all else to kindle the world's shame of slavery as a vice'.[39] As Hearn signals, but is loath to recognise, the shame of slavery adheres to his own 'white' race. Slavery is the vice to which miscegenation points, and slavery articulates a selfish corruption central to the ideology of civilisation and progress.

In his Martinique researches, Hearn records stories of the zombie, even though the term was, he said, a 'weird word' that defied clear explanation. Characteristically, Hearn's narrator presents not only a gothic story, but also an account of folkloric research. In 'La Guiablesse' (The Devil-woman), the narrator discusses the nature of the *zombi* with Adou, the daughter of the old woman in whose house he lodges. Adou knows about and believes in ghosts, and is a prime source of 'creole stories' – equivalent to an 'informant' in the discourse of anthropology. However, at the narrator's question 'What is a zombi?', Adou's dazzling smile evaporates. While she has not seen one, and does not want to, the narrator's probing questions solicit a series of enigmatic answers. The zombi, Adou says, 'makes disorder at night'. In answer to the narrator's suggestion, Adou states that the zombi is not 'the spectre of a dead person, . . . *one who comes back?*' – even though she is so scared of the *moun-mò* (the dead folk) that she is unable to cross the cemetery at night. But the 'dead folk' are not zombies: rather, Adou restates, the zombi is the origin of 'all those noises at night one cannot understand'. Old Théréza, Adou's mother, adds that 'the word "zombi" also has special strange meanings' beyond that sense indicated by the 'vague expressions "afraid of ghosts", "afraid of the dark"'.[40] To Old Théréza, the zombi is an uncanny event: a great fire observed from the road at night that recedes as it is approached; or a three-legged horse passing on the road.

After this limpid introduction to the zombies (ghosts) who appear at night, 'La Guiablesse' relates one story of a zombie encountered in broad daylight. The deliberately estranged almost hallucinatory tone creates a subtle gothic effect which all but masks the story's carefully contrived construction. The narrative relates an encounter between two rustic plantation hands surprised by the sudden appearance of a tall, beautiful and seductive black woman, dressed all in black: 'a black poem of artless dignity, primitive grace, savage exultation of movement'. Mesmerised by her erotic walk and libidinous manner, the younger man Fafa agrees to accompany her on her journey, drawn by an unidentifiable but 'libertine' urge. Traversing hills and valleys as day shades into evening, the mysterious woman leads Fafa off the path, and up a hill towards the top of a cliff. Expectation is slowly raised through the accretion of uncanny effects, each of which amounts to little but which cumulatively succeed in estranging the story: she claims to have no soul; she answers to no name; she does not sweat or tire; her hand is cold. The tale's incipient sexuality suddenly crystallises at the edge of the cliff, in a half-understood clarification, as Fafa realises simultaneously that this mysterious figure is a demon, a devil-woman or *Guiablesse* (Hearn's transliteration of the

Creole word for *diablesse* or devil-woman), and that she has pushed him over the edge.

> And she, suddenly – turning at once to him and to the last red light [of the setting sun], the goblin horror of her face transformed – shrieks with a burst of hideous laughter:
> "Atò, bo!" ["Kiss me now!"]
> For the fraction of a moment he knows her name: – then, smitten to the brain with the sight of her, reels, recoils, and backward falling, crashes two thousand feet down to his death upon the rocks of a mountain torrent.[41]

The climactic structure of the story, ironically recapitulating the shape of male desire, celebrates the zombi's unearthly seductions. Like the vampire, Hearn's zombie has an enigmatic desirability that, in the concluding crisis, equates sexual concupiscence with death.

II. TWENTIETH-CENTURY GOTHIC AND THE ZOMBIES OF MODERNITY

In the eighteenth and nineteenth centuries, the term 'zombie' referred to a constellation of gothic properties related to slave culture in the Caribbean: the leader of maroon rebels, a ghost or revenant, or a demon-lover in the shape of an impossibly seductive young woman. In the first decades of the twentieth century, the figure of the zombie is revived and rewritten, remade in new circumstances. The new zombie of the modern era, nonetheless, does not forget its slave heritage, the status of the revenant, or its role in colonial desire. The modern zombie retains an explicit connection to syncretic religion in the Caribbean, especially Haitian voodoo, and the politics of imperialism and independence, again especially in Haiti. The zombie's gothicisation of imperial labour and miscegenation articulates competing issues of modernity, race and capitalism. The subsequent migration of the zombie in the 1930s to the pulp fictions and B-movies of popular culture rewrites this discourse on modern imperialism as an imperial critique of modernity itself.

To most observers, Haiti at the turn of the century was an exceptional place, a land outside progress, modernity and history. The American president, Theodore Roosevelt, on a cruise in the Caribbean in 1906, saw in Haiti a 'beautiful, venomous, tropical' island, which recalled to him 'the hot, evil, riotous life of the old planters and slaveowners'. Haiti's violent history of slavery and revolution, he concluded, had led to 'the decay of most of the islands, the turning of Haiti into a land of savage negroes, who have reverted to voodooism and cannibalism'. Against this gothic atavism, Roosevelt argues, civilising American 'effort' will bring the Caribbean forward, out of 'wild and bloody romance' into modernity.[42] Commercial competition between the United States, France, and Germany intensified after the Spanish-American War of 1898–9, and US foreign policy became more notably imperial in its ambitions, seeking to establish protectorate status over Haiti (equivalent, many thought, to a colony). Political instability and economic decline came to a head in May 1915 when the US armed forces invaded and occupied Haiti, both to forestall German designs and to protect American railroad interests. The Marines established a client military dictatorship that ruled until 1934: under a Haitian president nominally elected by the National Assembly, the US forces exercised complete hegemony over the island. Resistance to the Marines by armed peasant irregular forces called *cacos* was provoked by the regime's re-institution of the *corvée*, a form of forced labour, to construct a network of roads. To many ordinary Haitians, this forced labour presaged the re-establishment of slavery. The uprisings and rebellions of *caco* forces, characterised in Marine reports as 'bandits', induced a systematic suppression by the Marines and the Gendarmerie d'Haiti (an armed constabulary under Marine command). This 'pacification' campaign – described as 'a reign of terror' even in Marine reports – killed at least 2,250 Haitians in the first five years of occupation.[43] Although peace and relative prosperity were established in the 1920s, resistance to the regime erupted into rebellion again in 1929. The Marines were withdrawn, and independence re-established in 1934.

The complex location of voodoo, and the zombie, in the discourse of the American occupation reinforced the notion that voodoo was a focus of Haitian resistance. On the one hand, voodoo priests and secret societies did play a significant role in the *caco* resistance.[44] The study of voodoo became a centre of cultural resistance to American imperialism, first in ethnographic work such as that of the anthropologist Jean Price-Mars and later by Haitian populist politicians such as Francois 'Papa Doc' Duvalier, later president of Haiti (1957–71).[45] As Michel Laguerre has argued, in Haiti, voodoo became indistinguishable from politics.[46] On the other hand, American representations of voodoo were often intended to legitimate their regime by demonstrating the 'savage' and 'barbarous' nature of Haitian rebels. In Brenda Gayle Plummer's terms, representations of voodoo constitute one of 'the instruments of power' of the occupation, by which Western writers controlled interpretations of Haitian society. As she notes, travel-writers repeated a 'durable repertory of myths, legends and simple gossip, which through constant use took on the patina of truth'.[47] Building on St John and Froude, Hesketh Pritchard's travelogue *Where Black Rules White* (1900) and F. A. Ober's travel-guide (1908) repeated lurid claims of ritual child sacrifice and cannibalism in voodoo ceremony.[48] John Houston Craige, a captain in the Marines radio service, relates a tale of voodoo and cannibalism in his *chronique scandaleuse, Cannibal Cousins* (1934). Aimed at demonstrating the illegitimacy of the President Borno's puppet regime in the run-up to evacuation, Craige relates the story of a Haitian politician, Dr Marbeuf, a former senator rumoured to be a 'voodoo magician'. Marbeuf, he recounts, had made a deal with the devil when he was a young man: Marbeuf was to supply a baby for cannibal sacrifice every year in return for the devil's aid in furthering his career. For thirty-nine years the devil advances Marbeuf's career, satiated by his prodigious fathering of children. However, advancing years render Marbeuf infertile, and in terror of the devil's power, he is forced to steal a baby from a nearby Syrian family. Discovery, arrest and humiliation follow. Craige constructs Marbeuf's despised ambition – he is one of those 'individuals who had risen from the swarming mass of primitives by virtue of their own native energy and ability'[49] – as both collaboration and Faustian necromancy.

— MODERN SLAVERY IN SEABROOK'S *THE MAGIC ISLAND* —

The inescapable politics of voodoo research is also legible in William Seabrook's *The Magic Island* (1929), the *locus classicus* for the modern zombie. Cast in a disquieting gothic mode, yet reliant on the methodologies of travel-writing, folklore and anthropology, this peculiar book is an account of a young American's travels in Haiti. *The Magic Island* was Seabrook's most successful work, selling more than half a million copies in the United States, although it caused resentment and bitterness in Haiti.[50] As a 'white' American, Seabrook's intimate treatment of voodoo was considered by contemporaries to be remarkable, if not scandalous. *The New York Times* commented in 1929 that Seabrook has 'travelled deeply. It is apparent that he has penetrated as few white men have done, perhaps as no white man has done in so short a time, to the soul of Haiti.'[51] Seabrook's Haitian journal records a journey across the racial boundary at the heart of the occupation. As Hans Schmidt has argued, racial segregation in occupied Haiti followed models, drawn from the American South, of systematic social discrimination supported by intense racial hostility. American personnel associated with the occupation authorities had no social contact with any Haitians, and social ostracism followed for those American businessmen who maintained social contact with the Francophone Haitian elite.[52] Although Seabrook retains throughout the book the racist essentialism upon which the colour bar was erected, his adoption of a gothic narrative model beseeches transgressive journeys across the boundary line, away from the light-filled world of civilisation into the dark mysteries of Haitian culture.

Seabrook relates how, almost by chance, he realises that Louis, his yard boy, inhabits a second world, that of voodoo.

> I learned from Louis that we white strangers in this twentieth-century city, with our electric lights and motor cars, bridge games and cocktail parties, were surrounded by another world invisible, a world of marvels, miracles and wonders – a world in which the dead rose from their graves and walked.

Surrounding the modern world is a secret world of voodoo supernaturalism. Seabrook's journey towards this 'world of marvels' is understood as an historical reversion to a primitive past. 'It was humble Louis', Seabrook says, 'who set my feet on the path which led finally through river, desert, and jungle, beyond the clouds, and at last to the Voodoo Holy of Holies.' As he journeys up into the mountainous interior of the island, he travels across the colour bar and down through the layers of Haitian society to become the lodger of Maman Célie, a *mamaloi* or Voodoo priestess, in her 'habitation, lost in the high mountains, . . . primitive and patriarchal'.[53] Reading his physical journey as travel back in history thus recapitulates a classically primitivist strategy. Through what Seabrook suggests is some sort of mystical sentimental community, Maman Célie is able to accept him for what he is (a *blanc* and a writer), and yet also permit his attendance at voodoo ceremony. Here he witnesses – to his evident satisfaction – animal sacrifice, orgiastic celebration and a girl possessed by the spirit of a goat, all related in a heady tone of sedulous credulity.[54]

Having narrated his credentials in the opening chapters, Seabrook turns, in the second part of the book, to 'Black Sorcery', a title which puns the notion of racial blackness with the putative necromancy of Haitian voodoo. The chapter teasingly entitled '. . . Dead Men Working in the Cane-Fields' presents his account of the zombie, and has a careful three-part rhetorical organisation: offering a definition, and an anecdotal example, before revealing Seabrook's most compelling evidence, his eye-witness account of his own encounter with a zombie. The manner of narrating these events is not unlike travel-writing, especially the loud 'I' of narrative observation and the luxurious loco-descriptive passages, emotionally laden and gothic in tone, while his extensive footnotes, offering more detailed authenticating evidence, justify the claims and amplify the intellectual ambition of the chapter. His guide to 'the ragged edge of things which are beyond either reason or superstition' is a literate

Haitian peasant farmer, Constant Polynice: a man familiar with, and sceptical about, every superstition of the nation's folklore. Their discussions range over fire-hags, 'who left their skins at home and set the cane-fields blazing'; the vampire, 'a woman sometimes living, sometimes dead, who sucked the blood of children' and the werewolf (*chauché* in Creole). Seabrook notes that as these demons are well known outside 'the tangled Haitian folk-lore', they were no novelty. However, there was one creature 'exclusively local' – the zombie. Unusually, the sceptical Polynice is convinced that the zombie 'is not a matter of superstition' but really exists.[55]

In his investigations amongst more credulous Haitians, Seabrook discovers that:

> while the *zombie* came from the grave, it was neither a ghost nor yet a person who had been raised like Lazarus from the dead. The *zombie*, they say, is a soulless human corpse, still dead, but taken from the grave and endowed by sorcery with a mechanical semblance of life – it is a dead body which is made to walk and act and move as if it was alive.

Unlike the biblical figure of Lazarus, miraculously restored to life, or an incorporeal ghost, the zombie is a dead body that acts as if alive (undead or dead-and-alive). This ambiguous state is the result of possession: 'People who have the power to do this go to a fresh grave, dig up the body before it has time to rot, galvanise it into movement, and then make it a servant or slave.' The zombie is a victim of possession, and their actions can be directed by the zombie master. This activity is clearly supernatural, but like Mary Shelley's vision of Frankenstein's reanimation of the creature, it is accomplished using a metaphor from science: that of galvanism. This theory, first advanced by Luigi Galvani (1737–98), proposed that the animal nervous system used a force analogous to electricity. Here it signifies the lifelike motion imparted to dead matter by applications of electricity, implying a mechanistic process of zombification. In Seabrook's account, the purpose of the zombie is utilitarian, in that the zombie provides a quiescent labour force. The zombie is created so as to act as a 'servant or slave, occasionally for the commission of some crime, more often simply as a drudge around the habitation or the farm, setting it dull heavy tasks, and beating it like a dumb beast if it slackens.'[56] Work is the destiny of the zombie: a labourer for whom there is nothing else but labour. While the profit of their work belongs to the owner-possessor, the zombies' corporeal maintenance costs almost nothing, since they are dead. The zombie, the absolute in cheap labour, recalls the condition of the slave: indeed, the zombie is an enslaved corpse. In Seabrook's construction, the zombie is the ghost of slavery made real.

Polynice, to illustrate his account, relates the story of the zombies of Hasco, a comic tale cast in a gothic mode. As the narrator explains, Hasco was an 'American-commercial-synthetic' word that 'stands for the Haitian-American Sugar Company'. The epitome of modernity, it was:

> an immense factory plant, dominated by a huge chimney, with clanging machinery, steam whistles, freight cars. It is like a chunk of Hoboken. It lies in the eastern suburbs of Port-au-Prince, and beyond it stretch the canefields of the Cul-de-Sac. Hasco makes rum when the sugar market is off, pays low wages, a shilling or so a day, and gives steady work. It is modern big business, and sounds it, looks it, smells it.[57]

The Haitian-American Sugar Company (HASCO), as the sole modern sugar refinery in Haiti, was the focus of much American commercial ambition. Lean years during the occupation had been turned to profit only by driving down the cost of labour. By subcontracting to Haitian gang bosses, HASCO took no responsibility for the low wages of its workers.[58] As the operator of a large-scale agricultural plantation, in which labourers were disciplined by gang bosses and worked for very low wages, HASCO unsurprisingly appeared to Haitians as a form of modern, commercialised and neo-imperial slavery.

Polynice's story, set in 1918, concerns the labourers offered to Hasco by 'an old black headman, Ti Joseph of Colombier'. These workers were a 'band of ragged creatures who shuffled along behind him, staring dumbly, like people walking in a daze'. Explaining their wordless expressions as the fear of simple rustics in the city, Joseph's gang is hired, and allowed to work in an out-of-the-way corner of the plantation, where the noise and smoke of the factory will not frighten them. In fact, of course, 'these were not living men and women but poor unhappy *zombies* whom Joseph and his wife Croyance had dragged from their peaceful graves to slave for him in the sun'.[59] Seabrook's use of the term 'slave' here is not accidental. The anthropologist Alfred Metraux observes that, 'A *zombi's* life is seen in terms which echo the harsh existence of a slave in the old colony of Santo Domingo'.[60] Having set them to work with beatings to make them move faster, Joseph reminds Croyance that their food must contain no salt or meat. Over the three-day Fête Dieu holiday, while Joseph spends the proceeds of their labour in the city, the zombies are left in the care of Croyance. She is charged with keeping them from straying and preparing their salt-less victuals, 'flat, tasteless *bouillie*' of savoury millet or plantains seasoned with dried fish and garlic. The narrator remarks, 'as every one knows, the *zombies* must never be permitted to taste salt or meat.'[61] As Wade Davis quips, salt is the antidote to the zombie process, as salt brings the zombie worker to an awareness of his condition of slavery (playing on salt's symbolic and literal association with honourable reward of labour in salary).[62]

However while Joseph is away, Croyance takes a fancy to see the crowds and processions of the holiday celebrations, and so she takes the zombies into town (see Figure 10). In the market square, she leads the zombies into a deserted market booth, where they 'sat like people asleep with their eyes open, staring but seeing nothing'. After the procession passes, Croyance makes her lunch of savoury dried herring and biscuit baked with salt and soda. As she dines, 'she pitied the *zombies* who had worked so faithfully for Joseph in the canefields, and who now had nothing.' From a passing market seller she purchases them some *Tablettes pistaches*, which the narrator explains are 'a sort of candy made of brown cane sugar (*rapadou*); sometimes with *pistaches*, which in Haiti are peanuts, or with coriander seed'. Croyance reasons with herself that as '"these *tablettes* are not salted or seasoned, they are sweet, and can do no harm to the *zombies* just this once"'. However, unbeknownst to her, the baker of the *tablettes* had salted the *pistache* nuts

> and as the *zombies* tasted the salt, they knew they were dead and made a dreadful outcry, and arose and turned their faces toward the mountain. No one dared stop them, for they were corpses walking in the sunlight, and they themselves and all the people knew that they were corpses.

As the zombies reached their own village, they were recognised by the villagers as fathers, brothers, wives and daughters. Rushing forward to welcome their departed loved ones, the villagers saw they 'were *zombies* who had been dragged dead from their graves'. But the zombies failed to recognise their family members, and shuffled past them to the graveyard, where they clawed at the ground to enter their graves again. 'As their cold hands touched the earth of their own graves, they fell and lay there, rotting carrion.' In revenge, the villagers discover Ti Joseph's name, have a *bocor* (voodoo priest) prepare a 'deadly needle *ouanga*' (charm) to poison him, and then to make sure, ambush him down on the plain, and hack his head off with a machete.[63]

This tale of 'walking dead men' relates not only the history of the 'zombie superstition' but also a homily about unforeseen consequences and female cupidity, observed in Croyance's treacherously silly behaviour. But the zombies, to Seabrook at least, do express material about the occupation, and the history of slavery. For these zombie-slaves, emancipation is equated with self-consciousness and self-realisation, not exterior agency. In this way, the zombies offer a particularly Haitian metanarrative of abolition and liberation. René Dépestre too connects the zombie with liberation struggles:

Figure 10. Alexander King, 'Croyance, Leading the Nine Dead Men and Women', William Seabrook, The Magic Island *(London: George G. Harrap, 1929), opp. p. 98. Reproduced with permission of University of Sydney Library.*

According to the myth, it was forbidden to put salt in the zombi's food since this would revitalise his spiritual energies. The history of colonisation is the process of man's general zombification. It is also the quest for a revitalising salt capable of restoring to man the use of his imagination and culture.[64]

In Dépestre's argument, the ubiquity of salt optimistically assesses the potential for revolutionary liberation from colonialism's oppression.

The narrator does not propose that Polynice's story is true or reasonable: indeed, he assumes it would persuade only a credulous and ignorant peasant. However, Polynice says that he will convince Seabrook as he was himself convinced, by showing him a zombie, one of these "'walking dead men" . . . with their faces and their eyes in which there is no life.'[65] Seabrook's own encounter with the zombies occurs in broad daylight one afternoon on the road to Picmy, where he and Polynice encounter three men and a woman labouring on a rough, stony terraced slope. The woman, called Lamercie, is the 'keeper' of three zombies, and as Seabrook approaches, he experiences a 'sickening shock' when he looks into the zombie's face.

The eyes were the worst. It was not my imagination. They were in truth like the eyes of a dead man, not blind, but staring, unfocused, unseeing. The whole face, for that matter, was bad enough. It was vacant, as if there was nothing behind it. It seemed not only expressionless, but incapable of expression.

Seabrook represents his shock – a 'mental panic' – not only in search of gothic effects, but also to persuade his readers. He reels from the scene:

for the flash of a second I had a sickening, almost panicky lapse in which I thought, or rather felt, "Great God, maybe this stuff is really true, and if it is true, it is rather awful, for it upsets everything." By "everything" I meant the natural fixed laws and processes on which all modern human thought and actions are based.[66]

His rehearsal of a drama of incomprehension and rational breakdown is an authenticating strategy: the zombie is a horror that defies representation, and can only be registered by feeling. Thus, while Seabrook relies on empirical description to create gothic effects, he saturates the scene with the trace of something more like sentiment. As Seabrook's reviewer for *The New York Times* noted, this makes him something of a 'mystic', credulous in the supernatural, and as such the book is 'not quite a scientific contribution'.[67] Accepting the truth of the zombie, Seabrook argues, means rejecting modern systems of rationality and science – and accepting an older world view in which the world of spirits has real force.

Seabrook's escape from this gothic *mis-en-abyme* comes when he proposes a rational explanation for the effects he has witnessed. Rather than 'dead men walking' the '*zombies* were nothing but poor ordinary demented human beings, idiots, forced to toil in the fields'.[68] Polynice's testimony that many people have witnessed their dead relatives being buried and then subsequently found alive working as zombies is given added force by Seabrook's footnote inaccurately recording an anecdote from Stephen Bonsal's *The American Mediterranean* (1912). This recounts the adventures of a well-to-do man in Port-au-Prince who fell ill, died and was buried, only to be found tied to a tree, in his grave clothes, some days later – although Bonsal ascribes the man's adventures to a blood sacrifice gone wrong, and he does not use the term 'zombie'.[69] Such stories, Seabrook replies, must be cases of mistaken identity, or mis-recognition of a double. Scrabbling for rational certainty, Seabrook explains that 'it is a fixed rule of reasoning in my country that we will never accept the possibility of a thing's being "supernatural" so long as any natural explanation, even far-fetched, seems adequate'.[70] Later again, Seabrook is told by another friend, Dr Antoine Villiers, a 'pragmatic rationalist', of his suspicions concerning certain voodoo ceremonies designed for inflicting a condition resembling death, a state of 'suspended animation'. An article from the Criminal Code of the Republic of Haiti is offered as evidence:

> *Article* 249. Also shall be qualified as attempted murder the employment which may be made against any person of substances which, without causing actual death, produce a lethargic coma more or less prolonged. If, after the administering of such substances, the person has been buried, the act shall be considered murder no matter what result follows.[71]

As Villiers notes, this document has 'nothing mysterious or esoteric' about it. For Seabrook, the scene of the zombie is offered closure with the reassertion of rational modernity. Staging a contest between rational science and the supernatural, the play of action here confirms, and denies, the political argument that the American occupation of Haiti is a rehearsal of an earlier phase of colonialism, in which folk-culture fosters resistance to tyranny. Seabrook's zombie story reiterates the argument from history central to other gothic narratives discussed in this book: dramatising and extrapolating a wider contest between rival forms of thought, between rationality and mysticism, between history and modernity.

'. . . Dead Men Working in the Cane Fields' offers a series of ritualised boundary crossings, managed through rhetorical techniques of persuasion and authentication. Borders are traversed between black and white society; public and secret; authority and the underground; official culture and the masses; scepticism and credulity; slavery and freedom; history and modernity; and life and death. From the light-centred white rationality of official public culture, with its ironic homologies of scepticism, modernity and civilisation, Seabrook crosses into a world of dark spirits, superstition and savagery, in reverse of the zombie's journey from death to life, associating a gothicised voodoo with deep history, slavery and mourning. The boundary crossing where Seabrook stops being a *blanc* and an American, inscribed in the gothic act of transgression, experimentally repudiates the terms of value of Seabrook's culture even as it also reconfirms them.

Seabrook's eyewitness report of a zombi in Haiti was validated, in a sense, by a series of writers and ethnologists who also claimed to penetrate through to the real Haiti. A German traveller, Richard Loederer, reports a conversation with a Haitian informant called only 'Uncle Dave', who relates a history of voodoo zombies based securely on Seabrook's account. 'Many of the workers on the sugar fields are mere soulless carcasses, brought back to life and now slaving for their masters.'[72] Edna Taft, a high-status American woman, immersing herself in 'the throbbing pulse' of Haitian popular culture, related a history (clearly incited by Seabrook) of the 'false zombis': 'the living dead . . . soulless, brainless. Their masters force them to work in cane or cotton fields at night, or out-of-the-way places where they will not be detected.' Taft likened her research into voodoo to 'crawling through' the 'Black Looking-Glass', like Alice, to a world where 'everything occurred illogically'.[73] A more academic approach was undertaken by the black American novelist and playwright Zora Neale Hurston. A trained anthropologist, Hurston was awarded a Guggenheim grant in 1938 to pursue research into voodoo in Haiti and obeah in Jamaica. Her account, again hybridising the laconic credulity of travel-writing with the intellectual curiosity of ethnography, was published as *Tell My Horse* in 1938 and under the more explanatory title *Voodoo Gods: An Inquiry into Native Myths and Magic in Jamaica and Haiti* in London the following year.[74] Addressing anthropological concerns, she refuses to use rationalism or science to repudiate the supernatural events she experienced. As Henry Louis Gates, Jnr, remarks, 'her work celebrates rather than moralises'.[75] Hurston's radical credulity underlines the creative potential of voodoo as a way of life: a credulity that she understands as a politics. Her work undertook to raise awareness of the black heritage in America, and is located in the contemporary Harlem renaissance. She begins her account thus: 'This is the way Zombies are spoken of: They are the bodies without souls. The living dead. Once they were dead, and after that they were called back to life.' In a deadpan tone, she recounts the process by which the *bocor* (a *boko* or voodoo priest) performs the rituals that result in the reanimation of the chosen dead victim. After collecting Haitian press reports regarding cases of supposed zombies, she describes meeting and photographing a zombie incarcerated in the hospital at Gonaives on 8 November 1936. Finding the woman cringing against a wall with a cloth hiding her face and head, Hurston eventually uncovers her face, despite the woman's reluctance to be inspected. 'Finally the doctor forcibly uncovered her and held her so that I could take her face. And the sight was dreadful. The blank face with the dead eyes. The eyelids were white all round the eyes as if they had been burned with acid'.[76]

— GOTHIC HYBRIDS AND THE WHITE ZOMBIES —

Following the publication of Seabrook's *Magic Island* in 1929, the zombie can properly be said to take on a life of its own in Western culture, as many writers, and film-makers, narrate versions of the zombie. The proliferation of zombie stories in print and cinema is a larger history than can be related here, but the examples which follow explore the creative potential of material developed from Seabrook, Hurston and the other popular travel writers. In adopting, adapting and reanimating their firsthand research, later writers feel no requirement to do their own fieldwork. The zombie becomes a property which can be deployed in a wide variety of contexts and locations. Some of these films and writings retain the Haitian setting, while others either substitute alternative exotic locations or domesticate the zombie by transporting the figure back to the metropolitan heart of civilisation.

Building on the figure of the zombie celebrated in Seabrook, Garnett Weston, using the pseudonym G. W. Hutter, published a short gothic shocker called 'Salt Is Not For Slaves' in the influential pulp-fiction magazine *Ghost Stories* for August 1931. Weston's story, elaborating the received notion that salt is an antidote for zombification, cannily rewrites the zombie trope as a counter-revolutionary argument, reversing Seabrook's gothic identification of the zombie with the slaves of modern capitalism. Weston's tale, set in Port-au-Prince, pits an encounter between the male American narrator and Marie, an ancient Haitian servant woman who comes to his attention as the result of a squabble when salt is accidentally spilt on her. The narrator inveigles Marie to tell her story, despite her warnings that 'Voodoo' is involved. As it unfolds, the narrator realises that her childhood stories of growing up on a large sugar plantation relate events that happened over 150 years ago. Raised a slave, Marie was instructed by her cruel master that if slaves ate salt then they would sicken and die. Her lover Tresaint leads a slave insurrection inspired by the stories of Christophe, the black revolutionary general later crowned king – although the story's version of Haitian history is hazily inaccurate. In the revolutionary mayhem, Tresaint ransacks his master's cellar, consuming huge quantities of the finest aged rum. Saluting the slaves' new freedom, Tresaint decides to prove that 'the master's power is gone' by consuming salt too. Marie watches in horror as her lover turns into a skeleton in front of her: 'I saw his face set in rigidity, the flesh seemed to drop away leaving nothing but cheek bones and eyes.' Screaming in horror, Marie concludes, 'He was dead! They were all dead! They were corpses treading a fantastic dance of death'. The shrieking spirits of the dancing dead whirl out of the house and make straight for the cemetery, collapsing onto their graves. The story refigures the rebellion not as freedom but as a new and worse tyranny. The healthful life of slavery – a commonplace argument of pro-slavery apologists – is exchanged through revolution for the rotten death of freedom, recalling by inversion Toussaint L'Ouverture's revolutionary slogan 'Liberty or Death'. In the present day, having accidentally swallowed the salt spilt on her, Marie dies: 'The flesh melted away under my terrified gaze. Nothing was left but the grim bones of the dead.'[77] By the conclusion of 'Salt Is Not For Slaves', the terrible history of the Haitian republic, troped in voodoo, revolution and the zombie, is finally laid to rest under America's benevolent gaze.

The zombie's contestation of imperialism and modernity is also explored in a short story by Manly Wade Wellman (1903–86) called 'The Song of the Slaves', published in another pulp-fiction magazine *Weird Tales* in March 1940.[78] Set in 1853 on a slaving voyage to Africa, the story depicts a cargo of slaves who sing a haunting African song in which they threaten to haunt the ship's captain after their death. The captain, pursued by a British warship enforcing the abolition of the trade in slaves, evades capture and punishment as a slaver, by drowning forty-nine slaves by throwing them overboard while they are still in their manacles. Aspects of this horrifying narrative recall the notorious Zong case of 1781, in which a slaver drowned 131 slaves from his cargo in order to claim the insurance on them.[79] In Wellman's story, on the slaver's return to his plantation in Charleston, he is visited and killed by the undead bodies of the drowned slaves, who have walked across the bottom of the ocean, still singing their haunting chant, and still in their chains. They exact their revenge by adding him to their chaingang, and marching him back into the sea to his death. Slavery, Wellman proposes, is the originating sin of the American polity.

The zombie stories of Vivian Meik, (1895–1959), a British journalist and travel-writer who wrote a volume of gothic horror tales set in a fictional African colony, called *Devils' Drums* (1933), conjoin themes of race and marriage. In 'White Zombie', Geoffrey Aylett, acting commissioner of the district of Nswadsi, is one night assailed by a suffocating heavy mist, 'a foul miasma reeking with all the horror of corruption' that seems to have been summoned up by the throbbing drums of African tribesmen. Recovering in a mission hospital, Aylett agrees with Padre Vaneken that in Africa 'Civilisation counts not' and that, as in Haiti, where Vaneken has also lived, strange events occur that surpass rational understanding. With suspicions aroused by Vaneken's tales of Haitian voodoo and zombies, Aylett visits the estate of an old army friend, John Sinclair, who had died in the previous year. Now managed by Sinclair's beautiful but hard widow, the estate is, to his surprise, in impeccable order. Mrs Sinclair explains that her labourers work so intently because she has got 'to the heart of Africa – the throbbing beating heart'. Aylett, who disapproves of the lone woman's success, cautions her that 'we don't encourage Europeans, especially European women, to go "native"'. Departing the estate at the end of his visit, Aylett secretly doubles back and observes the house from the surrounding trees. There he sees Mrs Sinclair, now only partially clad in a leopard skin, in the company of a witch-doctor, 'a gigantic native who looked like some obscene devil . . ., sinister and grotesque'.[80] As the drums beat, a 'grotesque procession' of labourers emerges, moving slowly and automatically to their work across the plantation. Aylett realises with horror that '*these pitiful automatons were dead – and they were not allowed to die . . .* Zombies'. As Aylett watches, he sees Mrs Sinclair's 'face distorted with perverted lust', and gasps 'in cold terror' that the last zombie in the line is his old friend Sinclair. Sinclair's widow has zombified her own white husband to make him work like a slave: not only reversing the commonplace notion of marriage as slavery, but further inverting supposedly inviolable colonial race hierarchies. As Meik comments in another zombie story of miscegenation, sexual relations between black men and white women contradict the central tenet of imperial order. 'There is a plane on which black and white may never meet on terms of intimacy.'[81] The horror in this story turns on a conception of race relations in the colony that is both misogynist and racist.

The 1930s white zombie tales offer a mapping of anxieties about slave insurrection and resistance to imperialism onto those about inter-racial sex, in such a way that one theorises the other. In Richard Goggard's noxiously racist zombie novel, *The Whistling Ancestors* (1936), a voodoo witchdoctor leads a gang of white slavers, kidnapping English women into prostitution. The investigations of the Buchanesque narrator uncover a global voodoo conspiracy to enslave the white races, aided by an army of zombies being manufactured in a basement in Cornwall by a mysterious Russian, Professor Kucynski.[82] As Robert Young observes, 'the forms of sexual exchange brought about by colonialism were themselves both mirrors and consequences of the modes of economic exchange that constituted the basis of colonial relations'.[83] In Dr Gordon Leigh Bromley's short story 'American Zombie', published in the late 1930s, the narrator, an American journalist with a keen interest in antiquarian books and 'Negro culture', undertakes a visit to Paris in 1936, where he reports a conversation with a fellow researcher, Henri Champley, about the 'occult side of the world' – found in Africa, the Orient and Haiti – and its relations to the 'civilised white' world. Champly concludes that, 'He was frankly alarmed at the intercourse of white men with coloured women, and – what seemed more serious to him – that of white women and the coloured men. He could understand, he said, the German revulsion against this biological revolution.' Mention of Seabrook's *Magic Island* causes Champley to recall his experience of meeting a white zombie in Harlem in New York, where he had gone to further his 'studies in Negro culture'. There, he relates with some revulsion, he had found a white woman living with 'a mysterious old Negro who had claimed the power to produce and control the zombies', who seemed to exercise some power over her similar to hypnotism or mesmerism. When Champley visits the woman, living in the garret of a Harlem rooming-house, he records his experience of 'one of the living dead':

> He drew back this cloth, revealing a deathly waxen face of a woman of perhaps thirty, dark-haired. He took the cover completely off. Her arms rested by her sides, and her torso and limbs glowed with a peculiar waxen pallor. There was not a spot of colour on her, no other hair, and the nipples were like white roots of some plant.[84]

The uncanny whiteness of the woman figures her as a zombie, playing upon a contrast between her master (black, empowered, lively) and the slave (white, passive, deathly). Gothic potential is derived from the revolutionary role-reversals of the scene. Bromley struggles to legitimise his voyeuristic curiosity about the spectacle of inter-racial sex by articulating it in a racist occult discourse. A similar strategy was also pursued in the cinema, where the earliest zombie films show a direct allegiance to the 1930s studies of voodoo by Seabrook and Craige.

III. THE OCCULTATION OF MISCEGENATION AND SLAVERY IN THE ZOMBIE FILM

White Zombie, directed by Victor Halperin, has been justly described as the 'archetype and model of all zombie-movies'.[85] It is certainly the first film to use that term, derived from William Seabrook's *The Magic Island* (1929). Produced outside the studio system by Edward Halperin, in the earliest days of the 'talkies', the film is closer in structure to a silent film. The production hinged upon Bela Lugosi, the famous star of Tod Browning's 1931 Universal Pictures hit *Dracula*. Playing a shadowy zombie master Murder Legendre, Lugosi's distinctive voice and accent, and his compelling eyes, were deployed in service of the film's theme of possession. The plot is powered by the motif of desire, centring on the blonde beauty of Madeline Short (played by Madge Bellamy), a young American woman visiting Haiti. She becomes the focus of a contest between her bank-clerk fiancé, Neil Parker (John Harron), and a rich Haitian plantation owner, Charles Beaumont (Robert Frazer). Despite her fidelity, Beaumont swears he is willing to sacrifice all to possess his object of desire (a Faustian theme). Persuading the couple to visit his estate, he decides to enlist the help of his neighbour, the mysterious plantation owner Murder Legendre. At Legendre's plantation, Beaumont is horrified to discover that the labourers are all zombies, over whose corpses Legendre has gained possession. The zombies slowly toil at their work with fixed expressions, and staring unfocused eyes: their mute and uncomplaining drudgery highlighted by the only sound present in the scene, the mournful creaking of the mill wheel.[86]

The Halperin film is often described as an adaptation of Seabrook's *Magic Island* – although the only writing credit is to Garnett Weston. The film does not attempt to cover all of Seabrook's wide-ranging book, although some scenes and anecdotes drawn from his examination of 'Black Sorcery' can be seen to have echoes in the film's narrative. The central Seabrook 'property' detectable in the film is Polynice's narrative of the zombie workers of HASCO. This tale, as examined earlier, reiterates the zombie's relation to slavery by representing the American occupation as a new imperialism and a renewed slavery. In *White Zombie*, the zombie theme again articulates the alienation endured by labour in modern capitalism, especially in the mechanised production of the factory. The illegitimacy of this mode of production is underlined when one of the zombie workers topples into the cane mill to a certain, and second, death, ground up by his unfeeling fellow workers – a scenario which recalls a notorious punishment on the slave plantations of the *ancien régime*.[87]

Using a potion provided by Legendre, Beaumont gains the same kind of magical possession of Madeline that Legendre has over his zombies. Like Dracula, Legendre claims a deep antiquity, using necromantic powers to master his own destiny. The poison he provides causes Madeline to appear dead; but after her burial, Legendre, Beaumont and his gang of zombies are able to steal her corpse. When she is reanimated, Beaumont possesses her according his previous desires. However, although Madeline as a zombie has retained both her beauty and her female accomplishments (she still plays the piano well), he discovers that she has no expression, desire or emotion. His gifts are accepted without excitement, her allure evaporates in enervation. Her state as a zombie, then, curiously seems to reveal more about her than was intended; a point underlined by Bellamy's unironically wooden acting, in which it is difficult to discern the difference between her self as a zombie and her prior state as a beautiful woman. As such, *White Zombie* both invests in, and offers a critique of, the emotional pathology of the domestic woman, whose characteristic passivity, dullness, and inactivity are here figured as zombification. Reflecting on the oxymoron signalled in its title – the white zombie (the dead white slave) – the film offers a woman quite literally possessed by a desiring man. Exploding the title's pun, the depiction of Madeline as zombie to Beaumont's will literalises the position of women within society, conventionally troped as slavery.

On discovering the disappearance of her corpse, however, Neil and Dr Bruno suspect that she has been abducted by a death cult with designs on her beautiful white body. As Neil understands it, 'the natives' want Madeline's body for sexual purposes, and she would be 'better dead than that'. The film's characteristic mixing of fears puns on the slavery theme of the zombie figure: Madeline's fate as a white slave suggests both prostitution and miscegenation. When Beaumont expresses his desire to free Madeline's soul ('I can't bear those empty staring eyes'), Legendre develops (or brings to fruition) plans for her himself, by zombifying Beaumont. As he does so, in a playful rupture of classical film language, the audience is placed in the position of Beaumont, and made subject to Legendre's staring mesmeric eyes.[88] The scene depends upon Bela Lugosi's telling countenance, and recalls his prior films playing an adept of the mysterious and supernatural, and intriguingly proposes that the audience can be identified as the zombie. Moreover, on two occasions the film implies a shot from the point of view of the zombie, whose blurred focus signals the loss of agency and consciousness.

Neil's island-wide search for Madeline draws him, by unspoken bonds of love (articulated using a cinematic language of dissolves and wipes), to a mysterious castle located on a cliff high above the sea, where Legendre has imprisoned Madeline. In the final showdown between Legendre, aided by his zombie gang, and the young couple, Legendre battles with Neil's sense of moral purpose. Madeline finds enough residual will to resist Legendre's orders to kill Neil with a sacrificial knife. As Legendre's powers over Madeline wane, a shadow lifts from her face (literally in a cinematic sense), and her gleaming, smiling countenance is restored. The film effects closure, in part, through this reassertion of the redemptive power of romantic love: Neil's power to save Madeline is his traditional and unproblematic love for her (which seeks expression through the normative channels of marriage). As in the Radcliffean gothic, closure signals the restoration of order, not only through the emblematic suppression of the figurehead of disruption, but also through the resolution of the romantic love plot.

Halperin's film initiated a series of B-grade zombie films in the 1930s, confirming the zombie's migration into Anglophone popular culture. Subsequent zombie films freely adapt the properties of the zombie trope however. Halperin's *Revolt of the Zombies* (1936) relocates the scene to Cambodia, where an expedition searches for a secret formula devised to turn men into zombies. In *King of the Zombies* (1941), directed by Jean Yarbrough, the passengers of a crashed plane find a basement factory manufacturing zombies on an island off the coast of South America, whereupon they incite the zombies to rebel against their master's tyranny. Monogram Pictures reprised this plot with *Revenge of the Zombies* (1943), directed by István Székely, in which a Nazi doctor creates armies for the Third Reich from the bodies of the dead in an old mansion in a Louisiana swamp. The tiredness of the genre is perhaps signalled by RKO's comic zombie farce *Zombies on Broadway* (1945), directed by Gordon Douglas. Renamed *Loonies on Broadway* for its British release, it was advertised with the tag-line 'Hee! Hee! What ghoulish glee!'.

The self-conscious vulgarity of the B-grade zombie film was contested by Val Lewton's *I Walked with a Zombie* (1943), which equally self-consciously repudiated crude pulp conventions by insisting on its own high-cultural values of beauty, history and liberty.[89] The film was the second of four low-budget horror films commissioned from the producer Lewton by RKO-Radio Pictures in 1942. The studio was alerted to the potential of such films by the notable horror successes of Universal Pictures in the 1930s, such as *Frankenstein*, *Dracula*, and *The Mummy*. The studio's understanding of horror-genre expectations was signalled by the title, chosen for Lewton, without consultation, by the studio's marketing department. Nonetheless, RKO studio boss, Charles Koerner, wanted to do something different with the four films, commenting that 'vampires, werewolves, and manmade monsters had been over-exploited.'[90] Pushed by the need to innovate, and drawn by the desire to make their own mark on the genre, Lewton's unit responded by producing four idiosyncratic horror films: *Cat People* (1943), *I Walked with a Zombie* (1943), *The Leopard Man* (1943) and *The Seventh Victim* (1943). These films eschew the grisly effects of horror and instead work towards emotionally ambiguous moments of tenderness with which to counterpoint uncanny or supernatural material. The four films were, and still are, strange and poetic in their narrative procedures, working with deep shadow and suggestive sound to produce telling gothic effects.[91]

Lewton assembled a strong production unit comprising young French director Jacques Tourneur, the veteran editor Mark Robson, and the screen writers Curt Siodmark and Ardel Wray. Lewton is reported to have disliked the title intensely, and the opening line of the film ironically comments that, 'It does seem an odd thing to say.' As the credits note, the screenplay was developed from Inez Wallace's story 'I Met a Zombie' in *American Weekly* magazine, which offered a series of zombie anecdotes and folklore from Haiti. But there are also higher cultural influences on the film. After being given the project, Lewton is reported to have told the unit that 'he would make a West Indian version of *Jane Eyre*'.[92] Lewton's identification of a West Indian historical resonance in Brontë's novel of 1847 was also pursued by Jean Rhys in *Wide Sargasso Sea* (1966).[93] The link between these materials is not always clear: from Brontë, Lewton derives the central romantic love plot; from Wallace (and her sources in 1930s voodoo studies) he derives the West Indian scenarios; and from the zombie trope, the central horror motif of the walking dead. Lewton prided himself on his literary sensibility and his drive for authentic detail.[94] Ardel Wray records that the unit's crew were 'all plunged into research on Haitian voodoo', locating 'every book on the subject Val could find'.[95]

At the centre of the film's narrative is Jessica Holland (played by Frances Dee), the beautiful but catatonic wife of Paul Holland (Tom Conway), an Anglophone sugar-plantation owner on the fictional West Indian island of St Sebastian (located near Antigua). The Holland family plantation, the first to import African slaves in the seventeenth century, had retained a faded grandeur and reduced profitability under the management of Holland's half-brother, the alcoholic American Wesley Rand (James Ellison). Holland's brooding intensity recalls the character of Rochester in Brontë's *Jane Eyre* just as Miss Jessica recalls Bertha Mason, the madwoman incarcerated in the attic of Thornfield House. The Jane

Eyre figure is played by a young Canadian nurse hired to care for Jessica: an innocent young woman called Betsy Connell, neither British nor American. Jessica's strange condition defies easy medical analysis: although she is physically unhurt, the resident doctor (Dr Maxwell) asserts that she suffers from mental paralysis after a tropical fever burnt out her cerebral cortex, leaving her without willpower, without speech, 'a sleep-walker who can never be awakened'. Her condition, buried alive in the house, is between that of life and death; and indeed, the island's people read her condition as that of a zombie. Nonetheless, it is clear that Holland considers himself in some way responsible for her psychological condition. The film never clarifies key aspects of Holland's secret family history, but it does emerge that Jessica had grown bored of island life, that she had found succour in a passionate affair with Wesley Rand, and their elopement was thwarted by Holland. The tropical fever that destroyed her sanity, then, is the lock on a prison already established in the contest for authority between the reserved English brutality of Holland (aristocratic, patriarchal, repressed) and the Americanised liberation promised by Rand (commercial, passionate, free).

When Betsy Connell arrives on the island, she is seduced by Holland's brooding charm, which she finds perversely erotic. Holland's seduction of Connell is essentially sadistic, taking place through a series of mannered linguistic chastisements. On the boat to St Sebastian, Holland dispels Connell's aesthetic contemplation of the scenery by explaining that the flying fish leap from the sea not in joy but in terror from their predators, and that the glittering water 'takes its gleam from millions of tiny dead bodies. It's the glitter of putrescence. There's no beauty here – only death and decay.' Their flirtation is almost entirely constituted through such encounters. The love (or passion) that Connell feels for Holland, however, is also perverse in its articulation: rather than trying to win Holland for herself, she states that she loves him so much that she will try to restore his wife to him (to reanimate Jessica's mind and his love for her). This inverted expression of desire again expresses some distinctly eighteenth-century gothic themes.

The film self-consciously elucidates the condition of the zombie, presumably unsure of audience comprehension. The zombie expresses an argument about the history of slavery, played out again in the perverse ideological contest between the brothers Holland and Rand. Nonetheless, both Holland and Maxwell are dismissive of these 'local legends', which they see as a kind of 'contagious' superstition. In a sense, they are right: Jessica has contracted through her brain fever both a mental condition and a status in local mythology. When Connell is first introduced to

Jessica by Maxwell, he states that she makes 'a beautiful zombie': which he explains, ironically, as 'a ghost, the living dead. It's also a drink'. Nonetheless, the film credits the zombie myth as a powerful tool in local folklore, and as such, in local politics. Although ignorant about what she is attempting, Connell resorts to voodoo to restore Jessica's sanity after the more orthodox electric-shock therapy fails. Although the voodoo ceremony leaves the viewer somewhat unresolved, the islanders confirm that Jessica is a zombie when she does not bleed from a wound to her arm. A more sceptical note is sounded when Holland's mother, Mrs Rand, reveals herself to be the mysterious voice of the goddess Dambala, whose supposedly supernatural presence haunts the voodoo temple. Exposed as primitive superstition, the houngan's voodoo rituals are manipulated by Mrs Rand's Christian mission to disseminate modern notions of public hygiene. Behind the primitive supernatural hides the latest turn of civilising values.

The ambiguous obscurity surrounding voodoo is maintained in the film's violent conclusion (played almost without dialogue). As the authorities and police close in on Holland's murky past, Rand proposes that Connell kill Jessica with a drug overdose to give her freedom. When Connell refuses (remonstrating 'she breathes and has life'), Rand opens the gate of the Holland compound to release Jessica to the calling drums of the voodoo *houmfort* (temple). In a simultaneous movement (enunciated by jump-cut montage), the *houngan* stabs his voodoo doll of Jessica with a needle just as Rand stabs her corporeal body with an iron arrow torn from the St Sebastian figurehead in Holland's garden (Ti Misery). Pursued by the stately zombie Carrefour (Darby Jones), Rand carries Jessica into the ocean to his death. Their bodies are recovered by night-fishing islanders. The sermonising declaration delivered perhaps by a preacher as the bodies are brought in torch-lit procession through the gates of the house – she was 'dead in her own life, yea Lord, dead in the selfishness of her own spirit' – suggest that Jessica's sin was self-regard or *amour propre*. By refusing to elucidate the nature of Jessica's zombification, or to clarify the meaning of the title, the film evades narrative closure and refocusses attention on mood and cinematics.

Lewton, constrained by the limited means of the small budget, had insufficient money for large-scale scenes or expensive special effects. In part, he resolved the difficulty by deploying techniques familiar to readers of gothic fiction, but recast in an innovative film language. The film exemplifies moments of purely cinematic terror, especially by postponing the appearance of the object of terror so as to prolong tension. The eventual pay-off (the moment of reification of terror) could be delayed, as in

Cat People, almost indefinitely, and such delay would only serve to extend and heighten the pleasurable sensations the audience derived from the film. To this end, Lewton explored a number of ways of restricting the audience's clear sight of the object of terror. He used off-screen sound (auratic) to intimate the unseen presence of a threatening agent. Shadows were as suggestive as a clear sight. The notorious still photograph used in the publicity for the film, though not actually from it, depicts the shadow of the zombie Carrefour falling across Betsy Connell's bed just as she starts from sleep. Elsewhere, threat is intimated by restricting the view. The film's most powerful instance of the chiaroscuro of gothic *film noir* is the scene in the cane field where Betsy, leading Jessica, first meets the haunting figure of Carrefour, the *houngan's* zombie-servant. As the women's eyes travel along the path between the waving sugar canes, the only source of illumination, Betsy's torch, picks up the various voodoo sigils (signs): a dead goat hanging in a tree, an animal skull. Finally, the light falls on Carrefour's feet. The torch travels up his body to meet – in a secondary terror – his bulging staring eyes. The terrifying event, when it comes, does not enter the viewer's sight by the edge of the frame, but out of the shadows within the shot, as if the terror is in the screen.

Lewton was by his own account a man of 'taste and refinement' who – despite and because of the B-status of his productions – wanted to produce elevated and literary productions. His films give evidence of references to, or the inspiration of, paintings by Goya, Gericault and Hogarth. Lewton's allusive adaptation of the Brontë novel, and the film's self-conscious cinematography, proposes a higher cultural status than mere B-grade horror, a gambit which allows *I Walked With a Zombie* to free itself from the creative slavery of mass culture and from zombie modernity.

— NOTES —

1. *Internet Movie Database*, Amazon.com Co. ([http://www.imdb.com], 8 July 1999).
2. See, for example, Peter Tremayne, *Zombie!* (London: Sphere Books, 1981); Curt Selby, *I, Zombie* (New York: Daw Books, 1982); Jamie Suzanne, *Steven the Zombie* (New York: Bantam Books, 1994); Michael Slade, *Zombie* (London: Hodder & Stoughton, 1996); Joyce Carol Oates, *Zombie* (New York: Plume/Penguin, 1996). None of these texts is recommended.
3. Alfred Metraux, *Voodoo in Haiti*, trans. Hugo Charteris (1957; London: Alfred Deutsch, 1959), pp. 378, 266–7, 281–5.
4. Hans-W. Ackermann and Jeanine Gauthier, 'The Ways and Nature of the Zombi', *Journal of American Folklore*, 104 (1991), pp. 466–94.

5. Maximilien Laroche, 'The Myth of the Zombi', in Rowland Smith, *Exile and Tradition: Studies in African and Caribbean Literature* (New York: Africana Publishing and Dalhousie University Press, 1976), p. 44.

6. Wade Davis, *The Serpent and the Rainbow* (1985; New York: Touchstone for Simon & Schuster, 1997); *The Serpent and the Rainbow*, dir. Wes Craven (Universal Pictures, 1987), 98 mins, colour; Wade Davis, *Passage of Darkness: the ethnobiology of the Haitian zombie* (Chapel Hill, NC: University of North Carolina Press, 1988).

7. Mark Kemp, 'Chemistry of Voodoo', *Discover*, 10, 1 (January 1989), pp. 26–8.

8. Ackermann and Gauthier, 'Ways and Nature', p. 491.

9. Richard Littlewood and Chavannes Douyon, 'Clinical findings in three cases of Zombification', *The Lancet*, 350, 9084 (11 October 1997), pp. 1094–7.

10. James Walvin, *Black Ivory: A History of British Slavery* (London: Fontana, 1992); Elsa Goveia, *Slave Society in the British Leeward Islands at the End of the Eighteenth Century* (New Haven and London: Yale University Press, 1965).

11. Bryan Edwards, *An Historical Survey of the Island of Saint Domingo, together with An Account of the Maroon Negroes in the Island of Jamaica* (London: John Stockdale, 1801), pp. 13–14.

12. John Locke, *Two Treatises on Government* (1690; London: Dent, 1978), II, p. 128.

13. Orlando Patterson, *Slavery and Social Death: a comparative study* (Cambridge, MA: Harvard University Press, 1982), pp. 38–45.

14. Bryan Edwards, *The History, Civil and Commercial, of the British Colonies in the West Indies*, 2 vols (London: John Stockdale, 1793), II, pp. 34, 62, 65.

15. Edwards, *British West Indies*, II, pp. 88–9.

16. Edward Long, *The History of Jamaica, or General Survey of The Antient and Modern State of that Island* (London: T. Lowndes, 1774), II, pp. 416–17.

17. Monica Shuler, 'Afro-American Slave Culture' in Michael Craton (ed.), *Roots and Branches: Current Directions in Slave Studies* (Toronto: Pergamon Press, 1979), p. 130. See also Michael Craton, *Testing the Chains: Resistance to Slavery in the British West Indies* (Ithaca: Cornell University Press, 1982), p. 258.

18. Edwards, *Historical Survey of Saint Domingo*, p. 319.

19. Philip Thicknesse, *Memoirs and Anecdotes*, 3 vols (London: for the author, 1788), I, pp. 120, 126.

20. Edwards, *British West Indies*, II, p. 89.

21. Benjamin Moseley, *A Treatise on Sugar. With Miscellaneous Medical Observations* (1799; London: John Nichols, 1800), pp. 189–93.

22. Maria Nugent, *A Journal of a Voyage to, and Residence in, the Island of Jamaica, from 1801 to . . . 1811* (London: n.p., 1839); Matthew Lewis, *Journal of a West India Proprietor*, ed. Judith Terry (1834; Oxford: Oxford University Press, 1999).

23. Robert Southey, *History of Brazil*, 3 vols (London: Longman, Hurst, Rees and Orme, 1810–1819), I, pp. 495–6.
24. Southey, *History of Brazil*, III, pp. 24–5.
25. R. K. Kent, 'An African State in Brazil', *The Journal of African History*, 6 (1965), pp. 161–75; Robert Nelson Anderson, 'The Quilombo of Palmares: a new overview of a Maroon State in Seventeenth-Century Brazil', *Journal of Latin American Studies*, 28 (1996), pp. 545–66.
26. Southey, *History of Brazil*, III, p. 24n.
27. Méderic Louis Élie Moreau de Saint-Méry, *Description Topographique, Physique, Civile, Politique et Historique de la Partie Française de L'Isle Saint-Domingue* (Philadelphie: by the author, 1797), pp. 47, 48, 50, 52.
28. See C. L. R. James, *The Black Jacobins: Toussaint L'Ouverture and the San Domingo Revolution* (1938; New York: Vintage Books, 1963); Michel S. Laguerre, *Voodoo and Politics in Haiti* (Basingstoke: Macmillan Press, 1989); Thomas O. Ott, *The Haitian Revolution, 1789–1804* (Knoxville: University of Tennessee Press, 1973).
29. Spencer Buckingham St John, *Hayti: or, The Black Republic* (London: Smith, Elder, & Co., 1884), pp. 182–227.
30. James Anthony Froude, *The English in the West Indies; or, The Bow of Ulysses* (London: Longman, Green and Co., 1888), pp. 56, 344.
31. J. J. Thomas, *Froudacity: West Indian Fables by James Anthony Froude* (London: T. Fisher Unwin, 1889).
32. Hearn to H. E. Krehbiel, 1878, *Life and Letters of Lafcadio Hearn*, ed. Elizabeth Bisland, 2 vols (London: Archibald Constable, 1906), I, p. 193.
33. Lafcadio Hearn, 'A Midsummer Trip to the West Indies', *Harper's New Monthly Magazine*, LXXVII, July-September, 1888, pp. 209–26, 327–45, 614–31; Lafcadio Hearn, *Two Years in the French West Indies* (London: Harper & Brothers, 1890).
34. Lafcadio Hearn, 'La Verette and the Carnival in St Pierre, Martinique', *Harper's New Monthly Magazine*, LXVIII, 461 (October 1888), pp. 737–48. The magazine essay is an edited version of that which appears in *Two Years* under the title 'La Vérette', pp. 202–40.
35. Hearn, 'La Verette and the Carnival', pp. 742, 740, 748.
36. Lafcadio Hearn, 'A Midsummer Trip to the Tropics' in *Two Years*, pp. 13–98.
37. Lafcadio Hearn, 'A Study of Half-Breed Races in the West Indies', in *Miscellanies*, ed. Albert Mordell, 2 vols (London: William Heineman, 1924), II, pp. 221–31, p. 221. Miscegenation is also discussed in 'La Fille de Couleur', in *Two Years*, pp. 311–37.
38. Robert Young, *Colonial Desire: Hybridity in Theory, Culture and Race* (London: Routledge, 1995), pp. 90–117.
39. Hearn, 'Half-Breed Races', pp. 221–2, 225–6.
40. Hearn, 'La Guiablesse', *Two Years*, pp. 185–90.
41. Hearn, 'La Guiablesse', pp. 193, 201.

42. Elting E. Morison (ed.), *The Letters of Theodore Roosevelt*, 8 vols (Cambridge MA: Harvard University Press, 1952), V, p. 495.
43. Hans Schmidt, *The United States Occupation of Haiti, 1915–1934* (1971; New Brunswick, NJ: Rutgers University Press, 1995), p. 102.
44. Laguerre, *Voodoo and Politics*, pp. 1–2, 80–1.
45. Jean Price-Mars, *Ainsi Parla l'Oncle* (Paris: Imprimerie de Compiègne, 1928).
46. Laguerre, *Voodoo and Politics*, pp. 101–20.
47. Brenda Gayle Plummer, *Haiti and the Great Powers, 1902–1915* (Baton Rouge and London: Louisiana State University Press, 1988), pp. 67–94, p. 71.
48. Hesketh Pritchard, *Where Black Rules White: a Journey Across and About Hayti* (Westminster: Archibald Constable & Co., 1900), pp. 280–2; Frederick Albion Ober, *A Guide to the West Indies and Bermudas* (London: T. Fisher Unwin 1908), pp. 267–8.
49. John Houston Craige, *Cannibal Cousins* (New York: Minton, Balch & Co., 1934), pp. 206–18, p. 207.
50. James G. Leyburn, *The Haitian People* (New Haven: Yale University Press, 1941), p. 334. See also Steven Gregory, 'Voodoo, Ethnography, and the American Occupation of Haiti: William B. Seabrook's *The Magic Island*', in *Dialectical Anthropology, Volume II: The Politics of Culture and Creativity: a critique of civilisation. Essays in Honour of Stanley Diamond*, ed. Christine Ward Gailey (Gainesville: University Presses of Florida, 1992), pp. 169–208,
51. R.L. Duffus, *The New York Times* (1 January 1929), p. 6; quoted in Gregory, 'Voodoo, Ethnography', p. 171.
52. Schmidt, *Occupation of Haiti*, pp. 136–8.
53. William Seabrook, *The Magic Island* (London: George G. Harrap, 1929), pp. 18–19, 35.
54. Seabrook, *Magic Island*, pp. 45–8, 65–71.
55. Seabrook, *Magic Island*, pp. 93–4.
56. Seabrook, *Magic Island*, p. 94.
57. Seabrook, *Magic Island*, pp. 95–6.
58. Schmidt, *Occupation of Haiti*, pp. 95, 169, 171, 178.
59. Seabrook, *Magic Island*, p. 96.
60. Metraux, *Voodoo in Haiti*, p. 282.
61. Seabrook, *Magic Island*, pp. 96–7.
62. Davis argues that salt may have some pharmacological effect in reducing tetrodotoxin poisoning, but that it more likely has a symbolic value. Davis, *Passage of Darkness*, pp. 179–80.
63. Seabrook, *Magic Island*, pp. 98–100.
64. René Dépestre, *Change*, Violence II, No. 9 (Paris: Seuil, 1971), p. 20; quoted in Maximilien Laroche, 'The Myth of the Zombi', in Rowland Smith, *Exile and Tradition: Studies in African and Caribbean Literature* (New York: Africana Publishing and Dalhousie University Press, 1976), p. 59.
65. Seabrook, *Magic Island*, p. 100.
66. Seabrook, *Magic Island*, p. 101.

67. R.L. Duffus, *New York Times*, 1 January 1929, p. 6.
68. Seabrook, *Magic Island*, p. 102.
69. Stephen Bonsal, *The American Mediterranean* (New York: Moffat, Yard, & Co., 1912), pp. 95–100.
70. Seabrook, *Magic Island*, p. 102.
71. Seabrook, *Magic Island*, p. 103. Metraux offers a different translation in *Voodoo in Haiti*, p. 281.
72. Richard A. Loederer, *Voodoo Fire in Haiti*, trans. Desmond Ivo Vesey (1932; New York: Double, Doran & Co., 1935), pp. 252–3.
73. Edna B. Taft, *A Puritan in Voodooland* (Philadelphia: Penn Publishing Co., 1938), pp. 257, 235.
74. Zora Neale Hurston, *Tell My Horse* (Philadelphia: J. B. Lippincott, 1938) and *Voodoo Gods: An Inquiry into Native Myths and Magic in Jamaica and Haiti* (London: J.M. Dent & Sons, 1939). The Lippincott edition is preferred here.
75. Henry Louis Gates, Jnr, 'Afterword: Zora Neale Hurston: "A Negro Way of Saying"', in Zora Neale Hurston, *Tell my Horse: Voodoo and Life in Haiti and Jamaica* (New York: Harper & Row, 1990), p. 295.
76. Hurston, *Tell My Horse*, pp. 189, 191–200, 206.
77. G. W. Hutter [Garnett Weston], 'Salt is not for slaves', in Peter Haining (ed.), *Zombie! Stories of the Walking Dead* (London: A Target Book by W.H. Allen & Co, 1985), pp. 47, 53.
78. Manly Wade Wellman, 'The Song of the Slaves', *Weird Tales* (March 1940), in *The Mammoth Book of Zombies*, ed. Stephen Jones (London: Robinson Publishing, 1993), pp. 45–56.
79. Walvin, *Black Ivory*, pp. 16–21.
80. Vivian Meik, 'White Zombie', in *Devils' Drums* (London: Philip Allan & Co., 1933), pp. 34–5, 41–2, 43–44.
81. Meik, 'The Man Who Sold His Shadow', in *Devils' Drums*, p. 168.
82. Richard E. Goddard, *The Whistling Ancestors* (London: Stanley Smith (Publishers), 1936).
83. Young, *Colonial Desire*, p. 181.
84. Gordon Leigh Bromley, 'American Zombie', in Haining, *Zombie!*, pp. 103–4, 106–7.
85. S. S. Prawer, *Caligari's Children: The Film as Tale of Terror* (Oxford: Oxford University Press, 1980), p. 68.
86. *White Zombie*, dir. Victor Halperin (Universal Pictures, 1932), 69 mins, B&W.
87. James Grainger, *The Sugar-Cane* (London: R. and J. Dodsley, 1764), III, p. 95.
88. Edward Lowry and Richard deCordova, 'Enunciation and the Production of Horror in *White Zombie*', in Barry Grant, *Planks of Reason: Essays on the Horror Film* (Metuchen, NJ: The Scarecrow Press, 1984), pp. 346–89.
89. *I Walked with a Zombie*, dir. Jacques Tourneur (RKO, 1943), B&W, 68 mins.

90. Joel E. Siegel, *Val Lewton: the Reality of Terror* (London: Secker and Warburg, 1972), p. 26.
91. Chris Fujiwara, *Jacques Tourneur: the Cinema of Nightfall* (Jefferson, NC: McFarland & Company, 1998), pp. 85–97; Sylvie Pierre, 'The Beauty of the Sea', in Claire Johnston and Paul Willemen, *Jacques Tourneur* (Edinburgh: Edinburgh Film Festival, 1975), pp. 45–7.
92. Siegel, *Lewton*, p. 41.
93. Jean Rhys, *Wide Sargasso Sea* (London: Deutch, 1966).
94. Edmund G. Bansak, *Fearing the Dark: the Val Lewton Career* (Jefferson, NC: McFarland & Company, 1995), pp. 141–61.
95. Siegel, *Lewton*, p. 41.

Select bibliography of gothic resources

This bibliography provides a selective guide to gothic criticism relevant to the argument of this book. Further references to related material are located in the end-notes.

Ackermann, Hans-W., and Jeanine Gauthier, 'The Ways and Nature of the Zombi', *Journal of American Folklore*, 104 (1991), pp. 466–94.

Armstrong, Nancy, 'The Nineteenth-Century Jane Austen: A Turning Point in the History of Fear', *Genre*, 23 (1990), pp. 227–46.

Armstrong, Nancy, *Desire and Domestic Fiction: A Political History of the Novel* (New York and Oxford: Oxford University Press, 1987).

Baker, Ernest A., *The Novel of Sentiment and the Gothic Romance*, Vol. V, *The History of the English Novel*, 10 vols (1936; repr. New York: Barnes and Noble, 1966).

Baldick, Chris, *In Frankenstein's Shadow: Myth, Monstrosity and Nineteenth-century Writing* (Oxford: Clarendon, 1987).

Bansak, Edmund G., *Fearing the Dark: the Val Lewton Career* (Jefferson, NC: McFarland & Company, 1995).

Barker-Benfield, Graham, *Culture of Sensibility: Sex and Society in Eighteenth-Century Britain* (Chicago: University of Chicago Press, 1992).

Beer, Gillian, *The Romance* (London: Methuen, 1970).

Belford, Barbara, *Bram Stoker: a Biography of the Author of Dracula* (London: Weidenfeld and Nicolson, 1996).

Birkhead, Edith, *The Tale of Terror: a Study of Gothic Romance* (New York: Russell & Russell, 1921).

Bohls, Elizabeth, 'Standards of Taste, Discourses of "Race," and the Aesthetic Education of a Monster: Critique of Empire in *Frankenstein*', *Eighteenth-Century Life*, 18, 3 (1994).

Botting, Fred, 'Power in the Darkness: Heterotopias, Literature and Gothic Labyrinths', *Genre*, 26 (Summer/Fall 1993), pp. 253–82.

Botting, Fred, *Gothic* (London: Routledge, 1995).

Brantlinger, Patrick, 'Imperial Gothic: Atavism and the Occult in the British Adventure Novel, 1880–1914', *English Literature in Transition*, 28 (1985), pp. 243–52.

Brooks, Peter, 'Virtue and Terror: *The Monk*', *ELH*, 40 (1973), pp. 249–63.

Brown, Homer Obed, *Institutions of the English Novel: From Defoe to Scott* (University Park: University of Pennsylvania Press, 1997).

Brown, Marshall, 'A Philosophical View of the Gothic Novel', *Studies in Romanticism*, 26 (Summer 1987), pp. 275–301.

Bruhm, Steven, *The Politics of Pain in Romantic Fiction* (Pennsylvania: University of Pennsylvania Press, 1994).

Butler, Marilyn, 'The Orientalism of Byron's *Giaour*', in Bernard Beatty and Vincent Newey, *Byron and the Limits of Fiction* (Liverpool: Liverpool University Press, 1988), pp. 78–96.

Butler, Marilyn, 'The first *Frankenstein* and Radical Science', *TLS* (9 April 1993), pp. 12–14.

Butler, Marilyn, *Jane Austen and the War of Ideas* (1975; Oxford: Oxford University Press, rev. edn 1987).

Butler, Marilyn, *Romantics, Rebels and Reactionaries, English Literature and its background* (Oxford: Oxford University Press, 1981).

Canuel, Mark, '"Holy Hypocrisy" and the Government of Belief: Religion and Nationalism in the Gothic', *Studies in Romanticism*, 34 (Winter 1995), pp. 507–30.

Castle, Terry, *The Female Thermometer: Eighteenth-Century Culture and the Invention of the Uncanny* (New York and Oxford: Oxford University Press, 1995).

Chappell, Miles L., 'Fuseli and the "judicious adoption" of the antique in the "Nightmare"', *Burlington Magazine*, 126 (1986), pp. 421–2.

Clark, Kenneth, *The Gothic Revival: An Essay in the History of Taste* (London: Constable, 1928).

Clemit, Pamela, *The Godwinian Novel: the Rational Fictions of Godwin, Brockden Brown, Mary Shelley* (Oxford: Clarendon Press, 1993).

Clery, Emma J., *The Rise of Supernatural Fiction, 1762–1800* (Cambridge: Cambridge University Press, 1995).

Cornwell, Neil, *The Literary Fantastic: from Gothic to Postmodernism* (London: Harvester Wheatsheaf, 1990).

Cosslett, Tess, *The 'Scientific Movement' and Victorian Literature* (Brighton: Harvester, 1982).

Craciun, Adriana, '"I Hasten to be disembodied": Charlotte Dacre, the Demon Lover and Representations of the Body', *European Romantic Review* 6, 1 (Summer 1995), pp. 75–97.

Craft, Christopher, '"Kiss me with those red lips": Gender and Inversion in Bram Stoker's *Dracula*', in Elaine Showalter (ed.) *Speaking of Gender* (London: Routledge, 1990), pp. 216–42.

Davis, Wade, *Passage of Darkness: the ethnobiology of the Haitian zombie* (Chapel Hill, NC: University of North Carolina Press, 1988).

Davis, Wade, *The Serpent and the Rainbow* (1985; New York: Touchstone for Simon & Schuster, 1997).

Day, William Patrick *In the Circles of Fear and Desire: a Study of Gothic Fantasy* (Chicago: University of Chicago Press, 1985).

Doody, Margaret Anne, 'Deserts, Ruins and Troubled Waters: Female Dreams in Fiction and the Development of the Gothic Novel', *Genre*, 10 (1977), pp. 529–72.

Duncan, Ian, *Modern Romance and Transformations of the Novel: The Gothic, Scott, Dickens* (Cambridge: Cambridge University Press, 1992).

Durant, David, 'Ann Radcliffe and the Conservative Gothic', *Studies in English Literature, 1500–1900*, 22, 3 (1982), pp. 519–30.

Ellis, Kate Ferguson, *The Contested Castle: Gothic novels and the Subversion of Domestic Ideology* (Urbana: University of Illinois Press, 1989).

Ellis, Markman, *The Politics of Sensibility: Race, Gender and Commerce in the Sentimental Novel* (Cambridge: Cambridge University Press, 1996).

Ferguson, Moira, and Janet Todd, *Mary Wollstonecraft* (Boston: Twayne Press, 1984).

Fleenor, J. E. (ed.), *The Female Gothic* (Montreal: Eden Press, 1983).

Frayling, Christopher, 'Vampyres', *London Magazine*, n.s. 14, 2 (June/July 1974), pp. 94–104.

Frayling, Christopher, *The Vampyres: Lord Byron to Count Dracula* (London: Faber & Faber, 1991).

Fujiwara, Chris, *Jacques Tourneur: the Cinema of Nightfall* (Jefferson, NC: McFarland & Company, 1998).

Gelder, Ken, *Reading the Vampire* (London: Routledge, 1994).

Graham, Kenneth W. (ed.), *Gothic Fictions: Prohibition/Transgression*, ed. Kenneth W. Graham (New York: AMS Press, 1989).

Grant, A., *Ann Radcliffe: a Biography* (Denver: Alan Swallow, 1951).

Greenway, John, '*Dracula* as a Critique of "Normal Science"', *Stanford Literature Review*, 3, 2 (1986), pp. 213–30.

Gregory, Steven, 'Voodoo, Ethnography, and the American Occupation of Haiti: William B. Seabrook's *The Magic Island*', in *Dialectical Anthropology, Volume II: The Politics of Culture and Creativity: a critique of civilisation. Essays in Honour of Stanley Diamond*, ed. Christine Ward Gailey (Gainesville: University Presses of Florida, 1992), pp. 169–208.

Groom, Nick, 'Celts, Goths, and the nature of the Literary Source', in Alvaro Ribeiro and James G. Basker (eds), *Tradition in Transition: Women Writers, Marginal Texts, and the Eighteenth-Century Canon* (Oxford: Clarendon Press, 1996).

Grudin, Peter, '*The Monk*: Matilda and the Rhetoric of Deceit', *Journal of Narrative Technique*, 5 (May 1975), pp. 136–46.

Guest, Harriet, 'The Wanton Muse: Politics and Gender in Gothic Theory after 1760' in Stephen Copley and John Whale (eds), *Beyond Romanticism* (London: Routledge, 1993), pp. 118–39.

Haggerty, George E., 'Literature and Homosexuality in the late eighteenth century: Walpole, Beckford, and Lewis', *Studies in the Novel*, 18, 4 (1986), pp. 341–52.

Henderson, Andrea, '"An Embarrassing Subject": Use Value and Exchange Value in Early Gothic Characterization', Mary A. Favret and Nicola J. Watson (eds), *At the Limits of Romanticism: Essays in Cultural, Feminist, and Materialist Criticism* (Bloomington and Indianapolis: Indiana University Press, 1995), pp. 225–45.

Hennelly, M. M., '"The Slow Torture of Delay": Reading *The Italian*', *Studies in the Humanities*, 14, 1 (1987), pp. 1–17.

Hindle, Maurice, 'Vital matters: Mary Shelley's *Frankenstein* and Romantic science', *Critical Survey*, 2, 1 (1990), pp. 29–35.

Holland, Norman, and Leona Sherman, 'Gothic possibilities', *New Literary History*, 8 (1977), pp. 279–94.

Hopkins, Robert, 'General Tilney and Affairs of State: The Political Gothic of *Northanger Abbey*,' *Philological Quarterly*, 57 (1978), pp. 213–24.

Howard, Jacqueline, *Reading Gothic Fiction: a Bakhtinian Approach* (Oxford: Clarendon Press, 1994).

Howells, Coral Ann, *Love, Mystery and Misery: Feeling in Gothic Fiction* (London: Athlone Press, 1978).

Hume, Robert D., 'Gothic Versus Romance: A Revaluation of the Gothic Novel', *PMLA*, 84 (1969), pp. 282–90.

Hunter, J. Paul, *Before Novels, The Cultural Contexts of Eighteenth-Century English Fiction* (London: Norton, 1990).

Jacobs, Edward, 'Anonymous Signatures: Circulating Libraries, Conventionality and the production of gothic romances', *ELH*, 62 (1995), pp. 603–29.

Janes, Regina M., 'On the Reception of Mary Wollstonecraft's *A Vindication of the Rights of Woman*', *Journal of the History of Ideas*, 39 (1978), pp. 293–303.

Jauss, Hans Robert, *Toward an Aesthetic of Reception*, trans. Timothy Bahti (Brighton: The Harvester Press, 1982).

Johnson, Barbara, 'My Monster/My Self', *Diacritics*, 12 (1982), pp. 2–10.

Johnson, Claudia, 'A "Sweet Face as White as Death": Jane Austen and the Politics of Female Sensibility', *Novel*, 22 (1988), pp. 159–74.

Johnson, Claudia, *Equivocal Beings: Politics, Gender and Sentimentality in the 1790s* (Chicago and London: The University of Chicago Press, 1995).

Johnson, Claudia, *Jane Austen: Women, Politics and the Novel* (Chicago and London: University of Chicago Press, 1988).

Jones, Ann H., 'Charlotte Dacre', *Ideas and Innovations: Best Sellers of Jane Austen's Age* (New York: AMS Press, 1986), pp. 224–49.

Jones, Wendy, 'Stories of Desire in *The Monk*', *ELH*, 57, 1 (1990), pp. 129–50.

Jump, Harriet Devine, *Mary Wollstonecraft: Writer* (Hemel Hempstead: Harvester Wheatsheaf, 1994).

Kelly, Gary, *English Fiction of the Romantic Period, 1789–1830*, Longman Literature in English Series (London and New York: Longman, 1989).

Kelly, Gary, *Revolutionary Feminism: The Mind and Career of Mary Wollstonecraft* (Basingstoke and London: Macmillan, 1992).

Kelly, Gary, *The English Jacobin Novel, 1780–1805* (Oxford: Clarendon Press, 1976).

Ketton-Cremer, R. W., *Horace Walpole: A Biography* (1940, 2nd rev. edn London: Faber and Faber, 1946).

Kiely, Robert, *The Romantic Novel in England* (Cambridge, MA: Harvard University Press, 1972).

Kiessling, Nicolas, *The Incubus in English Literature: Provenance and Progeny* (no place: Washington State University Press, 1977).

Kilgour, Maggie, *The Rise of the Gothic Novel* (London: Routledge, 1995).

Kliger, Samuel, 'The "Goths" in England: an introduction to the gothic vogue in eighteenth-century aesthetic discussion', *Modern Philology*, 43 (1945), pp. 105–17.

Kliger, Samuel, *The Goths in England: a Study in Seventeenth and Eighteenth Century Thought* (Cambridge, MA: Harvard University Press, 1952).

Knoepflmacher, U. C., and George Levine (eds), *The Endurance of Frankenstein: Essays on Mary Shelley's Novel* (Berkeley: University of California Press, 1979).

Laguerre, Michel S., *Voodoo and Politics in Haiti* (Basingstoke: Macmillan Press, 1989).

Laroche, Maximilien, 'The Myth of the Zombi', in Rowland Smith, *Exile and Tradition: Studies in African and Caribbean Literature* (New York: Africana Publishing and Dalhousie University Press, 1976).

Leask, Nigel, *British Romantic Writers and the East: Anxieties of Empire* (Cambridge: Cambridge University Press, 1992).

Leatherdale, Clive (ed.), *Bram Stoker's Dracula Unearthed* (Westcliff-on-Sea, Essex: Desert Island Books, 1998).

Leatherdale, Clive, *Dracula: the Novel and the Legend: a Study of Bram Stoker's Gothic Masterpiece* (Wellingborough, Northamptonshire: The Aquarian Press, 1985).

Longueil, Alfred, 'The word "gothic" in eighteenth century criticism', *Modern Language Notes*, 38 (1923), pp. 453–60.

Lowry, Edward, and Richard deCordova, 'Enunciation and the Production of Horror in *White Zombie*', in Barry Grant, *Planks of Reason: Essays on the Horror Film* (Metuchen, NJ: The Scarecrow Press, 1984), pp. 346–89.

MacAndrew, Elizabeth, *The Gothic Tradition in Fiction* (New York: Columbia University Press, 1979).

MacDonald, D. L., 'The Erotic Sublime: The Marvellous in *The Monk*', *English Studies in Canada*, 18, 3 (1992), pp. 273–85.

Macdonald, D. L., 'Bathos and Repetition: The Uncanny in Radcliffe', *Journal of Narrative Technique*, 19, 2 (1989), pp. 197–204.

Macdonald, David, *Poor Polidori: a Critical Biography of the Author of The Vampyre* (Toronto: University of Toronto Press, 1991).

Madoff, M., 'The Useful Myth of Gothic Ancestry', *Studies in Eighteenth-Century Culture*, 9 (1979), pp. 337–50.

Marshall, Tim, *Murdering to Dissect: Grave-robbing, Frankenstein and the Anatomy Literature* (Manchester: Manchester University Press, 1995).

McCarthy, Michael, *The Origins of the Gothic Revival* (New Haven: Yale University Press, 1987).

McGann, Jerome, '"My Brain is Feminine": Byron and the poetry of deception', in Andrew Rutherford (ed.), *Byron: Augustan and Romantic* (Basingstoke: Macmillan, 1990), pp. 26–51.

McKeon, Michael, *The Origins of the English Novel, 1600–1740* (Baltimore: The Johns Hopkins University Press, 1987).

McNally, Raymond T., and Radu Florescu, *In Search of Dracula: the History of Dracula and Vampires* (London: Robson Books, 1994).

Mellor, Anne K., *Mary Shelley: her Life, her Fiction, her Monsters* (London: Routledge, 1988).

Metraux, Alfred, *Voodoo in Haiti*, trans. Hugo Charteris (1957; London: Alfred Deutsch, 1959).

Miles, Robert, 'The Gothic Aesthetic: The Gothic as Discourse', *The Eighteenth Century*, 32, 1 (1991), pp. 39–57.

Miles, Robert, *Ann Radcliffe: The Great Enchantress* (Manchester: Manchester University Press, 1995).

Miles, Robert, *Gothic Writing, 1750–1820: A Genealogy* (London: Routledge, 1993).

Mishra, Vijay, *The Gothic Sublime* (Albany: State University of New York Press, 1994).

Moers, Ellen, *Literary Women* (London: W. H. Allen, 1977).

Moretti, Franco, *Signs Taken for Wonders: Essays in the Sociology of Literary Forms*, trans. Susan Fischer, David Forgacs and David Miller (London: Verso Editions and NLB, 1983).

Morris, David, 'Gothic Sublimity', *New Literary History*, 16 (1985), pp. 299–319.

Mowl, Timothy, *Horace Walpole: The Great Outsider* (London: John Murray, 1996).

Mullan, John, *Sentiment and Sociability: The Language of Feeling in the Eighteenth Century* (Oxford: Clarendon Press, 1988).

Napier, Elizabeth, *The Failure of Gothic: Problems of Disjunction in an Eighteenth-century Form* (Oxford: Clarendon, 1987).

Nethercot, Arthur H., *The Road to Tryermaine: a Study of the History, Background and Purposes of Coleridge's 'Christabel'* (Chicago: The University of Chicago Press, 1939).

Norton, Rictor, *Mistress of Udolpho: a Life of Ann Radcliffe* (Leicester: Leicester University Press, 1999).

Novak, Maximillian E., 'Gothic Fiction and the Grotesque', *Novel*, 13 (1979), pp. 50–67

Parreaux, André, *The Publication of 'The Monk': a literary event 1796–1798* (Paris: Didier, 1960).

Paulson, Ronald, *Representations of Revolution (1789–1820)* (New Haven and London: Yale University Press, 1983).

Peck, Louis F., *A Life of Matthew G. Lewis* (Cambridge, MA: Harvard University Press, 1961).

Poovey, Mary, 'Ideology and *The Mysteries of Udolpho*', *Criticism*, 21, 4 (1979), pp. 307–30.

Poovey, Mary, 'Mary Wollstonecraft: The Gender of Genres in Late-Eighteenth-Century England', *Novel*, 15, 2 (Winter 1982), pp. 111–26.

Poovey, Mary, *The Proper Lady and the Woman Writer: Ideology as Style in the Works of Mary Wollstonecraft, Mary Shelley, and Jane Austen* (Chicago and London: The University of Chicago Press, 1984).

Powell, Nicolas, *Fuseli: 'The Nightmare'* (London: Lane, 1973).

Prawer, S. S., *Caligari's Children: The Film as Tale of Terror* (Oxford: Oxford University Press, 1980).

Punter, David, '1789: The Sex of Revolution', *Criticism*, 24 (1982), pp. 201–17.

Punter, David, 'Social Relations of Gothic Fiction', in David Aers, Jonathan Cook and David Punter (eds), *Romanticism and Ideology: Studies in English Writing 1765–1830* (London: Routledge, 1981), pp. 103–17.

Punter, David, *The Literature of Terror: A History of Gothic Fictions from 1765 to the Present Day* (New York: Longman, 1980).

Railo, Eino, *The Haunted Castle: a Study of the Elements of English Romanticism* (London: George Routledge & Sons, 1927).

Richter, David, *The Progress of Romance; Literary Historiography and the Gothic Novel* (Columbus: Ohio State University Press, 1996).

Richter, David, 'From Medievalism to Historicism: Representations of History in the Gothic Novel and Historical Romance', *Studies in Romanticism*, 4 (1992), pp. 79–104.

Richter, David, 'The Reception of the Gothic Novel in the 1790s', in *The Idea of the Novel in the Eighteenth Century*, ed. Robert W. Lansing (East Lansing, MI: Colleagues Press, 1988), pp. 117–37.

Richter, David, 'The Unguarded Prison: Reception Theory, Structural Marxism, and the History of the Gothic Novel', *The Eighteenth Century*, 30, 3 (1989), pp. 3–17.

Rivers, Christopher, 'Safe Sex: The Prophylactic Walls of the Cloister in the French Libertine Convent Novel of the Eighteenth Century', *Journal of the History of Sexuality*, 5, 3 (1995), pp. 381–402.

Roberts, Bette, *The Gothic Romance: its Appeal to Women Writers and Readers in Late-eighteenth century England* (New York: Arno Press, 1980).

Roberts, Marie, *Gothic Immortals: the Fiction of the Brotherhood of the Rosy Cross* (London: Routledge, 1990).

Rogers, Deborah D. (ed.), *The Critical Response to Ann Radcliffe* (Westport, CT and London: Greenwood Press, 1994).

Rogers, Deborah D., *Ann Radcliffe: a Bio-bibliography* (Westport, CT and London: Greenwood Press, 1996).

Sabor (ed.), Peter, *Horace Walpole: The Critical Heritage* (London and New York, 1987).

Sage, Victor, *Horror Fiction in the Protestant Tradition* (London: Macmillan, 1988).

Samson, John, 'Politics Gothicised: The Conway Incident and *The Castle of Otranto*', *Eighteenth-Century Life*, 10, 3 (1986), pp. 145–58.

Schiff et al, Gert, *Henry Fuseli, 1741–1825* (London: Tate Gallery, 1975).

Sedgewick, Eve Kosofsky, 'The Character in the Veil: Imagery of the Surface in the Gothic Novel', *PMLA*, 96 (1981), pp. 255–70.

Sedgewick, Eve Kosofsky, *The Coherence of Gothic Conventions* (London: Methuen, 1986).

Sedgwick, Eve Kosofsky, 'Jane Austen and the Masturbating Girl', *Critical Inquiry*, 17, 4 (1991), pp. 818–37.

Seed, David, 'Gothic Definitions', *Novel*, 14, 3 (1981), pp. 270–4.

Senf, Carol A., *Dracula: Between Tradition and Modernism* (New York: Twayne Publishers, 1998).

Siegel, Joel E., *Val Lewton: the Reality of Terror* (London: Secker and Warburg, 1972).

Simmel, Georg, 'The Sociology of Secrecy and of Secret Societies', trans. Albion Small, *The American Journal of Sociology*, XI, 4 (1906), pp. 441–98.

Smith, Allan Lloyd, and Victor Sage (eds), *Gothick Origins and Innovations* (Amsterdam and Atlanta: Rodopi, 1994).

Smith, Crosbie, 'Frankenstein and natural magic' in *Frankenstein, Creation and Monstrosity*, ed. Stephen Bann (London: Reaktion Books, 1994), pp. 39–59.

Smith, R. J., *The Gothic Bequest: Medieval Institutions in British Thought, 1688–1863* (Cambridge: Cambridge University Press, 1987).

Spencer, Jane, *The Rise of the Woman Novelist: From Aphra Behn to Jane Austen* (Oxford: Basil Blackwell, 1986).

Summers, Montague, *The Gothic Quest* (London: Fortune Press, 1938).

Summers, Montague, *The Vampire: His Kith and Kin* (London: Kegan Paul, Trench, Trubner & Co., 1928).

Tanner, Tony, *Jane Austen* (London and Cambridge, MA: Macmillan, 1986).

Thompson (ed.), Gary, *The Gothic Imagination: Essays in Dark Romanticism* (Pullman: Washington State University Press, 1974).

Tinkler-Villani, et al (eds), Valeria, *Exhibited by Candlelight: Sources and Developments in the Gothic Tradition* (Amsterdam: Rodopi, 1995).

Tomalin, Claire, *The Life and Death of Mary Wollstonecraft* (London: Weidenfeld and Nicolson, 1974).

Tomory, Peter, *The Life and Art of Henry Fuseli* (London: Thames and Hudson, 1972).

Tuite, Clara, 'Cloistered Closets: Enlightenment Pornography, the Confessional State, Homosexual Persecution and *The Monk*', *Romanticism on the Net* 8 (November 1997): (Online: Internet, 2.8.98 <http://users.ox.ac.uk/~scat0385/closet.html>).

Twitchell, James, 'The Vampire Myth', *American Imago*, 37 (1980), 83–92.

Varma, Devendra, *The Gothic Flame. Being a History of the Gothic Novel in England: Its Origin, Efflorescence, Disintegration, and Residuary Influences* (1957, repr. New York: Russell & Russell, 1963).

Vasbinder, Samuel H., *Scientific Attitudes in Mary Shelley's Frankenstein* (Ann Arbor, MI: UMI Research Press, 1976).

Wacke, Jennifer, 'Vampiric Typewriting: *Dracula* and its Media', *ELH*, 59 (1992), pp. 467–93.

Wagner, Peter, *Eros Revived: Erotica of the Enlightenment in England and America* (London: Secker & Warburg, 1988).

Warner, William B., 'The Elevation of the Novel in England: Hegemony and Literary History', *ELH*, 59 (1992), pp. 577–96.

Watkins, Daniel P., 'Social Relations in Byron's *The Giaour*', *ELH*, 52 (1985), pp. 873–92.

Watt, Ian, 'Time and Family in the Gothic Novel: *The Castle of Otranto*', *Eighteenth Century Life*, 10, 3 (1986), pp. 159–71.

Watt, Ian, *The Rise of the Novel: studies in Defoe, Richardson, and Fielding* (London: Chatto, 1957).

Watt, James, *Contesting the Gothic: Fiction, Genre and Cultural Conflict, 1764–1832* (Cambridge: Cambridge University Press, 1999).

Wolff, C. G., 'The Radcliffean Gothic Model: A Form for Feminine Sexuality', in J. E. Fleenor (ed.), *The Female Gothic* (Montreal: Eden Press, 1983), pp. 207–33.

Wolstenholme, Susan, *Gothic (Re)Visions: Writing Women as Readers* (Albany: State University of New York Press, 1993).

Index